Crossing the Bay of Bengal

Crossing the Bay of Bengal

The Furies of Nature and the Fortunes of Migrants

Sunil S. Amrith

HARVARD UNIVERSITY PRESS

Cambridge, Massachusetts

London, England

2013

Library of Congress Cataloging-in-Publication Data

Amrith, Sunil S., 1979–
    Crossing the Bay of Bengal : the furies of nature and the fortunes
of migrants / Sunil S. Amrith.
        pages cm
    Includes bibliographical references and index.
    ISBN 978-0-674-72483-9 (hardcover : alk. paper)
    1. Asians—Migrations—Bengal, Bay of, Region—History—
19th century. 2. Immigrants—Bengal, Bay of, Region—History—19th
century. 3. Bengal, Bay of, Region.—Commerce—History—19th
century. I. Title.

JV8490.A728 2013
304.809182'4—dc23   2013010984

For Ruth

Contents

Crossing the Bay of Bengal

The Bay of Bengal in History

The Bay of Bengal was once a region at the heart of global history. It was forgotten in the second half of the twentieth century, carved up by the boundaries of nation-states, its shared past divided into the separate compartments of national histories. The regions that gave shape to the postwar organization of academic knowledge—the "areas" of area studies—drew a sharp distinction between "South Asia," on one hand, and "Southeast Asia," on the other: the line between them ran right through the middle of the Bay. The rise and decline of the Bay as a connected region is a story almost completely untold. It is the story of one of the largest movements of people in modern history, and of environmental change on an enormous scale. It is also a story with important consequences today—perhaps even a key to understanding Asia's future.

For centuries the Bay of Bengal was crossed by troops and traders, by slaves and workers. It was a maritime highway between India and China, navigable by mastery of its regularly reversing monsoon winds. As European states and armed chartered companies expanded into Asian waters from the end of the fifteenth century, the Bay became a crucial arena in their competition with each other—and with their Asian rivals. Portuguese advances were reversed in the seventeenth century by the growing power of the Dutch and the English. By the dawn of the eighteenth century, the English, Dutch, and French East India companies had footholds all around the Bay's arc of coasts. Their fortresses (called "factories") clung close to the shoreline; a deeper entanglement with local politics followed. By 1800 the British dominated the Bay of Bengal as no previous power had ever done. Already the Bay

1

was linked by bonds of culture, by constant migration, by the movement of holy men and relics, by the exchange of high-value luxuries and staple goods. Already a process of ecological specialization had advanced: some of the "spice islands" of Indonesia were, by the sixteenth century, entirely dependent on food imports. Now the littorals of the eastern Indian Ocean were linked in new ways by British imperialism—by the movement of soldiers, the posting of garrisons, the exchange of legal codes, and the circulation of officials.

In the second half of the nineteenth century, the connectedness of the Bay of Bengal underwent a change in scale. It was remade as a region at the heart of the global, imperial economy. It was soldered by the force of capital in search of new profits on Southeast Asia's forest frontiers. It was animated by the power of fossil fuels as steamships made the ocean crossing faster, cheaper, and easier than ever before. It was governed by imperial laws that both uprooted and immobilized people, locking some communities in place (as "peasants") while compelling others to travel under contracts of indenture or under the weight of debt. It was shaped, above all, by human labor—and human suffering.

Migrant workers, alongside local people, cleared land, planted trees, harvested cash crops, and turned the forests to enormous profit. The impact of these changes is difficult to overstate. The Bay of Bengal's circuits of migration both responded to and fueled change on a global scale. Malaya's rubber—tapped by Tamil migrant workers—fed the American automobile industry. Malaya became the most economically valuable tropical colony in the whole of the British Empire. Burma became the largest rice exporter in the world, in a boom backed by Indian capital and drawing millions of Indian migrant workers into every sector of its economy. Somewhere in the region of 28 million people crossed the Bay of Bengal, in both directions, between 1840 and 1940. The region was home to one of the world's great migrations—but almost certainly the least well-known.

This large story of economic integration and mass migration can be told from the inside, as a history of cultural contact and mixture. The material transformation of Southeast Asia's forests, for example, is tied intimately to an emotional history of displacement. The suffering of the workers, whose blood stained the landscape, left an imprint on cultural memory on both sides of the sea. The "inner history" of the Bay of Bengal as a region is also a history of encounters with cultural difference.

The port cities of Southeast Asia, where the Bay of Bengal met the South China Sea, were as plural as any on earth, and more so than most. A rich exchange of ideas and languages was the result of transient encounters or cross-cultural relationships. Ethnic conflict and cultural cosmopolitanism coexisted in uneasy balance, a result of this meeting of many Asian diasporas. Those who crossed the Bay left us few letters and fewer memoirs, but traces of their journeys—even their ideas and sentiments—remain in legal testimony, in identity papers, in architecture, and in sacred rituals. These can shed new, if sometimes oblique, light on millions of Asians' experience of modernity.

The history of the Bay of Bengal as a connected region points, above all, to the limitations of the artificial distinctions between economic, political, cultural, and environmental history—and of those between South Asian and Southeast Asian history.

However densely it was woven together, the world of the Bay of Bengal collapsed with astonishing rapidity in the middle decades of the twentieth century. Crossings were interrupted, first by the global economic depression and then by World War II, which arrived in the Bay of Bengal in December 1941, with the Japanese invasion of Southeast Asia. New, revolutionary visions of citizenship and belonging emerged from the trauma of war. But the ultimate effect of the conflict was to cement the division between "South Asia" and the lands across the Bay ("Southeast Asia"). The fragmentation was rapid, because however closely linked the Bay of Bengal's coasts—by kinship, by commerce, by cultural circulation—there was never a corresponding political structure to encompass the sea. Not even the British imperial frame could hold the Bay together. The region was governed as a patchwork of separate territories, often deliberately kept apart. Lacking political coherence, the Bay did not emerge as a meaningful unit for the planned economic development and social mobilization that held such promise for so many in mid-twentieth-century Asia. Almost without exception, the policymakers of postwar Asia took the nation-state as the most natural foundation for their dreams of a better future.

Instead, the region—defined, most fundamentally, by its mobility—was now divided by controls over trade and migration. This forced choices upon many who previously had seen no reason to choose between homes and had circulated between India or China and Southeast

Asia; now they crossed international boundaries where access was regulated by passports and rationed by visas. Communities that had crossed the Bay of Bengal in the age of empire sought a place for themselves as "minorities" within new nation-states. Their journeys to citizenship were hard, and many of those journeys remain unfinished.

The rise and decline of the Bay of Bengal as a region parallels the rise and collapse of British imperialism in Asia. Imperialism provided the motive force—and the brute force—for the mass migration that tied the Bay's coasts so closely together in the nineteenth century. Its disintegration could be seen as an inevitable function of empire's end: the writing was on the wall from the 1930s. But there are too many jagged edges, too many fugitive pieces, to support such a tidy story. The Bay of Bengal's precolonial history shaped its colonial history in many ways, and many forms of connection across the sea outlasted and outlived empires. However abrupt the shifts in political architecture around the Bay, however constrained its paths of migration came to be, connections did not simply cease. The rhythms of human relations, the capacity of societies to expand their cultural boundaries, were not so easily decreed by political borders or economic policies. Even at the low ebb of trade between India and Southeast Asia, the Bay of Bengal lived on as a regional arena through family connections, through enduring links of pilgrimage—and in the cultural imagination.

Many of Asia's states turned their backs on the sea, instead looking inward: toward the development of their resources, toward the mobilization of their workforces, toward securing themselves against the fluctuations of trade and fortune that, so many remembered, had proved disastrous in the 1930s and 1940s.

Paradoxically, as the sea no longer provided the lifeblood of commerce and as it faded from the imagination, human activity began to affect the sea itself. As the political and economic connections across the Bay came apart, a new ecological interdependence took root: a new phase in its environmental history began. Realization of this shift was slow to dawn, until its demands became insistent and its effects undeniable. Beginning in the 1950s, and with growing force from the 1970s, the effects of population growth and land clearance, the effluent of industrialization and the damming of rivers, have altered the very nature of the Bay of Bengal. At the same time, processes on a planetary, not regional, scale have disrupted the oceans. The warming of the earth's atmosphere as a result of human activity has thrown the world's seas off balance; the notoriously turbulent Bay of Bengal, terror of mariners past, is acutely vulnerable.

At the turn of the twenty-first century, the Bay of Bengal is once again at the heart of international politics. A history that seemed of little relevance in the heyday of postcolonial nation building now seems urgent again. In two key ways, the region is at the forefront of processes that are shaping Asia's future. First, the Bay of Bengal is now, as it was in the eighteenth century, an arena for strategic competition between rising powers. Today those powers are Asian rather than European: India and China both eye the Bay of Bengal as a crucial frontier in their competition over energy resources, shipping lanes, and cultural influence. Second, the Bay of Bengal's littoral stands at the front line of Asia's experience of climate change: its densely populated coastal zone is home to nearly half a billion people. In this new context, the Bay of Bengal's history can be a source of insight and explanation.

A historical perspective can explain the potential for and the obstacles to greater regional integration. It can show us that many of the region's current environmental challenges are the (often unintended) outcome of earlier movements of capital and labor. It can show us, too, that informal networks of mobility have always outstripped official attempts to control them—and that these old paths assume new salience today, as climate change threatens to displace millions of people. The Bay of Bengal's history is, finally, an archive of cultural resources that might help us to reimagine solidarity across distance and to comprehend planetary change on a regional, even human scale.

1

The Life of the Bay of Bengal

Ahmad Rijaluddin traveled across the Bay of Bengal, from Penang to Calcutta, in late 1810. He accompanied Robert Scott—son of James Scott, one of Penang's first residents and wealthiest merchants. Rijaluddin was himself the son of a rich local family: his father was a Tamil trader, his mother was Malay. He worked as an interpreter for the European merchants of Penang, which had been established in 1786 as a settlement of the British East India Company. Rijaluddin's memoir, written in the Malay language, is probably the first modern account published by an Asian traveler of crossing the Bay of Bengal.

Passing quickly over the sea voyage, Rijaluddin's account begins with his arrival at the Bay of Bengal's northern basin. By the time of his voyage, Bengal's fame had "spread to the east and to the west, as far as Constantinople, Egypt, China, Mecca and Medinah." Rijaluddin delved into the life of Calcutta. "Ships visit the capital without a break," he wrote, "there is no let-up day or night, thousands of ships arrive and depart and from the west to the east, from the north-west to the south-east." Sailors from around the world took their pleasure in port. "In every street, you will find different sorts of *street entertainers*," he told his readers. Most enticing was the "winding lane near the shipyards" where "the whores live, thousands of them . . . Pathans, Indians, Mughals, and Bengalis." Their clientele was equally diverse: "people of different races—English, Portuguese, French, Dutch, Chinese, Bengali, Burmese, Tamil and Malay—visit the place morning, noon and night." The street was always "as noisy as if they were celebrating the end of a war." Rijaluddin described an open field nearby, with "hundreds of people cooking rice, chappatis and roast meat, and others selling sweets and rice crisps." The scene "sounds like the roaring of thunder," he wrote, "you can't imagine the noise produced by such a great crowd."[1]

Rijaluddin could have been writing about any port in the world in the age of sail. They had in common their mixed crowds, the landed conviviality that followed weeks at sea, the many trades that fulfilled sailors' desires. But his account also describes something more specific: a maritime world surrounding the Bay of Bengal. The peoples he describes—"English, Portuguese, French, Dutch, Chinese, Bengali, Burmese, Tamil and Malay"—were the peoples of the Bay's rim: the imperial rulers and adventurers, the traders and merchants and sailors and laborers that made the Bay of Bengal "a far more tightly knit unit of interaction . . . than the Indian Ocean as a whole."[2]

More than a century later, in 1937, Palanisamy Kumaran crossed the Bay of Bengal the other way, from the South Indian port of Nagapatnam to Penang. Palanisamy has not written an account of his travels; he narrated it to me over several hours in a series of interviews at his house in Sungai Petani, in Kedah. Sungai Petani was once a frontier outpost in Malaya's "wild west" and is now a midsized and bustling town. Traveling with few possessions, Palanisamy paid twenty-seven rupees for his place on the steamer. The worst of the Depression was over, and Malaya's rubber plantations needed new hands. A freak accident, a house fire, sent the young man to seek his fortune abroad at a time of family trouble. His destination was obvious: "Lots of guys came and went from Malaya, so I thought I would go, too, see what it was all about," he told me. His first sight of shore was the quarantine station on Jerejak Island, where he was detained for five days. His first job was to carry buckets of "rubber milk" on a long pole balanced on his shoulders, at a wage of fifty cents a day. Mr. Palanisamy was part of the vast movement of South Indian laborers across the Bay at the height of the British Empire, to Malaya, Burma, and Sri Lanka. But he insisted that "not one single person came here with the idea that they'd get married, settle down; they just wanted to earn money for a couple of years and go back," he said. When I met him, in 2007, he had been in Malaysia for more than seventy years.[3] During his lifetime he had seen the political transitions of modern Asian history: he had lived in British India, the Federated Malay States, Japanese Malaya, British Malaya, and independent Malaysia.

In the century between Rijaluddin's journey and Palanisamy's, millions of people crossed the Bay of Bengal as sail gave way to steam. If Rijaluddin, a wealthy merchant's son, epitomized the voyager in the early nineteenth century, Palanisamy, a laborer destined for the rubber plantations of Malaya, typified the migrant of the early twentieth. Their journeys, under such different circumstances, frame the narrative of this book and provide a sense of its span. They also hint at a longer history. Rijaluddin's family was formed over centuries of commerce, movement, and marriage across the Bay; Palanisamy's story reminds us that this is a history that endures in the Indian diaspora remaining in Southeast Asia.

This began as a history of the migration of Tamil labor to the Malay Peninsula—a history of journeys like Palanisamy's. Over time it metamorphosed into a history of the sea. The history of Tamil migration is our recurring motif, but we will hear many other voices—Chinese, Malay, Burmese, Bengali, English, Dutch—along the way. Tamil migration was among the largest and most enduring movements across the eastern Indian Ocean, and it is a good starting point from which to approach the history of the region as a whole. Sometimes a simple, even naive question can reframe our vision—how far can we see South India as part of the Southeast Asian world, as closely linked to the coasts across the Bay of Bengal as it was to the centers of power in India? We have become so accustomed to national histories and nationalist maps that it is difficult to put the Bay of Bengal, with its traffic of people, ideas, and things, at the heart of our story. But to do so opens new perspectives on the past and the present.

Picture the Bay of Bengal as an expanse of tropical water: still and blue in the calm of the January winter, or raging and turbid with silt at the peak of the summer rains. Picture it in two dimensions on a map, overlaid with a web of shipping channels and telegraph cables and inscribed with lines of distance. Now imagine the sea as a mental map: as a family tree of cousins, uncles, sisters, sons, connected by letters and journeys and stories. Think of it as a sea of debt, bound by advances and loans and obligations. Picture the Bay of Bengal even where it is absent—deep in the Malaysian jungle, where Hindu shrines sprout from the landscape as if washed up by the sea, left behind. There are many ways of envisaging the Bay of Bengal as a place with a history—one as rich and complex as the history of any national territory.

Today one in four of the world's people lives in a country that borders the Bay of Bengal. More than half a billion people live directly on the coastal rim that surrounds it. This is a region that has long been central to the history of globalization: shaped by migration, as culturally mixed as anywhere on earth, and at the forefront of the commodification of nature. It is also now being transformed by global warming. The coastal frontiers of the Bay are among the most vulnerable in the world to climate change; they are densely populated, ecologically fragile, and at the fault lines of new dreams of empire.

The Bay of Bengal is a large triangular basin in the Indian Ocean, and the largest bay in the world. It is an enclosed sea, surrounded by thousands of miles of coastline—an arc stretching from the southeastern edge of India, up and along the coasts of present-day Bangladesh and Burma, and down to the western coast of Thailand and Malaysia. It has a narrow continental shelf, and "islands are scarce and small except for Ceylon" in the west and the smaller Andaman and Nicobar Islands in the east. At its southeastern edge, the Bay of Bengal meets the waters of Southeast Asia—the Straits of Melaka, the Java Sea, and the South China Sea—which are, by contrast, shallower, fresher, warmer, and "thickly strewn with small islands." Ceylon and the southern tip of the Indian subcontinent, at Kanyakumari, mark its western boundary with the Arabian Sea.[4]

Many of Asia's great rivers empty into the Bay of Bengal: the Ganges, the Brahmaputra, the Meghna, the Godavari, the Kaveri, the Krishna, and the Salween spill 200 cubic kilometers of water into the sea each monsoon season. The Bay "receiveth into its bosome many navigable rivers, which lose their note and names in the eminent neighborhood of the famous Ganges," wrote the English trader William Methwold in the 1620s.[5] Many of these rivers begin high in the Himalayas, and by the time they reach the sea, having passed through many countries, they carry enormous accumulations of silt. Each year the Ganges alone discharges more than two and a half billion tons of sediment into the Bay. "In a sense," historian Willem van Schendel writes, "Bangladesh *is* the Himalayas, flattened out."[6] If you could look down upon the sea floor, it would appear "virtually featureless." Sediment coats the sea floor more than twenty kilometers thick in the north, thinning out to several hundred meters toward the south. Silt creates many sandbars in the active

Bengal delta, making the northern part of the Bay especially shallow. But the "generally smooth" sea floor has significant "valley-like features" in the north and "isolated highs" in the south.[7]

The India tectonic plate runs far beneath the Bay of Bengal; it meets the Burma microplate near the Andaman Islands. The India plate moves gradually northeast toward the Eurasian landmass at a rate of around sixty millimeters a year. The friction between the India and Burma plates, where both meet the Sunda plate, has created a submarine volcanic arc subject to periodic eruptions. In December 2004 a rupture more than a hundred kilometers wide occurred on the floor of the Andaman Sea, causing a massive undersea earthquake—magnitude 9.0 on the Richter Scale—and a devastating tsunami that swept across the Indian Ocean. As many as a quarter of a million people died.[8] The 2004 tsunami, Sugata Bose writes, "brought to light the deep and unique bonds that tie together the peoples of this interregional arena of human interaction." It also laid bare the deep forces that have given life, and continue to bring death, to the Indian Ocean as a whole and to the Bay of Bengal in particular, where the 2004 tsunami took its greatest toll.[9]

The Asian monsoon animates the Bay of Bengal; it is "one of the most dramatic climatic phenomena on Earth."[10] This region is the beating heart of "monsoon Asia," which in the old colonial vision stretched from the Arabian Sea up to southern China and down to the northern tropics of Australia. In this region climate was thought to determine every aspect of human society and culture, an idea that scientists have been slower than historians to abandon.[11] The monsoon—from the Arabic *mawsim*, or "season"—is a weather system of seasonally reversing winds. Colloquially, it refers specifically to the heavy rains, or "monsoon rains," that these winds bring in the summer months. Between April and September the southwest monsoon moves roughly from southwest to northeast; between November and March the northeast monsoon moves in the opposite direction. In the Bay of Bengal these regular patterns are broken by depressions, cyclonic storms, and strong countercurrents, particularly at its northern head during the southwest monsoon, when the accumulation of water from the south has no other outlet but to turn back on itself.

The differential heating of sea and land drives the monsoon. "The Air which is less rarified or expanded by heat and consequently more ponderous," Edmund Halley wrote in his 1686 essay on the monsoons, "must have a Motion towards those parts thereof, which are more rarified, and less ponderous, to bring it to an Equilibrium."[12] The monsoon's intensity comes from the sheer mass of the Tibetan mountains, the "largest mountain chain seen on Earth for more than five hundred million years." The summertime heating of the Tibetan plateau creates low-pressure cells, drawing in moist winds from the cooler sea; in winter, cold dry winds blow out from the mountains to the warmer ocean, which has a greater capacity than the land to store heat.[13]

The southwest monsoon begins its path across the Bay of Bengal in April. By May the summer rains reach the island of Sri Lanka, a "meeting or dividing point for the currents of the Indian Ocean, the Arabian Sea, and the Bay of Bengal."[14] Witnessing the May rains drifting in from the Bay of Bengal during his stint as Chilean consul in Ceylon, the poet Pablo Neruda wrote of "the seasonal wind, the green wind, laden with space and water."[15] By early June the rains reach the Bengal delta; the winds accumulate such moisture from the sea that Cherrapunji, in the mountains north of the Bay, is the wettest place on Earth. Moving up the coast the other way, the monsoon reaches the eastern littoral of the Bay: the coasts of Arakan, lower Burma, and southern Thailand. Everywhere it intensifies in July and August, "steadiest in the central and western parts of the Bay," bringing heavy rains to most of its coastal arc. As the southwest monsoon begins to retreat in September, it settles upon the Malaysian Peninsula. There the heaviest rains come in the period of the summer monsoon's retreat, in the transitional months of October and November. But this region "below the winds" is less affected by the monsoons: the pattern of wet and dry seasons gives way to more constant rainfall at these latitudes. The Bay of Bengal is at its most unsettled as the southwest monsoon retreats in October and November. In October the Bay's notorious cyclones are most common. The term *cyclone* came into use in the 1840s, first presented at the Asiatic Society of Calcutta by ship's captain and president of the Marine Courts Henry Piddington (1797–1858), based on his detailed study of a devastating storm that had hit the Orissa coast in 1789. He derived the word from the Greek *kukloma*, "wheel, coil of a snake."[16]

Reporting on a cyclone that had swept in from the Bay to inundate the districts of Midnapore and Burdwan, in Bengal, on the fifteenth and sixteenth of October 1874, W. G. Willson observed that the "storms of October and November are usually generated in the eastern part of the

Bay of Bengal near or a little north of the Andaman islands," and warned that "there are usually no weather indications along the Bengal coastline of the coming storm until a day or two before its arrival."[17] In November the northern basin of the Bay of Bengal frequently experiences storms known in English as nor'westers: their arrival is marked by "a low bank of dark clouds in the north-west, the upper outline of which has the appearance of an arch."[18] By the second half of October, the winds have reversed and the northeast monsoon arrives on the Coromandel Coast, bringing the heaviest rains of the year there. Dry, fine weather spreads across most of the region from November until February or early March, when again the clouds begin to thicken and the waters stir.

The monsoon sustains life in the Bay. The upper layer of its waters are warm, low in salinity, and rich in nutrients and oxygen, nourished by the sheer volume of silt-laden water discharged into the sea. Great biodiversity thrives. The Bay is home to hundreds of species of fish, including some 215 demersal species, 65 pelagic, and 40 cartilaginous; shrimp, yellowfin, and skipjack tuna are plentiful.[19] Francis Day, an English fisheries officer, observed in 1873 that the waters around the Mergui Archipelago, off Burma's coast, were "literally alive with fish."[20] The aquatic life of the sea provides a crucial source of energy—calories—for human life on its coasts. Far inland, the monsoons set the rhythm of human agriculture across large parts of South, Southeast, and East Asia. In Asia the monsoon "drew the frontiers of cereal cultivation" and established the boundaries of rice production.[21] The surplus produced by rice cultivation allowed for the early development of centralized states and large urban centers and sustained some of the largest populations in the premodern world.[22] The arid, irrigated grain-raising tracts of the Indian subcontinent depend on the summer rains; so, then, do the livelihoods of a major part of the world's population.

The monsoons—cyclical, repetitive, *natural*—appear to be outside history. But the monsoons have changed; they change constantly. On the longest timescale, the monsoons have altered over "millions or tens of millions of years." On the scale of centuries, it appears that the Asian summer monsoon has strengthened during warm interglacial periods, as during the Medieval Warm Period, which ended in the middle of the thirteenth century, and weakened during periods of planetary cooling, as during the Little Ice Age, which lasted until the eighteenth century.

Monsoon patterns vary over even shorter periods and have changed particularly rapidly over the past fifty years. Often these shifts have been linked to changes in other parts of the global climate system, including the El Niño–Southern Oscillation, in the Pacific Ocean, and the North Atlantic heat conveyor.[23] From year to year the monsoons are fickle. Asian agriculture is so dependent on the monsoons that a slightly late onset can wreck a harvest; proverbs in many languages foretell the consequences of a week's, or a month's, delay. A lasting intensification in the monsoon's variability is one likely result of climate change.

The regularity, even predictability, of the monsoon winds has made the Bay of Bengal easier to cross than many other seas. This feature of its geography has shaped its history. Monsoon winds were a threat to early mariners but also an ally. For centuries the crossing was made in ships built in the Indo-Arab tradition, seen throughout the Indian Ocean from the Persian Gulf and the coast of East Africa to Melaka—from the dhows in the western Indian Ocean to the "ark-like" thonis on the Coromandel Coast and the smaller coasting vessels, catamarans and manches. Constructed from teak planks and bound with coir (coconut fiber), these vessels were sturdy and flexible.[24] The dhows' triangular lateen sails took them closer to the wind than traditional square sails. Where the Bay of Bengal met the Straits of Melaka, the Indian Ocean vessels shared the waters with local craft built in the Indonesian tradition—prahus and sampans. Small and fast, these shell-built craft with square sails carried cargoes on regional journeys and along inland waterways. By the fourteenth century, Chinese ships—"junks," the Europeans called them—crossed the Bay, as they had long crossed the South China Sea. Larger than Indian Ocean vessels, the Chinese ships could carry up to a thousand passengers and crew and a thousand tons of cargo. They had flat bottoms for shallow waters and a keel that could be lowered for deep-sea voyages.[25]

The Bay of Bengal was for centuries the maritime thoroughfare between India and China. The outer limits of the Bay lie at the Straits of Melaka. The Straits divide, in Herman Melville's words, the "long unbroken Indian Ocean from the thickly studded oriental archipelagoes." Though he sought to convey the irresistible dynamism of "the all-grasping Western world," *Moby Dick*'s narrator, Ishmael, paused to consider the "endless procession of ships before the wind"—each "freighted with the costliest cargoes of the east"—which "for centuries past" had sailed in the waters that the *Pequod* now traversed.[26] Mountain ranges on either side of the Straits, the "spines" of the Malay Peninsula and Sumatra, sheltered ships from the strength of the winds. This shelter turned the Straits into a crossroads of trade: a transit point for ships traveling between China and India, the Middle East and Europe. Lying at the end of both the southwest and the northeast monsoons, the Straits became a favored place of replenishment and commerce as ships waited for the winds' reversal. As such, the Straits of Melaka formed the pivot point of cultural interactions across a very wide region that Leonard Andaya calls the "Sea of Melayu": "one sea, stretching from India to Vietnam." It was an aqueous world in which "rivers and seas formed unities," while "land formed the link between bodies of water." The bead trade between India and Southeast Asia flourished long before the common era, as we know from archaeological evidence in Thailand and Vietnam. Buddhism formed a "common cultural bond" that linked the coastal regions of South, Southeast, and East Asia. Statues, relics, and sacred objects crossed the waters along with pilgrims.[27]

The Bay's littorals grew closer in the first millennium of the common era. Under the rule of the Pallava dynasty in South India, from the middle of the sixth to the middle of the eighth century, the trade between India and Southeast Asia flourished. The Pallavas influenced statuary and temple architecture across Southeast Asia. The period between the ninth and thirteenth centuries marked a high point in the premodern history of commerce in the region, coinciding with the rise and collapse of the Chola Empire in South India. An ancient dynasty with roots in the fertile Kaveri belt of the Tamil country, the Cholas reached the height of their power between the ninth and thirteenth centuries, when they ruled over much of South India. Under the Cholas, Indian merchants' overseas activities expanded, led by powerful merchant guilds known as the Ayyavole and Manigramam. Javanese inscriptions record the presence of South Indian merchants in cities across Indonesia; the reach of Coromandel cotton textiles left its trace on the garments drawn or engraved upon Javanese statues.[28]

Chola power expanded through South India in the tenth century. By the early decades of the eleventh, the Cholas moved into Sri Lanka, the Maldives, and the Laccadives, announcing their arrival as a regional maritime power.[29] Theirs was the first Bay of Bengal empire. The region

Figure 1 Fragments of a Hindu religious structure excavated in the Bujang Valley, Malaysia: evidence of a thriving Indian settlement in Kedah in the first millennium of the common era. *Photograph by Sunil Amrith.*

became a site of imperial and commercial rivalry. Challenging the Cholas for control over the Bay was the empire of Srivijaya, which sought a commanding position around the Straits of Melaka while advancing on its rival to the east, the Javanese kingdom of Mataram. On the Southeast Asian mainland, the Cambodian kingdom of Angkor expanded south, in competition with the Dai Viet and Champa polities (in present-day Vietnam). The Burmese kingdom of Pegu, on the northeastern rim of the Bay of Bengal, faced both east and west, developing Buddhist connections with Ceylon while linking the Bay's northern commerce overland with Yunnan. The great prize for all was the China trade. The new Song dynasty in China (AD 960) fostered overseas trade, breaking with the inward-looking, xenophobic policies of the Tang dynasty in decline. Between the tenth and the thirteenth centuries, trade in Asia expanded rapidly; few parts of the region were unaffected by the gravitational pull of China's coastal commerce.[30]

The competitive quest for Chinese favor reached its apex in the 1020s. In 1025 the Chola ruler, Rajendra, launched a military expedition across the Bay of Bengal to raid the lands of Srivijaya. It was the first attempt to assert naval supremacy over the Bay; many others would try it in the centuries that followed, including the Portuguese, the Dutch, the British, and the Japanese. The causes and the course of the Chola raid on Southeast Asia remain obscure. The most likely explanation is that Srivijaya attempted to monopolize the Bay's trade with China, and the raid was retaliation. The Chola leadership might also have been pressured into the expedition by merchant guilds wanting to shore up their own position in Southeast Asia.[31] The impact of the Chola naval expedition appears to have been modest, and after a few quiet years, the Srivijaya rulers again sent a large diplomatic mission to China. Commercial ties between China and India were well established by the thirteenth century; direct contacts between them prospered. Archaeologists have found evidence of a large South Indian merchant community in the Chinese city of Quanzhou, in the form of a Hindu temple dating from around the thirteenth century, containing hundreds of sculptures. In the Indian port of Nagapatnam, the ruins of a three-storeyed Chinese pagoda could be seen until their demolition in 1867.

The efflorescence of commerce between strong regional states was a connected process—connected on a Eurasian scale, as Victor Lieberman has shown in his pathbreaking work. Recent climatological evidence suggests that the period of planetary warming between the ninth and thirteenth centuries, known as the Medieval Warm Period (c. 900/950 to c. 1250/1300), played a coordinating role in this expansion. By extending the growing season, shifting the intertropical convergence zone several degrees to the south, and strengthening the Asian monsoon, this climatic anomaly supported a period of state building, agricultural colonization, population growth, and overseas trade. After around 1240, "not only in Southeast Asia but in Europe, South Asia, and China, major states collapsed, societies and cultures fragmented, and populations and economic output fell sharply." One plausible explanation for this coordinated collapse was the onset of a period of global cooling that reversed the gains of the Medieval Warm Period, sharpening the social and political tensions fueled by the earlier period of expansion. In both China and South Asia, this coincided with a fresh wave of conquest and invasion by seminomadic armed groups from Inner Asia, which "profoundly disrupted regional politics." The Turkic founders of the Delhi sultanate had conquered much of North India by 1231; in the early fourteenth century, they expanded south into the Deccan and beyond, destabilizing regional polities. The Mongol Yuan invasion of China defeated the Song dynasty and succeeded in unifying north and south China by 1279. In both India and China, Inner Asian conquest reoriented patterns of exchange away from seaborne commerce and toward overland trade at the frontiers between settled lands and the steppes—the trade of the Silk Road.[32] Levels of integration around the Bay of Bengal declined until the wave of European expansion that began in the fifteenth century both revived and transformed the region.

Throughout that interregnum, the commercial and cultural life of the Bay of Bengal moved in new directions. The growth of Islam in South and Southeast Asia between the thirteenth and fifteenth centuries gave new prominence to Muslim trading communities from South India. The Delhi sultanate placed India at the center of the Islamic world: in the early fourteenth century its power expanded into South India. Dispersed communities of Telugu- and Tamil-speaking Muslims connected South and Southeast Asia to the Arab world. Muslim traders and teachers provided an element of continuity with the past once the region came under European control, they added another layer to the earlier, Buddhist, cultural traffic that bound the Bay's coasts together.

Over centuries interregional trade produced a "family resemblance" in material culture, religious practices, and ritual across a wide area, giving South and Southeast Asia the feel of sharing "a neighborhood."[33]

There is much we do not, and may never, know. Amidst the uncertainty and speculation, the British archaeologist H. G. Quaritch Wales, working in Malaya in the 1930s, insisted that "one cannot of course, at any period, exclude contact more or less direct from across the Bay of Bengal."[34]

The Bay of Bengal was for many centuries, and in many languages, known as the "Chola Sea" or the "Chola Lake"; the Portuguese gave it the name "Golfo de Bengala." At the 1938 International Congress of Geography in Amsterdam, Portuguese scholars Armando Cortesão and Avelino Teixeira presented a paper on the "first account of the Far East in the sixteenth century," in which they discussed the manuscript of Francisco Rodrigues's *O Livro,* held in the library of the Chamber of Deputies in Paris. Rodrigues produced one of the first known maps of the Bay of Bengal. In a letter to the Portuguese king, Manuel, in August 1512, Afonso de Albuquerque called Rodrigues a pilot "with very good knowledge and able to make maps." In "178 folios of thick white paper, $263 \times 377\,mm$," Rodrigues sketched the route from Europe to China. The following year he participated in the first Portuguese expedition to the Red Sea, and in 1519 he captained one of the ships in the disastrous Portuguese expedition to China.[35]

European navigators relied on local nautical knowledge. Rodrigues's map of the route to China depended on information gleaned from Malay seafarers. Among the first to inscribe this nautical wisdom was the Arab navigator Ahmad Ibn Majid in the late fifteenth century. Ibn Majid's work was a compendium of local seafaring wisdom, distilled through his keen intelligence. He declared that the navigators of the Coromandel Coast of India knew the Bay of Bengal best. "It is sensible," he wrote, "that every man knows his own coast best, although God is all-knowing, and it is certain that the Cholas live nearer to these coasts than anyone else, so we have used them and their *qiyas* as a guide."[36] Ibn Majid saw the monsoon above all as a specific *date* for sailing from a port. His treatise shows how regular and predictable were the sailing schedules for each of the Indian Ocean's seas. He cautioned mariners that to take advantage of the favorable winds of the northeast monsoon,

the timing had to be just right as they embarked on the westward journey across the Bay of Bengal, from Southeast Asia back to eastern India.
He advised them not to set out too late in the season and reminded
them that the northeast monsoon did not usually arrive in Sumatra
before the beginning of January. He warned of the particular unreliabil-
ity of the winds when the monsoons changed over in March and April,
and the threat of fearsome storms in October and November.

Ibn Majid's work was a faithful companion to sailors for hundreds of
years. By the eighteenth century Europeans were no longer satisfied
with the state of navigational knowledge. When the British East India
Company commissioned a chart of the Bay of Bengal in 1772, the famed
mapmaker Alexander Dalrymple declared that "it must appear very
extraordinary, when it is considered how long the Europeans have had
an intercourse with Bengal, that there is not hitherto a particular Chart
of the Bay of Bengal published in any language."[37] Portuguese maps no
longer met the exacting requirements of modern cartography. English
attempts to formalize and extend their knowledge of the sea had clear

Figure 2 A New Map of the East Indies, by J. Bayly (c. 1782). *From the author's
collection.*

political motivations. "The whole of the Coast of Choromandel being now under the Government of the English or of their Friends and Allies," Dalrymple concluded, "it will be very proper to take the present opportunity to make a compleat Survey of it."[38] Keen though the English were to minimize the prior achievements of the Portuguese, their bibliographies are littered with references to Portuguese and French manuscripts, themselves imbued with (borrowed or stolen) Arab, Indian, and Javanese expertise. As K. N. Chaudhuri has written, "the greatest achievement of Spanish and Portuguese hydrographers was to bring together the work of theoretical mathematicians and combine these with the practical experience of seamen." By the seventeenth century English and Dutch navigational charts surpassed those of the Portuguese; the captains of East Indiamen were "carefully trained to follow generalized methods on their voyages to the Indian Ocean."[39] Their knowledge of the Bay of Bengal emerged from fragments. A 1787 list of available maps details an accumulating series of sketches, "views," and charts as exploration intensified and navigational techniques improved.[40] Seagoing chronometers improved the accuracy with which sailors could measure time. Sailing directions for the Bay of Bengal proceeded by experiment: they reflect the practical knowledge of many voyages, preserved for posterity in ships' journals.[41]

As British power expanded and as scientific knowledge advanced, maps and sailing directions were codified in the *Bay of Bengal Pilot* in 1879, which would go through several editions into the 1960s. The *Pilot* was one of several guides published by the British Admiralty, alongside those to the "Eastern Archipelago," the Straits of Melaka, and the China Sea. "These business-like books," Somerset Maugham wrote, did not allow their "stern sense of the practical" to "dim the poetry that, like the spice-laden breeze that assails your senses . . . when you approach some of those magical islands of the Eastern seas, blows with so sweet a fragrance through the printed pages."[42] The *Pilot*'s warnings and advice spanned centuries. It explained how the crossing was hastened or hindered by the monsoons. It contained many general indicators: at all times, "keep as far west of the Andamans as possible"; on the Coromandel Coast, make land to the north of the port during the northeast monsoon, and to the south during the southwest monsoon.[43]

The threat of cyclones loomed large. By the middle of the nineteenth century English sailors had begun to collect systematic observations of

cyclones in the Bay of Bengal, of interest to meteorologists and navigators alike. Captain Henry Piddington, who coined the term "cyclone,"
spent his retirement in the painstaking compilation of observations
that filled the pages of the Asiatic Society of Bengal's *Journal*. The log-
book of the *Belle Alliance,* published by Piddington, was a testament to
how dangerous a stormy crossing could be. On the way from Madras to
Calcutta, the ship was blown off course, toward the center of the Bay,
by a cyclone. It was the end of April 1840, late in the changeover period, as the southwest monsoon was beginning to blow. Between 1:00
and 5:00 in the morning on April 30, the ship's crew felt the "gale increasing, with violent gusts of wind and heavy rain." By six o'clock the
ship was "plunging deep, with a heavy confused sea." The gale "carried
away the flying jibboom." Hours later, the desperate crew had to cut
away the ship's fore and main topgallant masts to stop the vessel from
"laying over and plunging deep." The log repeated the invocation of a
"heavy, confused sea." After a "sudden calm," the ship was again battered by "most awful gusts of wind and heavy rain"—such were the
vicissitudes of the cyclonic winds. Only after midnight did a semblance
of calm return with "thick hazy weather." The *Belle Alliance* and her
crew were lucky: they lived to resume course for Calcutta.[44]As accounts
of the Bay's cyclones became widely known, navigators sought general
principles for steering through them safely. C. W. Brebner, veteran
ship's captain from Mauritius, wrote in the 1880s that "the mariner
navigating the Bay at this [monsoon] season should always be in a state
of complete preparedness," senses at the height of alertness, "carefully
watching the barometer for any indication of a rising wind and sea, as a
low and falling barometer with dark gloomy weather may safely be considered the precursor of a cyclonic storm."[45]

This nautical wisdom appeared timeless. Advice and observations
from the late seventeenth century sat alongside accounts from the mid-
nineteenth. One gets little sense that by the time the first edition of the
Bay of Bengal Pilot was published, a fundamental transformation had
compressed space and time on the crossing. The rise of the steamship
brought about a wholly different relationship with the winds and the
sea: "not so much a contest," Joseph Conrad wrote, "as the disdainful
ignoring of the sea." Steam power liberated shipping from the monsoons.
Conrad contrasted the steamer's "disdain" for nature with the sailing
ship's reverence for it, "bordering upon the magic of the invisible

forces, sustained by the inspiration of the life-giving and death-dealing winds."[46]

In the 1920s the Bay of Bengal was crossed by air for the first time. British and Dutch exploratory missions culminated in a Dutch plane reaching Batavia in 1927. On October 1, 1931, "one of the great days in the history of air transport," the Dutch Airline KLM began scheduled passenger service from Amsterdam to Batavia, carrying four paying passengers; flying time was eighty-one hours. From Calcutta, the route followed the coastal arc around the Bay to Akyab, Rangoon, Bangkok, Medan, Palembang, and Batavia. In 1933 KLM extended its service to Singapore. Its British rival, Imperial Airways, had yet to get that far.[47]

The following year Richard Upjohn Light—neurosurgeon at Yale University's medical school, amateur aviator, and later president of the American Geographical Society—crossed the Bay of Bengal in a Bellanca Skyrocket seaplane as part of a 29,000-mile journey around the world. His companion was Robert Wilson, a Yale graduate in electrical engineering and an expert in radio technology, who had never previously flown. "The airplane recognizes no geography save that of altitude and temperature," Light insisted. Yet the monsoons shaped his journey. "The onset of the monsoon forced a change in plans," he noted, "it was now impossible to round the southern tip of the Indian peninsula with the sea plane." Despite advanced navigational aids, Light depended on mariners' faithful guides: charts and lighthouses, and the reassurance of land. Setting course for Akyab, crossing the Bay of Bengal where the Brahmaputra River met the sea, Light checked his plane's position "with a lightship far out in the bay" and "soon had a first close view of the rocky shore that was to be our guide for thousands of miles." But from the air Light pictured the arc of coasts in a new way—through aerial photographs. His images charted the shift from dense cultivation along the river deltas to the threatening, lucrative jungles of the frontier. He was the first to capture the "traffic-heavy" Irrawaddy from the air, glittering as the evening sun broke through a bank of dark clouds.[48]

The Bay of Bengal marks the eastern frontier of the Hindu cosmos. Of the four *dhams* (sacred dwellings) of Hindu mythology that span the four corners of the subcontinent—Badrinath, Puri, Rameshwaram, and Dwarka—Puri fronts the Bay of Bengal along the Orissa coast, and the island of Rameshwaram, where the Indian subcontinent juts into the sea, is the southernmost of the *dhams*. Today, as in the past, the "footsteps of pilgrims create a lived landscape," Diana Eck writes. Rameshwaram plays a pivotal role in the *Ramayana*—it is from there that Rama builds his bridge (*setu*) to the isle of Lanka to rescue his wife Sita, held in captivity by Lanka's demon-king, Ravana. Many Indian pilgrims believe that a visit to the holiest of cities on the banks of the Ganges, Varanasi (Banaras), should be followed by a journey to Rameshwaram; today the Rameshwaram temple receives pilgrims from every corner of India. Many of their journeys culminate in ritual bathing in the Bay of Bengal. Farther south, at the southern tip of the Indian subcontinent, Kanyakumari is the abode of the goddess Kumari, guardian of India's shores. India's eastern coast is full of sacred places (*tirthas*), where India's rivers meet their "lord"—the ocean.[49]

But the Indian sacred imagination has long extended beyond the subcontinent and across the eastern seas. For ancient Indian storytellers, the sea promised risk, temptation, and untold riches at the end of the crossing. Across the sea lay Suvarnabhumi, the "land of gold," nothing less than "an eastern eldorado." The story literature of South Asia, both religious and secular, captures the "adventurous spirit and acquisitive ethos" of early voyagers to the east.[50] The imaginative power of the Bay of Bengal stems from its fury.

Reaching the "land of gold" entailed crossing the Bay and confronting its dangers. Malevolent beasts inhabit the "black waters." The sea's demons threaten to swallow ships whole. The Buddhist *Jatakas*—stories of the previous births of the Buddha, dating back to the fourth century BCE—are a rich source of such narratives, among them the story of Prince Polajanaka's voyage to Suvarnabhumi. The prince sets out to recapture the throne that his father had held before it was usurped by his brother. Living in exile with his mother, the prince declares, "I will go to Suvarnabhumi and get great riches there." His mother is full of foreboding. "The sea has few chances of success and many dangers," she warns. As he crosses the Bay of Bengal, disaster strikes. "Having gone too violently in its course," the ship's "planks gave way, the water rose higher and higher," and "the ship began to sink in the middle of the ocean while the crew wept and lamented and invoked their different gods"—an early invocation, this, of the multireligious world of Asian seafarers. As the ship goes down the prince is steadfast, hard up against the mast that "stood upright" as the vessel sinks. The sailors "became food for the fishes and tortoises, and the water all round assumed the color of blood." The prince survives the ordeal; he "crossed through the jewel-colored waves" and traverses the sea "like a mass of gold."

In midcrossing the prince meets Manimekhala, daughter of the gods and guardian of the seas. At first she doubts his resilience:

> Here in this deep and boundless waste where shore is
>   none to meet the eye
> Thy utmost strivings are in vain,—here in mid-ocean
>   thou must die.

The prince convinces the guardian of the seas that he will "not yield" to the turbulent waters. Manimekhala praises his courage:

> Thou who thus bravely fightest on amidst this fierce
>   unbounded sea
> Nor shrinkest from the appointed task, striving where
>   duty calleth thee
> Go where thy heart would have thee go, nor let nor
>   hindrance shall there be.[51]

The Bay of Bengal, before it bore that name, was just the "fierce unbounded sea."

The *Jatakas* are not the only tales of seaborne trial. In another well-known story, the *Kathasaritsagara,* an eleventh-century collection of Indian tales, the princess Gunavati, on her way from Kedah to India, finds herself shipwrecked off the coast of Suvarnadvipa.[52] Early Chinese travelers, too, faced turbulence on the maritime highway from India to China. Fa Xian (Fa-Hsien) was a fifth-century Buddhist pilgrim who journeyed from China to India. His return journey from the Buddhist lands, in the year 413, led him to cross the Bay from Ceylon to Java. He left Ceylon on a "large merchant-vessel which carried about two hundred men." Two days into the crossing the ship encountered a storm and developed a dangerous leak. The storm "lasted thirteen days and nights," until eventually the ship found shelter on an island, where the sailors were able to restore it to seaworthiness. "In the sea are many pirates," Fa Xian warned, and "any one who falls in with them is lost." He thought the Bay of Bengal was "boundless"; "it is impossible to know East from West," and "in dark rainy weather one must run before the wind in ignorance of its direction." In the "darkness of night," anyone crossing the Bay would see "nothing but great waves striking one another and shining like fire and one sees sea-monsters of various descriptions." After ninety days Fa Xian arrived in Ya-Va-Di (probably Java). Stranded by the turn of the monsoon, he stayed in Java until the following May, when finally he set sail for Canton.[53]

Folk traditions, still alive in the twentieth century, present the Bay of Bengal similarly, as a place of terror and adventure. Student ethnographers—recipients of Ramtanu Lahiri research fellowships—recorded ballads from eastern rural Bengal in the 1920s. In these Bengali songs the sea was simply "the terrible Bay—the *kalapani*." The ballads imagined the sea's waves "high as mountain summits." Such were the waters' furies that boats "were raised to a great height to be thrown down to the lowest point," and "ships with sails puffed by winds struggled hard to preserve themselves." Bengali oral traditions evolved to include human as well as natural terrors: the Harmads, Portuguese "pirates," were a particular threat. A history of imperial plunder was incorporated into legends of the sea's "few chances" and its "many dangers." "In the immense deep, the Harmads were a terror"; they lurked in the Bay and "plundered the boats," and "captains of the sea-side trembled in fear" of them. In an ironic reversal of the spice trade, local fishermen seize armfuls of pepper—the lucre that brought Portuguese gunboats to the Indian Ocean—and blind the Harmads.[54]

By the twentieth century crossing the Bay of Bengal was a matter of routine, and with routine came disenchantment. Only a privileged few experienced the romance of flight, but hundreds of thousands of deck passengers crossed the sea every year. Their voyage came under the control of a regular bureaucracy of sanitary inspectors, ships' nurses, magistrates, and licensed cooks. The journey was quicker. Shipwrecks were rare. Conditions on board improved. But an element of seasickness and disorientation remained. One's first sight of Southeast Asia's modern docks—industrialized, bustling, and regimented—from the deck of a steamer bore little resemblance to the enchanting vista of Marlowe's first encounter with "the East" in Joseph Conrad's story "Youth": "I see it always from a small boat, a high outline of mountains, blue and afar in the morning; like faint mist at noon; a jagged wall of purple at sunset . . . And I see a bay, a wide bay, smooth as glass and polished like ice, shimmering in the dark."[55] By contrast, as the Japanese ship *Tosamaru* pulled into port in 1916, Rabindranath Tagore stood on deck and surveyed the belching chimneys of Rangoon's skyline, commenting that "it looked as if Burma was lying on its back and smoking a cigar." Approaching Rangoon's jetties, Tagore remarked that they were like "so many hideous, giant, iron leeches."[56]

More prosaic is the account of M. K. Bhasi, a schoolteacher who traveled from Madras to Singapore in the late 1940s in search of a better life. Penang provided his first glimpse of Southeast Asia. It was fleeting, but it left an impression. "We were allowed to come out [of the ship] in Penang only for a few hours. And we just took a taxi or something, and just went around," Bhasi recalled. What struck him most were "the various races" of people. This was "quite uncommon in my old village, or even in Trivandrum or Madras; they didn't have that cosmopolitan look."[57] Crossing the Bay of Bengal, he had arrived in the "plural society."

"The sea was the same," Derek Walcott writes, "except for its history."[58] The Indian Ocean was "global" long before the Atlantic. Merchants roamed from China to the Arabian Peninsula, settling in port cities around the ocean's rim, setting up shop, marrying into local families, shipping spices and jewels and elephants and horses over long distances. Shared faith created trust among strangers; where faith was disputed, other rituals cemented bonds. Centuries before the first Atlantic crossings, pilgrims moved from the Indonesian archipelago and India to the Hejaz, or they followed Buddhist routes from China and Japan to India and Sri Lanka. Slaves crossed the sea under duress. Mariners navigated the monsoon winds with growing precision. People spoke many languages; some of their languages—Arabic, Malay, Swahili—broke through the barriers of ethnicity. On the grandest scale, the Indian Ocean brought many civilizations into contact and blurred their boundaries; perhaps they were never pure, sealed off, to begin with.[59]

It is a world that is strangely familiar from the vantage point of the early twenty-first century—a world of polyglot traders and cross-cultural marriages, a world in which long-distance travel is a common experience. The Indian Ocean's past recasts contemporary globalization in a "very new yet very old framework." At the same time, that past is deeply unfamiliar, in ways that explain the rise in scholarship on the Indian Ocean world since the 1980s. Many histories of the Indian Ocean evoke an open, cosmopolitan world of trade and intercultural exchange. Often they end their stories at the point when Portuguese gunboats brought violence to a peaceful ocean, disrupting its ancient bonds; or they end with the triumph of nationalism, which rooted political belonging in the bounded territories marked out by European conquerors. There is a clear—sometimes irresistible—tendency to romanticize the Indian Ocean's precolonial history, downplaying earlier episodes of violence and older forms of predatory behavior in favor of a world in equilibrium.

The narrowness of postcolonial nationalism compounded the loss of connection across the region, mourned in the late twentieth-century context of rising religious violence and bloody internecine wars across the postcolonial world. In a pivotal scene in Amitav Ghosh's *In an Antique Land,* a young Indian anthropologist (Ghosh himself) and an Egyptian imam find themselves in an argument that degenerates into a discussion of the relative strength of the two countries' armed forces in the 1980s. "The Imam and I had participated in our final defeat," Ghosh writes, "in the dissolution of centuries of dialogue that had linked us: we had demonstrated the irreversible triumph of the language that had usurped all the others in which people once discussed their differences." Ghosh evokes that earlier "dialogue" in the other part of his book, through the story of Abraham bin Yiju, a twelfth-century Jewish trader, whose letters, preserved in Cairo's Genizah, recount his travels across the medieval Indian Ocean world. But perhaps that "defeat" was never complete. Well into the age of European world dominance, the Indian Ocean continued as a highway of scholars, pilgrims, merchants, and journalists, an "interregional arena" with its own rhythms and its relentless flow of ideas. In the Indian Ocean's port cities, encounters between Asians and Europeans, Muslims and missionaries, Buddhists and rationalists, gave rise to a "historically deep archive of competing universalisms."[60]

For centuries, commerce and culture created a "strong sense of unity" across the Indian Ocean; for those who made their living from oceanic trade, the far shores of the sea's littoral were often closer—culturally, economically, imaginatively—than their own hinterlands. Nevertheless, the western and eastern divisions of the Indian Ocean (known to us as the Arabian Sea and the Bay of Bengal) were each more closely integrated within themselves than with the Indian Ocean as a whole. The Arabian Sea's networks linked western India's coast most closely with the Persian Gulf, eastern Africa, and the islands of the southern Indian Ocean; the Bay of Bengal's web of commerce and migration joined eastern India with mainland and island Southeast Asia.[61]

Surprisingly, however, most histories of the Indian Ocean have ignored the Bay of Bengal in favor of the ocean's western reaches; surprising, because the coasts of the Bay were more closely linked than any other part of the Indian Ocean. Its distinctiveness within the wider Indian Ocean comes from the sheer scale of movement that tied its coasts together, and in the nineteenth century this movement underwent a step change. Far more people crossed the Bay of Bengal than any other part of the Indian Ocean. Of the nearly 30 million people who left India's shores between 1840 and 1940, all but 2 million of them traveled back and forth between eastern India and just three destinations: Ceylon, Burma, and Malaya. This was overwhelmingly a circular migration around the Bay of Bengal. The migration of labor, in turn, made the region the most economically important segment of the Indian Ocean world.

One explanation for this neglect is that scholarly interest in Islam's binding role across the Indian Ocean has directed attention to the links between South Asia and the Middle East. Yet the Islamic connections across the eastern Indian Ocean were quite as intensive as in the west: traveling traders and teachers from India and China deepened the influence of Islam across Southeast Asia. Under European imperial rule, Indian (and Arab) Muslim traders continued to move across the Bay. There is no question that Islam provided a cultural and ritual thread binding Indian Ocean societies together; but many millions crossed the Indian Ocean who were not Muslims. The region also hosted intensive connections between the Indian Ocean and the Chinese maritime sphere. The Bay of Bengal's role in global history stems from its position as a corridor between India and China, a position that it retains today. When (Hindu and Muslim) migrants from India crossed the Bay in the nineteenth and twentieth centuries, they encountered not only the peoples of Southeast Asia but also the rich and complex society of Chinese overseas. The Bay of Bengal and the South China Sea—and, through them, Indian and Chinese migrant worlds—converged on the Malay Peninsula, which is our story's eastern stage, where much of the action takes place. Crossings were never smooth. Cultural encounters were dangerous as often as they were productive. In the modern world, the Indian Ocean's cosmopolitanism was messy and inconsistent, and often it shattered under pressure. It developed as a cultural response to the demands of living in a world of strangers; its archive lies in popular culture, in the unwritten conventions of urban sociability, and in the shape of the landscape as much as in the writings of poets and visionaries.

Any history of an ocean must confront the question of boundaries—between sea and land, between fresh water and salt, between the seas that make up an ocean; from that question "all others flow."[62] Often these boundaries are arbitrary, and they shift over time. According to the strict definition of the International Oceanographic Commission, the Bay of Bengal's southern limits are south of the Nicobar Islands, intersecting the northern edge of Sumatra. From the perspective of political and cultural history, to write of the Bay of Bengal without considering the Malay Peninsula would be meaningless. At particular moments the reach of the Bay of Bengal could be greater still. Braudel wrote of the "global" Mediterranean: in the sixteenth century, its "world horizons" reached "as far as the Azores and the New World, the Red Sea, and the Persian Gulf." Similarly, we are concerned with the Bay of Bengal in global history. To anticipate just one example, Malaya supplied the majority of the American automobile industry's rubber by the 1920s, most of it tapped by Indian migrants who had crossed the sea; the Bay was, for a time, central to Henry Ford's revolution and the rise of an oil-hungry capitalism. At every stage, the life of the Bay of Bengal was shaped by its embeddedness in the wider Indian Ocean, and by connections of trade and culture on an intercontinental scale, underpinned by the power and the violence of empires that were global in their reach.

And what of the sea itself? "Most novelists," Orhan Pamuk writes, "sense that reading the opening pages of a novel is akin to entering a landscape painting."[63] Most oceanic historians begin by evoking a seascape. Braudel insisted that this was no mere backdrop; after all, he noted, "ships sail on a real sea that changes with the seasons." But in his history of the Indian Ocean, K. N. Chaudhuri invokes Braudel to argue that the history of the sea is one "in which all change is slow, a history of constant repetition, ever-recurring cycles." If the sea had a history, it was one of "depth and semi-immobility."[64] The French philosopher Paul Ricoeur described the first volume of Braudel's epic as a "geohistory whose hero is the Mediterranean." Yet the hero is, in one sense, passive: the unchanging sea provides a backdrop for very human adventures. "Here, now, are the waters, their coastlands and their islands," Ricoeur wrote, but "they, too, enter this geohistory on the scale of human beings and their navigation."[65]

In its cyclical life, the Bay of Bengal is more dramatic than the Mediterranean; from month to month it changes more. Each monsoon season, the average sea level on the Bay's northeast shore, near Chittagong, fluctuates by four feet, "the largest on record in the world."[66] Dramatic change comes to the Bay seasonally, annually. But change is not just seasonal. The sea—its currents, its shoreline—has changed gradually, over millennia. Its coasts have been carved away by floods; they have expanded as mangrove colonies spread and sandbanks shifted. Such changes have occurred ever more rapidly over the past century. In the twentieth century the effects of human intervention became so pronounced and so fundamental that they began to reshape the sea, breaking the Bay of Bengal's "constant repetition" and its "ever-recurring cycles."[67] The landscape of the coasts changed first, and they changed dramatically. The mass migration of the age of empire turned tropical Southeast Asia into a flood of commodities: the forests of Malaya cleared and replanted by Tamil workers crossing the Bay of Bengal, its tin mined by Chinese laborers crossing the South China Sea. For a time the valleys of South India seemed to open directly onto the frontiers of Southeast Asia, a great river of labor that spilled into the Bay. Until the twentieth century, changes in the land left barely a trace on the sea. Since the 1950s, and with greater force since the 1970s, the sea displays the effects of human activity—it is choked with refuse, its fish stocks have dwindled, its level rises as it heats up. The Bay of Bengal is no longer the same sea.

These transformations in the sea are an outcome—unintended and unpredictable—of a history of migration, imperial expansion, and technological change that knit the littorals of the Bay of Bengal together, then pulled them apart. The natural history of the Bay of Bengal has become inseparable from its human history; environmental history became inseparable, in the twentieth century, from the history of migration.

Environmental historians rightly caution us against "ventriloquism": seeking to give voice to the waters, or to the fish, in ways that could only ever project upon them human understandings or fantasies.[68] This book does not attempt to make the Bay of Bengal "speak"; it does, however, treat the sea as more than an empty space to be traversed.[69] The Bay of Bengal has a life. The sea's role in human history—and the consequences of that history for the sea—deserve more serious consideration than they have received.

2

That Vast Sea's Emporium

Nagore is a modest town a few hours' drive south of Pondicherry. There are few signs here of India's new prosperity. Washed by the Bay of Bengal, this stretch of Tamil Nadu's coast was among the places worst hit by the Indian Ocean tsunami of 2004. When I visited four years later, I saw many reminders of the devastation, with rehabilitation projects still lining the main road. There were reminders, too, of a past far more distant. "The locality of the town may be recognised from seaward by its five well known mosque towers, which are white and visible long before the low coast in their vicinity comes into view," the *Bay of Bengal Pilot* wrote of Nagore; the same minarets dominate the horizon a century later.[1] The "well known mosque" is a tomb shrine (*dargah*) to the saint Shahul Hamid, built in the seventeenth century.

The shrine complex feels like a self-contained township. The passageway leading to the first courtyard is lined with stalls selling pieces of foil imprinted with images—a wounded leg, for healing; a ship, to symbolize a safe journey—compact discs, prayer beads, mats, cloth, rubber balls, toys, kites, sweets, and drinks. Visitors to the shrine are Muslim and Hindu; they come from nearby, and from as far away as Central Asia. I am struck by the multitudes who have taken up residence at the shrine. Those who cannot afford the simple rooms offered for rent are stretched out on the floor; many of them are unable to move, clearly very ill. The shrine remains a site of healing, and plants from its garden are renowned for their curative power. The genial trustee, my host, points out to me the number of Hindus worshipping at this "Muslim" *dargah* as we walk through the compound. "You will

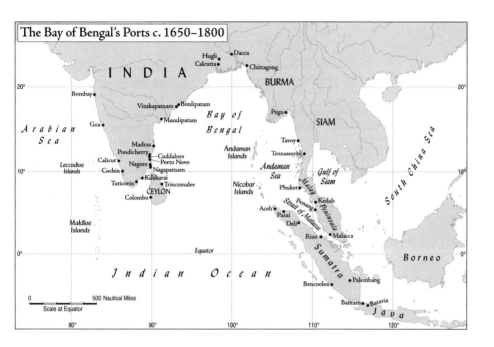

The Bay of Bengal's Ports c. 1650–1800

INDIA

Hugli • • Dacca
Calcutta •
• Chittagong

BURMA

Bombay •

Vizakapatnam • • Bimlipatam

Bay of
• Masulipatam
Bengal

Pegu •

SIAM

Arabian
Sea

Goa •

Madras •

Tavoy •

Andaman
Islands

Tennasserim •

Pondicherry •
Calicut •   • Cuddalore
Nagore • • Porto Novo
Cochin •   Nagapatnam
Tuticorin • • Kilakarai
• Trincomalee

Laccadive
Islands

Andaman
Sea

Gulf of
Siam

Phuket •

South China Sea

Nicobar
Islands

Malay

CEYLON

Colombo •

Penang • • Kedah

Aceh •
Pasai •
Deli •

Strait of Malacca

Maldive
Islands

Peninsula

Riau • • Malacca

Borneo

Sumatra

Equator

Indian   Ocean

Bencoolen •
• Palembang

0   500 Nautical Miles

Scale at Equator

Bantam • • Batavia
Java

80°   90°   100°   110°   120°

Figure 3 One of the minarets of the Dargah of Shahul Hamid, Nagore, Tamil Nadu. *Photograph by Sunil Amrith.*

hear music here like you won't hear at any other mosque," he says as Hindu devotional songs blare from a shop's speakers. He shows me the parts of the complex that Hindu devotees have donated, including two of the minarets and a gold doorway to the inner sanctum. The Nagore shrine has long fostered interreligious community. It also commemorates the long-standing connections between Nagore and Southeast Asia.[2]

For centuries local merchants have bound this stretch of the Coromandel Coast to Southeast Asia. Alongside the Tamil Muslim merchants of Nagore and Nagapatnam, Chettiar, Sindhi, and Gujarati traders from India sojourned in the port cities of the Malay world. Starting in the fifteenth century they were joined by European trading companies, attracted by the commercial opportunities of the Bay of Bengal. Europeans' routes to and through the Bay followed those of Indian, Malay, Arab, and Chinese ships that had gone before them. Europeans brought with them new ideas of territory, law, and religious mission; they had different conceptions of human difference (including the idea of "race") and different ways of governing it. They made new demands on the land. In search of profit, and in defense of their monopolies, European trading companies reorganized and intensified production by inducement or by force of arms. Their appetite for the earth's products appeared limitless—spices, timber, food to feed their workers, and eventually coal to power their ships.

The lands around the Bay's rim were no tabula rasa for European newcomers to reshape in their own image. The Bay was thick with traffic and crowded with family firms and business relationships that antedated the Europeans' arrival. The Asian commercial world was the substratum on which the Europeans constructed a new layer of trade—and which, eventually, haltingly, they came to dominate. By the turn of the nineteenth century the British dominated the Bay of Bengal as no previous power had ever done. But even British control rested on long-established Asian webs of trade that remained relatively autonomous. Until the era of "high imperialism" in the second half of the nineteenth century, British dominance should not be overstated. Despite British attempts to drive local shipping merchants out of business, Nagapatnam—just a few miles from Nagore—continued to enjoy a "considerable trade with the straits of Singapore, Penang, Rangoon, and Maulmain," and "upwards of 3000 passengers are annually carried by

Figure 4 Inscription commemorating the donation to the Nagore shrine by a haji in Rangoon. *Photograph by Sunil Amrith.*

native vessels of 150 to 700 tons to the ports of Burmah and Singapore."
Nagore's Muslim merchants, British observers saw, "carry on a large
trade with Penang, the coast of Sumatra, Maulmain and Rangoon,
whence teak is imported for the repair of vessels."[3] At these ports the
old world of Asian commerce met the expanding world of European
empires. Their paths across the Bay of Bengal intersected—and at times
they clashed over taxes and monopolies, rights and duties.[4]

Islam crossed the Bay of Bengal along many routes. By the eighth century of the common era, Arab traders had settled along the Coromandel
Coast and brought their faith with them. In South India, as elsewhere,
Sufi mystics spread Islam to the interior.[5] Islam established a foothold
in trading towns along the southern coast—Kilakkarai, Kayalpatnam,
Nagore, Nagapatnam, Porto Novo, Karaikal, and Pulicat. Across the
Bay, Islam expanded its reach starting in the late thirteenth century: its
first foothold was the kingdom of Pasai, in northern Sumatra. Parts of
the northern Malay Peninsula, eastern Java, and the southern Philippines followed in the fourteenth century. These settlements formed a
connected world of faith and commerce. The turning point in the rooting of Islam in Southeast Asia came at the beginning of the fifteenth
century with the conversion of Melaka, the region's foremost trading
center, in 1419. The years between 1400 and 1650 witnessed the "major
successes of Islam" in Southeast Asia.[6]

European scholars of Southeast Asia were obsessed with the search
for the "origins" of Islam in the region. The initial conviction that Arab
traders and settlers had brought Islam gave way to speculation about
direct connections across the Bay of Bengal. No single origin can explain the spread of Islam in so diverse an area as Southeast Asia. Islam
came to the region from multiple sources—Arabic, Persian, Indian,
Chinese—and spread through the travels of itinerant scholars, charismatic mystics, and intrepid merchants across the Bay and the Arabian
Sea. Often the agents of religious change were Southeast Asians who
traded with and traveled to the Middle East, returning home with
new ideas.[7] Early modern South and Southeast Asia formed part of a
shared world, linked by the movement of holy texts, citations, and
translations—and linked, too, by the Arabic language. Investigating
Tamil, Malay, and Javanese translations of the *Book of One Thousand
Questions*—a staple work in the Islamic canon—Ronit Ricci shows that

a sphere of shared references bridged the "Arabic cosmopolis" of the Bay of Bengal. This cultural realm expanded as distinctive local cultures of Islam, distinctive local engagements with Arabic script and vocabulary, took root.[8]

The flow of people, as much as the movement of texts, created Islamic connections across the Bay of Bengal. A diaspora of Persian merchants, scribes, poets, and administrators fanned out across the region in the fifteenth and sixteenth centuries. They dominated the trade of Masulipatnam, they advised the courts of Ayutthaya and Arakan, they installed Persian as the language of administration in polities on both sides of the Bay. The Arab diaspora from Hadramawt (in Yemen) reached even farther. Over a period of 500 years, Hadramis formed a creole diaspora of merchants and religious scholars that spanned the Indian Ocean. "Hadramis and their offspring became Swahilis, Gujaratis, Malabaris, Malay, Buginese, Javanese and Filipinos," Engseng Ho writes; "they became natives everywhere." Pilgrimage and genealogy tied them to the Hadrami homeland, and to Hadramis elsewhere. Ho writes of a "skein of networks" through which the Hadrami diaspora "brought together hitherto-separated people in single families and in a single religion." These networks were "asymmetrical": though Hadrami sons traveled the Indian Ocean and married local women, Hadrami daughters were forbidden to leave their homeland.[9]

The Tamil Muslims of the Coromandel Coast, too, created an enduring web of culture and commerce around the Indian Ocean. They, more than any other group, focused on the region around the Bay of Bengal, where their networks were deepest and widest. The community's elite were known as Maraikkayars, the name conveying their maritime heritage, as it comes from the Tamil word *marakkalam*, "boat." Coastal Maraikkayar communities had grown prosperous from the trade in horses with West Asia; they dominated the pearl and chank fisheries of the Coromandel Coast and Ceylon, where they competed with (and often surpassed) the Portuguese. They moved into the textile trade and shipping. Of lower status than the Maraikkayars were Tamil Muslims known as *lebbais*. Many observers suggested that they formed a separate community (even a "caste"), but more recently a careful scholar of Tamil Muslim society has argued that *lebbai* is simply a religious title, denoting "petty scholars or educated laymen."[10] Elite and lay Muslims were involved in reciprocal but unequal relations: as patrons and clients, as employers and employees, and as fellow travelers across the Bay of Bengal.

Over centuries Maraikkayars forged a distinctive culture, rooted in the Tamil language while embracing a wider Islamic world. Tamil Muslims made an "important contribution to Tamil literature by way of expanding the limits of existing genres, and of introducing novel combinations and entirely new models," Ricci writes. The *Cirappuranam* of Umaru Pulavar, the preeminent Tamil Muslim poet of the seventeenth century, encapsulates this cultural versatility. Umaru Pulavar's was a "Muslim creation in a Hindu form," produced under the patronage of Sidakaddi—a leading Maraikkayar merchant, close to the Hindu court of Ramnad—and under the tutelage of the renowned scholar Sheikh Sadaqatullah. It brought together the Arabic genre of the *sirah* (biography of the Prophet) with the Hindu *puranam* (narrative epic) to relate the Prophet's life using Tamil literary conventions. The poem bore the influence of the Tamil version of the *Ramayana*, composed by Kampan. In its construction, it was a *kavya*—lyric verses linked together in a narrative.[11] The blending of forms and vocabularies also expressed a melding of sacred landscapes. The *Cirappuranam*'s opening description substitutes the wet-rice landscape of the Tamil country for the Arabian desert:

> Milling in crowds, those who labor in the fields
>   gather and praise Earth.
> Their right hands shake the sprouting seeds
>   and scatter them thick on the ground.
> They fall like golden rain on earth.[12]

As the Tamil Muslims of the Coromandel Coast traveled, their sacred geography expanded to encompass the eastern as well as the western Indian Ocean.

Tamil Muslims settled in Kedah, Aceh, and Java; they traded across the breadth of the Indonesian archipelago. Textual fragments of their journeys remain. Malay chronicles refer often to South Indian Muslim teachers, traders, and holy men. The *Sejarah Melayu* (*Malay Annals*), a sixteenth-century genealogy of the rulers of the Malay Peninsula (based on an earlier chronicle written in Melaka), recounts Pasai's conversion to Islam, in which an Indian emissary from Ma'abar, the Arabic term for the Coromandel Coast, plays a pivotal role. A decisive story of intrigue in the Melaka court involves a Tamil Muslim called Raja Mudeliar, who, as master of the port, was "easily the richest man of his time." Raja Mudeliar and the king's advisor, the Bendahara, are great rivals: "That's just what one would expect from a Kling [Tamil] who doesn't know how to behave!" the Bendahara says to Raja Mudeliar after a misunderstanding over money. Using the help of "a certain man of Kalinga named Kittul," Raja Mudeliar persuades the sultan to have the Bendahara executed; when he later learns of the shenanigans, the sultan orders Raja Mudeliar himself to be killed.[13] This combination of myth and chronicle hints at how prominent Tamil Muslims were in Melaka's court, and it is likely that they played a similarly important role in other port polities across the region.

When Afonso de Albuquerque's Portuguese forces attacked Melaka in 1511, they conquered a port city at the heart of Asian commerce. The apothecary Tomé Pires arrived in Melaka in 1512; he served as "scribe and accountant of the trading warehouse and controller of the drugs"; he became rich, "more than you can imagine."[14] In his travel account, the *Suma Oriental,* Pires counted no fewer than eighty-four languages spoken on Melaka's streets and in its bazaars. He lists the peoples he encountered—a Babel of names, places of origin ("men of . . ."), ethnonyms, and terms of religious affiliation:

> Moors from Cairo, Mecca, Aden, Abyssinians, men of Kilwa, Malindi, Ormuz, Parsees, Rumes, Turks, Turkomans, Christian Armenians, Gujaratees, men of Chaul, Dabhol, Goa, of the kingdom of Deccan, Malabars and Klings, merchants from Orissa, Ceylon, Bengal, Arakan, Pegu, Siamese, men of Kedah, Malays, men of Pahang, Patani, Cambodia, Champa, Cochin China, Chinese, Lequeos, men of Brunei, Lucoes, men of Tamjompura, Laue, Banka, Linga (they have a thousand other islands), Moluccas, Banda, Bima, Timor, Madura, Java, Sunda, Palembang, Jambi, Tongkal, Indragiri, Kappatta, Menangkabau, Siak, Arqua, Aru, Bata, country of the Tomjano, Pase, Pedir, Maldives.[15]

The map of his words stretches from China to the Middle East.

Trading diasporas from across Asia converged upon the port towns that dotted the Southeast Asian littoral. Until their near-simultaneous collapse in the middle of the thirteenth century, the major cities of Southeast Asia had been agrarian settlements of the interior—Angkor, Pagan, and Sukhothai were the largest among them. Situated along river deltas in areas of intensive wet rice cultivation, often far from the sea, they were centers of royal power; sophisticated schemes of hydraulic engineering allowed them to flourish. As Denys Lombard has shown, urban centers gravitated to the coasts in the fifteenth century. Port polities emerged in quick succession, each founded on entrepôt trade; maritime relations were more significant to many of them than links with their own hinterlands. In Burma, the seat of power shifted from Pagan to the coastal settlement of Pegu. Along the western coast of the Malay Peninsula, Melaka emerged as the greatest of the region's ports. The conversion of Melaka's ruling family in 1419 cemented the relationship between Islam, trade, and the port polities of the Indian Ocean rim; port cities with Muslim rulers were hospitable to Muslim and non-Muslim merchants from across Asia. Along Java's northern coast, Gresek, Tuban, Demak, and Banten all rose to prominence in the fifteenth century. In the sixteenth and seventeenth centuries, Ternate, Hitu, Brunei, Aceh, Makassar, and Manila flourished—Manila under the rule of a local sultanate before the Iberian conquest.[16]

The port cities of Southeast Asia evolved a new urban form, one that persisted through European conquest; arguably, its contours are still faintly discernible today.[17] Where the inland cities depended on their agrarian base, the new port polities had the encouragement of trade as their main aim. Where the old capitals' structure reflected a holistic royal cosmology, the new port polities' layout was testament to the diversity of their residents. After the ruler, the most important political office in many of the Southeast Asian polities was the harbormaster, the *shahbandar,* who was very often a foreigner. The *shahbandar*'s chief aim was to grease the wheels of commerce, showing visiting and resident merchants that prices were fair and taxes were moderate, that agreements were honored and disagreements resolved honorably. The larger communities—Gujaratis, South Indians, and Fujianese—each had a nominated representative (the Portuguese newcomers labeled them *kapitans*) with a voice in decision making. The residential structure of the port cities was distinctive, too. Each was a mosaic of ethnic quarters, distinct but overlapping. This was the world that Portuguese carracks had stormed; this was the world their crews of adventurers, traders, and apothecaries tried to subdue.

The Portuguese entry into the Indian Ocean depended on superior weaponry—cannons made of sturdier metal—and on efficient sailing ships furnished with effective navigational aids; their advance was driven by Christian fervor, pulled by Asia's fabled wealth. The maritime expansion of this small country in southwestern Europe had begun a century earlier, with the conquest of Ceuta (in Morocco) in 1415, followed by exploratory voyages into the Atlantic and along the west coast of Africa. The creeping conquest of the Canary Islands in the fifteenth century produced the earliest agricultural "plantations" in the New World; enslaved people, both Africans and local Guaches, worked alongside indentured Europeans and "free" adventurers to make them productive. By the century's end, Iberian expansion was on the threshold of a world-historical transformation. In the decade of Vasco da Gama's Indian Ocean crossing, the Genoese navigator Christopher Columbus sailed west to the New World, in the service of his Spanish masters, and da Gama's countryman, Bartolomeu Dias, rounded the Cape of Good Hope in 1497–1498, paving the way for the seaborne passage from Europe to Asia.

Excluded from Europe's lucrative spice markets by Muslim powers' control over the heartlands of Eurasia, the Portuguese forced a maritime route into a world of riches. Imbued with the spirit of the Crusades, they waged war on the Muslim powers of the Indian Ocean. The result of their quest was messier and less absolute than they planned: the Portuguese became one power among others. Brutal, their power was concentrated at strategic coastal fortresses. Fragile, it never reached far inland. Afonso de Albuquerque extended the Portuguese presence in Asian waters between 1500 and 1515. From their fortress at Goa (established in 1510), they expanded both east and west. In 1511 Albuquerque captured Melaka, "that vast sea's emporium" where the Bay of Bengal met the China Sea; having failed to capture Aden in 1513, Portuguese forces took Hormuz, gateway to the Arabian Sea, two years later.[18]

The pursuit of riches fed Portuguese expansion around the Bay of Bengal more plainly than was the case in the western Indian Ocean. In the Bay Portuguese adventurers and private merchants played a greater role: more distant from the power of Goa, they had greater autonomy. In the words of Luís Filipe Thomaz, "Beyond Ceylon—that is in the Bay of Bengal, in the seas of the archipelago and in the Far East—the Portuguese enterprise was closer to the Guinea model: first, fortresses became less frequent and even factories were placed at distant intervals, secondly, the dominant type of trade was a seasonal one along the coasts."[19] By the middle of the sixteenth century Portuguese outposts littered the Bay of Bengal's coasts, anchored in a small fortress at Nagapatnam and in a civilian settlement in São Tomé (Mylapore), an ancient center of textile production. "For with this famous city of Mylapore," poet Luís de Camões wrote, "the Bay of Bengal begins its curve," and Portuguese poet Luís de adventurers followed it.[20] By the 1540s they were active in the northern Bay of Bengal, where "the River Ganges joins the domain of salt." In Bengal, "a province which boasts of its wealth," they established a foothold in Chittagong and Satgaon, and they reached the coast of Arakan. Portuguese authorities established protected crown routes, or *carreiras*, between pairs of ports around the Bay.

But private traders thrived outside the authorities' control. Portuguese settlers, known as Harmads, engaged in raiding, and their depredations were recalled even in twentieth-century Bengali ballads. "Many Portugals," an English resident of Masulipatnam wrote, "decayed in their estates or questioned for their lives, resort hither and live [in Bengal] plentifully, yet as banished men or out-lawed, without government."[21] Portuguese mercenaries flocked to serve the king of Arakan. One of them, Filipe de Brito e Nicote, received the "crown" of Pegu in 1602 and ruled the port of Syriam—across the river from Rangoon—as his private kingdom. De Brito was notorious for his brutality toward the local population and for sacking Buddhist temples. He acted both for his own profit and for the benefit of the Portuguese crown, seeking reinforcements from Goa to take the eastern coast of the Bay for the Portuguese empire. He was finally captured by the king of Ava in 1613 and impaled.[22] Along the northern rim of the Bay of Bengal, the Harmads entered transient alliances with the indigenous Magh raiders of Arakan: they traded, as we will see, in slaves.

Portuguese gunboats brought violence to a peaceful and cosmopolitan Indian Ocean: in this proposition lies both an element of truth and a degree of exaggeration.[23] Plunder and raiding were widespread in the Indian Ocean long before the arrival of Europeans. What was new were the claims of exclusive sovereignty that European chartered companies—backed by states and navies—asserted over land and sea. The Portuguese *cartazes* epitomized this new order. The Portuguese king, Dom Manuel (r. 1495–1521), envisaged himself as a universal Christian ruler, the "lord of the sea." The Portuguese were never in a position to challenge the power of Asia's great empires on land; by the late sixteenth century those rivals threatened their position in the Bay of Bengal. Under the emperor Akbar (r. 1556–1605), Mughal power pushed east into Bengal, which was declared a Mughal province (suba) in 1575–1576. The Mughals gained direct access to the eastern Indian Ocean through the ports of Pipli and Satgaon. By the dawn of the seventeenth century, the Portuguese confronted a new challenge at sea.

Conflict in a distant corner of western Europe altered the course of the Bay of Bengal's history. In 1579 Dutch elites rebelled against their Spanish rulers, beginning a decades-long war. The Dutch revolt was a rebellion of ardent Protestants against an official Catholicism they found oppressive, compounded by resentment at the heavy taxation necessitated by the Spanish war against France.[24] As Dutch merchants were driven from the great spice exchanges of Lisbon and Antwerp, the city of Amsterdam emerged as the leading financial center in northwestern Europe. Shippers and investors, insurance brokers and speculators met in Amsterdam's stock market; there they exchanged information about prices and markets and opportunities around the world. The Amsterdam bourse came to "attract the supply of and the demand for idle money and credit from all over Europe."[25] The English, too, were excluded from Spanish and Portuguese markets in retaliation for privateering raids on Spanish shipping in the Atlantic. Dutch and English merchants broke the Portuguese monopoly over the spice trade, seeking direct access to the "spice islands" in the far east of the Indonesian archipelago. In the 1590s the first English and Dutch voyages to the spice islands disappointed their sponsors, but they heralded the rise of chartered trading companies, which would change the world.

The first of them was the English Levant Company, formed in 1581 to trade with the Ottoman Empire; the East India Company was established in 1599 and given a royal charter by Queen Elizabeth I in 1600. Two years later autonomous Dutch trading ventures to the East were amalgamated into the United East India Company (VOC). The VOC was formed as a federation of regional chambers of commerce—those of Amsterdam, Hoorn, Enkhuizen, Middelburg, Rotterdam, and Delft—mirroring the federal structure of the United Provinces. The Dutch state granted the VOC a monopoly on the eastern trade and gave it the power to make war, build fortresses, and conclude treaties with foreign sovereigns. The VOC accumulated military resources, allowing it to "internalize protection costs."[26] A new structure revolutionized the operations of the trading companies: as joint-stock companies, they could pool capital on an unprecedented scale, shareholders' liability was limited, and ownership of capital was divorced from the daily running of the business. The VOC began its rise to dominance in Asia by avoiding areas of Portuguese control. But the European conflict—the Portuguese were under the Spanish crown, arrayed against the Dutch—spread to Asian waters. The Dutch refused to recognize Portuguese sovereignty over the sea. The maritime highway between India and China, with the Bay of Bengal at its heart, became a corridor of conflict.[27]

On February 25, 1603, three Dutch ships under the command of Jacob van Heemskerk seized a 150-ton Portuguese carrack, the *Santa Catarina,* in the waters just off Singapore. The *Santa Catarina* was on its way from Macau to Melaka, fully laden with a cargo of Chinese and Japanese goods, including more than a thousand bales of silk and a valuable store of musk. The battle raged through the day, but by nightfall the Portuguese had surrendered. When the Dutch sold the *Santa Catarina's* cargo, judged to be a legitimate "prize" by the admiralty courts, it brought in double the existing capital of the VOC. To justify its actions, the VOC deployed the talents of a young jurist, Hugo Grotius: he published *Mare Liberum (The Free Sea)* in 1608, though it was in fact part of a larger work, *Commentary on the Law of Prize and Booty.* Grotius's text—one of the foundations of modern international law—defended the right of the Dutch to use force against Portuguese claims of monopoly in the east. "The Portuguese are not sovereigns of those parts of the East Indies to which the Dutch sail, that is to say, Java, Ceylon, and many of the Moluccas," Grotius wrote. Freedom of trade, on his view, derived from natural law—"for do not the ocean, navigable in every direction with which God has encompassed all the earth, and the regular and occasional winds which blow . . . offer sufficient proof that Nature has given to all peoples a right of access to all other peoples?" Property came from possession. But the sea could not be occupied, and "a ship sailing through the sea leaves behind it no more legal right than it does a track." By violating these provisions of natural law, the Portuguese left themselves open to legitimate attack by Dutch captains defending the freedom of the seas (though, in practice, asserting their own claims to monopoly). To satisfy his paymasters, Grotius allowed for some ambiguity: he envisaged partial forms of sovereignty over "territorial" waters—such as the Dutch exercised around the spice islands.[28]

Between 1600 and 1663, the Portuguese Estado da India "suffered catastrophic reverses" at the hands of the Dutch. By the second half of the seventeenth century the Dutch faced a growing challenge from the English.[29] The Dutch and English companies adopted the Portuguese model of the *feitoria,* or "factory": fortified coastal settlements where they concentrated their power and conducted their trade. Before long, they formed a deeper entanglement with local powers and local politics. As map 1 illustrates, a chain of fortresses threaded around the coast; they were linked by ships and letters and account books. Beginning in the Maluku islands (the Moluccas), with a sole factory in Amboina (1605), the Dutch gained a foothold on the Coromandel coast of India, establishing factories at Pulicat and Masulipatnam. The Dutch made Batavia (today's Jakarta) their base in the Indonesian archipelago in 1619; it became the heart of their Asian empire. By midcentury, Dutch forces had seized key Portuguese possessions: Melaka (1641), Colombo (1656), and, in 1663, Cochin. The Dutch then expanded farther into southern India from their base at Nagapatnam. By the 1680s the VOC was by far the biggest employer in the Netherlands, perhaps even largest employer in the world. Its staff at home and overseas grew from 7,700 in 1625 to 21,900 in 1688. The VOC's rival, the British East India Company, established factories in Masulipatnam (1611), Petapuli (1611), and Madras (1639); on the west coast of India, they had bases at Surat (1615) and on the island of Bombay, acquired from the Portuguese in 1668. By the century's end the East India Company had established another factory in a small Hugli village—Calcutta.

European newcomers could not ignore the prevailing political order of the Bay of Bengal any more than individual European traders could ignore the Asian merchant networks that preceded them. The Bay marked the eastern extent of the Muslim land-based empires that dominated the heartlands of Eurasia in the middle of the second millennium—the Ottoman, Safavid, and Mughal Empires. It was also the maritime thoroughfare, alongside the overland Silk Road to the other great Asian empire, China. Europeans expanded around the Bay of Bengal's seaboard while the Mughals stamped their authority over much of the Indian subcontinent. Under the reign of Akbar (r. 1556–1605) and his successors Jahangir, Shah Jahan, and Aurangzeb, Mughal domains grew to encompass most of South Asia and a population of 100 million people. In 1583 Mughal domains reached the coast with the conquest of Bengal, though it would be another thirty-five years before they subdued local resistance to their rule in eastern Bengal. The fabulous wealth of Bengal impressed contemporary Europeans (William Methwold wrote in the 1620s of the "abundance of such things as that countrey produceth, that is the most plentifull in the East"): this prosperity was the relatively recent product of Mughal conquest, settlement, and land clearance. The Bay of Bengal was an ecological and religious as much as a political frontier. Groups of settlers led by Muslim holy men (*shaikhs*)—encouraged by the Mughal authorities to subdue the uncultivated, uncivilized forest—pioneered the transformation of eastern Bengal into a region of intensive rice cultivation.[30]

Along the Coromandel Coast the political situation in the seventeenth century was more fragmented, characterized by shifting alliances of principalities and small kingdoms. With the slow decline of the Vijayanagar Empire in the second half of the sixteenth century, South India was contested by many powers. Among the successor states, the Qutb Shahi dynasty of Golconda had consolidated its position as the leading power along the coast by the 1640s. A Shi'a kingdom, Golconda forged close ties with Safavid Iran. Persian merchants played a leading role in the trade of its main port, Masulipatnam ("quite the most famous market on the coast"), which had dense connections to the eastern and western arms of the Indian Ocean. A Dutch resident of Masulipatnam in the early seventeenth century observed that "ships sail every year to the coast of Bengal, Arakan, Pegu, and Tenasserim, carrying a variety of cotton cloths, glass, iron, cotton yarn (red and white), tobacco, and certain shells which are used instead of coins in Bengal and Arakan." In turn the merchants imported "rice, butter, oil, gingelly seed, sugar, a variety of woven cloths, some fine embroidered quilts, rubies, sapphires, lac, benzoin, China root, gold, tin, eagle-wood, [and] sappan-wood." William Methwold noted the importance of the China trade: goods from Masulipatnam were transported to Tenasserim, and "from thence to Syam fourteene dayes journey over land; from whence by the like conveyance they bring all sorts of China commodities."[31]

The kingdom of Bijapur, less powerful than Golconda, controlled key southern ports of Cuddalore, Porto Novo, and Puducheary (Pondicherry). Further south, the disintegration of the Vijayanagar Empire allowed the rise of formerly subordinate *nayaks* (military rulers) and small sultanates to power: south of Madras, the *nayak* of Thanjavur, the *thevar* of Ramnad, and the *nayak* of Madura all claimed succession from Vijayanagar.

Local rulers were landlords to European trading companies. Golconda was the largest of them all, possessing the land settled by the English in Madras, the English and the Dutch in Masulipatnam, the Dutch at Pulicat, and the Portuguese in São Tomé—from where they were expelled by Golconda (with Dutch support) in 1664. Europeans exploited every opportunity to intervene in local conflicts—succession disputes and interstate tensions alike—to negotiate better terms for themselves. Neighboring states competed to attract European trade to their ports. Europeans enjoyed favorable terms, including reduced customs and transit duties. By backing one side in a clash with arms and capital, European powers gained leverage over their clients.

The political order exploded in the 1670s as Mughal power reached South India. In 1687 Golconda submitted to Mughal authority, giving the Mughal state direct access to the Coromandel Coast. The Mughal thrust into South India destabilized society as it undermined local polities. Warfare brought economic upheaval; combined with drought, it caused famine and a cholera epidemic in 1685–1686. Mughal expansion was challenged on many fronts, including by the fugitive Maratha king at Jinji, by Telugu warriors north of Madras, and by Kam Baksh's attempt to establish a Deccan kingdom in Hyderabad. South India's political tumult beckoned to the Europeans. They proved ready to use their naval power, as the Dutch did when they blockaded the port of Masulipatnam in the 1680s after a dispute over a debt. A leading historian of Indian Ocean trade has concluded that "in the seventeenth century Coromandel became a region of prime commercial interest for every European trading power in the east." By the end of the century, when local powers were weakened by the Mughal assault, a proliferation of domestic conflicts paved the way to European expansion.[32] Competition between ports, the patchwork of jurisdictions, multiple political regimes, close trading connections with Southeast Asia—these features of early modern Coromandel would shape the Bay of Bengal's history well into the nineteenth century. But the creeping and, from the second half of the eighteenth century, rapid consolidation of authority in English hands saw a fundamental redistribution of power along India's Coromandel Coast.

Along the Bay of Bengal's eastern littoral the political order was equally fluid around 1600: the stretch from Burma down to the Malay Peninsula and the Indonesian archipelago was divided between centralizing states, maritime trading ports, and smaller principalities. Along the Bay's northeastern shores, the kingdom of Arakan maintained its independence, and its capital, Mrauk-U, flourished between 1540 and 1640. Regular raids captured thousands of slaves from eastern Bengal and came to an end only with the Mughal conquest of Chittagong in 1665. Inland, the Toungoo dynasty ruled much of upper Burma, Chiengmai, and Ayutthaya, until its collapse at the end of the sixteenth century. Further south, Melaka's conquest by the Portuguese allowed many other port states to flourish as Asian traders escaped Portuguese control: Patani, Johor, Pahang, Banten, and Aceh above all. Under the rule of Sultan Alau-d-din Ri'ayat Syah al-Kahar (r. 1539–1571), Banda Aceh became "the principal Muslim entrepôt in the Straits of Malacca region."[33] In Southeast Asia, as along the Coromandel Coast, the seventeenth century brought major political change—and political consolidation. Under pressure from European trading companies and from their regional rivals, Southeast Asian states extended royal monopolies over trade, developing a mercantilism in their own fashion. The Thai king Narai (r. 1656–1688) boosted the system of royal trade, and Siamese royal ships began to compete on the Coromandel route. Aceh's "absolutist" sultan Iskander Muda (r. 1607–1636), too, sought a monopoly over external trade: starting in 1622, the English and the Dutch were excluded from trading in Aceh, and Iskander Muda sent his own "great ship" to the Coromandel Coast each year.[34]

The expansion of European trading companies into Asian waters coincided with the Little Ice Age. This era in global climate history lasted—on the broadest definition—from the fourteenth until the nineteenth century and had economic, ecological, and political effects across Europe, South and Southeast Asia, and China, though it remains unclear how far these changes were globally synchronous.[35] The transition from the Medieval Warm Period to the Little Ice Age brought a 500-year-long southward shift in the intertropical convergence zone and a resultant weakening of the Asian monsoon. The scale of monsoon fluctuations diminished somewhat after 1450, but the monsoons failed many times in the 1600s, inflicting prolonged periods of drought on the Bay. The region's interconnected climatic system intersected with commercial expansion and diplomatic ambition to upset the prevailing political order.[36]

Technological innovation and an increase in states' capacities meant that "societies became less vulnerable to climatic fluctuation" over time; nevertheless, "recurrent political crisis" in Europe, China, South Asia, and Southeast Asia in the seventeenth century "reflected, in some uncertain degree, the effects of Little Ice Age cooling." From the interaction of these multiple political crises a new imperial order emerged in the Bay of Bengal—and almost everywhere else in the world. The impact of the Little Ice Age on the Bay remains difficult to measure, but certain broad patterns are clear. The years from 1629 to 1635 (possibly up to 1640) brought "appalling droughts and drought-induced famines all around the Bay of Bengal" and swelled the traffic in enslaved people across the eastern Indian Ocean. Along the Coromandel Coast, the years 1660 and 1661 were among the driest on record. The late seventeenth and early eighteenth centuries were a "mega" El Niño era.[37]

The effects of climate on the political order were not mechanistic— political crises were not *caused* by a cooling planet. In the words of historian Victor Lieberman and climatologist Brendan Buckley, we need "greater attention to climate, whilst avoiding climatic determinism."[38] The influence of climate change on agriculture and settlement help to explain why there were so *many* crises, increasingly connected, in this period, as economic relations thickened, and new forms of interdependence arose. Monsoon failure in one part of the Bay of Bengal reverberated in other parts of the region through the traffic in rice, on which many lives depended, and through the traffic in people, which expanded to encompass a much wider area in the seventeenth century. Climatic change provoked an overarching set of material pressures that interacted with new forms of state, with changing relations of property, and with new ideologies (including variants of "mercantilism") to create an environment of political ferment.

Spices lend the Indian Ocean's history its romance—they are what the Europeans came for. Cairo's Jewish merchants corresponded about exotic spices from the east as early as the tenth century, but they were prohibitively expensive in Europe until the end of the fourteenth. There followed a boom in European demand for spices, which arrived in the markets of Venice at the end of a maritime and caravan route that linked the eastern Indonesian archipelago to the Mediterranean. Before the late eighteenth century, the finer spices—clove, nutmeg, and mace— were exclusive to the Maluku islands. Cinnamon came only from Ceylon. "The most important tree, the island's own, is the cinnamon tree," wrote François Valentijn in the late seventeenth century.[39]

Pepper was more widely dispersed, spreading to Southeast Asia from its source on the Malabar coast of southwestern India. In the mid-fourteenth century Ibn Battuta described Mangalore's thriving spice market, and the pepper trees that "resemble grape-vines; they are planted alongside coco-palms and climb up them in the same way that vines climb." "In the autumn," he observed, the people "gather the grains and spread them on mats in the sun, just as is done with grapes in order to obtain raisins."[40] By 1400 pepper cultivation had spread to the island of Sumatra, either directly from India or, possibly, by way of Java. In 1500 Malabar supplied most of the pepper purchased in Europe and the Middle East; half a century later, Sumatra's pepper exports equaled or exceeded India's.

Spices played a minor role in the bulk of the Indian Ocean trade, but they were its main source of profit, with pepper accounting for the largest share. When the Portuguese stormed the Indian Ocean, one of their aims—as well as extending the Christian realm—was to monopolize the spice trade by diverting it away from the Mediterranean and away from the control of Muslim merchants. Initially they succeeded. In 1501 the Venetian diarist Girolamo Priuli lamented that "to-day, with this new voyage by the King of Portugal, all the spices which came by way of Cairo will be controlled in Portugal, because of the caravels which will go to India, to Calicut, and other places to take them. . . . And truly the Venetian merchants are in a bad way, believing that the voyages should make them very poor."[41] Portuguese dominance did not last long. By the middle of the sixteenth century "enormous quantities of spices were reaching the Mediterranean" once again, coming across the Red Sea or overland on the caravan route to Aleppo and Cairo. The independence of Aceh, the "principal commercial and military rival of the Portuguese in Southeast Asia," secured an alternative supply of pepper: Aceh's relations with the Ottoman Empire revived other routes across the Bay of Bengal and the Indian Ocean, including the southerly track from Aceh, via the Maldives, to the Arabian Sea. Only when the Dutch captured eastern Indonesia did they secure a lucrative spice monopoly, consolidated with brutal force. Beginning in the 1620s, the oceanic route around the Cape of Good Hope had triumphed. This "second European age in the Indian Ocean," Fernand Braudel concluded, was "more catastrophic to the Levant than the imperfect domination of the Portuguese."[42]

The spice trade depended on the commerce in cloth across the Bay of Bengal. Even before the arrival of Europeans, Indian textiles were the linchpin of the region's trade; their circulation connected the economies of South and Southeast Asia to those of China in the east and the Mediterranean in the west. Indian cloth opened Southeast Asia to long-distance trade. In return for Indian cotton textiles, Southeast Asia's distinctive products—spices, aromatics, medicinal plants, tin, and gold—flowed across the Bay and beyond. In the sixteenth century's "age of commerce," cotton from Gujarat, Coromandel, and Bengal was traded across Southeast Asia—in Pegu and Tenasserim, in Melaka, in Sumatra and Java.[43] The apothecary Tomé Pires surveyed Melaka's spice marts and saw pepper, cardamom, edible camphor, and benzoin, all brought to market by the promise of Indian textiles. "A junk goes from Bengal to Melaka once a year, and sometimes twice," Pires observed. The Bengal ships brought "five white cloths, seven kinds of *sinabafos*, three kinds of *chautares, beatilhas, beirames* and other rich materials. They will bring as many as twenty kinds." In their holds came "very rich bed-canopies, with cut-cloth work in all colors and very beautiful," and "wall hangings like tapestry." Pires concluded that "Bengali cloth fetches a high price in Melaka, because it is a merchandise all over the east." In return, Indian traders exported from Melaka "camphor and pepper—an abundance of these two—cloves, mace, nutmeg, sandalwood, silk, seed-pearls a large quantity, copper, tin, lead, quicksilver, large green porcelain ware from the Liukiu, opium from Aden . . . white and green damasks, *enrolados* from China, caps of scarlet-in-grain and carpets; krises and swords from Java are also appreciated." A century later the Dutchman Augustijn Stalpaert confirmed the popularity of Indian textiles "all over the east" when he surveyed the marketplace in Banda in 1602 and counted twenty-one kinds of Coromandel cloth.[44]

Words convey the reach of India's empire of cotton: into every language and lingua franca across the Bay passed detailed descriptions of Indian cloth. Ships' cargo lists have a mesmerizing quality that comes from their endless terms for textiles: longcloth, salempories, moris, gingham, dungarees, guinea cloth, kaingulong. Indian weavers' products targeted diverse markets, their weaves, patterns, colors, and designs all adapted to local tastes.[45]

With little of value to offer Asian markets, European traders paid for their purchases with precious metals and then relied on profits from inter-Asian trade to finance their business. "To ensure an adequate and timely supply of textiles for Bantam and the Moluccas," wrote the VOC's governor-general, Jan Pieterzoon Coen, in 1617, it was "essential that Coromandel be kept well provided with cash specie and goods." Braudel insisted on the importance of tracing the "world context" of the spice trade, "from the American silver mines to the Moluccas." He described "a steady flow of gold and silver coins of every description, traveling from west to east, following the rotation of the earth . . . and loosing in the opposite direction a rich and varied stream of different commodities and precious goods from east to west." The trade boom of the seventeenth century was fueled by a dramatic increase in the availability of silver from its two key sources in the world: the mines of Potosí in Spanish Peru (today's Bolivia) and Japan. In both places, and almost simultaneously, new techniques of extraction increased supply. China and the VOC absorbed most of the Japanese supply, until its export was prohibited in the 1680s; the other European trading companies used mostly South American silver to finance cloth purchases in India. In the first half of the seventeenth century, the Spanish silver real became the most widely accepted currency in Southeast Asia.

The export of Indian cloth to Southeast Asia in exchange for spices peaked in the middle of the seventeenth century. Between 1620 and 1655, Southeast Asia imported cloth to the value of forty tons of silver each year; thereafter it declined steeply. An increasing proportion of Coromandel, Bengal, and Gujarat textiles went to Europe. A collapse in the price of pepper reduced the purchasing power of Southeast Asian consumers, combined with an increase of up to 45 percent in the price of Indian cloth, inflated by European demand.[46] By the turn of the eighteenth century the China trade supplied the lion's share of European traders' profits; they sought new ways to finance their purchases in the

Middle Kingdom, as political economists at home warned against an unsustainable "drain" of precious metals. Through its factory in Canton, the British East India Company enlarged its imports of Chinese tea, which grew fivefold, from 20,000 pounds in 1700 to 100,000 pounds six years later, and to 5 million pounds annually by 1760. In the first half of the eighteenth century huge quantities of silver entered China to finance these purchases, a lot of it by way of India. Much of this silver was in the form of Mexican pesos, of which well over a billion were minted in the eighteenth century—they were widely trusted, their silver content guaranteed. Eventually the Chinese market grew saturated with silver; as the relative value of silver declined in China, an alternative medium arose to finance the relentless demand for tea. That alternative was Indian opium.[47]

Ecological exchange antedated European incursion: pepper cultivation spread from India to Southeast Asia around the fourteenth century. So large was the market for Southeast Asian spices, and so great the reciprocal demand for Indian cloth, that certain of the islands of eastern Indonesia specialized early on in export production. Tomé Pires observed in the early sixteenth century that "the islands of Banda have hardly any foodstuffs. The surrounding islands bring foodstuffs."[48] Commercialization made economies around the Bay more interdependent, increasingly specialized—and increasingly vulnerable.

One clear sign of this interdependence was the growing trade in bulky subsistence goods over longer distances—rice above all. Wet rice cultivation is a cultural and ecological link between the territories bordering the Bay of Bengal, and between them all and the rim of the South China Sea. Rice is the staple food across this expansive area, and it is a powerful symbol of sustenance, reciprocity, and good fortune—"a key tenet of rice culture is that rice is a sacred food divinely given to humans that uniquely sustains the human body in a way no other food can."[49] Rice had been traded around the region for centuries. With good reason, early European traders described the ports of eastern India as the "rice ports." The interregional commerce in rice accompanied the movement of luxury items of lesser bulk, and in the seventeenth century both trades grew in scale.

Around the Bay, growing towns demanded food. Rice gravitated from regions of surplus to those of deficit, the patterns of trade shifting with the seasons. Frequent warfare—cause and consequence of European expansion—devastated harvests, increasing demand for imports from those who could afford them. In years of surplus, the northern Coromandel ports of Bimilipatnam and Ganjam, with their fertile hinterlands, exported rice to southern India and to Southeast Asia; the southern Coromandel ports imported rice from the north—and, in good years, sent their surplus to Aceh, Melaka, Ceylon, and Malabar. Many times during the 1620s Dutch authorities at Batavia demanded rice from Coromandel or Arakan "irrespective of cost," though "without cutting into orders for cloths." As Southeast Asia's port cities focused on long-distance trade, they grew dependent on food imports. Augustin de Beaulieu, who came to Aceh to purchase pepper in 1620, observed that Aceh's main town was "insufficiently cultivated to feed its residents, so much so that a good part of its rice comes from abroad"—from the Malay Peninsula, and from the Coromandel Coast. To meet the demand for rice, paddy cultivation breached new frontiers. In both the Mekong and Irrawaddy delta regions, state-supported movements of peasant colonization expanded production. By the end of the nineteenth century, these two areas, together with the Chao Phraya delta in Siam (Thailand), would become the "rice bowl" of the whole Bay of Bengal region.[50]

Spices and rice flowed across the Bay of Bengal. Human beings were the other commodity in demand. In Aceh, slaves from India cultivated the little rice that was grown locally. The slave trade in the western Indian Ocean was always larger than in the Bay, and it is better known. Yet competition between empires stimulated the coerced movement of people across the Bay, too, a movement that would reach massive proportions in the nineteenth century. The modern history of migration across the Bay begins with slaves as much as with merchants.

For a time, Dutch authorities in Batavia imagined a future world filled with slaves. Writing to his counterpart in Masulipatnam in 1622, Coen declared that "a large number of boys and girls from various quarters of Asia were needed to populate Batavia, Amboina and Banda with servile people." He was sure that "even hundreds of thousands of such people would be welcome." He felt that the Dutch had lessons to learn from the "Portuguese precedent" and even from "how the Moors had extended their rule over Asia." Coen issued his instructions: "All places in Coromandel, Ceylon, and Bengal were to be instructed to buy as many slaves as possible." The same day Coen wrote to his lieutenant in Surat and reiterated his point: "Any number of slaves, particularly young people, could be sent to Batavia. Even if this number was 100,000, the Dutch territories were quite extensive and productive enough to support them."[51]

It proved impossible to recruit nearly so many slaves. "Batavia's disappointment in the matter of the supply of slaves was understandable," Van Uffelen replied from Masulipatnam, "but Coromandel would be unable to increase the number supplied except in a year of famine." The Dutch authorities then turned to private traders. Free burghers used VOC ships to transport slaves from India back to the East Indies, even as they were forbidden to trade in cloth. Captives bought their freedom with slaves. A man known as Machomet of Masulipatnam was a pilot on a Portuguese yacht captured by the Dutch; to redeem his freedom, the VOC permitted him to return to the Coromandel Coast to procure slaves to sell back in Batavia, and "he had been allowed to use the Company's ships to transport as many slaves as he wanted." So, too, had Alberto Gomes, an Englishman "who had been with the Portuguese since his boyhood and had married in Macao."[52]

By the 1620s the borderlands of Bengal and Arakan had emerged as the region's most important slave market. The court of Toungoo supported raids on eastern Bengal by Maghs from Arakan, often undertaken in concert with Portuguese Harmads; these raids enslaved thousands of people. But a great many of the captives died before they could be sold or transported. Reports reached the hopeful Dutch that a raid in 1625 had captured more than 10,000 people, but an epidemic killed nearly half of them before they reached the Arakanese capital, Mrauk-U. The Dutch ships *Medemblink* and *Jager* transported 544 of the survivors. Only 130 of them arrived at the Coromandel Coast alive. Coen—back in Batavia for a second stint as governor—reconsidered his eagerness for slaves. "The old, the unsuitable, and the useless are to be left out," he instructed his factors in India.[53] Dutch records contain cursory mention of the numbers of enslaved people who died as they crossed the Bay. The letters are prosaic in their brutality: "These ships had also brought 400 slaves of which 100 had died," one wrote. Another missive noted that "the large scale mortality among the slaves in Coromandel has been compounded by the death of another ninety-three of them on the trip to Batavia," lamenting that this had increased "the cost of the surviving slaves per unit."[54] The inhuman calculus of the slave trade—more familiar to us in its Atlantic context—was present in the Bay of Bengal, too, if on a smaller scale.

Historians have pierced the silence that shrouds the slave trade in the eastern Indian Ocean.[55] Between the 1620s and the 1660s, India—the Coromandel Coast, Arakan, and Bengal—was the chief supplier of enslaved people to the VOC's empire. The company and private traders shipped an average of 150 to 400 slaves each year. They went to Batavia, to the eastern islands of Indonesia, and to Ceylon; they worked on the docks, as domestic servants, as miners and construction workers and fishermen and cultivators. Slaving thrived on agrarian distress and flourished through warfare; the coincidence of crop failures and conflict could be particularly devastating, and this explains the large slave traffic from Coromandel in the early 1620s, in 1646, in 1659–1661, in the 1670s, and in 1688. Arakan was a more consistent source of slaves from the 1620s, until the Mughal conquest of Chittagong, in 1666, put a stop to the traffic. By the 1660s, Southeast Asia's own circuits of slave raiding supplied the Dutch, with a significant slave trade flourishing around Bali and Makassar.

The slave trade from the English settlement in Madras also fluctuated with circumstances. "The use of slaves for domestic purposes in Madras had always been recognized," an English chronicler noted, though "the iniquitous practice of stealing children for export was, of course, illegal." Company authorities changed their minds often about the scope of iniquity. In 1687 they reversed an earlier ban on the export of slaves overseas, and the trade was "sanctioned under regulation." Records from the office of the sea customer showed that in the month of September 1687, 665 slaves were exported; the following year, however, "in deference to the aversion of the Mogul power to the trade," the ban was reinstated. The debates at Fort St. George set a precedent. The distinction between different forms of enslavement, the concern with "the stealing of children," faith that "regulation" would mitigate the evils of slavery—these assumptions shaped the British regulation of migration around the Bay until the twentieth century.

In the Bay of Bengal, as everywhere in Asia, slavery was a powerful mover of men, women, and children: "the interregional movement of slaves helped to integrate peoples, economies, and cultures of South

Asia with those of Central Asia and the Indian Ocean rim." In Southeast Asia, too, "the movement of captive peoples and slaves was the
primary source of labor mobility" before the nineteenth century. Until
the nineteenth century most residents of Southeast Asia's cities were
slaves or captives. The taste for spices sparked an ecological transformation across Southeast Asia; to meet investors' demand for labor,
thousands of people lost their freedom.[56]

By asserting their naval power, European companies had acquired settlements, concessions, factories, fortresses, and colonies around Asia's
coastal rim. But at the end of the seventeenth century their foothold
was far from secure.[57] In the west, European companies confronted the
resurgent naval power of the Ottoman Empire, and the Mughal Empire
expanded its reach to the western shores of the Bay of Bengal; powerful
states in Burma and Arakan secured their hold over the Bay's eastern
littoral, and the kingdom of Aceh sat defiant at the region's edge. Rivalry
was intense between European powers. Europeans' profits depended on
Asian merchants.

At the end of the seventeenth century Thomas Bowrey, an English
merchant, wrote an account of his "nineteen years continuance in East-
India wholly spent in Navigation and Trading in most places of those
Countries." His narrative depicts a world in transition—a world in
which the balance of force and advantage was fairly even. When the
unpublished manuscript was discovered and edited two centuries later
by Sir Richard Carnac Temple, he called it *A Geographical Account of the
Countries Round the Bay of Bengal*. Little is known of Bowrey's life before he arrived in India around 1669, but from then on, his writing is a
window on the commercial connections between India and Southeast
Asia, and on the growing presence of Europeans throughout the region.
From South India, Bowrey traveled to Formosa, Mindanao, Java, Singapore, and Tenasserim.

Asia, Bowrey declared, "comprehendeth many Vast and plentifull Islands of riches and what else necessarie for mankinde." Translation was
crucial in this world of strangers. Bowrey's only work published during
his lifetime was his *Dictionary of English and Malayo* (1701), written
from memory on the long voyage home to England at the end of his
Asian sojourn. Deposited with Bowrey's manuscript in the British Museum was an anonymously authored leaflet containing "the Chinese

Compass of The Points, the Names of the Solar half-months, ordinary Numbers (Learned and Vulgar) and the Private Numeral Notes used only by the China Merchant." Another fragment found with his manuscript takes us from Asia to North America: "A Dictionary of the Hudson Bay Indian Language"—whether this was written by Bowrey himself or by someone else we do not know.

Bowrey's world was insecure and violent. He wrote of "robbery or Murther," raids and massacres, slaves and jailors. He experienced personally the sudden reversals of fortune that befell so many of his contemporaries. In 1687 Bowrey wrote in distress to the East India Company's officers in Porto Novo, informing them that he was in captivity following an altercation with a local merchant, Ahmad Maraikkayar. Ahmad Marakkayar had sent an agent with a consignment of goods on the ship Bowrey owned. Rather than heading for Kedah and Aceh as planned, the ship stopped at Junk Ceylon (the island of Phuket), where its cargo was sold. Ahmad Maraikkayar claimed that the sale was in a "bad market," bringing in less than the goods would have fetched in Aceh, and as compensation, he withheld the cloth his agent had purchased on Bowrey's behalf. In the fight that ensued, Bowrey physically assaulted one of Ahmad Maraikkayar's assistants; in retaliation, he was detained by the local magistrate, who "kept me this three days with a pair of Irons on my leggs and putt me in his peons Cookroom for a Prison." Bowrey faced a further liability. A hundred slaves belonging to Mir Jang Maraikkayar, another local merchant, had traveled on Bowrey's ship without customs dues being paid to the Golconda rulers of Porto Novo. The slave owner had disappeared, so Bowrey was held responsible for his debt. This episode shows how close the relationship was between European and Asian merchants in the Bay of Bengal, and how quickly relations could sour. "I hope in God I shall have a time to have my satisfaction from Amad Marcar for making me wear Irons," Bowrey wrote. The problems of jurisdiction that emerged everywhere in maritime Asia, prompting aggressive European intervention, were clear in this case: East India Company officials in Porto Novo claimed that local authorities were not "competent Judges to punish the offences of one of our owne people."

The lands where Bowrey sought his fortune were linked to the far reaches of the world, often by the ships and by the commercial reach of Asian merchants. Of the trade of Fort St. George (Madras), Bowrey observed that "great Stores are transported and Vended into most places of note in India, Persia, Arabia, China, and the South Seas, more particularly Moneela [Manila]." On the other side of the Bay, the port of Aceh was "never without ships of English, Danes, Portuguese, Moors, Chuleas, Chineses and others."[58]

European travelers such as Bowrey remarked on the wealth of Tamil Muslim traders across Southeast Asia. He wrote of the Tamil Muslims that "the Chulyars are a People that range into all Kingdoms and Countreys in Asia." He noted that "by theire rangeing much," the Maraikkayars "doe learne to write and Speake Severall of the Eastern languages." Bowrey's hostility toward them was unremitting: "I am not at all Sorry for this massacre," he wrote after a local conflict culminated in attacks on Tamil merchants on Phuket Island. Envy motivated Bowrey's animosity. "Wherever these rascalls be," he admitted, "we cannot sell any goods to a Native of the Country."[59] The diaries of John Adolphus Pope, who traveled around the Bay in the 1780s, convey the depth of Tamil Muslims' role in Southeast Asian society. A young man of just fourteen, he was less tainted than Bowrey by prejudice. Arriving in Kedah in April 1786, Pope wrote that "it is inhabited by Malays, Chulias, natives of Choromandel, and Chinese"; the king's merchant was a Tamil Muslim. In the town of Alor Setar, he found "the shops almost all kept by Chulias and Chinamen." Throughout his travels around the Malay world Pope relied on "Chulia" interpreters and intermediaries, and he befriended many of them. In Aceh, he found "Chulias without number." And in every small port he called at, there were Chulia settlements, and Chulias in high office.[60]

Throughout these accounts we can see the mutation of names across the Bay: Maraikkayar becomes "Marcar" or "Merican"—a form still used in Malaysia today. Early European accounts provided the terms of identification that would attach to Tamil Muslims until the twentieth century, and which even became terms of self-description: "Chulia" and "Kling." Both had their origins in the names of ancient Indian kingdoms—Chola and Kalinga, respectively. The terms left an imprint on the street names and neighborhoods of Melaka, Penang, and Singapore, where "Kampong Kling," "Kapitan Kling," and "Chulia Street" betray their origins. Over time, the term "Chulia" came to refer to Tamil Muslim merchants, whereas "Kling" was a more general term, which acquired pejorative connotations. Only with the advent of mass migration from South India in the 1870s would "Tamil" emerge as an overarching category to describe both Muslims and Hindus, and by this time Muslims were in a minority.

In many respects the European advance in Asian waters was parasitic on Asian networks and on Asian trade. The European newcomers inserted themselves into a regional economy that had already turned ecological contrast to profitable specialization. Indian textiles, Southeast Asian spices, and Chinese pottery already coursed through global circuits of exchange; initially the Europeans' (fortuitous) command of the New World's silver allowed them favorable entry into a market to which they had little of their own to offer. Europeans tried to control, but could not monopolize, the Bay's commercial networks. However, the changes they brought to the eastern Indian Ocean were fundamental. Shaped by centuries of internecine conflict born of an unusually competitive interstate system, imbued with the fervor of religious wars, carrying with them distinctive ideas of property and possession, and armed with lethal weapons, the militarized European trading companies effected a sea change in sovereignty.

By the end of the seventeenth century, European factories were spread along the Bay of Bengal's rim, from southern India and Ceylon to Melaka. Their expansion over 150 years was fitful; their power was uneven; their fortresses rarely held sway beyond the coasts. The Portuguese established their foothold first, driven by adventurers in an uneasy relationship with Goa. As the Dutch revolt spread to the eastern seas, the VOC displaced the Portuguese around the Bay, and the British East India Company followed. The northern Europeans saw themselves as different from the swashbuckling Portuguese: more ordered, more rational, more enlightened. Many twentieth-century historians of empire upheld this contrast. But the European powers had much in common. They came for Asia's wealth in spices and textiles. They shared their dependence on inter-Asian trade. They struggled to balance their public and private interests. But at the peak of its power in the seventeenth century, the Dutch East India Company combined commerce and militarism to devastating effect. The fusion of state power, commercial interests, and new institutional forms characterized the Dutch brand of capitalism. Dutch success spawned imitation—not least in the Baltic, the crucial and proximate regional market on which that success depended, however far-flung the Dutch commercial web. Eventually, competing mercantilisms eclipsed Dutch power altogether, the English variety with most success.[61] At their height, the Dutch took advantage of preexisting networks to profit from inter-Asian trade, but they also used the force at their disposal, and an exceptional degree of brutality, to gain a stranglehold over the Maluku Islands. They interposed their own need for labor upon established slave markets, in the process increasing the scale of the slave trade and turning a regional traffic global: quite literally, the Dutch empire took its captives to the ends of the earth.

The European powers brought with them new ideologies of rule and new ideas of personhood. Viewed from Asia, a triumphalist account of the "birth of human rights" in the Dutch Republic looks odd indeed. In the chapters to follow we will track the progress of these new ideas as they circulated around the Bay of Bengal, undergoing many translations and many iterations and having unpredictable, unintended consequences. At particular times, in particular places, they had liberatory potential; at other moments, in other lands, they were profoundly disempowering for those who already had little power. Often the language of freedom was used—sometimes sincerely, sometimes cynically—to justify plunder. Arguably, the English were the most effective of all at combining moralism and self-interest.

In his masterpiece of early American history, Daniel K. Richter points to the importance of understanding "layered pasts." Likening his work to an effort of "geology," Richter argues that "earlier strata of society, culture, and politics" in North America were submerged as planters, imperialists, and revolutionaries staked their successive claims. But "these ancient worlds remain beneath the surface"—they influenced what followed, and their traces survive.[62] The merchants, workers, slaves, and soldiers who crossed the Bay in the early modern world shaped a maritime sphere around its arc of coasts. In the nineteenth century, the force of modern empires would both transform and build upon it.

3

Turbulent Journeys, Sacred Geographies

In May 1786 the *Eliza* set sail from Calcutta to Penang, at the head of a small fleet. Francis Light was in command. The illegitimate son of a Suffolk landowner, Light grew up in the port of Woodbridge; "watching the busy scenes and mingling with mariners doubtless aroused young Light's spirit of adventure," his biographer speculates. He first entered the Royal Navy in 1759, and joined the East India Company's service in 1765. He tasted success as a "country trader" moving between Madras, Aceh, and Kedah; in Kedah he developed close links with the sultan, and found love in the royal court. Light's fleet arrived in Penang on July 16, after long negotiations with the sultan of Kedah, who sought English aid against Bugis maritime raiders in exchange for a trading concession. To his friend Andrew Ross, Light wrote that even "before we could get up any defense we had visitors of all kinds, some for curiosity, some for gain, and some for plunder."[1]

The English coveted a "Port to the Eastward, the situation of which would connect the Bengal trade with that of China and at the same time serve as a Windward Port of refreshment and repair." Penang was not the only option. For several years English sailors trawled the waters off the Straits of Melaka in search of alternatives, among them the island of Phuket—known by Europeans as Junk Ceylon (Ujung Salang)—the Andamans, and even Aceh. Correspondence from the time conveys visions of a sea under English control. In the view of J. Price, Penang was better than Phuket because it was right on the Straits: "the latter lies so far to the northward as to endanger the loss of passage." It was also more likely to be a success than Aceh, which had "ever distressed and at length driven out every European Nation who has attempted to settle there." Crucially, Price remarked, "the situation of Pinang is such that the communication with the Presidencies of Bengal and Madras is at all times open and not more than a month or six weeks at the most unfavourable season is necessary to send or receive advices from both." In the vision of adventurer James Scott, a settlement in Penang promised no less than "a second Bombay, more Central in its location."[2] When he wrote his account of a voyage from Penang to Calcutta, two decades after Light's arrival in Penang, the translator and scribe Ahmad Rijaluddin gestured to the new imperial world in which Penang was now a strategic fortress: by 1810, British power across the Bay was so well established that, Rijaluddin observed, "if any case arises which presents difficulties, the Governor of Penang Island is informed, who thereupon sends an envoy to Bengal."[3]

By the 1820s the British Empire had an enviable position around the Bay of Bengal's coasts. "The events of history often lead to the islands," Braudel wrote of the Mediterranean, and the Napoleonic Wars did just that in the "eastern seas."[4] British expansion around the Bay was secured by strategically central islands, east and west: of these, Penang, Singapore, and Ceylon were most important. With the growth of territorial power in India, with the rising importance of Indian revenues to the British Empire, India's defense became an end in itself. The Bay's strategic advantages grew as the factories of northern England, in the first spurt of what would later be called the "industrial revolution," created new demand for Asia's raw materials, while a growing English bourgeoisie demanded Asia's luxuries. The power of this modern, industrial empire boosted older paths of mobility across the Bay while creating new ones; crossing the Bay of Bengal, thousands of boatmen, day laborers, soldiers, and plantation workers created a new world.

By the turn of the eighteenth century, power along the eastern Indian coast had grown concentrated. Bengal displaced Coromandel as the leading producer and exporter of textiles. European companies consolidated their position at a few key settlements. The Dutch withdrew from many of their smaller factories, focusing on the southern reaches of the Coromandel Coast. After 1740, Dutch commercial primacy in Europe declined steeply, though their financial role remained prominent—many

Dutch investors plowed their capital into English ventures. By the early decades of the eighteenth century, the French Compagnie des Indes had established a major presence in the Asian seas, from a base in Pondicherry.

English power in South Asia expanded in the crucible of European wars, now wars of global consequence. The decades of intra-European conflict—played out in South Asia and North America and on the high seas—began with the War of Austrian Succession (1744–1748). François Dupleix, the French governor-general in India, saw this as an opportunity to challenge English dominance in South India. In 1746, Dupleix's forces besieged Madras and drove out the English; he intervened in succession disputes in regional states including Hyderabad and Arcot. The English retook Madras under the treaty of 1749 and themselves intervened in the politics of Arcot, allowing the East India Company's ally to prevail and causing Dupleix to suffer humiliation. The Seven Years' War (1755–1763) was even more far-reaching in its effects: it precipitated the defeat of French power in South Asia, now restricted to the enclaves of Pondicherry and Karaikal; it precipitated the East India Company's penetration of India, leading up to the conquest of Bengal. The conflict also had a decisive impact on the future of North America.[5] The scale, the expense, and the sheer length of the wars produced an assertive new nationalism in Europe that relished military glory and celebrated territorial expansion. Bloody warfare also consolidated Europe's "military-fiscal" states, with their unparalleled capacity to raise men and resources for war.

The watershed in India came at midcentury, with the Battle of Plassey in 1757. Victory gave the English control over the Mughal province of Bengal, to which they acquired the *diwani,* or the right to collect revenues, in 1765. The story of their subsequent expansion is too well known to need repeating here; it was the beginning of the British territorial empire in India. From their "Bengal bridgehead," the Company moved into Awadh and the heartlands of northern India; by war and threat of war, by treaty and alliance, by inducement and deception, the East India Company deepened its hold. The Company faced fierce resistance from the Marathas in the west and from Tipu Sultan's Mysore in the south; with their rivals' defeat, the English stood virtually unchallenged. They controlled a vast territory, interspersed with a patchwork of suborned princely states.[6]

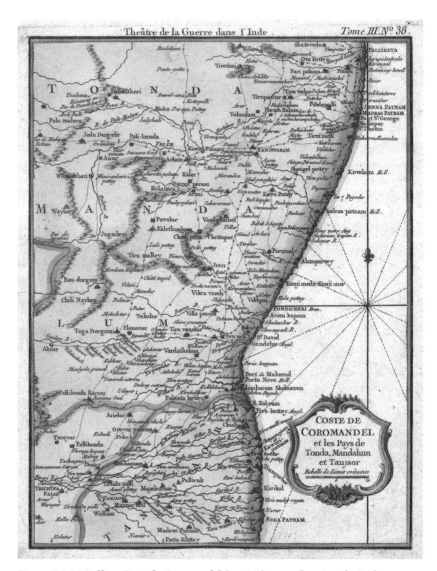

Figure 5 J. N. Bellin, *Coste de Coromandel* (c. 1762): map showing the Indian "theater of war." Bellin was the official hydrographer to the French king and one of the most prolific French cartographers of the mid-eighteenth century. *From the author's collection.*

This fundamental upheaval in South Asian and global politics coincided with a particularly intensive and widespread drought around the Bay of Bengal. Between 1756 and 1768 a "spatially broad and persistent 'megadrought' from India to Southeast Asia" marked "one of the most important periods of monsoon failure" in a millennium.[7] A further drought in 1770, combined with the cumulative social and economic dislocation brought by the early years of Company rule, brought famine to Bengal—up to a third of the population died. To Adam Smith, the Company's disastrous policies bore responsibility for the disaster. He observed:

> In rice countries, where the crop not only requires a very moist soil, but where in a certain period of its growing it must be laid under water, the effects of a drought are much more dismal. Even in such countries, however, the drought is, perhaps, scarce ever so universal as necessarily to occasion a famine, if the government would allow a free trade. The drought in Bengal, a few years ago, might probably have occasioned a very great dearth. Some improper regulations, some injudicious restraints imposed by the servants of the East India Company upon the rice trade, contributed, perhaps, to turn that dearth into a famine.[8]

Many British observers at the time drew different lessons from the Bengal famine of 1770. They began to imagine the "rice countries"— not only India but lands around the Bay of Bengal as well—as "prisoners" of their climate: lands in which every aspect of society, and every aspect of human character, was shaped by natural forces. In the nineteenth century, the notion of "monsoon Asia" encapsulated these assumptions.[9]

South Asia's natural wealth, not its poverty, lent territorial conquest such incalculable importance to Britain's world power. The British government waged the Napoleonic Wars virtually free from foreign debt, thanks to the enforced tribute levied upon India—and this alone allowed for a sixfold increase in public spending between 1792 and 1815. Massive government spending, in turn, boosted the British capital goods industry, and so spurred Britain's industrialization. Levies on opium accounted for up to 20 percent of revenues from India. By the end of the eighteenth century, control over Indian opium—its cultivation was enforced and expanded as British control extended into Bihar—provided the East India Company's greatest strategic advantage in the China trade.[10] Edward Thornton, chief statistician at East India House, put it this way: "India, by exporting opium, assists in supplying England with tea. China, by consuming opium, facilitates the revenue operations between India and England. England, by consuming tea, contributes to increase the demand for the opium of India."[11] A perfect equation.

The ultimate instrument of English power was the Indian Army, financed entirely from Indian revenues. Its separate regional forces—the Madras, Bombay, and Bengal native armies—grew in size; the defeat of rival powers glutted India's "military bazaars." The Madras Army was 24,000 strong in 1796; by 1805 it had more than doubled in size, to 53,000. At the height of the Napoleonic Wars, the Indian Army as a whole counted more than 150,000 men, constituting one of the largest standing armies on earth.[12] By the 1820s, the Company's armies had been pressed into service overseas, in Java, Burma, Ceylon, Penang, and Singapore. They formed the military vanguard of this new Bay of Bengal empire. Many of the Indian soldiers stayed on to enrich the cultural mix of Southeast Asia's port cities in the nineteenth century.

The world conflict of 1793–1815 saw the decisive expansion of British power eastward beyond South Asia. The British set out to "purge the Orient of all of their European rivals." Of the Napoleonic Wars, C. A. Bayly writes that "it is the global interconnectedness of the economic and political turbulences of this era which is so striking." Indian revenues contributed heavily to the British war effort; this encouraged the East India Company's territorial expansion in search of additional land to tax. Under the aggressive leadership of Lord Wellesley, the Company secured an unassailable position in India. By 1818 they had defeated both Tipu Sultan's Mysore and the Maratha Confederacy. The Napoleonic Wars also created an opening for the British east of India. The Dutch were embroiled in war with France, and their possessions in Asia became vulnerable to English attentions. Napoleon's forces occupied Dutch lands in 1795. Communications between Asia and Europe were interrupted, bringing the VOC to bankruptcy. British forces, including many Indian troops, occupied Dutch territories in the east: Melaka, Java, and Riau. Concern with the balance of power in Europe led the British government to be conciliatory toward the Dutch, returning those three territories in 1816.[13]

A decade after the settlement in Penang, in 1796, the British took over Dutch possessions in Ceylon during the war with France, consisting of the northern part of the island and its coasts. More than twenty years later, in 1818, British forces sacked the capital of the inland kingdom of Kandy and occupied the whole island, which the Portuguese and the Dutch had never attempted. Ceylon occupied a crucial position at the western gateway to the Bay of Bengal—the junction of the Bay, the Arabian Sea, and the southern Indian Ocean. "The island seduced all of Europe," Michael Ondaatje writes. "The Portuguese. The Dutch. The English. And so its name changed, as well as its shape—Serendip, Ratnadipa ('island of gems'), Taprobane, Zeloan, Zeilan, Syllan, and Ceylon." Surveying the island soon after the British occupation, Robert Percival wrote of the "vast importance of the island, both in a commercial and a political view"; "with the exception of Bombay," he noted, "it contains the only harbor [Trincomalee] either on the Coromandel or Malabar coasts, in which ships can moor safely at all seasons of the year." The harbor alone, the best harbor in the eastern Indian Ocean, made "Ceylon one of our most valuable acquisitions in the East Indies," with "easy access to our settlements in the Bay of Bengal."

Another attraction was Ceylon's natural wealth: the thriving pearl fishery in the Gulf of Mannar and, above all, the island's wealth in cinnamon. "The best cinnamon is rather pliable," Percival observed, "and ought not much to exceed stout writing paper in its thickness." Early British administrators in Ceylon showed enthusiasm for their Dutch predecessors' experiments in planting cinnamon, which until then "grew entirely in its wild state." These experiments were inspired by the visit to Ceylon, in 1777–1778, of the Swedish botanist Carl Peter Thunberg (1743–1828), one of Carl Linnaeus's most talented pupils; Thunberg collected and cataloged plant specimens from around the Indian Ocean. Percival was convinced that "plantations" designed to "rear cinnamon trees by art" were "infinitely more commodious," productive, and aesthetically pleasing than harvesting from the wild.[14]

The British occupation of Java was short-lived. But it was not long before they acquired a base as well positioned on the eastern frontiers of the Bay as Ceylon was in the west—the island of Singapore, at the end of the Straits of Melaka, which serves as a hinge between the Indian Ocean and the South China Sea. Stamford Raffles and his friend William Farquhar (who had governed Melaka during the British occupation) negotiated terms for an English base in Singapore, leased from the ruler of Johor. Raffles presented his move to Calcutta and London as a fait accompli; the higher authorities in Britain worried about the potential of the settlement to antagonize the Dutch and to upset the balance of power in Europe, but they saw the value of its location.

Singapore was even better situated than Penang to protect and foster the Company's China trade, which was now the most lucrative part of its business. "It breaks the spell," Raffles wrote in 1819, "and [the Dutch] are no longer the exclusive sovereigns of the eastern seas." On Raffles's second visit to Singapore, in May 1819, he declared that it "bids fair to be the next port to Calcutta." His assessment grew audacious: "as far as naval superiority and commercial interests are concerned," Singapore was "of much higher value than whole continents of territory." Within three years of its founding, more than 3,000 vessels had called at Singapore's harbor. Junks from Siam, Cambodia, and Vietnam flocked to Singapore, attracted by its status as a free port and the absence of duties—in February 1821, the first junk arrived from Amoy, on the China coast.[15] Soon Singapore became home to one of the most diverse populations on earth.

In 1824, the English negotiated the Treaty of London with the Dutch, for the purpose of "Respecting Territory and Commerce in the East Indies." In exchange for their Sumatran factory at Bencoolen, the British acquired Melaka: the Straits formed a border between the British and Dutch territories in the Malay archipelago. Melaka, Singapore, and Penang together constituted the Straits Settlements, ruled from Calcutta as an eastward extension of British India.[16] In a final thrust around the arc, the Indian Army conquered the Burmese province of Tenasserim in the 1820s, along the Bay of Bengal's eastern coast.

The three islands—Ceylon, Penang, and Singapore—reflected the competing imperatives of imperial rule around the Bay. Singapore developed as a free port, Ceylon as an agricultural plantation, and Penang as a port city that would become the gateway to the Malay Peninsula. The free trade of Singapore might have been more valuable than "whole continents of territory," but the British Empire depended increasingly on "whole continents" to profit from it. The East India Company depended on its control over India's land revenues and opium production; Britain's expanding and ceaseless demand for the products of the tropical forest was fed by Ceylon and Malaya in the nineteenth century.

Tamil Muslim merchants prospered in Penang. On some accounts, the very day Light's fleet landed there, Tamil traders from Kedah set up a market stall selling produce to the new arrivals. News traveled and their numbers grew, as did the flow of Chinese visitors and settlers. A census undertaken in 1788 counted more than 200 "Chooliar inhabitants" in seventy-one "houses and shops." Within a few years, the Penang authorities noted that "the Native Vessels which come over from the Coast of Coromandel are always full of people a great many of whom are Merchants having each a small adventure." Some early Tamil Muslim settlers in Penang were "originally from the Coast" but "the Greatest part of them have their families at Queda."[17]

Tamil Muslim traders married local Malay women, creating a creole community that would come to be known in the nineteenth century as the Jawi Peranakan (*peranakan* denoting "local-born," and applied more commonly to locally born Chinese).[18] They blended Tamil and Malay culture; they evolved distinctive modes of dress, speech, and ritual, bound by a shared adherence to Islam. This contact of cultures brought painful dilemmas as well as linguistic and social versatility: the dilemmas would grow sharper with the rise of new ideas about race and nationality. Through their patronage of shrines, Tamil Muslim merchants shaped the sacred architecture of Southeast Asia's port cities. Through their control of shipping from India, they transported workmen across the Bay of Bengal. Through their command of capital, they financed a torrent of textiles and rice and pepper.

The biographies of two prominent figures from within the creole Tamil Muslim community of the Straits evoke a world of multiple affiliations across the Bay of Bengal.[19] Abdullah abd al-Kadir, also known as Munsyi Abdullah, worked as a scribe and translator for the East India Company. He is famous in Malay history as a social reformer, as author of the "first Malay autobiography," and as a servant of the British Empire. Abdullah's great-grandfather was a Hadrami Arab from Yemen who settled in Nagore and married a local Tamil woman. The couple had four sons. The first, Abdullah's grandfather, traveled to Melaka, where he met and married a Tamil Muslim woman, "Peri Achi, the daughter of Schaikh Mira Lebai." The other three sons all traveled to "Java" (in this case a general term for Indonesia), where they settled in Ambon, Sumatra, and Java, married, and had children.

Abdullah's father, Abdul Kadir, was born in Melaka. He mastered the Malay language and "became a merchant trading in sundry goods between Melaka and the hinterland," where he would also "impart his

knowledge of the Koran and Muslim prayers to the upcountry people."
At the same time, he "spoke the 'Hindu' language, i.e. Tamil, well; and
he used to write and keep accounts in it." Abdullah describes his
mother as an "Indian from Kedah who had embraced the Muslim
faith." Abdul Kadir deployed his cultural versatility to act as an inter-
mediary between Indian, Malay, and European worlds, and he made
himself rich in the process. He served the Dutch as a *shahbandar,*
and—in his son's wry description—he "might be compared to the
mouse that falls into the rice-bin, living as he was then in the most af-
fluent circumstances."

As a boy Abdullah creatively bridged the many sides of his cultural
inheritance. He writes that "my father sent me to a teacher to learn
Tamil, an Indian language, because it had been the custom from the
time of our forefathers in Malacca for all the children of good and well-
to-do families to learn it. It was useful for doing computations and accounts, and for purposes of conversation because at that time Malacca
was crowded with Indian merchants." "Many were the men," he continued, "who had become rich by trading in Malacca, so much so that the
names of Tamil traders had become famous. All of them made their
children learn Tamil." Munsyi Abdullah saw no contradiction in recog-
nizing his Tamil heritage while devoting himself to the uplift of the
Malay "race" (*bangsa*), with which he identified most closely.[20]

With the settlement of Penang by the East India Company in 1786,
new opportunities opened for Tamil Muslim merchants. Mohamed
Noordin Maraikkayar—known locally as Mohamed Merican Noordin—
arrived in Penang from Nagore in the 1820s.[21] Within a decade he as-
cended to a position of wealth and influence among Penang's merchants. Mohamed Noordin used his links of kinship, language, and
trust with communities across the Indian Ocean—from his native
South India to Burma, Aceh, and even China—to build his business. In
1838 he dispatched seventeen ships from Penang, destined for "Chittagong and Arakan, Deli, Aceh, Pudu and the Pedir Coast, Cuddalore,
Bombay, Nagapattinam, Cochin and Calcutta, Aleppey and Singapore."

Details of Mohamed Noordin's life are scattered through the legal
record thanks to his family's taste for litigation. After his death, the
family engaged in long proceedings in the colonial courts over his
will.[22] Among his wives were a Malay, a European, and an Indian, and
possibly also a Chinese woman. He had six sons and five daughters:

some of his family were registered with the authorities as "Kling," others as "Malay." The children, in turn, married others from the Tamil-Malay community, recently arrived Tamil Muslims from India, and local Malays. Mohamed Noordin's lavish philanthropy cemented his public reputation. Like many other Muslim merchants across the Indian Ocean, he endowed land to be used for religious purposes *(waqf)*. He established a school "for the learning of English, Hindoostanee, Malay, Tamil, Malabar and the Al-Koran," at a charge of twenty Straits dollars each month. He financed Penang's municipal water supply. He donated money to Christian institutions of charity and education. Upon his death, the Noordin family tomb became a site of veneration. It was this veneration, however, that took Noordin's family to the courts: he had provided for an annual *kandoori* (procession) in his honor, but the Supreme Court of Penang decreed that this was not lawful under the law of charitable gifts and that this money should go to his next of kin. The case dragged on for thirty years, through appeal and counter-appeal, ending in a landmark case in the Privy Council that helped to define the law of estoppel.[23]

The islands of the Bay were remarkable for their ethnic variety. They were heirs to Melaka, where Tomé Pires had heard eighty-four languages on the street. British power brought new kinds of free and unfree movement to the Bay of Bengal, rooting and uprooting in unequal measure: immobilizing those who had once been mobile, forcing the movement of sedentary people. Francis Light wrote of the "great number of Strangers constantly coming and going" from Penang. He recommended the "strict police" of the "great diversity of Inhabitants differing in religion, laws, language, and customs." A few years later, Robert Percival observed of Ceylon that "there is no part of the world where so many languages are spoken or which contains such a mixture of nations, manners and religions."[24]

The colliding currents of the Bay of Bengal brought people into contact. They created new societies under the anvil of a new empire; they welded new and old routes across the sea. A voracious and unprecedented appetite for labor distinguished the mobility of the nineteenth century from earlier times. The militarized competition between empires called for soldiers. The demand for tropical products, now cultivated in plantations, required labor to clear the land. The port cities, swelled by commerce and by war, needed workers: men for their dockyards, men to pull carriages, men to build roads, men to dispose of waste. These were frontier societies of many men and few women. The cities they forged were relatively free of social constraint but suffused with violence. Rough justice prevailed, but gradually new norms evolved over the use of public space, over proper behavior, over sharing resources. The port cities of the Straits were places of linguistic innovation, as strangers were thrown together and had to learn to speak to one another. The distinction between forced and free migration blurred. Soldiers, slaves, transported convicts, and migrant workers toiled together. Their collective biography is the story of the Bay of Bengal as a human sea—a sea connected by ships and money, but also by ideas, struggles, and shared suffering.

The soldiers came first. Indian sepoys fortified the sea. By the early nineteenth century, English garrisons formed a ring around the Bay of Bengal. On the first English ship to dock in Penang were a hundred Indian soldiers, twenty lascars, fifteen artillerymen, and five British officers. Within a year of its settlement, Alexander Kyd reported that "Penang as yet can be said to have no Inhabitants of its own or even any but the servants of Government and the followers of the Troops that are firmly established." With the Indian soldiers came the "bazaar contingent": camp followers, washermen, groomsmen, cooks, artificers, performers, and "peons." They set to work on the island's topography. "The little of the woods that are cleared," Kyd wrote, "and all the works about the point has been done by the Lascars of the Detachment" working alongside Malays from the mainland for a daily wage.[25] The first contingent of soldiers made Penang their home—"they have stock sufficient to begin with and many of them have already portions of land with cattle." But the government needed an army, and the governor made an urgent request for more troops. Of the two original regiments, "the greater part of these will prefer remaining as Riotts [cultivators] rather than to return to Bengal, they only require their families to be sent to them." As well as cultivating the land, Indian troops were a mainstay of the bazaar: they thrived as moneylenders, traders, and day laborers. After the settlement of Singapore in 1819, many members of the Bengal Native Infantry settled in the town after their tours of duty, gravitating toward the Serangoon neighborhood.[26]

In frontier settlements, where might was right, British and Indian soldiers helped themselves to what was on offer. "I have heard frequent complaints from the Malays and Chooliars who supply the market, of the sepoys having gone into their Prows, and taken whatever they wanted," the island's provost complained in 1794. James Scott, the island's commercial pioneer and freebooter in chief, complained that "every female slave brought to market is purchased [by the sepoys] at price hitherto unknown to the Natives." A local magistrate heard the case of the unfortunate Syedpilly Marikan, a Nagore merchant who had traveled to Kedah to trade after his family had been "reduced to poverty" by the British capture of Nagapatnam. Having lost his return passage, he went to Penang hoping to find a place on a vessel crossing the Bay back to India, but his small trading boat was raided "by a European and a sepoy," and he was left with nothing.[27]

Soldiers crossed the Bay of Bengal both ways in the era of the Napoleonic Wars. They forged an archipelago of fortifications, formed communities, left traces on the land and in language. Indian troops spearheaded the British occupation of Java between 1811 and 1816. The Dutch had raised a "Malay regiment" for service in Ceylon, which the British later incorporated into their regular forces; these men formed the nucleus of a Malay community that continues to thrive in contemporary Sri Lanka. The British military force in Ceylon was a microcosm of the Indian Ocean world: it included 450 "Gun Lascars," "inhabitants originally of the lower parts of Bengal and Chittagong"; a regiment of "Coast sepoys"; the "Corps of Malays . . . most of whom had been in Dutch Service"; and the "Baillies," 800 "Caffrees imported from Mozambique and Goa."[28]

Neither soldiers nor local people sufficed for this labor-hungry empire. Just months after his arrival in Penang, Light demanded "a further supply of one hundred coolies, as the price of labor here is enormous." Land clearance was a high priority; within a few years a concerted land grab was under way. "A vague and indiscriminate order seems to have been given on the moment of settling," Penang's superintendent, F. R. MacDonald, complained in 1796, "entitling every person able to handle an axe to the possession of such Ground." MacDonald reserved his harshest judgment for the "wanton manner in which Europeans, on speculations of its future value, have seized upon, or acquired by trifling

Purchases, extensive Tracts of our finest lands." MacDonald was not the first to criticize Light's free-for-all, in which even Penang's warehouses were given over to private merchants and rented back from them by the Company. But "hands" were needed to make Penang productive. "The large trees are first cut down at the distance of six or seven feet from the ground, after which the Earth is dug away from the roots" W. M. Hunter noted in 1802; once the tree trunks were cut up, "the whole mass is reduced to ashes, which answers the purposes of manure." The coerced, but still remunerated, labor of convicted prisoners combined with the efforts of Malay workers on a daily wage; thereafter, "the remaining operations necessary to bring the ground into a state fit for Cultivation are performed by the Chinese."[29]

English authorities turned first to the "Caffrees," enslaved people from Mozambique who were transported to the Company's factory at Bencoolen, in Sumatra, and from there to Penang, as forced laborers. They were the survivors of an earlier traffic in slaves across the Indian Ocean. Many had settled in Goa, serving in the Portuguese and then the British armies; exiled to Madras, some were uprooted again and transported to Southeast Asia. The first group of them arrived in Penang on the *Ravensworth* in June 1787. Within a few months they were "employed at various work," and "the women do by far the most labor." As well as clearing land, the enslaved Africans worked as "sawyers and carpenters and brick makers." As late as 1808 British officials envisaged a further traffic of "Caffrees" from Mozambique, to provide a military force for Ceylon that was "possessed of no local prejudices of feelings." Thomas Maitland was careful to insist that this could be done "without violating any of those principles which recently led to the abolition of the Slave Trade in England," though he did not specify how.[30]

The enslaved people from Mozambique remain mostly invisible in the archives, but occasionally their voices intrude in petitions and demands. When the East India Company ceded Bencoolen to the Dutch in 1824, the "Free Bengalis" who moved from Bencoolen to Penang were a diverse group of people—a mixed community of African slaves and Indian convicts, many of them married to local Sumatran women. They had "emigrated . . . to this place in different situations," and had by the 1820s "inter-married with Natives of this place, and we are now fathers and Husbands of families."[31] The end of the archival trail is abrupt: there is no further trace of the "Caffrees" or the "Free Bengalis" in the record, and one might assume that their few descendants melded, unnoticed, into the working class of the port cities.

There were few slaves in the Straits Settlements. Governors and planters turned to another, much greater source of forced labor: convicted prisoners from India. The British imperial system of punitive transportation spanned the Indian Ocean, depositing convicts from India in a network of island prisons stretching from Robben Island to Mauritius, from the Andaman Islands to Singapore. The movement of convict labor was a global phenomenon. In the age of sail, mobility embraced captivity. Between 30,000 and 50,000 prisoners were transported from Britain to the North American colonies in the seventeenth and eighteenth centuries; around 160,000 traveled to Australia in the eighteenth and nineteenth. The Indian Ocean's penal circuit was on a comparable scale. In all, 80,000 convicted prisoners were transported overseas from India between 1787 and 1943. Of these, around 20,000 went to the Straits Settlements (between 1790 and 1860), 5,000 to 7,000 to Arakan and Tenasserim (1828–1862), and 50,000 to the Andaman Islands (1858–1943). A smaller number of prisoners crossed the Bay the other way: Chinese, Malay, and Burmese convicts were exiled to Madras, Bengal, and Bombay.[32]

Discipline and punishment were foremost in the minds of British administrators in India. They favored transportation because of its capacity to provoke "terror" in the "native mind": the sea voyage across the "black waters" (*kala pani*) threatened loss of caste, and the prospect of physical isolation instilled fear in the convicts. Political prisoners were among the first to be exiled to Southeast Asia. Madras authorities banished seventy-three Poligar rebels to Penang after their defeat of the Sivaganga Revolt in 1799–1801; there many of them died and the survivors languished until, in 1815, they petitioned the Penang authorities to "beg . . . [to] return to the Coast." Straits officials were sympathetic, arguing that they "have all equally conducted themselves with propriety" and that their liberation would be an act of "Justice and humanity," but the Madras Government refused them the right to return. Across the Indian Ocean, small groups of political prisoners turned their places of exile into new homes: transported rebels from the Dutch East Indies formed the core of the "Cape Malay" community, and their journeys continue to evoke powerful memories to this day.[33]

On the Indian Ocean's eastern frontiers, however, the convicts were first and foremost laborers. In 1793 the Bengal authorities experimented with a prison settlement on the Andaman Islands, to make these forbidden islands productive. Three hundred convicts were sent; the scheme was a disaster. Most of the prisoners died of disease or exhaustion; some of the survivors returned to Bengal, others went on to Penang.[34] In 1790 the first two convicted prisoners from India, Eyenodien Sheikdar and Mahomed Heiant, landed in Penang. "You may employ them in any manner that you think proper," the Bengal government advised, "consistent with the security of their persons." By 1824 nearly 1,500 convicts had been sent to the Straits Settlements. The mortality rate was over half, with the average number of new arrivals each year 192 and the number of deaths averaging 103; desertions averaged 15.

The Straits authorities divided the convict labor force into "classes," giving them greater or lesser privileges depending on the nature of their offenses and the value of their labor. A "convict census" of 1824 showed that fifty-six convicts had been "freed from irons" to work as *sirdars* (labor bosses) or as *munshis* (scribes); at the other end of the spectrum were those on the "criminal gang," who "worked from six to twelve and two to five every day in heavy irons clearing the streets and drains of Georgetown." Convicts worked as cooks and servants, as orderlies and hospital attendants, as gardeners and syces and grass cutters. Some were hired out to private residents, for which the government received a payment and the workers received nothing; others, with rarer skills, earned a daily wage for themselves. Building roads and digging ditches, convicts were dispersed across the island. Often they worked without restraint: the prisoners were "their own warders" to an extent that astonished visitors and disturbed European settlers.[35]

The centrality of convict labor to the development of the Straits Settlements was clear to many observers. In 1796 F. R. MacDonald wrote that convicts "might in a new settlement be of great advantage": they "can usefully be employed on the island owing then to the difficulty at that early stage of our society, in obtaining coolies and servants." In Burma, similarly, convict labor promised to transform the land. "I entertain strong hopes of seeing the cultivation of Cotton, Sugar & Coffee 'ere long extensively engaged in," wrote E. A. Blundell (future governor of the Straits Settlements) from Arakan. He reassured Calcutta that the convicts were "proving profitable to Government," and he listed their occupations: "sawyers, 60; brick and tile workers, 220; potters, 7; weavers, 12; blacksmiths, 2; brass founders, 2; hired out and private servants, 88."[36]

His counterpart in Akyab, A. C. Phayre, was less sanguine. There the settlement was engaged in an unending battle against nature—the monsoons and vegetation threatened to engulf it. Phayre insisted on the need for convict labor "on the public roads," because "the heavy rain in Arracan, averaging more than two hundred inches per annum . . . make[s] an unremitting attention to the roads and drains" essential. In Phayre's view, convict workers had transformed not only the land but the very climate as well. The "presence of a large body of prisoners disposable at a moment's warning"—giving "constant attention" to the roads, and clearing jungle from the shoreline—"made such a salutary change to the climate of this station, which we all acknowledge to be very different indeed, to what it was seven or eight years ago." He issued a stark warning to his bosses in Calcutta: "Were this neglected for even a month or two, it is to be feared that the consequence would be a return of the severe fevers & sickness which formerly prevailed so fatally." The immobility of the convicts was useful precisely because of the mobility of others. Phayre observed that migrant laborers from Chittagong "who come down yearly" would do a season on the fields in Arakan and return home with their earnings "as the southwest monsoon arrived in April." In Burma, as on the Malay Peninsula, convict labor coexisted with many other kinds of circulation.[37]

Meanwhile, convict labor created the sinews of the Straits Settlements. The "numerous and extensive Roads which intersect the island in every direction, the extensive Public Buildings . . . the swamps and marsh grounds which have been drained and raised" all stood as a testament to their industry, and to their sacrifices. Convicts socialized with soldiers and camp followers; they formed relationships with local women; they worked alongside Chinese and Malays. They asserted a sense of worth in identifying themselves as "company's servants," *kampani ke naukar.*[38]

The panic that followed the Indian Rebellion of 1857 hardened settler opinion against convict labor in the Straits. A mutiny in the Company's army developed into a general revolt of dispossessed artisans and deposed aristocrats across North India, with the old Mughal emperor, Bahadur Shah, as its symbolic leader. The rebellion posed the greatest challenge to English rule in the nineteenth century, and it was defeated with savage violence by the British Army. The revolt of 1857 spelled the end for East India Company rule in India and around the Bay of Bengal, as the British crown took over control and the Raj was born. The Straits government refused to accept the exiled rebels of 1857, and local European opinion grew hysterical; a rift developed between the Straits and India, which would culminate in the separation of the Straits from Indian control a decade later and its establishment as a crown colony. The *Singapore Free Press* lamented that the island had become "the common sewer . . . for all the scum and refuse of the population of nearly the whole British possessions in the east"; a petition of "Christian inhabitants" asserted that "we are no longer an infant colony—that state has been passed when convict labor is either desirable or necessary." Governor Blundell feared, above all, the effect that "any outbreak on the part of the convict body" might have on the "turbulent disposition of the lower classes of our Chinese population."[39] The convict settlement in the Straits was finally disbanded in 1873.

By the last quarter of the nineteenth century, the expansion of trade and cultivation had brought forth a surge of migrants—free and unfree—across the Bay of Bengal. Convict labor was superfluous: other solutions had been found to the problem of "obtaining coolies and servants."

The commercial life of the Bay of Bengal had long sustained a maritime labor force. Fishing was the lifeblood of the coastal economy. The shipbuilding industry was ancient and well established. In the eighteenth century, Bombay emerged as the most important center of Indian shipbuilding, dominated by Parsi craftsmen from Surat. Under their initiative, Indian hardwoods and construction techniques melded with European designs. Under the command of the master builder Lowji Nuserwanji Wadia and then his sons, 159 ships over a hundred tons were built in Bombay between 1736 and 1821. Bengal, too, was an ancient center of ship construction, and Calcutta and Chittagong continued to thrive in the eighteenth century, rising to new demand from European country traders. In the first two decades of the eighteenth century, 237 ships were built on the Hugli, many of them at the Kidderpore dry dock, inaugurated in 1803 under the watch of J. and R. Kyd, master builders. These ships were made of "teak and timber planks, imported from Pegu; saul and sissoo timber from Behar and Odh, and the inexhaustible forests that skirt the hills which form the northern boundaries of Bengal and Behar," Anthony Lambert observed in 1802. The Indian shipping industry tumbled in the 1820s: pushed to the margins by the rise of steam technology, squeezed by political pressure from British shipbuilders to restrict entry to Indian ships.[40]

Dockworkers and boatmen, pilots and navigators filled the ranks of maritime labor. Beginning in the seventeenth century, Portuguese and English ships employed Indian sailors—known as *lascorin* by the Portuguese and as lascars in English—trained to operate artillery guns. Drawn from the Urdu word *lashkari,* "soldier," the term assumed a maritime connotation in the European lexicon. Europe's expanding empires absorbed thousands of Indian sailors, who worked alongside Malays, East Africans, Chinese, and southern Europeans. Writes Amitav Ghosh: "it is unlikely that there were ever any more diverse collections of people—albeit only men—than the crews of merchant ships in the age of sail." To take one example of many, the *Princess Royal,* the ship on which the young John Pope traveled in 1786, had on its crew Innes from Malta, Jean Le Fevre from Guernsey, and Manu, Manuel and Pedro from Bengal as seacunnies; the *serang* was Hadjee Dosa, of Surat, who died on the journey; the *tindals* came from Bengal and Madras; the thirty-five lascars were from Madras and Lucknow and Chittagong. The ship's cook was from Mozambique, and the captain and chief mate had each an "African slave boy." The officers, inevitably, were Europeans. As sail gave way to steam in the nineteenth century, sailors from around the Indian Ocean world continued to form the vanguard of the maritime working class.[41]

On shore as much as at sea, European companies relied on local labor. Panic gripped Fort St. George in 1784 when the master attendant reported to the governor that nearly 300 boatmen of Madras harbor had fled to the French territories of Pondicherry and Karaikal, and to Danish Tranquebar. The boat owners and the master attendant demanded that soldiers be sent to track down the "deserters" and bring them back. On their own admission, Company officials could see that it was a question of freedom: by leaving Madras, the boatmen could "work when they please and are not obliged to it." Furthermore, the ports they went to experienced "less Surf and therefore the work is easier," and there the workers' subsistence was ensured, as "they have liberty to fish when they choose." The contractors, by contrast, argued that the boatmen were bonded to them "forever" by debt. The contactors' complaints—and their own self-interest—led the Madras authorities to declare that "the necessary public services on the beach will be extremely endangered if the men are permitted to go away," adding that the contractors had "purchased their Future Services by large advances of money." In an increasingly commercialized economy, debt could lock people in place—or it could force them into long journeys to serve, or to escape, their creditors.[42]

Right around the coastal rim, labor was mobile—but it was particularly mobile between southern India and Ceylon.[43] For centuries, workers and artisans moved temporarily or permanently from South India to Ceylon. For centuries, fishing communities and petty traders lived across both sides of the Palk Strait. For centuries, too, "the sanctity of certain mountains and temples in Ceylon which have been the object of pilgrimage from time immemorial has served to maintain an uninterrupted intercourse between the Natives of India and this Island." British attempts to exploit more intensively the island's natural riches created a hunger for Indian labor. The conquest of Ceylon's interior—by force, with roads and bridges—depended on Indian soldiers and corvée labor. With the decline in the value of cinnamon, British planters staked their fortunes on coffee, which required labor on a larger scale. "An immense alteration will be effected in the heretofore desert wastes of the island," one British observer predicted. Ceylon embraced the "West India system of cultivation," as the equalization of the coffee tariff between the two regions in 1835 set them up as competitors. Planters moved with their "system": while many of Ceylon's coffee planters were novices, a few had prior experience in the West Indies. R. B. Tytler, longtime president of the Planters' Association, arrived in Ceylon after working on a Jamaican coffee plantation in the last years of slavery. He brought with him his experience of wielding whip and chain.[44]

Labor migration between South India and Ceylon flourished in the 1840s. It rose to an early peak of nearly 80,000 arrivals in 1844, falling away as the coffee industry sank into depression, reviving with the planters' fortunes to approach 100,000 arrivals annually by the late 1850s. On average, between half and three-quarters of the migrants returned home within a year or two.[45] Labor recruiters, known in Tamil as *kanganies,* marshaled the process. They would become key figures in the Bay of Bengal's history of migration. In the early years, most *kanga-nies* were simply the appointed spokesmen of gangs of laborers who traveled together from South India. Others became professional labor recruiters, who gathered up willing (and, at times, unwilling) migrants in South India and delivered them to coffee plantations in Ceylon looking for workers. Many *kanganies* were existing plantation workers, sent back to India by their employers to recruit more men on commission. Debt galvanized the system. *Kanganies* advanced money to the families of recruits in India—the "coast advance," it was called—which they used to free themselves from servitude, or to pay off debts incurred in times of dearth. Once indebted, the migrants were in the *kangany*'s power. Where they operated on a small scale, recruiting largely among their fellow villagers, relations of caste and kinship could moderate the *kanganies*' power, but such intimacy could also make the bonds of debt more pervasive.[46] The "coolie" had to be mobilized in India, loosened from his social ties, transported, immobilized again on the plantations, prevented from moving on except when it suited the planters, and placed under the "traditional" authority of the *kangany*.[47]

As British power expanded eastward across the Bay, Indian labor followed. Writing in 1873, John Geoghegan, a civil servant charged with investigating the previous century of Indian emigration, found that "the earliest emigration seems to have taken place from the southern portion of the continent." He wrote of a Tamil "exodus to the Straits Settlements" that "had begun before the end of the last century." Indians in the Straits, Geoghegan noted, "were employed both as domestic servants and as agricultural laborers." Already by 1794 Penang's rulers had observed that "about one thousand . . . Chulias, or People from the several ports on the coast of Coromandel," were "settled" in Penang, "some with families." They "are all shop keepers and coolies," and many had moved to Penang from older settlements in Kedah. Light estimated that "the vessels from the Coast bring over annually 1500 or 2000 men who by traffic and various kinds of labour obtain a few Dollars with which they return to their homes and are succeeded by others." It was a community in flux.

For the large number of sojourners who returned to India, a few stayed behind. By the 1820s, Tamils constituted the largest single group in Georgetown, the urban settlement on Penang Island. "The numerous vessels of their nation bring annually, with the setting in of the westerly monsoon, shoals of these people, literally to seek their fortunes in a country richer by nature," John Crawfurd observed. In Penang, as in Singapore, new arrivals from the Coromandel Coast melded into an already diverse South Asian population, which included Company soldiers and convicts from Madras and Bengal, as well as a large and growing society of Chinese migrants.[48]

Mobility across the Bay surged in the mid-nineteenth century. The sheer number of boats crossing the Bay elicited government concern for the first time; beginning in the late 1840s, Tamil emigration features in the Madras archives. Cases came to light in which seriously overcrowded "native vessels" crossed the water. As one observer wrote in 1848, "It is notorious the crowded manner in which the vessels arrive at Penang"; "the consequences this year have been very fatal, many of the passengers having died on the way." Regulation appeared impossible. So dispersed was the traffic, from smaller as well as larger ports, that if regulations were tightened in Penang, "Asiatics wishing a passage can readily embark from the adjacent Malay coast."[49] Hindu and Muslim shipping merchants advanced to thousands of laborers the cost of their passage overseas, and matched them up with employers in Penang and Singapore.[50] We know little about how these recruiters worked; until the 1870s, the relationship between Indian shipping merchants and labor migrants to Southeast Asia remains opaque. It seems likely, however, that early Indian migration to Malaya was similar in nature to Chinese migration, which is better documented—that is to say, it was in local hands, embedded in local networks, and organized around debt. The main difference, even before 1870, was that many Indian migrants worked for Europeans, whereas Chinese migrants tended to have Chinese employers.

By the end of the 1860s, the chief secretary of the Straits Settlements observed that there was "a regular cooly emigration from the Coast to Penang. Many ships belonging to Hindus and Mussulmen are employed in it, and the number of persons who are thus brought over is believed to average 4,000 per annum." He saw that "almost all the boatmen, caulkers, and laborers on board ships and in the town,—syces, watermen, and a large number of hawkers, traders and domestic servants, are men from the Madras Coast."[51] Unheralded, their stories untold, many of the boatmen were from seafaring communities along the coast of

Orissa.[52] The port cities at the eastern edge of the Bay of Bengal were made by the labor of migrants who had crossed it as soldiers and convicts and workers. Their world was shared with—and fought over with—many others: Chinese traders and miners, Malay fishermen, European jailers and innkeepers.

In the contest between empires, the Straits of Melaka were prized as the narrow point where the Indian Ocean met the China Sea. Indian and Chinese migrants encountered each other for the first time in the Malay archipelago, a region with its own seafaring traditions. Wherever Europeans went in Asia, they found thriving communities of Chinese. The commercial links between China, Southeast Asia, and India were of long standing. In the period 1405–1431 Chinese maritime expeditions led by the admiral Zheng He—a Muslim eunuch of Mongol origin, who rose within the court of the Yongle Emperor—traversed Southeast Asia and crossed the Indian Ocean to eastern Africa. He called at the Sri Lankan port of Hambantota, where he left an inscription; his forces attacked and kidnapped the royal family of Kotte after a dispute over a Buddhist relic. Members of his vast crew settled at the many stops along their journey; when they died, some of their places of burial became sites of pilgrimage, as we see at Gedung Batu at Semarang, the tomb of one of Zheng He's pilots, who converted to Islam and married a local woman.[53] Even after the Chinese state turned its back to the sea, faced with a restive inner Asian frontier, Zheng He's voyages left small communities of Chinese along its route, "precursors of China's modern emigration history." Early European settlements in Southeast Asia hosted Chinese populations, and so too did many indigenous kingdoms.[54]

The British Empire expanded Chinese merchants' commercial opportunities. Penang and Singapore were declared "free" ports. From the outset, Chinese traders and laborers flocked to both; Singapore was, by the 1820s, overwhelmingly a Chinese city, its elite infused by the exodus of Hokkien-speaking Chinese from Melaka. A steady and increasing flow of labor followed the Chinese merchants to the southern seas. Social networks were the crucial mechanism of this migration. Some were rooted in kinship, while others were based on native place, surname, dialect group, or region. Overseas Chinese associations were a clearinghouse for news of jobs, and they also arranged credit for the journey, connections with employers, housing, and even armed protection. Such was the importance of knowing the right people and having the right contacts that one village with many sons abroad might have neighbors with none; over time, these networks tended to reinforce themselves.

The sheer diversity of occupations in which working-class Chinese migrants found themselves is clear from J. D. Vaughn's dizzying list in his "observations" on the Chinese in Penang. "The Chinese are everything," he wrote:

> they are actors, acrobats, artists, musicians, chemists and druggists, clerks, cashiers, engineers, architects, surveyors, missionaries, priests, doctors, school-masters, lodging-house keepers, butchers, pork-sellers, cultivators of pepper and gambier, cakesellers, car and hackney carriage owners, cloth hawkers, distillers of spirits, eating-house keepers, fish-mongers, fruit-sellers, ferrymen, grass-sellers, hawkers, merchants and agents, oil-sellers, opium shopkeepers, pawn-brokers, pig-dealers, and poulterers. They are rice-dealers, ship-chandlers, shop-keepers, general dealers, spirit shop keepers, servants, timber-dealers, tobacconists, vegetable sellers, planters, market-gardeners, labourers, bakers, millers, barbers, blacksmiths, boatmen, book-binders, boot and shoe-makers, brick-makers, carpenters, cabinet makers, carriage builders, cartwrights, cart and hackney carriage drivers, charcoal burners and sellers, coffinmakers, confectioners, contractors and builders, coopers, engine-drivers, and firemen, fishermen, goldsmiths, gunsmiths and locksmiths, limeburners, masons and bricklayers, mat, kajang and basket makers, oil manufacturers, and miners. To which we may add painters, paper lantern makers, porters, pea-grinders, printers, sago, sugar and gambier manufacturers, sawyers, seamen, ship and boat builders, soap boilers, stone cutters, sugar boilers, tailors, tanners, tin smiths and braziers, umbrella makers, undertakers and tomb-builders, watch-makers, water-carriers, wood cutters and sellers, wood and ivory carvers, fortune-tellers, grocers, beggars, idle vagabonds or "samsengs" and thieves.[55]

In some of these many trades, the Chinese competed or formed partnerships with Indian merchants. Chinese laborers also worked alongside Indians and Malays, and they observed and even participated in each other's festivals. But never did the Indian migrants to the Straits have the same density of associations as the Chinese, who had *kongsis* and other associations that linked capitalists in the towns and miners in the hinterland. Nor did they have the freedom of maneuver that Chinese migrants gained almost by default, by virtue of the colonial state's ignorance of Chinese society, which colonial writers readily described as an "imperium in imperio."

Indian and Chinese migrants to the Straits landed in port towns full of kinsmen—and full of strangers. Singapore and Penang, by the 1860s, were among the most diverse cities on earth. John Thomson, a British photographer who traveled across the "eastern archipelago," noted that "on landing from the steamer it is difficult to discover that one is actually on a Malayan island," since Penang hosted "descendants of the early Portuguese voyagers, Chinese, Malays, Parsees, Arabs, Armenians, Klings, Bengalees, and negroes from Africa." In the marketplace, Indians and Chinese were most prominent. Thomson described "a Kling bazaar" in Georgetown, "where all sorts of foreign commodities are sold, and at prices which rarely exceed the sums they can be bought for, in the countries where they are manufactured." He saw "grog-shops and lodging houses," and evidence wherever he went of the "large Chinese

Figure 6 A typical shop house in Georgetown, Penang. The city's urban landscape was shaped by the meetings of migrants in the nineteenth century. *Photograph by Sunil Amrith.*

population, made up of merchants, shopkeepers, and handicraftsmen, immigrants from the island of Hainan, Kwangtung, and from the several districts of Fukien province."[56]

This world of transient people led to many exchanges, of goods and currencies and favors and words. In his novel *River of Smoke,* Amitav Ghosh imagines in rich colors Singapore's clothes bazaar in the 1830s—the "Wordy Market," the lascars call it: a "noisy melee of a mela." "Where else," Ghosh writes, "could a woman exchange a Khmer sampot for a Bilaan jacket? Where else could a fisherman trade a sarong for a coattee, or a conical rain-hat for a Balinese cap?" The market's stalls were piled up with goods that had been "robbed, purloined or pirated at distant corners of the Indian Ocean."[57]

Migration revived ancient paths across the Bay of Bengal. Coastal shrines belonged as points of effulgence in an archipelago of others, scattered along the shoreline. Sojourners' temples gave thanks for safe voyages; they resounded with prayers for the arrival or the timely departure of the monsoons, or for a bountiful catch from a season's fishing. Maritime traditions crossed the boundaries between Hindus, Muslims, Buddhists, and Daoists. As the clocks and the cartography of modern Europe refigured time and space, coastal spiritual traditions offered a different understanding of history and geography: proximity was measured by spiritual intensity rather than by physical distance, and time was cyclical rather than linear. Every migrant in a new place seeks to re-create some trace of home; arrival becomes a kind of return. Building replicas of shrines they had known, migrants made new landscapes familiar. Sharing rituals, they made intimates of strangers. Seeing their journeys in the footsteps of holy men, they overcame their fears of the unknown. European travelers who set foot in new lands found that their Asian crew already knew where to pay their respects. The location of graves and shrines was passed down through generations, in stories and in rumors. John Pope's diary records that in 1787 he was "on a small island in the roads" off Sumatra, "about a mile in circumference only," and there "a Mahometan saint is interred . . . to whom our Lascars paid much respect."[58]

The Bay of Bengal's littoral was an arc of holy places. Sir Richard Temple—ardent orientalist and amateur ethnographer, editor of Thomas Bowrey's travel account—remarked on the presence across the eastern

Indian Ocean of shrines built by Muslim sailors, which he called "Bud-dermokan" (badr-mokan). They were "equally holy," he suggested, to Muslims, Hindus, Chinese, and Buddhists. They were built in memory of Badr al-Din Awliya', who lived in the first half of the fifteenth century; the temples watched over the safety of sailors. Half a century later, Moshe Yegar found that the Badr was worshipped in coastal Burma as "a nat by Burmese Buddhists, a Deva by Hindus, as a spirit by Chinese, and as a saint by Muslims." Among the shrines that Yegar identified were one in Akyab that had been built in 1756, one in Sandoway, and one on an island of the Mergui archipelago. They were frequented by sailors and fisherman, and "the architectural style, with minaret and cupola and the niche on the west side (mihrab), synthesizes the Burmese pagoda and the Muslim mosque."[59]

Tamil traditions, too, evoked the power of the sea. The sea shapes the legend of Shahul Hamid of Nagore, at whose gravesite chapter 2 began. Stories of the saint's life recount his journey from the plains of North India to Mecca and back across the Indian Ocean, stopping in the Maldives and at Adam's Peak in Ceylon before settling in Nagore, where he died. Shahul Hamid's protection of voyagers incorporated the coming of Europeans. A modern chronicler narrates one of his miracles:

> A Dutch ship was on her way to Nagapattinam port. At a little distance from the shore that ship had been caught in the midst of sudden storm, that caused a big hole on the bottom of the ship . . . At the critical moment some one on board the ship suggested the name and help of our Quthub be invoked. The captain and crew did so. What a miracle! The inflow of the sea water suddenly ceased. The ship was saved.[60]

To this day, shops that line the passageway leading to the main Nagore shrine sell small pieces of foil imprinted with the images of boats, which devotees offer at the shrine when they pray for the safety of their voyages. And, to this day, these journeys often have Southeast Asia as their destination.

Shahul Hamid's story reaches back to his descent from Sayyid Abd al-Qadir al-Jilani—founder of the Qadiri tariqa in twelfth-century Baghdad—and forward to the dispersal of his followers across Southeast Asia in the nineteenth and twentieth centuries. A trustee of the dargah in Nagore told me that alongside the surviving Nagore dargahs in Singapore and Penang, there were once shrines to the saint of Nagore dispersed in Burma, Ceylon, Indonesia, and Vietnam. These signs of the saint's presence charted his followers' travels. Susan Bayly has argued that the Nagore saint and his cult were always situated "in a wider world of *hajj* pilgrimage, trade, and teaching, which his devotees still visualized [in the 1980s] . . . as a living and expansive arena in which the saint continued to radiate his presence."[61]

To a newcomer from across the Bay, the urban landscape of the Straits Settlements would have seemed strangely familiar: strange in its variety, familiar in its forms. The temple roofs and minarets of South India and southern China were transplanted, juxtaposed, translated. Deities of the sea were especially likely to travel. There stand, to this day, *dargahs* to Shahul Hamid of Nagore on Telok Ayer Street in Singapore and on Chulia Street in Penang. The Penang shrine, pictured in figure 7, was built in 1801, and the structure in Singapore, shown in figure 8, during the late 1820s; both were replicas of the original *dargah*. In transit, they absorbed a wider range of architectural influences, both

Figure 7 Nagore Dargah in Penang. *Photograph by Sunil Amrith.*

European—seen in the Palladian features of the Singapore *dargah*—
and from the wider Islamic world. They became places of devotion and
healing, attracting local worshippers beyond the Tamil Muslim community, just as the original shrine in Nagore had always attracted Hindu
devotees. One British observer claimed to have seen the saint's followers in Penang throw their valuables into the sea, firm in the belief that
they would cross the Bay of Bengal and wash up on Nagore's shores.[62]
The boatmen of Penang harbor set aside a portion of their earnings to
sponsor a day's feasting and procession in the saint's honor each year.
In a poem written at the end of the nineteenth century (and published
by a Chinese printer), Koca Maraikkayar describes the annual procession through Penang in honor of Shahul Hamid, naming the streets
and sights and notables along its route. The poet describes, too, the diversity of peoples who witnessed or participated in the procession:
"Klings" and "Hindus," Malays, Burmese, Chinese, Chettiars, Bengalis,
Japanese, "Coringees," "Pariahs," and Portuguese. In 1857, when the
annual procession in Singapore led to a confrontation between march-
ers and the police, the legal proceedings that followed revealed a list of

Figure 8 Nagore Dargah in Singapore. *Photograph by Sunil Amrith.*

Figure 9 Mariyamman Temple, Singapore. *Photograph by Sunil Amrith.*

Figure 10 Mariyamman Temple, Penang. *Photograph by Sunil Amrith.*

witnesses from virtually every ethnic and linguistic group on the island. A nineteenth-century painting, once part of the collection of Singapore's Raffles Museum, shows a vibrant street scene outside Penang's Nagore *dargah,* the flags fluttering on its minarets.[63]

Tamil Hindu landscapes overlapped with Tamil Muslim ones, and both of them with the social and sacred worlds of the local Chinese. Chettiar merchants financed, and migrant workers constructed temples dedicated to South Indian deities in Singapore and Penang in the first three decades of the nineteenth century. Some were little more than makeshift shrines, but more-permanent structures soon arose. In 1823 Narayana Pillai, a Tamil building contractor who had arrived in Singapore with Raffles, erected the Sri Mariyamman temple in Singapore (figure 9), on land granted by the Company.[64] It was built by convict laborers. A similar structure, pictured in figure 10, had been erected on Queen Street, in Georgetown, by the 1830s.

The temples formed the heart of Tamil neighborhoods. A petition from the trustees of the Mariyamman temple in Singapore recorded that the Company had given early Tamil Hindu settlers "sufficient ground for our occupation, and also for the Church, near the banks of the Fresh Water River, and [we] accordingly observed that place, and builded the houses and Church." The Hindu "Church" was built in immediate proximity to another place of worship: the largest Tamil Muslim mosque, the Masjid Jamae (figure 11), which channeled a parallel but distinct spiritual connection—an Islamic one—between South India and the Straits Settlements. As early as 1827, a dispute arose between the trustees of the mosque and the temple as to the use of the public road between the two structures, generating much correspondence within the colonial archive.[65]

Tamil settlements in Singapore were a microcosm of South Indian society, reflecting the physical juxtaposition, even sharing, of Hindu and Muslim places of worship, and their periodic conflicts over public space. But Tamil cultural symbols shared space with many others. Telok Ayer Street in Singapore stands as a symbolic point of intersection between the Bay of Bengal and the South China Sea. Within a few steps of one another stand the Nagore *dargah,* the Chinese Temple of Heavenly Blessings—dedicated to Mazu, protector of seafarers—shown in figure 12, and another mosque built in the Tamil style, the Al-Abrar (also known as *kuchi palli,* or "small mosque"), pictured in figure 13. In

Figure 11 Masjid Jamae, Singapore. *Photograph by Sunil Amrith.*

the nineteenth century the street was on the shoreline—but thanks to decades of land reclamation in Singapore it is no longer on the coast.

In a world of sojourners, religious performances found ready audiences. The Straits government tried to impose new norms of public behavior on this migrant society. Observing in 1834 a performance in Penang of the rite of *thaipusam*—an annual celebration of Murugan, son of Siva and Parvati—James Low, chief military officer of Province Wellesley, wrote that "when people forsake their own country and voluntarily settle in another, they should be satisfied with the permission to celebrate their religious rites only which do not outrage the proper feelings of the other portions of the community, and which are not injurious to public morals, the decencies of life, and order." Decades later, in 1860, the trustees of the Mariyamman temple in Singapore were denied permission to perform the rites of the *thimithi* fire-walking ceremony in public, the governor's council declaring it to be its responsibility to "prevent the Peace of the Town being in any way disturbed."[66]

Figure 12 Chinese Temple of Heavenly Blessings, Singapore. *Photograph by Sunil Amrith.*

There was always more cultural mixing than this public doctrine of toleration recognized. At times "Indian," "Malay," and "Chinese" ritual performances came together. In Penang, a hybrid, local version of the Shi'a Muharram procession, called Boria, attracted Tamil and Malay Muslims (overwhelmingly Sunnis), Tamil Hindus, and Chinese. Around the Indian Ocean, Muharram drew large followings and reached beyond the lines of community. In Trinidad it was called Hosay, and its annual performance allowed plantation workers, both Hindus and Muslims, to assert a claim to public space; in Bombay, Muharram provoked conflict between neighboring localities, which did not necessarily follow divisions of faith.[67] Everywhere it was a major public celebration, and one that seemed to invert the prevailing social order, if only for a day. In Penang, Boria drew participants from local Chinese society: it became the site for the commemoration of bonds of solidarity that transcended, if only fleetingly, race and community. One English observer warned that this would "unite into one brotherhood men of such different customs and ideas as Malays, Klings, and Chinese." Colonial authorities were alarmed by the confluence of "secret societies"—both

Figure 13 Al-Abrar Mosque, Singapore. *Photograph by Sunil Amrith.*

Chinese and Malay—which brought together a cross-section of Penang society for "mutual help and protection of their women," essential to people "living in a mixed society." The Penang Riots of 1867 brought to light the rivalry between opposing alliances: their solidarities and conflicts were based on locality rather than ethnicity.[68]

The origins of the "riots" remain obscure. "Formidable disturbances" erupted on the streets between the Ghee Hin and Toa Pek Kong societies—each of them allied to a rival "native" society with Malay and Indian members. They engaged in pitched battle. British authorities lost control of the town. The sole native regiment was away on an exploratory mission to the Nicobar Islands. Penang's governor, Harry Ord, lamented after the riots that the suppression of the "secret societies" was "a task altogether beyond the power of the Government." The lieutenant governor, A. E. H. Anson, had arrived only months earlier and was haunted by news of the Morant Bay rebellion in Jamaica. As Anson was "going about town" during the riots, shooting "from muskets and small petards" in "all directions," his head "became addled with the names of people and places that were continually being brought to me. These were Chinese names, Malay names, Mohammedan names, Hindoo names . . ."[69] Names, names, names: the garbled lists of the people arrested after the riot give a sense of how mixed these societies really were. A statement pledging to keep the peace, signed by six of those arrested, was written in Tamil but signed—variously—in "Malayan characters," in "Tamil characters," and with "marks" by those who were illiterate.

European observers understood the diversity of peoples they ruled over in Southeast Asia through the emerging category of "race." John Crawfurd, a Scottish administrator and amateur ethnographer, observed that the "race" of people from the Coromandel coast was "shrewd, supple, unwarlike, mendacious and avaricious." The Chinese, on another view, were "the most successful traders and most patient toilers in the East," whose "love of combinations, of the guilds and unions in which all Chinamen delight, tempts them too far." Southeast Asia's creole communities caused Europeans particular anxiety. Of the Jawi Peranakan, Crawfurd wrote that "the motley race formed by these unions is a compound character of no very amiable description, partaking of the vices of both parent stocks." Peranakan Chinese families, too, represented "a race inferior in energy and spirit to the original settler."[70] Many British governors and administrators around the Bay of Bengal believed fervently in the immutable divisions of race—and in the explanatory, even predictive power of racial categories; many ruled to make this a self-fulfilling prophecy in Southeast Asia. But ideas about "race" were confused and incoherent.

From the start, there were cracks in the edifice. Race could never fully explain the reality of these migrant societies. Terms of ascription mutated into terms of self-description; racial categories struggled to incorporate the sheer diversity of origins, languages, and practices seen on the street. An official report concluded in 1856 that "although this Asiatic population is classed under three heads, Chinese, Mahometan and Hindoo, no correct opinion can be formed of its composition from these distinctive appellations."[71] The Straits Settlements, like many other ports along the Bay of Bengal's rim, possessed the openness of frontiers. And in the workplace, on the street, and in "secret societies," migrants formed relationships—sometimes transient, sometimes lasting—with strangers who had crossed other seas.

Jealous empires parceled out a region connected by the flow of people, goods, and ideas. By the 1820s the "related cultures" of South and Southeast Asia "were now seen as separate unities: 'India' and 'Ceylon,' 'Malaya' and 'Indonesia' respectively." To this day, the Anglo-Dutch agreement of 1824 marks the border between contemporary Malaysia and Indonesia—a border that makes little historical or cultural sense. Facing each other across the narrow Straits of Melaka, peninsular Malays and Malay-speaking inhabitants of eastern Sumatra "are ethnically related, understand each other's speech"—and regard each other as foreigners. Yet, as Benedict Anderson noted, "these same Sumatrans . . . have come to understand the Ambonese as fellow-Indonesians," despite sharing neither language nor religion and being separated by thousands of miles of sea.[72] It is a commonplace worth restating: the colonial borders of the nineteenth century have had a long life.

The Bay of Bengal's connections followed the lineaments of imperial power. Colonial rule failed to stamp out, and in some ways even fostered, older forms of cultural and commercial connection across the Bay, and it created new ones. Indian, Chinese, and Arab merchants continued to play a crucial role in the region's commerce: without them, many

European projects would have collapsed. Unfree labor continued to cross the sea, and at moments of crisis the small-scale traffic surged into larger migrations. In the nineteenth century this forced movement paved the way for the "new system of slavery" that was indentured labor. The monsoons continued to connect the Bay of Bengal, but now its constituent parts were more interdependent. The "commercialism without capitalism" pursued by precolonial states—and often independent of European initiative—gave way to "primitive accumulation" in the forests of Southeast Asia. In the nineteenth century, the bonds thickened between densely settled areas of wet rice cultivation and sparsely populated frontiers where capital investment reaped greater profits.[73] The movement of people—enslaved, indentured, and "free"—created a new world.

4

Human Traffic

In early 1870 W. L. Hathaway, subcollector of the South Indian district of Thanjavur, condemned the "traffic" in people across the Bay of Bengal. He alleged that migration between South India and Malaya was "a regularly organized system of kidnapping." Time and again, "captives were shipped from Negapatam for Penang and other countries, where the males were employed as coolies, and the females sold to a life of prostitution." This "traffic," Hathaway wrote, "is contrary to the law . . . [that] makes it illegal to assist any native of India in emigrating." He insisted that the Madras government intervene to stop the traffic, and embarrassed the authorities in a long letter to the *Friend of India,* a journal read by British and Indian critics of imperial policy.

Hathaway made the "traffic" his personal mission. From his base in Nagapatnam he pursued shipowners and labor contractors. At the start of 1870's "emigration season," he ordered a raid on a warehouse where migrants waited to board ships for Southeast Asia. The problem arose when their cases came before the local magistrate. Each migrant insisted that he acted of his own free will. Young boys declared that the labor recruiters were their "fathers" or "uncles"; they hadn't signed contracts, so there was no evidence that they were "migrating for the purposes of labor." "It is useless to attempt to unravel the real facts of the case," Hathaway lamented; "people themselves will not reveal the truth." This was an old problem. The local *Police Weekly Circular* had reported a similar case a few years earlier. On finding a warehouse full of "coolies crowded together like beasts," the police superintendent refused to let their ship depart. Questioning the detained men, he concluded, "I

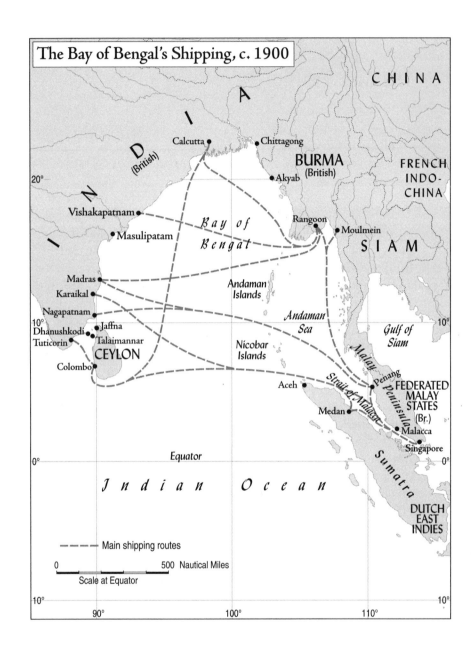

The Bay of Bengal's Shipping, c. 1900

CHINA

I N D I A (British)

Calcutta • • Chittagong

BURMA (British)

• Akyab

FRENCH INDO-CHINA

20°

Vishakapatnam •

Bay of Bengal

Rangoon •

• Masulipatam

• Moulmein

SIAM

Madras •
Karaikal •

Andaman
Islands

*Andaman
Sea*

Gulf of
Siam

Nagapatnam •

10°
Dhanushkodi • • Jaffna
Tuticorin • • Talaimannar

CEYLON

Nicobar
Islands

10°

Malay

Colombo •

Aceh •

Strait of Malacca

Penang •

FEDERATED
MALAY
STATES
(Br.)

Medan •

Peninsula

• Malacca

Equator

• Singapore

0°

0°

I n d i a n   O c e a n

S u m a t r a

DUTCH
EAST
INDIES

- - - - Main shipping routes

0   500 Nautical Miles

Scale at Equator

10°

10°

90°   100°   110°

fancy they had got their stories cut and dried ready for use; for they answered satisfactorily enough; and they all produced parents, uncles, or guardians." The superintendent thought, "This coolie trade has reached such large dimensions that there is plenty of room for an Emigration Agent here."[1] This goal was finally secured in 1873, when a protector of emigrants was appointed to oversee migration to Southeast Asia.

By 1870 circulation between South India and the Straits Settlements was entrenched, and it looked set to grow. Already cases of overcrowded ships and fugitive shipowners had come to the government's attention. With the planters of the Straits crying for more labor, Hathaway and his colleagues in local government argued that it would be disastrous to lift legal restraints on movement between India and Malaya. British planters and their spokesmen in the Straits responded with the case for free migration. Connections across the Bay, they argued, were entirely natural. Malaya was really an extension of India; Indian laborers hardly thought it a "foreign" land. The tension between freedom and migration would resurface time and again in the years to come.

The last quarter of the nineteenth century was pivotal in the Bay of Bengal's history. The slow intensification of "traffic" through the nineteenth century was jolted into expansion, and the trickle became a torrent. Steam energy made the crossing faster, easier, and cheaper. Imperial power charged into the interior. By treaty and by conquest, colonial states moved beyond their coastal strongholds, preceded or followed by European, Chinese, and Indian investors. Coffee. Sugar. Tea. Tobacco. Rubber. Southeast Asia's frontiers promised vast profit. Wherever in the world they found local communities stubborn in their economic independence—cultivators who found wage labor unattractive, or people who resisted enslavement—European settlers perpetuated the "myth of the lazy native." "No gain," Alexander Kyd wrote from Penang, "will induce a Malay to constant and unremitted Industry." So labor, like capital, had to be imported. Chinese capitalists had a ready source: through their brotherhoods and regional associations they mobilized men in ever greater numbers as steamships brought the China coast nearer. Europeans, without access to Chinese networks, turned where the sugar planters of Mauritius and the Caribbean had first resorted after the abolition of slavery—to British India.[2]

A few figures convey the scale of change. The exodus to Ceylon began first. Starting in the 1840s, tens of thousands of Indian laborers a year arrived in Ceylon to work on the coffee plantations. By the end of the 1850s this had grown to nearly 100,000 arrivals annually. Between half and three-quarters of them returned to India each year. The longer journey across the Bay of Bengal to Malaya involved much smaller numbers until the 1880s, but by the end of that decade 22,000 people were arriving annually at the ports of the Straits Settlements from South India. Beginning in the 1880s, Burma was the third great destination for Indian labor, and it would attract the most migrants of all. By 1911 more than 100,000 people each year arrived from India in each of these three destinations across the Bay of Bengal.[3]

The statistics are notoriously imprecise, but in the century between 1840 and 1940 somewhere around 8 million people traveled from India to Ceylon, 4 million to Malaya, and between 12 million and 15 million to Burma; a varying but large proportion, well over half, returned to India within three to seven years. Most of this movement occurred after 1870. Whole families moved to and from Ceylon; to Malaya and Burma, the migrants were mostly men until the 1920s. Consider this in the context of the totality of Indian migration overseas: from the beginning of organized Indian emigration in 1834 until 1940, well over 90 percent of *all* Indian emigrants went to Ceylon, Burma, and Malaya. Put simply, the Bay of Bengal region accounts for nearly the sum total of India's emigration history in the age of empire.

Now consider this in a global context. Migration around the Bay was comparable in scale to transatlantic migration in the same era. Some 26 million people arrived in the United States between 1870 and 1930 from southern and eastern Europe, East Asia, and the Pacific. Add Chinese migration to Southeast Asia to the equation—around 19 million people in the century after 1840, more widely dispersed than their Indian counterparts—and it is clear that the region where the Indian Ocean met the South China Sea was home to one of the world's great migrations. The main difference between the Asian and Atlantic circuits lies in the numbers of those who settled rather than returned. Between 6 million and 7 million people of Indian origin, and a similar number of Chinese, had settled overseas by the end of the 1930s; American demographer Kingsley Davis contrasted this with the 85 million people of British origin who lived outside the British Isles by that time.[4]

"The piercing of the Isthmus of Suez, like the breaking of a dam, let in upon the East a flood of new ships, new men, new methods of trade,"

Joseph Conrad wrote.[5] The opening of the canal in 1869 reshaped the Bay of Bengal's geography. It meant that a journey from Europe to the Bay was a matter of weeks, not months. Suez reconnected the Indian Ocean with the Mediterranean. Through the sliver of the canal, steam power reordered the world. Conrad's "new ships, new men, new methods of trade" sparked mass migration, east and west, and stimulated commodity production across the tropical world. As steamships glided over the oceans, no longer at the mercy of the prevailing winds, undersea telegraph cables engirdled the world beneath the seas' surface. By 1870 the British India Submarine Telegraph Company had connected Bombay with the Red Sea. A year later cables crossed the Bay of Bengal. News of prices and harvests now traveled instantaneously. On land, railroads compressed time and distance and attracted huge capital investment. As the transcontinentals snaked their way across the North American continent, so the Indian railways provided the sinews of imperial power in South Asia. Land and sea routes converged as radials upon port cities that pulsed with people, the cities' fabric sagging under the weight of new wealth and new misery. In the nineteenth century fossil fuels broke almost every conceivable limit to growth.[6]

Rails, rivers, and seas intersected. As the Suez Canal brought the Bay of Bengal closer to Europe, the railways extended the sea's reach beyond the coasts. Like a "magnetic field," Braudel wrote, the Mediterranean cast its influence far from its shores. Similarly, the life of the Bay of Bengal drew the products of the land, and the sons of the soil, into its steam-powered web. By the 1880s migrants came not only from the coastal regions but also from further inland. Most of those who crossed the Bay were no longer from traditional seafaring communities. On the other end of their voyages, railroads brought the ports closer to the frontiers: once Ceylon's railways reached the Kandyan highlands, the infamous "long walk" from port to plantation was eased. Railway construction in Burma was slower to take off, given the country's thousands of miles of navigable waterways, but as the railways developed, Indian migrants followed the steel lines from Rangoon.

For more than a millennium the Bay had been a highway between India and China. Throughout that time, traders and states sought shortcuts around it, and ways around the vulnerable choke point of the Straits of Melaka. In the first millennium traders had used overland portage across the Isthmus of Kra—the narrow strip of land in southern Thailand before it widens out into the Malay Peninsula—to connect the Bay to the South China Sea. The rise of Melaka as Southeast Asia's great emporium diverted traffic to the south. But in the nineteenth century the railways renewed the promise of a northerly route to China's interior, feeding into its internal waterways. The engineer Arthur Cotton imagined eastern Bengal's railways as the first step in a line from Calcutta to Canton. Competing proposals envisaged a line from Chittagong to Yunnan via Bhamo, and another cutting through the Shan states. A rail link between India and China remained a perennial dream. In 1904 the British government signed an agreement with the consul general in Yunnan to build a railroad from Burma to China; in the 1930s the plans remained under consideration—not for the last time.[7]

Steam power demanded new sources of energy and made new demands on the land. Before the age of steam, "more energy could be captured from the wind . . . by changing the number, arrangement, and operation of sails on ships." The clippers of the early nineteenth century represented the highest achievement of these incremental adjustments. They were elegant, streamlined craft that could reach unprecedented speeds. But the energy that steam could provide surpassed even the most efficient use of wind; steam engines harnessed matter buried deep in the earth for thousands of years.[8] By the middle of the nineteenth century, steam-powered vessels were a common sight on the Ganges. The East India Company owned ten river steamboats by 1850, and a number of oceangoing steamships. All these vessels demanded supplies of coal. The mid-nineteenth century saw the rapid development of coalfields in eastern India—in Burdwan, Sylhet, Assam, Palamau, and Cuttack. Where coal was unavailable, the Company sought firewood as an alternative, creating a thriving market for fuel. Burma's untapped energy resources, located centrally along the Bay of Bengal's routes, beckoned to British administrators and shipping companies.[9]

The Irrawaddy Flotilla Company was formed in 1865: owned by the brothers Henderson, originally from the village of Pittenween in Fifeshire, Scotland. The family's fortunes rose from the adversity of George Henderson, shipwrecked while commanding a sailing vessel "trading to the near east." He survived the ordeal and installed himself in Italy, where he flourished in the marble trade to Britain—the Glasgow end of the business was handled by his three brothers. By the 1850s the Hendersons had abandoned marble and moved into long-distance shipping: they owned a small fleet that sailed initially between Scotland, New York, and Quebec. At the turn of the 1860s they were at the forefront of the "emigrant trade" to New Zealand. On the return journey the Hendersons' vessels began to call at Rangoon, where they took on cargoes of rice and teak. Before long the Burma rice trade proved so profitable that the Hendersons abandoned the antipodean leg of the voyage altogether; around the same time, they purchased a small fleet of steam-powered river craft to profit from the Irrawaddy's flourishing trade.

A promotional booklet of 1872 assured potential investors that "there is no trade to the east more capable of . . . continuous expansion than that of Burmah." The Irrawaddy had "its banks studded with towns and villages, crowded with an active, industrious population to whom this river is the great highway." Until the advent of steam, "the whole traffic on the river was conducted by native boats"—up to 25,000 of them. Now steam power, "by its speed, regularity, and safety, is gradually superseding native craft"; all that was needed was a "sufficient supply of plant to monopolise, in great measure, the traffic." For two decades the Irrawaddy Flotilla Company imported its coal directly from Britain; beginning in the 1890s, supplies began to arrive from the coalfields of Bengal. Already by 1890 Dalah, across the river from Rangoon, had developed into a thriving dry dock and repair station: "here also were situated Boiler Shops, Erecting Shops, Machine Shops, Carpenters Shops and all the other type of shops which go to make up a shipyard."[10]

But steam triumphed over sail more gradually than we might imagine. Scale and state protection gave European transportation firms a competitive advantage, but Asian shipping merchants fought back. Well into the 1870s sailing ships followed their old routes around the Indian Ocean and across the South China Sea. Crossing the Bay of Bengal remained risky.[11] But by then the advance of passenger steam travel was under way. Beginning in the 1860s the British India Steam Navigation Company (BISNC) grabbed the largest share of passenger traffic across the Bay. In 1861 the BISNC launched a monthly steamer between Calcutta, Akyab, and Rangoon. Within a decade, fortnightly and then weekly steamer services connected Rangoon with the ports of the eastern Indian coast, north of Madras: Coconada, Vizagapatnam, Bimlipatnam,

Calingapatnam, Baruva, and Gopalpur. By the 1880s a weekly steamer service ran from Madras, Pondicherry, Cuddalore, Karaikal, and Nagapatnam to Penang, Port Swettenham, and Singapore. Today many of these ports are faded provincial towns. Visitors might struggle to imagine them as thriving maritime centers, but for older people, the places' names, many of which have since changed, evoke another world: a Bay of Bengal world that encompassed eastern India and Southeast Asia. The annual number of passenger journeys between South India and Malaya in both directions grew from an average of 15,000 in the 1870s to nearly 40,000 by the end of the 1880s.[12] The traffic between Madras and Ceylon, even larger in scale, was dominated by ships on the short crossing (under two hours) between Talaimannar and Dhanushkodi; a supplementary steamer service between Colombo and Tuticorin ran twice a week.[13]

By the end of the nineteenth century, indigenous shipping was pushed to the margins of both legality and commercial viability.[14] As the great rivers Kaveri, Krishna, and Godavari spilled into the Bay of Bengal, so

Figure 14 The Myanmar Port Authority building, previously the headquarters of the Irrawaddy Flotilla Company. *Photograph by Sunil Amrith.*

the sons of their valleys crossed it, pouring in their thousands into Burma and Malaya. The steamship changed people's sense of proximity. New routes linked port cities but also braided distant hinterlands—the Kaveri delta and the Malayan forest, coastal Andhra and the rice fields of Lower Burma. As families fanned out across the Bay, "the names of villages" were "plaited into one map."[15]

The "breaking of the dam" redistributed power around the Indian Ocean. Although they began as coastal trading enclaves, European empires developed a terrestrial obsession in the nineteenth century; they pursued "whole continents of territory." Dutch rule in Indonesia epitomized this shift. Desperate for revenue after the Napoleonic Wars, the Dutch administration put Java to work, instituting a system of forced cultivation and corvée labor. They retreated from inter-Asian trade, staking their fortunes on plantation production.[16] After the Indian Rebellion of 1857—the most widespread revolt against British rule in India until the 1940s—the Raj consolidated its hold on the land as the basis of imperial rule: mapping, surveying, and assessing territory; settling nomadic peoples; and seizing commons and forests for the state.[17] With lethal military technologies from the foundries and shipyards of industrial Europe, a renewed thrust of aggressive expansion brought almost all of Southeast Asia, with the exception of Thailand, under European control. Lower Burma fell to British conquest after the Anglo-Burmese War of 1852. The French assumed direct control in Indochina, piecemeal, a decade later. In the 1870s the British "forward movement" pushed into the Malay Peninsula, suborning Malay sultans in a series of treaties. By 1885 the British conquest of Burma was complete. The Dutch conquest of Indonesia took longer, provoking a bloody war of resistance in Aceh that lasted from 1873 to 1908.

With the opening of the Suez Canal, India became the "nodal point" of the Indian Ocean, allowing the projection of British power eastward, to Southeast Asia, and westward, to the coast of eastern Africa. Indian systems of governance (varieties of indirect rule), Indian legal regimes (the Indian Penal Code), and Indian district officers moved out across the Indian Ocean. English officials, schooled in the Indian administration, implemented and adapted Indian models of rule in the Straits Settlements, in Egypt, and in East and West Africa. Indian soldiers secured the ocean's rim for the British Empire.[18] Above all, Indian laborers fanned out to sustain the capitalist transformation of the land—they cleared bush, planted trees, built railways. By far the greatest numbers of them moved to just three destinations across the Bay of Bengal: Ceylon, Burma, and Malaya. Ceylon's mutation from a strategic trading post to a plantation colony set the stage for a sweeping change around the Bay's littoral; within decades the region became one of the world's foremost suppliers of raw materials. The conversion of its forests into monoculture plantations and its valleys into acres of paddy fields set in train a migration of labor so vast that it dwarfed the earlier movement of indentured workers to Mauritius and the Caribbean.

Proximity, precedent, and policy explain why migrant labor to Southeast Asia came almost entirely from particular regions of southern and eastern India. The "uninterrupted intercourse" between South India and Ceylon, and between South India and the Malay world, provided a base on which to build. Networks of transportation, methods of recruitment, and sources of finance already existed, ripe for expansion under the power of steam. In the second half of the nineteenth century the channels of communication between South India and Southeast Asia deepened. Ceylon's planters, accustomed to working with Tamil labor, maintained this source of supply when they moved across the Bay to Malaya. Colonial officials, accustomed to seeing India as a land of too many people, turned to the subcontinent when labor was scarce elsewhere. The concept of race, accustomed to conflating circumstantial behavior with immutable traits, held Tamil labor to be, always and everywhere, "docile"—feckless, but amenable to discipline. As migration reached massive proportions, drawing in many from inland communities not previously connected with the world of the Bay of Bengal, the churning effects of colonial capitalism clashed with enduring forces of immobility.

South India had long been a place where people moved around: priests and mendicants, artisans and warriors. In his classic work on medieval South India, Burton Stein wrote of the "peripatetic ways of many in South Indian society," highlighting the succession of migration and conquest, and the gradual integration of newcomers. Initially the circulations that knitted South India together were small in scale but culturally significant: they involved the movement of Brahmin ritual specialists, poets, and scribes. Military mobility gained in importance—throughout the medieval era, communities of Telugu peasant-warriors invaded and settled in the Tamil country. Under the rule of the Chola Empire in the second millennium, "expanding trade and agrarian systems" enmeshed lower peasant groups. Urban settlements clustered around large temples. Religious change both shaped and responded to economic transformation. The rise of the Saiva devotional movement saw the growth of wealthy temple complexes supported by peasant groups. The twelfth century "introduced the great age of religious pilgrimage in the Tamil country": a widening circle of itinerancy that stretched across the southern peninsula.[19]

The natural environment shaped circulation and exchange. The Tamil country encompassed three distinct ecological regions: the river valleys, based on irrigated rice cultivation, wealthy temple towns, and Brahmin ritual authority; the plains, where a harsher climate encouraged herding, hunting, and the cultivation of hardier grains; and the Konku region, a frontier that combined characteristics of plains and valley societies and had interactions with both. The valleys had long looked outward, exporting rice to Ceylon and to Southeast Asia, and importing luxuries from distant shores, so it is no surprise that they would dominate the mass migration to Southeast Asia after 1870. Plainsmen exchanged specialist services for surplus food from the valleys: short-term migration from plains to valleys became widespread, for military service or for construction labor. Over time, distinctions "broke down the land and sea boundaries which had kept Tamilnad in relative isolation": greater *internal* mobility between complementary environments interacted with the greater *external* mobility between the coast and the other side of the Bay of Bengal.[20]

But movement took place amid servitude. The most common form of immobility in the Tamil districts was the *pannaiyal* system of "permanent farm servants," compared by British commentators at the time to European serfdom. Servants were tied to the land, but there were instances when *pannaiyals* could be sold independently—sold, on most definitions, as slaves. Such forms of tied labor, according to Dharma Kumar's account, "spanned a wide range from near-freedom to near-slavery." Often bondage came with a corresponding entitlement, even a right, on the part of the servants to demand employment, access to land, and support for subsistence. Inevitably such customary rights came under greatest strain during periods of dearth and famine. At the turn of the nineteenth century bonded agricultural laborers made up a "sizeable proportion of the total population"—up to 20 percent—of many Tamil districts. The British abolitionist movement focused its attentions on Indian "domestic slavery," yet the interventions of the colonial state did little to change the structure of agrarian society until the last quarter of the nineteenth century.[21] Alongside these ancient institutions, newer forms of immobility spread with the consolidation of colonial rule over South India. For weavers, artisans, and professional soldiers, among many others, British conquest brought economic ruin. Cheap Lancashire textiles flooded the Indian market. The traditional mobility of Indian weaving communities declined as their productivity fell behind that of Britain's mechanized textile mills. Contrary to the predictions of contemporaries including Karl Marx, South Indian society underwent a process of deindustrialization, rather than modernization, in the nineteenth century. It experienced a shift toward lower-quality, lower-value-added production and a decline in hand weaving, which was particularly important in securing women's livelihoods. Urban residents were thrust onto increasingly marginal lands, where they found a hardscrabble subsistence. South India's acute vulnerability to famine in the nineteenth century was one result of this enforced decline.[22]

The power of steam promised the conquest of the monsoons. Less than a decade after the opening of the Suez Canal, the monsoons demonstrated their enduring power over human life—they failed. The failure was global and catastrophic. The El Niño–Southern Oscillation in 1877–1878 was the worst "since records began." The rains failed across lands as far apart as southern India, China, Java, Egypt, and northeastern Brazil. Primary producers were already vulnerable when the drought came—jolted by the burst bubble of American railroad stocks, the global economic depression of the 1870s caused a downward spiral in commodity prices and squeezed producers who had expanded too far and too fast into cash crops, often at the expense of food production. Drought turned to catastrophe in part because of the economic orthodoxies of the British Empire: British officials, loath to interfere with market forces, were niggardly with relief, having dismantled many preexisting systems of social support.[23] In India, the famine was worst in the South and across the Deccan plain. William Cornish—a doctor and humanitarian, harshly critical of British famine policy—wrote that "we saw children of all ages in such a condition of emaciation that nothing but a photographic picture could convey an adequate representation of their state."[24] "When the dead are so numerous that they lie unburied," Cornish lamented, "when people leave their villages by wholesale and when village officials fly from their posts in panic, we can never get accurate accounts of vital statistics." Even in their absence, the death toll is estimated in the millions.

At the time and subsequently, observers assumed a direct connection between the famine of the 1870s and the increase in Indian emigration, which accelerated at that very moment. Famine was the ultimate "push factor," to use a term first popularized by the American geographer Harry Jerome in the 1920s. George Grierson—folklorist, linguist, and colonial administrator—toured Bengal and Bihar in early 1883, charged with investigating the causes and consequences of Indian emigration. "Surely emigration may be looked upon as an engine of immense power for good to India," he wrote, as "the more safety-valves there are for a pent up population in time of famine, the greater chance there will be of saving life." Migration, on Grierson's account, was a natural flow of population governed by economic and environmental conditions. He correlated the price of rice with levels of emigration and found that the "agreement between these two lines is almost complete." Emigration, on this view, was a "vent" for India's surplus population: as the New World absorbed Europe's poor in increasing numbers, so the frontiers of the Indian Ocean and Southeast Asia promised to do the same for India. The governor of the Straits Settlements wrote that clearing the forests of the Malay Peninsula would open new opportunities to "numbers of labourers of a country already greatly overstocked, and which is periodically visited by famine to a most lamentable extent."[25]

The link between famine and migration was, in truth, more complex. Faced with a chronic shortage of labor, British administrators across the Bay of Bengal saw opportunity in the famine. One official in Burma wondered, in March 1877, if "in view of the prevalence of very widespread famine in the Presidency of Madras, an impulse could not be given, by special arrangements, for a more extended emigration of labourers from the distressed tracts to British Burma, partly as a measure of relief from the famine, and partly in promotion of the settlement of population in this province."[26] The plans failed. A year later the government of Burma again offered work on public construction projects to famine victims in Madras, but the scheme was suspended because only 800 people volunteered. Numerous other schemes to resettle famine victims overseas faltered.[27]

By contrast, Ceylon did see an upsurge of migration because of the famine. The number of Indian laborers arriving in Ceylon doubled between 1875 and 1876 and exceeded 160,000 in each of the two worst years of the famine, 1876 and 1877; return migration from Ceylon to India fell significantly. The migrants to Ceylon came almost entirely from those regions "already accustomed to short-term labor migration": the dry regions of Thanjavur and southeastern Madurai. That is, those who saw emigration to Ceylon as a means of survival came from regions that already had close connections with the island. Migration to Ceylon had begun decades earlier and was already well established by the 1870s. "In view of the severe and protracted nature of the famine," David Arnold concludes, "it might be asked why the exodus from Madras was not even greater." Obstacles stood in the way of those who migrated—panicked officials tried to stop them from leaving their villages, and recruiters at the emigration depots rejected them as unfit for labor. The relative paucity of famine-induced emigration showed the "limited extent to which rural labor in Madras had ceased to be tied to the land and villages."[28]

Economic opportunity and cheaper transportation eased the way for young men, and a smaller number of women, to leave their homelands and seek their fortunes in Southeast Asia at a time of catastrophe. But they did not react blindly to the furies of nature. What appears to be natural takes work: policies and legislation, chance and intention, technology and energy—not famine alone—combined to "push" migration across the Bay of Bengal. Migration was not simply a natural movement of population between regions of surplus and deficit population, or rainfall, or land; each act of migration arose from the hopes of individuals or the grim calculations of family survival; as often as not, migration was spurred by the coercion enshrined in laws written in distant chambers.

The essential link between crisis and opportunity was provided by what today we would call the "migration industry." Labor recruiters, shipping agents, petty financiers, and speculators worked together with—and, at times, against—the colonial state and European planters. They un-moored the South Indian countryside. They channeled labor across the Bay. The migration industry of South India fused very old features of the indigenous labor market with the capital of European agency houses and the force of colonial laws of contract. The law made a clear distinction between migrants under contracts of indenture and those who made their own arrangements through intermediaries, but these were points on a spectrum. Each form of recruitment used a combination of inducement, coercion, and above all debt to mobilize workers in South India, and then to immobilize them on the plantations of Ceylon or Malaya.

Ceylon was the first to undergo a transformation, beginning in the 1830s, as coffee plantations spread on the island. As we have seen, the 1840s witnessed an early peak in labor migration, with nearly 100,000 people arriving from India in 1844. But migration fell with the decline in the fortunes of the coffee industry—in part because of competition between producers around the world. In the late 1860s, as the Suez Canal invigorated global trade, coffee leaf disease ravaged Ceylon's plantations, ruining many planters. After experimenting with alternatives, investors settled on tea. In the 1880s the number of acres planted with tea grew from 9,000 to more than 150,000, while the area of coffee plantations diminished from 252,000 acres to 98,000. Many coffee plantations were converted directly into tea estates. With tea came a surge in migration. State-operated ferries ran between Paumba and Mannar, and between Tuticorin and Colombo; the disaster of famine in South India made Ceylon all the more attractive. The North Road—which had been built by Indian workers—ran for 110 miles between the port of Mannar and the Kandyan highlands; it was a marked improvement on the brutal walk through swamp and jungle that had greeted arrivals from India a few decades earlier. The migrants now "practically never belonged to nomadic and marginal groups, but were recruited among the settled populations of the rice-growing districts." And although low-caste and *dalit* communities were well represented, so, too, were the landed and dominant castes of the southern Tamil region.[29]

The *kangany* dominated recruitment from the start in Ceylon. The Tamil word means "overseer" (*kan* means "eye" in Tamil); in the Tamil Bible, *kangany* is the term for a bishop, the overseer of the congregation.

By the 1870s, "head" *kanganies,* who supplied several estates, emerged as powerful brokers: each of them employed many subordinates, in charge of the workforce on individual plantations. The cultivation of tea, unlike coffee, required labor year-round, and the rhythms of work on tea plantations made them more suitable for women and children. Whole family groups now dominated the movement from India to Ceylon. Here, as elsewhere, debt was at the heart of the system. The "coast advance" that the *kangany* made to the families of the laborers—or to the masters of bonded servants, to free them—kept the workers in his control, and these advances ballooned. Debts migrated with the workers. If they died on the plantations, as so many did, the debts passed to their families. The cost to the workers of their food and lodging and their purchases from the estate stores (which the *kangany* often owned) added to their financial burdens.

Migration to Ceylon was an extension of earlier traditions of movement, building on proximity, habit, and deep connections of caste and kinship. Movement over longer distances demanded greater initial efforts by the state and employers. In Malaya, *kangany* recruitment coexisted with, and eventually displaced, the system of indentured labor, adopted from the earlier migration of Indian workers to the sugar colonies of the Indian Ocean and the West Indies. "The soil is good," one Malayan planter wrote in 1836, "the climate is fine," and "nought is waiting but the hand of man to bring abundance to our doors."[30] In the nineteenth century, those hands came almost exclusively from South India. As sugar cultivation expanded in the 1850s in Province Wellesley—on the Malayan mainland, across the water from Penang—demand for Indian labor intensified.[31] Distance meant shipping costs to Malaya were greater than to Ceylon: to recover their investments, brokers and planters insisted that laborers sign contracts of indenture of between three and five years. Planters were obsessed with desertion. They enforced iron discipline. Speculators in India gathered up willing or unwilling recruits and dispatched them across the Bay, confident that the growing demand for labor would bring handsome profits. Planters raised recruits on their own, too, working through their Indian agents: Adamson, Taggart and Company (the Scottish presence was ubiquitous) and two Indian firms, Ganapathi Pillai and the Madura Company. The recruitment of low-caste Hindu or *dalit* workers for Malaya, along with many from the cultivating castes, changed the balance of migration across the Bay of Bengal, once dominated by Tamil-speaking Muslims. Between 1866, when detailed statistics began, and 1910, when indentured labor was abolished in Malaya, as many as 250,000 workers moved from India to Malaya under contracts of indenture. In the 1870s and 1880s, between 70 and 80 percent of Indian workers went under indenture. But, as the rest of this chapter will show, their experience stimulated a chain reaction that would eventually displace altogether the system of indenture. By the turn of the twentieth century, *kangany* recruitment was paramount in Malaya. This had everything to do with the rise of "Raja rubber."[32]

The fortunes of coffee and sugar planters in Malaya had been disappointing, as neither crop turned the rapid profits that investors had hoped for. By the early twentieth century, rubber was so lucrative that Malaya had become the most valuable tropical colony in the whole of the British Empire. Rubber trees were indigenous to the Malay Peninsula, but the Victorian quest for "improvement" led imperial agronomists and botanists to experiment with transplantation. The Brazilian *Hevea* species was more productive and hardier than the native rubber trees of Malaya. Henry Wickham, an English prospector working in the Amazon, harvested thousands of wild *Hevea* seeds in the 1870s and sent them to Kew Gardens, the "botanical heart" of the British Empire. In 1876–1877, seedlings were exported to Ceylon, and a small number to Singapore, where their potential was truly realized. Henry Ridley was curator of the Botanical Gardens of Singapore; he saw Malaya's commercial future in the cultivation of the *Hevea* tree. Ridley devised the "herringbone form of excision, peeling away a limited area of the outer bark, but leaving the inner cambium intact," so that tapping rubber would not kill the trees. The angle of the cut and its depth, the overpowering smell of the sap—these would become second nature for tens of thousands of young men from South India. Expansion was rapid. In 1905, 20,000 hectares were planted with rubber in Malaya. By 1910, plantings covered more than ten times that area.[33]

Rubber planters recognized that the *kangany* system represented the quickest and most efficient way of getting labor. Unlike their counterparts in Ceylon, Malaya's *kanganies* recruited for single estates on which they were already employed, and so operated on a smaller scale. Their success in Malaya is clear from the numbers of workers the *kanganies* managed to recruit. By the end of the 1880s more than 20,000 people arrived in the ports of the Straits Settlements from South India each year; in 1911 that number was over 100,000. The migrant population rapidly moved inland. In 1881 Singapore and Penang still accounted for 39,000 out of the 44,000 Indians resident in Malaya at the time of the census; by 1901, the two cities' combined population of 55,600 was matched by a plantation population of equal size, mostly in Selangor and Perak.[34]

In his pioneering investigation of the history of Indian emigration to Malaya, undertaken in the 1960s, Kernial Singh Sandhu noted that "almost every laborer who was questioned . . . invariably included the recruiter or agent among his 'reasons'" for migration. Traveling through Malaysia's plantation lands forty years later—and, in so many ways, this is a work in Sandhu's footsteps—I had the same experience. In the narratives and family memories of most Tamil migrants to Southeast Asia, fate, chance, and decision are personified in the figure of the *kangany*. The *kangany* was usually a known person; his chance reappearance in the village, which eventually the villagers came to expect, started millions of journeys across the Bay of Bengal. The *kangany* created tight connections between South Indian villages and particular Malayan plantations, and between local shrines at home and estate temples overseas.

In different guises, the *kangany* appears as a brutal agent of the power of the European planters, or as the person who provided alienated Tamil estate workers with a sense of community.[35] By the early twentieth century, British officials and Indian nationalists agreed that the *kangany* was a shark, and it is mostly through their eyes that we see this essential, but almost invisible, figure in the Bay of Bengal's history. The Calcutta nationalist daily, *Amrita Bazar Patrika*, mocked the *kangany* as "like a tin god clothed in gorgeous velvet coat and lace turban and bedecked with costly jewels in his ears and his fingers." Another newspaper commented that "he instils in the minds of these ignorant seekers of fortune" the idea of Malaya as El Dorado: "his gold attracts like [a] magnet."[36] In one recent reminiscence, the *kangany*'s affectations appear more humble, and for that reason perhaps more believable. The family of Palanisamy, who worked as a *kangany* in the late 1910s or early 1920s, recall his frequent trips to India to recruit workers, during which he cut a striking figure with his short trousers and shirt, his close-cropped hair, and a whistle that dangled from his waistband.[37]

In Burma, a similar system of recruitment prevailed under a different name and under different conditions. There the recruiter was known as a *maistry*. The movement from India to Burma really took off in the 1880s and was far more diverse in its composition than migration to Ceylon or Malaya. Most migrants to Burma came not from the Tamil districts of the far south but from the Telugu-speaking area north of Madras—today's Andhra Pradesh coast. They were joined by migrants from the Tamil region, from Orissa, and from Bengal. Adding to the arrivals by sea, an older, overland movement continued, back and forth, across the watery frontier from Chittagong into Burma: movement across a realm that once had been ruled by the kingdom of Arakan. In Burma development did not depend on plantation agriculture. There, Indian migrants dispersed into a wide range of occupations. They were as likely to work in small-scale industry as on the land, and they were less concentrated in particular workplaces. In this sense, migration to Burma was the freest of the three, but the system of debt and advances played a similar role in enabling migration and in binding indebted migrants. Two further contrasts stood out between Burma, on one hand, and Ceylon and Malaya, on the other. The first was juridical. Burma was ruled as a province of British India, and so Indians who moved to Burma were "domestic" migrants, despite having crossed the Bay. As such, they came under far less control and surveillance by the colonial state. Second, in Burma, South Indian capital, not just labor, was essential to the metamorphoses of the late nineteenth century.

Imagine, for a moment, the experience of a Chettiar agent, still a youth, crossing the Bay of Bengal to Burma in the 1880s. He receives his initiation from the man he is sent to replace. Together they live in an isolated compound, iron bars on the windows, in Hanthawaddy district of Lower Burma, surrounded by the emerald sea of paddy fields along the Irrawaddy delta. The Chettiars develop the intimacy and intuition to decide who in the village is trustworthy. It is a lonely life. They spend their days crouched over writing desk and account ledger; their records are immaculate. They are part of the life of the village, yet always removed. We do not know in what language they speak, but most likely it is a pidgin Burmese, spiced with English, Tamil, and Hindustani. The Chettiars take in deposits after the harvest; they lend directly to cultivators, and also to Burmese moneylenders who work the bazaar, reloaning the money at higher interest. They finance the flow of trinkets and manufactures from England and from India: canned milk, biscuits, soap, glassware, crockery, "portraits of Queen Victoria and Kaiser Wilhelm, Christmas cards, and pictures cut from the illustrated magazines of the day."[38]

Though isolated physically, the agent is never cut off from the flow of information and capital, which are like blood circulating through the arteries of the Chettiar community, from its heart in India's deep south to its limbs in Burma, Siam, Malaya, and Indochina. Once a week, the community's elders convene at the Chettiar temple in Mogul Street, Rangoon, which stands "at the centre of an international web of finance closely connected with the banking systems in Madras, Colombo, Penang, Singapore, and Saigon." They discuss community affairs. They set interest rates for different kinds of loans and deposits, beginning with the internal rate for transactions between Chettiar firms. They assess market conditions. They distill rumors of war, faltering monsoons, and new shipping lines into a single figure: the interest rate. They do business with European exchange banks, which are quite willing to lend to Chettiar firms, and with Chinese traders and bankers. People move back and forth. Our new apprentice will soon be alone, as his mentor returns home for a period of rest.

The Chettiars began as a caste of salt traders. By the eighteenth century they had moved into banking and grown experienced in the use of sophisticated financial instruments. Their first forays abroad were to Ceylon, where they financed the early expansion of coffee. Alongside Tamil Muslims, they imported rice and textiles to the island and exported areca, cinnamon, and coffee. Until British banks muscled in, they also handled currency exchange. The Chettiars followed the British military into Southeast Asia, to the Straits Settlements and Tenasserim, and then moved beyond the British Empire to Indonesia and Indochina. Southeast Asia's frontiers brought a better return on their capital than the Indian market, and the "wild east" saw fewer restrictions on their activities. By the turn of the twentieth century far more Chettiar capital was invested overseas than in Madras; above all they invested in Burma.[39]

When they arrived in Lower Burma, Chettiar bankers found the Irrawaddy delta paved with gold. After the Second Anglo-Burmese War (1852), British authorities lifted the ban on rice exports from Burma that the ruling Konbaung dynasty (1752–1885) had imposed. As the global conflicts of midcentury unsettled the international rice market—the 1857 rebellion in India; the American Civil War, which disrupted rice supplies from the Carolinas—Burma emerged as a major rice exporter. The Suez Canal brought Burmese rice to the world. Initially most of it went to Europe. Around the turn of the twentieth century, demand from Burma's neighbors grew. The thousands of migrant laborers on Malaya's plantations had to be fed, and Malaya could not produce rice on that scale. Burmese production soared just as population growth put pressure on the rice-producing heartlands of eastern India, and by the 1920s Burmese rice would flood the domestic Indian market, too.

The weakness of Burma's credit markets gave the Chettiars their opportunity. Before the 1870s, Burmese pioneers expanded into the Irrawaddy delta and increased rice cultivation slowly but steadily. They relied on relatives and shopkeepers for credit to tide them over until the harvest or to finance occasional cash purchases. As new lands were colonized in a headlong rush after the opening of the Suez Canal, the need for credit became acute. The Chettiars were the only group that could supply it. European exchange banks dominated the export economy but had no desire to lend to Burmese cultivators—though they were willing to lend to Chettiar firms, with whom they had established a sound relationship. Indigenous Burmese moneylenders were active but lacked the capital to lend on a large scale. Initially Chettiar firms stayed close to Rangoon and financed cultivation in its immediate hinterland. By the 1880s the Chettiars had moved along Burma's railway lines. They made loans directly to Burmese cultivators, who pledged land and property as collateral. The results were dramatic. Burma exported 162,000 tons of rice in 1855; by 1905–1906 the figure was 2 million tons. In the same period, the land area devoted to paddy grew from 700,000 acres to more than 6 million. Over those years the price of rice rose from 45 rupees to 120 rupees for a hundred baskets. By the turn of the twentieth century, around 350 Chettiar banking firms operated in Burma, with a working capital of 150 million rupees.

Burma's rice revolution was both consequence and instigator of the changes sweeping the Bay of Bengal. As Indian migrant workers poured in, they found diverse occupations, which paid better than plantation work in Malaya or Ceylon. Many were employed in small-scale industry: milling and packing and processing rice, working on the docks or on the railways. The movement of Indian labor to Burma was seasonal. It followed the syncopated rhythms linking cycles of cultivation and rainfall in eastern India and Burma. By the turn of the twentieth century more than half of the Indian residents of Burma lived outside Rangoon— in Bassein and Moulmein, in market towns such as Henzada, Toungoo, and Myaungmya, and in rural hamlets in the lower delta, where they occupied huts on the edges of the rice fields. But it was in Rangoon that the transformation of Burma was most startlingly on display. Rangoon had become an "Indian city" by 1900; it remained so until the catastrophic 1930s. More Indian migrants traveled to Burma than to any other destination: between 12 million and 15 million in all, the vast majority of them in the years from 1880 to 1940. Theirs remains almost an untold story.[40]

Three routes: Ceylon, Burma, Malaya. Viewed in aggregate, each had its own distinct social and geographical contours. The Telugu districts provided Burma with most of its labor, whereas the deep south of Tamil Nadu was most closely linked with Ceylon, and Thanjavur, Tirunelveli, and the area around Madras with Malaya. But there was sufficient overlap between these routes that they intersected and the lines became tangled. Within particular villages, even within single families, men would take their chances with different destinations, one brother going to Burma, another to Malaya. They spread their bets, mitigating the enormous risks they took. Others' journeys encompassed the Bay within a lifetime: a few years in Ceylon, a period back home, and then on to Burma or Malaya. Choice was not always in the hands of migrants, for chance and accident played their roles in determining who ended up where. For some, the world overseas remained abstract until they set sail, not knowing quite where they were headed. Echoes remained of the old idea of Suvarnabhumi, a mythic frontier in the east. Ceylon and Malaya had an especially close relationship, beginning with the planters who took coffee from Ceylon to Malaya, and with them a preference for Tamil labor. By the late nineteenth century, Tamil families in Sri Lanka sought new frontiers in Malaya, working as plantation managers and *kanganies*; starting in the early twentieth century, an educated class of Ceylon Tamil migrants filled the ranks of the Straits Settlements' bureaucracy and its law courts. We do not need a view from on high to see the Bay of Bengal whole: many itineraries, many family histories, were built upon circulation around this maritime world.

Marx wrote in the 1860s that Britain had "indirectly exported the soil of Ireland" by transporting the products of the Irish land over thousands of miles, as food and as cloth; producers failed to replenish the soil's essential nutrients, breaking its "metabolic" balance.[41] We can imagine soil moving alongside human labor on the ocean currents of the Bay of Bengal, too: soil in the Burmese rice exported to India, soil in the Malayan rubber exported to the world, from trees reared on plantations cleared from jungle by the hands of Indian workers.

The supposed familiarity of the "tropical" Malayan climate to Tamil emigrants furnished part of the ideological defense of indentured labor. Against the humanitarian concerns of the Madras government, the governor of the Straits Settlements defended migration from India, insisting that "the emigration which has hitherto existed from India to the Straits is beneficial to the emigrant who finds himself in a climate well suited to his constitution."[42] The contrary proposition also proved useful: planters argued that Tamil laborers in Malaya experienced high rates of sickness and death because of the unfamiliarity of the climate, and not because of abuse or overwork. Justifying their policies to the government of India, officials in the Straits argued that they provided free passage home for Indian laborers not as a matter of right but out of climatic charity. "Immigrants were sent back by this Government from motives of humanity," A. E. H. Anson wrote, "it being considered that they might, to some extent, recover health by the return to their native climate."[43]

The presumed fit between particular peoples and particular lands informed the search for "ideal" emigrants from different Indian regions. "Owing to the similarity of the climate of Borneo to that of the West Coast of India," one Malayan official wrote, contemplating a new stream of migration to British North Borneo, "natives of Malabar and South Canara would probably thrive better" than those from drier districts in the southeast.[44] Another observer put it more strongly. "The Straits climate is totally different to that of the East Coast of India, whence most of the emigrants are drawn," he insisted. "I am informed that in the Straits there is constant rain all the year round. If, then, men are to be recruited at all I would urge that the most suitable for the purpose are the West Coast natives, who are acclimatised to a heavy rainfall."[45] But the recruiting networks, the shipping lines, the government emigration depots—all of these ran from the east coast of India to Malaya, and it was from the east coast that migrants continued to come.

To colonial geographers, the differences in climate between India and the tropical plantation colonies made migration seem a natural redistribution of population to where the soil was most fertile. "A glance at the map . . . will show that the colonies importing Indian labour are in the belt of the tropics," Grierson argued, and those colonies possessed "an equable climate, free from sudden or extreme variations, and an amazing fertility." Grierson's historical account of the need for Indian labor in tropical colonies combined culture and climate. "When an Indian cooly is transported to a tropical colony," Grierson concluded, "he finds himself in a place quite beyond his experience. He finds a soil capable of yielding good crops with hardly any cultivation." What Grierson neglected to note was that—in contrast to the situation facing the white settlers of the New World—the obstacles in the way of Indian emigrants' acquiring land of their own were almost insurmountable, as the products of the "good soil" went straight to the planters.[46]

Sensitive observers could see that migrant labor changed the ecology and landscape of Malaya, and even its climate, rather than experiencing them passively. As early as 1849 the naturalist James Low expressed concern that the pace of deforestation in Penang, as the island was opened to both English and Chinese capital, would have an unwanted impact on its climate. He echoed a view common in other parts of the British Empire at the time, known as the "desiccationist" theory. "Climate concerns the whole community," Low wrote, "and its protection from injury is one of the duties of government." If "dense, leafy forests" were "consigned to destruction," he warned, then "every successive drought will prove more baneful than the preceding." On the mainland, in Province Wellesley, "the great extent to which the plain . . . has been shorn of its forests would of itself produce an urgent necessity for a stop being at once put to a war with nature, which must entail severe calamities on the future."[47] The war with nature continued, and for those whose labor reshaped the landscape of Malaya, the future held many calamities.

In collective memory, passed down over generations, many Tamil migrants recalled their first encounters with the damp heat of Malaya as a shock; those who moved to the highlands of Ceylon had an even more difficult adjustment to make. The relatively unchanging nature of the Malayan climate, with constant rain year-round, contrasted with the alternation of wet and dry seasons in South India; that unvarying climate was ideally suited to rubber cultivation. Together with the clockwork regularity of the working day on the plantations, from the roll call before six in the morning to the midday break, climate shaped how Tamil migrant workers in Malaya experienced the passage of time, imposing a new rhythm of life. The disorientation was tempered by the preservation of rituals from home. Muthammal Palanisamy, a retired schoolteacher—a vigorous and warmly intelligent woman, with a passion for local research—has collected and recorded folk songs sung by older people, mostly women, in Malaysian Tamil communities. The continued performance of Tamil harvest songs into the late twentieth century in Malaysia, where most Tamils worked as wage laborers and not as cultivators—and where, for most of the year, the last thing one needed to pray for was rain—was part of the imaginative transition underpinning migration.[48]

Others searched for the familiar—hills that reminded them of the landscapes of their native land, upon which to construct small temples; familiar trees and herbs, to provide the material for healing. Shoreside temples flourished, but now they were joined by shrines deep in the Malayan jungle, founded on the Tamil belief in what David Shulman has called "a rooted, totally localized godhead." The erection of a new shrine on a rubber plantation would be seen in terms of a "pre-existent relationship between the god and the site." Workers felt that their deities had crossed the seas before they had, and so they constructed shrines where they already felt the deities' power. The workers brought with them the Saiva devotional tradition of the Tamil country, worshipping the youthful Murugan and the powerful Mariyamman (the Mother Goddess). The migrants believed in the divine power animating the earth, and their rituals embraced "violence, death, blood-sacrifice and impurity."[49] A scholar of Indian religion has written of the "everywhere of the sacred" in South Asia: "the supreme lord who is right here where the rivers meet, right here where the herons wade, right here where the hillock rises." The sacred geography of India crossed the Bay of Bengal and implanted itself on the Malayan landscape. This, too, was how workers experienced, and made sense, of a changing climate.[50]

The first generation of Indian indentured workers in Malaya endured infernal conditions: racked with fever, beaten when their efforts flagged, consumed by the dangers that lurked in uncleared jungle. The early years of plantation agriculture in Southeast Asia dramatized Marx's observation that "capital comes dripping from head to toe, from every pore, with blood and dirt."[51] Most workers who crossed the Bay were not seafaring people—unlike the Muslim merchants and mariners who had crossed the sea for centuries before them—and this is one reason why the 1870s are a moment of rupture in the Bay of Bengal's history; another such moment came in the 1920s, when women crossed the sea in large numbers for the first time. Most labor migrants were cultivators of the land in India, or laborers on others' land. And it was the land, Southeast Asia's forests and river valleys, that their efforts reshaped. "Nature can be known through labor," Richard White reminds us;

Figure 15 A small tree shrine on a rubber estate in Malaysia. Hundreds of similar shrines were built on plantations in the nineteenth century. *Photograph by Sunil Amrith.*

through their labor, Tamil workers came to know the Bay of Bengal's eastern shores—"the real structure of the land, its systems of bones and muscles."[52] The migrants learned their work on the land, which had first to be cleared and then, constantly, weeded. Sugar cultivation, which came first, was the most arduous of all, and the most destructive of the environment. Tea needed attention year-round, in plucking and sorting and drying the leaves; rubber tappers learned just where to make the incision to bring forth the sap of the tree without killing it— the instinct lodged itself in their bodies

Henri Fauconnier won the Prix Goncourt in 1930 for his novel *Malaisie*, based on his experience in Malaya, where he arrived in 1906 to manage a plantation cultivating West African oil palm. His is a lyrical description of the horror of the early plantations. The land clearing was done by gangs of Malay contract laborers and by Tamil and Chinese workers. Fauconnier witnessed their struggles. "Then they attack the forest trees," he wrote, "on all sides I hear axe-blows biting steadily into the trunks." Then "I would hear the rending shriek of a tornado; then a moaning sound, a sort of long drawn out neigh that ended in a roar. The earth shook beneath my feet"; in a "cloud of flying wreckage," he wrote, "a whole stretch of jungle had crashed." The early plantation workers left no written accounts to balance planters' fantasies such as Fauconnier's, but in oral tradition and in song they recall the creation of the plantations by their hands. As he flew down the "great crescent" in the mid-1930s, Richard Upjohn Light, Yale University neurosurgeon and aviator, wrote that "the vegetation of the peninsula did not change much as far as Penang." But "from that point to Singapore the wild country had been tamed and given over to rubber plantations, laid out with the regularity of carefully kept gardens." This aerial snapshot of the land is, in a way, an archive of the Bay of Bengal's history of migration.[53]

The forest posed another great threat to the workers' lives—the threat of disease. In a view still common in the nineteenth century, the soil of the Malayan jungle harbored miasma; the newly developing science of bacteriology taught that the local ecology was home to pathogens to which migrant workers had little natural resistance. Dysentery, diarrhea, and "fevers" were a constant presence. Water supplies to the workers' dormitories were inadequate and poorly maintained, and "doubtless had some influence in inducing diarrhoea and dysentery."[54] Boosters and labor recruiters boasted of Malaya's "healthful climate," but death rates on the plantations were higher than in almost any other part of the British Empire. Malaria posed the greatest risk of all. The disease was hyperendemic in the Malayan jungle, unlike in southern India; Tamil migrant workers had little natural immunity to it. The ecological rupture caused by land clearance might even have worsened the problem. Only in the 1910s did death rates decline, with the abolition of indentured labor, with the gradual improvement of sanitation, and, perhaps, with growing immunity among workers now more used to Malayan conditions. As late as the 1920s, a Malayan medical officer lamented that "the wastage was too rapid; it was not worthwhile to bring coolies over from India, however strictly they were bound to fulfil their term of contract if, in fact, they died before the term was up."[55]

A map of blame divided India from Malaya. To justify the high rates of mortality among indentured laborers, planters argued that recruits had arrived from India in poor health to begin with, and lacked the resilience to adapt to Malaya's climate. The Tamil estate workers were responsible for their own suffering: "the filthy habits of the natives as regards conservancy are too well known to require explanation," a Malayan magistrate wrote, in defense of the planters.[56] By contrast, Indian officials argued—timidly at first, and then with greater force—that "ill usage" and poor conditions turned healthy emigrants into "sickly" returnees. A Nagapatnam port surgeon put it starkly in 1880: "For the authorities on the other side of the water to pretend that the sickly, starved, ill-used looking wretches who return to this port from Penang . . . owe their present appearance to the weakly state in which they were when they emigrated," he wrote, was "a contention far worse than ridiculous."[57]

Many workers on the plantations lacked the most fundamental relationship that human beings have with the soil—the cultivation of food. The estates of Malaya were fed on rice imported from Burma or Thailand; in Malaya, far fewer estate workers than in Ceylon (or in Assam) had their own plots on which to grow vegetables or raise poultry. Malnutrition was an insidious cause of debility, even death. A Tamil worker rescued from the notorious Malakoff Estate in Province Wellesley was found to be suffering from what the examining medical officer called "a degree of emaciation unsurpassed in my experience." If the Malayan government argued that Indian emigrants should be grateful for the escape that Malaya offered them from famine, a port surgeon in India had quite a different view: he saw workers returning from Malaya "in a worse state than the famine-stricken and diseased creatures I have seen in the hospitals of famine camps."[58]

For the least fortunate among the workers, the land that had been made by their efforts swallowed their battered bodies. In the 1870s and the 1880s the brutality on the worst of Malaya's plantations stands comparison with conditions on the slave plantations of the Caribbean. When local coroners began to investigate deaths on Malaya's plantations, the workers' testimonies sketched a horrifying map of the plantation land populated with unmarked graves, where workers had been beaten or tortured and buried. "Some died of flogging and were buried," one coroner's investigation concluded. Workers' knowledge of the land included knowledge of the trees under which their fellows lay.[59] Ramasamy, an enfeebled man, forty-five or fifty years old, was found buried in a shallow grave under some coconut trees on the estate where he worked. The coroner's investigation found evidence of at least fourteen wounds on his body inflicted by a rattan (bamboo cane) and indications that Ramasamy had received an additional hundred lashes with a cat-o'-nine-tails. Muthusamy, who witnessed the murder, had arrived from Madras with Ramasamy three months earlier, and took the coroner to the spot where his friend lay buried.[60] In Tamil, the word for estate—*thottam*—is the word for "garden."

"Blood and dirt" gave the frontiers of Southeast Asia their dynamism— the human suffering of migrant workers reshaped the land. We tend to think of environmental history as something that happens to us. Environmental history on the largest scale is made by the forces of nature that shape human society: human beings are "biological agents" alongside plants and pathogens, competing for supremacy. Alternatively, we think—anthropocentrically—that environmental history is driven by the state, particularly in its modernist incarnation, in a drive to conquer nature and make it productive at any cost.[61] But what would it mean to turn this around, to think of those who crossed the Bay of Bengal as agents of environmental transformation? They crossed the sea to alter the land. Small decisions within families, small acts of coercion—the motive force of debt, or the glitter that adorned the *kangany's* promises—accumulated to shift the "metabolic balance" of the Bay of Bengal.

Crossing the Bay of Bengal, Indian migrants crossed many frontiers: ecological, cultural, and legal.[62] By the turn of the twentieth century, migration across the Bay was governed by many rules, and rules full of contradictions. For Chettiar moneylenders or European investors, for migrant families from Thanjavur or Godavari, the Bay of Bengal was an unbroken region within which people and money flowed back and forth. For the imperial state, it was an area transected by borders—borders between British, French, and Dutch empires; borders between different sorts of British territory, ruled differently. The control of migration arose in tandem with its growth.

"The Tamil emigrant does not find himself wholly a stranger" in the Straits Settlements, wrote Octavio Hume in 1875. Hume was at the time a civil servant; a decade later, he would be a founding member of the Indian National Congress. Invoking both history and geography, Hume argued that connections across the Bay were part of the natural order of things.[63] Gradually that view changed. Migration between India and Southeast Asia came under careful regulation from both sides over the next half century. The establishment of new rules linked the coasts of the Bay more closely together, and at the same time introduced new distinctions between different kinds of migration—free and unfree, "assisted" and "unassisted," Chinese and Indian—and between immigrants and indigenous populations. By the 1880s, the scale of migration across the Bay had provoked official intervention. Of the three main destinations across the Bay of Bengal, migration to Malaya was the most closely regulated. Only in Malaya did indentured labor coexist with "free" migration, in which laborers were recruited by *kanganies*. Tamil migrants to Malaya were, by the early twentieth century, among the most intensively governed populations in the British Empire.

British authorities invested time and energy to uphold the ideology of free labor, satisfying liberal consciences that every migrant to Malaya crossed the Bay willingly, in full knowledge of what awaited him on the other side. Adopting the legal regime that had been put in place in the 1830s to oversee migration to Mauritius and the West Indies, the government of India introduced the post of protector of immigrants to supervise migration from Madras to Malaya in 1873, following Hathaway's condemnation of the "regularly organized system of kidnapping." In the Bay of Bengal, where people had moved unimpeded for centuries, the protector's task was significantly more complicated than in the case of the distant sugar colonies.

From the outset, the interrogation of emigrants made the Madras government uncomfortable, yet it continued, almost as a play performed daily for an audience of imperial policy makers. Officials were unsure whether they could trust the migrants' testimony and uneasy about what that testimony told them of migrants' intentions. "It very often happens that a native is tempted to emigrate for the most inadequate reasons," Bowness Fischer wrote from the French-controlled port of Karaikal to the authorities in Madras. These "inadequate" reasons included "debt, domestic discord, [and] a transient discontent with his lot," and were rooted in "a weak inability how to make a choice." As such, the "free" migrant was all too often "easy prey to an insidious recruiting agent." The migrant, in this situation, was not an agent at all. Fischer pleaded that each migrant should be "examined by some experienced and judicious official, and his motives subjected to the test of analysis," and that this should happen "before he has caught the contagion of the depot, or been able to compare the superior comfort it promises with that which he has left behind."[64] Colonial officials saw dissimulation everywhere, and it was not always clear who was responsible for the manipulation—recruiters or the migrants themselves. They resorted to widespread assumptions about the gullibility of the "credulous" peasants, pointing to "the facility with which the Indian coolie can be induced to say anything when he is brought before the Protector" and to the propensity of "the emigrant" to make statements that "may be to his own disadvantage."[65]

By making each Indian migrant legally responsible for his decision to emigrate, the government of British India sought initially to absolve itself of responsibility for migrants' welfare, in the full knowledge that they were passing into a different jurisdiction, entering into contracts of indenture that were onerous if not unjust, bound by a harshly punitive labor code that punished even minor "misdemeanours."[66] The examination involved migrants and magistrates in an encounter of confession and deception. Many of the officials involved distrusted the process. Even as magistrates made each and every migrant legally responsible for his actions, the state lacked the information to establish the identity of individuals over time and space. The entry of the migrants' names was far from simple: while some were accompanied by detailed histories—the names of their fathers, the villages they come from, their castes and occupations—others were identified only by their generic caste names, so much so that a common name, Ramasamy, became a noun of sorts, a derogatory term for any plantation laborer in Malaya ("Ramasamy is happy in the fields"), effacing his individuality quite deliberately. "At its most brutal," John Berger writes, "home is no more than one's name—whilst to most people one is nameless."[67]

The protector could not possibly examine each and every migrant, and "he must too often both see and hear through the medium of others' eyes and ears." Few British officials were as critical of the process as Fischer. A veteran of the Madras Army, Fischer was appointed the British consular agent in Karaikal in 1880, where he remained until his retirement in 1888, untiring in his efforts to increase his consular powers. He became obsessed with illicit emigration from French India to the Straits Settlements—that is to say, emigration evading British control. Standing at the margins, outside the boundaries of British India, Fischer reflected on the weaknesses in the law. Pugnacious and arrogant, Fischer left a running commentary on emigration from Karaikal and Pondicherry. He insisted that "no term has been more unfairly used or has less accurately represented actual facts" than the notion of "free" migration from south India. "There was not the slightest doubt," he argued, "that the majority of persons who left our coasts for the Straits Settlements were *not* free in any proper sense of that term." Some "chose to say they were," and "repeated by rote certain statements"; this was an absurdity, Fischer concluded, for these migrants were people who "by birth or circumstances, could not possibly" be free.[68] The larger question, he wrote, was "whether the Indian agricultural laborer as we at present know him, is really fit to look after his own interest." He thought not. The Indian migrant, synonymous with the Indian peasant, needed "protection both from himself and from others."[69]

In theory, the whole edifice of migration around the Bay of Bengal region assumed that migrants were moving of their own volition, rather than as slaves or as human cargo. This was perfectly compatible with the notion that they had given up willingly some part of their freedom by signing agreements of indenture or long-term contracts. In practice, however, British officials charged with regulating migration suspected that Indian migrants were incapable of agency, in two senses of that term. British liberal theorists, from John Locke onward, believed that personhood "belongs only to intelligent agents, capable of a law, and happiness, and misery," and the likes of Bowness Fischer saw none of these attributes in the crowds of the depot. They felt that the people they called "coolies" lacked the ability to evaluate their own desires or to ask themselves whether they were migrating for the "right" reasons.[70] Second, officials felt that the real "agents" were the labor recruiters, known precisely by that term: as agents. Acting on their own behalf, or on behalf of their principals—the planters of Malaya or Ceylon—the agents practiced deception to lure the laborers with false promises, turning them into passive victims.

What worried the state most was the autonomy from British control that recruiting agents continued to enjoy. The sharpest contrast between migration across the Bay and the indentured migration to the distant sugar colonies was that the eastward movement was far from new, even if now it took place on an unprecedented scale and under different conditions. Long-standing systems of recruitment across the Bay continued to operate into the later nineteenth century. The colonial state's anxiety about migrants' agency expressed, at least in part, anxiety about the limits of its own control. Throughout the region, "a significant traffic in human labor existed outside of the power of Europeans . . . Javanese, Boyanese, Banjarese, Dayaks, Kelantanese, Tamils, and Chinese were all in motion."[71] When Hathaway described the "illegal traffic" in people across the Bay, he expressed two overlapping concerns: first, the humanitarian anxiety that these people were being "kidnapped," enslaved, or otherwise taken against their will, and second, that the trafficker—like the pirate—was independent of British control, perhaps neither more nor less oppressive of his human cargo than those who went through official channels.

Indigenous commercial arrangements connecting South India and Southeast Asia—consortia of shipping merchants, labor recruiters, and financiers—reconstituted themselves in space and time; we might say they had long memories. Many of these connections across the Bay had their origins in a world of multiple, competing ports along the

Coromandel Coast: a world in which merchants would move, bag and baggage, to a neighboring coastal settlement when conditions or taxation became oppressive. When British shipping regulations and migration controls at Nagapatnam became too stringent, Tamil Muslim shipping merchants did as their predecessors had done and simply set sail from the adjacent French port of Karaikal—this was precisely Fischer's concern. The stretch of coast from Nagore to Karaikal was the heartland of the Maraikkayar community, and the region of Ramnad the home of the Chettiars; to these groups, colonial borders had little meaning. Migrants and migration agents—often they were indistinguishable to European eyes—switched passports at will, as in the case of the emigrant from Karaikal who, Bowness Fischer remarked incredulously, "held a pass-port from the local police, which had been granted to him as a French subject!"[72] To the chagrin of Indian government officials, the Supreme Court of Singapore confirmed in 1878 that migrants from French India were excluded from the laws governing migration between India and the Straits.[73] And it was never easy to determine who was a British subject and who a French subject, certainly not "with the strict judicial precision required in Courts of Justice." Frustrated British officials ascribed this to the "indifference of the coolie to questions of nationality"; it is equally plausible that many used the "question of nationality" quite strategically.

An angry Fischer lamented his lack of control over what went on in Karaikal: the French did not seem to care. The "deeply laden vessels" of the mid-nineteenth century had "given place to steamers . . . but the native maistries or speculators of the Lubby caste remain," he wrote—an apt summary of the enduring vitality of earlier Bay of Bengal networks. The categorical distinction between "coolies," who migrated "under agreement to labor," and "free" migrants, whose travels within the British Empire were unregulated, caused further problems for those charged with law enforcement. In practice, the coolie could evade detection by blending in with the "continual ebb and flow of petty traders pursuing their small gains over the black water": the "discontented cooks, butlers and maties," the "speculative barbers, dhobies and peons," the "shoals of journeymen artisans."[74]

Repeatedly the colonial authorities became aware that indigenous brokers exceeded the writ of the Raj. Both Chettiar and Lebbai Muslim merchants did their own recruiting; they advertised their services openly in the Penang press. One such firm, M. Kanapady Pillai and Company, announced in the *Penang Standard* that "any gentleman requiring the services of Indian agricultural labourers can be supplied with any number of men of strong and sound constitution at moderate brokerage and within a reasonable time after notice."[75] They shipped their workers out from Karaikal, evading the restrictions imposed by the British authorities.[76] Although the British controlled the map, the Bay of Bengal remained a stage with many players. In the early 1880s Spanish and German vessels took migrants from Karaikal to the Straits: the Spanish vessel *Zamboga* and the German ships *Septima* and *Decima* were all regular visitors to Karaikal, and "the substitution of these foreign steamers entirely removed the captains and crews of these vessels from the moral influence of [British] consular authority." Worse still, in British eyes, a privately owned Dutch ship with a Chinese name, the *Kongsi,* ran directly from Karaikal to Sumatra.

Crossing the Bay of Bengal, migrants and their recruiters crossed political boundaries faster than governments could track their movements. Several thousand Tamil migrants arrived in the Straits Settlements only to be shipped "illegally" beyond the British Empire to the tobacco plantations of Sumatra, where they worked alongside a much larger number of Chinese who also arrived there, whether legally or illegally, after transiting through Singapore.[77] To the north, Indian workers deserted their plantations and slipped over the border into Siam. "The runaway coolies from the estates can always obtain employment" north of the border, the Malayan protector of immigrants noted, "and the greatest difficulties are invariably thrown in the way of any one attempting to find them." The protector, F. H. Gottlieb, made the clerk from his office double "as a detective to seek out the offenders and to secure evidence to enable me to prosecute"; he was aided by Inspector Timmins of the Penang police. Their local officers were less enthusiastic: "One man lost his life in such an attempt and his men now refuse to cross the frontier."[78]

Even within British territory in Malaya, migrants and recruiting agents exploited the patchwork of jurisdictions that indirect rule had brought. Desertion from the plantations was more or less constant. Some of the fugitive plantation workers disappear from the record. Oral tradition suggests that a small number of them settled among Malay villagers; others died trying to escape. The most fortunate were often those who managed to escape from Perak or Selangor to the Straits Settlements, where they could use the juridical distinction between direct and indirect rule to their advantage. In 1913 Sellappan Kavandan, known as Sellea, escaped from Braunston Estate in Selangor and fled to Singapore. He was arrested there, and the planters tried to use the law of extradition to get him back, on the grounds that, by leaving Selangor and crossing into the Settlements, he was a fugitive in another jurisdiction. The magistrate ruled in the planters' favor, but the Supreme Court of Singapore overturned the decision, arguing that Sellea's offense was "trivial" and that extradition would be "too severe" a punishment. At the outbreak of World War I a similar case came to light: seven workers escaped to Singapore from Midlands Estate in Klang when their employers failed to pay their wages. There, too, the judge in Singapore found in their favor and refused their extradition. Strikingly, these cases of desertion and flight appear in the standard manual of extradition law in the British Asian empire, written by Aloysius de Mello—a Goan lawyer trained in Cambridge and Paris, and a member of Gray's Inn.[79] So many of the distinctions we now take for granted in discussing migration—those between internal and international movement, and between legal and illegal migration—emerged from the debates of the early twentieth century, and many of the formative debates, the test cases, were in the Bay of Bengal region.

By the first decade of the twentieth century, Indian labor contractors and British authorities had found a modus vivendi. In both Ceylon and Malaya, the *kangany* system had proved its efficiency: the colonial state stopped trying to interfere so directly with the process of recruitment as governors and planters alike saw no further value in the system of indentured labor, now defended only by a dwindling number of diehard conservatives. In 1903, the Madras government affirmed that "checks formerly exercised by the Superintendent of the Emigration Depot, Negapatam, over *kangany* recruitment had been deliberately relaxed." The *kangany*, with his networks of information and credit and kinship, had prevailed. On the other hand, the colonial state had gained leverage over the system of debt and advances. In 1901 the "tin ticket" system was introduced in Ceylon, under which the government paid for the passages of migrants, and recovered the money from the planters; in 1907 a similar system was introduced in Malaya.[80] "Trafficking" and persistent forms of slavery became much less common as colonial controls achieved their aims.[81] In a strange way, both Hathaway and his enemies had won.

The lives of Indian migrants circulated on paper through the archival labyrinth of the British Empire. Documents, like people, moved from colony to colony, from department to department, from coast to coast. The earliest days I spent working on this project at the National Archives of India were filled with confusion, as multiple handlists and catalogs lay open before me. Official deliberations on migration moved around among the institutions of state every few years: from the Department of Revenue and Agriculture to the Department of Home, Revenue and Agriculture; from there back to Revenue and Agriculture; and then to Commerce and Industry. Each of these shifts in administrative logic reveals a change in the way the state envisaged and defined the "problem" of migration in relation to agricultural production, taxation, land, and industrialization. In Burma, Malaya, and Ceylon, debates on immigration came under the Departments of Labor and under the Protectors of Indian Immigrants. And stories of migration appear in other records—consular and diplomatic correspondence, for instance—where migrants' journeys crossed political boundaries. The organization of the archive of migration illustrates the choices, and the accidents, that determined who would be responsible for the journeys of millions of people overseas.

Before the language of citizenship became widespread, the law provided a way in which even the most disadvantaged could appeal for protection, assert claims to public respect, and defend customs that remained sacrosanct even where abuse was widespread—though the odds, always, were in favor of the wealthy and the powerful. The voices of migrants were "heard" in Madras or Calcutta, and so survive to be heard by historians, only when they were expressed in particular ways—in petitions (though only if they followed convention), in legal testimony (though this testimony was not always believed), and, above all, if they arrived through British intermediaries: medical officers, magistrates, and missionaries.[82] As correspondence between Malaya and India grew, the inhumanity of plantation life became harder to ignore; evidence mounted that Tamil laborers in Malaya were "habitually flogged."[83] British officials with the courage of their convictions—among them Subcollector Hathaway of Thanjavur—concluded that the government should act to prevent further emigration to Southeast Asia because the system was so open to abuse. But Malaya's planters needed their labor, and they had powerful backers in London.

The planters justified unrestrained migration by invoking the Victorian shibboleth of free trade: freedom of movement within the empire was fundamental. Furthermore, they insisted, circular migration around the Bay of Bengal was rooted in local tradition. "To the traditional connexion of the Straits with India," they argued, "we may fairly enough trust to ensure the immigrants' interest." There was no further need for government intervention.[84] But the language of freedom was double-edged. Indian administrators and humanitarians argued that restrictions on freedom of movement would enhance the human freedom of their Indian subjects, saving them from unjust contracts, which they were never truly free to enter into. And even purely economic arguments in favor of freedom could undermine the planters' case as much as bolster it.

Hathaway's successor, Henry Sullivan Thomas, collector of Thanjavur between 1874 and 1878—he made his career as an administrator, and later would write a treatise on the history of the fishing rod in India—argued that "the principle should be that nothing more is to be attempted or countenanced than the unabused removal of the obstructions to the spontaneous flow of labour from a cheap to a dear market." Contrary to the planters' claim that the flow of labor between India and Malaya was natural and spontaneous, he showed that it would be impossible without government intervention at every stage of the process: "primitive accumulation," as Marx saw clearly, depended on the power of the state. As such, Thomas wrote, "if the Government legalizes and aids a blind contract for labor at a price below the market-price of the place to which it is going, then it directly injures the emigrant and indirectly injures the two countries." He was particularly concerned that "if it were good policy for India to interest herself in sending labor anywhere, it should [be] . . . in distributing it to the less-populated parts of India, where it is most wanted as, for instance, to its own coffee and tea planting industries." Thomas's conclusion was stark: "If English capital in Burma, the Straits, Ceylon or anywhere else, has gone where it cannot live without unfair bolstering at the expense of India, then the sooner it finds it out and remedies its mistake the better." Thomas was prescient: the debate over freedom of migration across the Bay would

continue into the twentieth century and by the 1930s Indian nationalists would be making exactly the arguments against emigration that
Thomas had outlined.[85]

Though the motivations for official concern were often self-interested,
even cynical—upholding the system by putting its horrors down to individual cases of "abuse"—government interest in the conditions of
Indian labor overseas had an unintended consequence: it opened up
the imperial state to claims by migrant workers, claims that held the
state to its own promises of justice. Initially Malaya's planters appeared
to win the argument, for the likes of Hathaway and Thomas were lone
voices. The desire not to "inconvenience" Malaya's planters prevented
Indian officials from "ordering at once the immediate cessation of emigration" to Malaya, which the weight of the evidence before them suggested they ought to do.[86] But if colonial administrators were unwilling
to follow through on the implications of their findings, Indian nationalists and social reformers took up the cudgels of reform.

By the first decade of the twentieth century, Indian and Chinese
journalists, social reformers, nationalists, and government officials
turned their attention to the condition of Indian and Chinese coolies in
the world. For both Indian and Chinese political leaders, their inability
to protect their countrymen abroad epitomized national weakness. As
"free" Asian migrants began to experience legal discrimination in, and
exclusion from, the settler colonies and the United States, the presence
of the coolie branded Indians and Chinese everywhere with the stigma
of unfreedom and humiliation.[87]

Led by veteran liberal politician Gopal Krishna Gokhale, Indian public figures raised once again the question of the condition of Indian labor migrants, as British humanitarians and antislavery campaigners
had done in the 1840s. Addressing the imperial legislative council, of
which he was a member, in 1912, Gokhale spoke of the "vast and terrible
amount of suffering" caused by the system of indentured labor, the
"personal violence" and "bitterness" that it brought.[88] He used the imperial authorities' own statistics on diet, wages, and mortality to draw
attention to the plight of Indian emigrants. Beyond the suffering of migrant workers, "disgrace" in the eyes of the world was the greatest concern of the Indian elites who condemned indentured labor.[89] Indentured labor, Gokhale declared in 1912, was "degrading from a *national*
point of view," for "wherever the system exists, there the Indians are

only known as coolies, no matter what their position might be."[90] Respectable Indian merchants and lawyers overseas, he implied, were tainted by association with their toiling countrymen.

The denial of political rights to Indians in South Africa became an urgent public issue in India, spurred by the activity of an increasingly prominent lawyer, Mohandas Gandhi. Racial discrimination in the settler colonies was particularly galling to many elite Indians, but this was not the only issue at stake.[91] Anxiety about Indian emigration stimulated wider concerns about India's poverty and its potential for economic development, including concerns about India's frontiers and its connections with the broader region. Because of its proximity to India and the historical connections across the Bay of Bengal, Malaya stood in a very different relation with India than did the distant sugar colonies of the Caribbean or Indian Ocean. The image of an Indian community marooned far from home carried little weight in the Malayan context. But the new awareness of Indian labor migration around the world placed the condition of workers within an imperial and international politics of reform: the problem of the coolie became at once more emotive and more general. By the 1910s, literate Indians in Malaya had begun to intervene in their own right in the debate on indentured and plantation labor.[92] A Kuala Lumpur–based Indian writer, J. D. Samy, wrote that in Malaya "the coolie is literally unrepresented," as he described in detail the "sufferings that the poor, illiterate and ignorant coolies daily undergo."[93]

The publicity given to the suffering of migrant labor by Indian politicians and social reformers was one of many challenges to the empire-wide system of indentured labor migration by the early twentieth century. Hugh Tinker's exhaustive consideration of the internal debates within the British Empire leading to the abolition of indentured labor concluded that a coalition of humanitarians, missionaries, and Indian liberal reformers first "condemned" and then "dismantled" the global export of Indian indentured labor.[94] Imperial authorities worried about the political opposition to indentured labor in India, which gathered force after Gokhale's intervention in 1912.[95] At the same time, the profitability of indentured labor declined, as planters across the British Empire found new ways to recruit "free" labor using ties of kinship and debt.[96]

These broader imperial pressures contributed to the specific decision to end indentured labor migration to Malaya, but there the economic arguments against the use of indentured labor were particularly powerful.[97] With the dizzying rise of rubber, planters found that the system of indentured labor simply could not provide them with a large or steady enough supply of workers. The last batch of indentured workers arrived in Malaya in 1910, and their terms of indenture expired in 1913, marking the end of the system's life in Malaya. In Ceylon and Burma, of course, the system of indentured labor was never used. Around the Bay of Bengal, the end of indenture had limited impact, for it was already a system in decline, and recruitment by *kanganies,* which both antedated and outlasted indenture, shared many of its vices.

Between the 1870s and the early twentieth century, connections across the Bay of Bengal underwent a change in scale. However imprecise the statistics, it is certain that a comparable number of people crossed the Bay as crossed the Atlantic. Indian and Chinese migrants were less likely than their Atlantic counterparts to settle permanently overseas. But were they necessarily less free? Many observers, at the time and since, would answer that they were. Writing in the 1870s, one British official in Madras declared that "any analogy" between Indian migration to Southeast Asia "and the spontaneous emigration of a free and intelligent people in England and elsewhere" would be "fallacious and illusory."[98] But the thousands of young men who crossed the Bay of Bengal did so with "different degrees of freedom," to borrow a phrase from Rebecca Scott's study of Cuba and Louisiana after slavery.[99]

Anthropologist Talal Asad makes a powerful case for moving beyond the perception, as widespread in the social sciences today as it was in the minds of British magistrates in the late nineteenth century, of people as *either* agents *or* victims. In "a world of accumulating probabilities rather than constant certainties," he writes, "behavior depends on unconscious routine and habit" and "emotions render the ownership of actions a matter of conflicting descriptions." Such "conflicting descriptions" abound in response to a simple question asked by nineteenth-century magistrates and by twenty-first-century oral historians: "Why did you migrate?" Asad argues that we should instead "think of moral agency in terms of people's habitual engagement with the world in which they live."[100] Through their "habitual engagement" with the new landscapes of the Kandyan highlands, the Malayan plantations, and the Irrawaddy delta—landscapes that their labor made unrecognizable—Indian migrant workers asserted their agency across the Bay of Bengal. We can think of this as moral, political, or even environmental agency. As investors recalibrated "land values" and watched their inexorable rise, laborers gave land a value of their own. This was expressed, often, in the temples they built on every rubber estate and tea plantation, sometimes little more than tree shrines. And like their counterparts who crossed the plains of North America headed west, the workers of the Bay of Bengal rim had their own pioneer narratives of cultivation and civilization wrested from the jaws of forbidding nature. In the words of one Telugu song of the early twentieth century:

> It was in the nineteenth century; we arrived in Malaya
> Those were the days of British rule over Malay Peninsula
> The days of flourishing Rubber and Coconut plantations

Figure 16 The remains of a temple excavated in the Bujang Valley, Malaysia's most important archaeological site. Many parts of the site were first discovered by laborers on local estates. *Photograph by Sunil Amrith.*

> The Telugus from Andhra country were brought by the
>   British to work in the plantation
> We cut the forests, cleared the land for plantations
> We laboured hard to make the country green and
>   prosperous.[101]

Clearing the land, Tamil workers in Malaya stumbled upon ancient memories buried in the soil. As they worked, laborers on the Sungai Batu Estate in Kedah found "an extensive but low mound, a drainage ditch in the banks of which they noticed laterite and stone." Others nearby, "engaged in the modern (and ancient) industry of collecting boulders," discovered a miniature bronze shrine. In creating the plantation landscape, coolies found Ganesha statues, coins, and relics. After H. G. Quaritch Wales's excavations in 1937–1938, aided by his wife, Dorothy—a graduate in law from the University of London—it was clear that the estate sat in the midst of the most significant archaeological site in Malaysia, the Bujang Valley, which testified to the thriving commerce across the Bay of Bengal more than a millennium earlier.

In time, the Bujang Valley—like other "Hindu" sites in Southeast Asia—would be appropriated by colonial orientalists and elite Indian publicists to argue that Southeast Asia was an extension of "greater Indian" civilization. But that came later. We can only imagine what the workers digging culverts and collecting boulders experienced when they came upon these buried traces: A flash of recognition? A sense that they had crossed the Bay in the footsteps of powerful ancestors? Or, perhaps, just a sense that this land, too, was where they belonged.[102]

5

Oceans' Crossroads

Ramasamy Narayanasamy boarded the S.S. *Rajullah* for Singapore in 1930, a boy of fourteen. Though the depression had stemmed the flow of Indian labor to Southeast Asia, young Ramasamy found work through his uncle, herding cattle along Singapore's Serangoon Road (still today the heart of the city's Little India) for local magnate Kadir Sultan. He moved on to work at the Krishna Vilas and Ananda Bhavan restaurants; he graduated from wiping tables to grinding rice for *thosai*, and then to selling them from a street stall for ten cents each. He lived at 40 Poplar Road, in the midst of a world in flux. People came and went from India. Their trunks carried cloth and gold; some of their hearts carried the bitterness of broken dreams.

Life in the city was more open than in the sequestered world of the rubber plantations. In town, family contacts were as likely as labor recruiters to land new arrivals a job. Wages were good—good enough to afford cinema tickets, cigarettes, and other pleasures. As a city of immigrants, Singapore in the early twentieth century had much in common with New York or Buenos Aires, in that the layout of neighborhoods in all three cities were palimpsests of successive migrations. Lodging houses and clubs furnished support, information, and social life to newcomers from home. Singapore's coffee shops sold toddy for ten cents a bucket, the better for lonely and hardworking young men such as Ramasamy to forget their troubles; they ate "fish curry, murukku, vadai, idli, thosai," and they drank. They listened to news from home and from the world around them. "Men would read the newspaper aloud," Ramasamy recalled. "Large groups would gather around the paper reader, and then they would go to bed." Sound recordings, too, crossed the Bay of Bengal. "People would put on the radios in the food shops," and Ashok Kumar's songs filled the air.

Ramasamy found himself among kinsmen and strangers. At first glance their world was a microcosm of South India: men from Thanjavur would congregate on one street corner, men from Tirunelveli on another. But their spheres were never self-contained. They jostled against one another. This society of Indian migrants—mostly male, mostly transient—met the even larger world of Chinese migrants in Singapore: a world very similar in some of its characteristics, yet with a different social and institutional structure.[1]

The encounter between Indians and Chinese in Malaya attracted attention from distant shores. Writing from across the Indian Ocean, in South Africa, Gandhi commented in 1905 that "Singapore can be said to be as near to the Chinese as it is to [India]." "Despite this," Gandhi lamented, "our people there cannot hold their own against the Chinese." The Chinese were wealthier than Indians in Singapore and, Gandhi pointed out, "some even own motor cars." Gandhi told the readers of *Indian Opinion* that the number of Chinese arrivals in Singapore the previous year was nearly ten times greater than the number of people who came from India. "This shows how much is yet to be achieved by our people in the matter of emigration to, and settling in, foreign territories," he wrote; "it is a shame that we cannot keep abreast of the Chinese." As Indian and Chinese public figures considered their place in a world of nations and empires, emigration was for them a matter of pride and anxiety.[2]

After the crescendo of trade and migration in the early twentieth century, World War I dented traffic across the Bay of Bengal. The German cruiser SMS *Emden* moved into the eastern Indian Ocean in September 1914, attacked the British merchant fleet, and closed the shipping lanes from Colombo to Singapore. Under the command of Captain Karl von Müller, the *Emden* launched a surprise attack on oil installations and merchant ships in Madras harbor on September 22, and targeted Penang at the end of October. The ship finally ran aground in battle with an Australian cruiser around the Cocos and Keeling Islands in November 1914. For the first time in nearly a century, British dominance in the Bay of Bengal came under threat—but only briefly.[3] The sense of imperial insecurity deepened the following year, in February

1915, when soldiers of the Fifth Madras Light Infantry in Singapore mutinied. The troops were predominantly Punjabi Muslims, and they were inspired in their actions by the anticolonial publicity of the Ghadar movement—spearheaded by Indian exiles in North America who sought to use the war as a spark for insurrection in India. The revolt was subdued, and thirty-six of the mutineers were executed in public, before an audience of 15,000.[4] Around the same time, the tide of migration receded: in 1914, the number of Indian migrants departing Malaya exceeded the number of arrivals.[5] Immediately after the end of the war, the global influenza epidemic tracked the resumption of shipping across the Indian Ocean and the South China Sea, sweeping through Malaya and taking a heavy toll on the migrant labor force of the plantations.[6]

With the end of the postwar slump, trade and migration across the Bay reached, and soon exceeded, their highest prewar levels. In 1926 and 1927 Asian migration reached an all-time peak. In those two years, more than 150,000 people arrived in Malaya from India, and nearly 300,000 in Ceylon. The number of journeys from India to Burma exceeded 400,000 each year from 1926 to 1929, with a peak of 428,300 arrivals in Burma in 1927. The peak of Chinese migration to Southeast Asia was reached the same year, involving more than half a million people. The Chinese moved more widely than the Indian emigrants, who tended to stay within the British Empire; Chinese migrants journeyed to Indonesia, Vietnam, Thailand, Australia, and North and South America—but they arrived in Malaya in the greatest numbers. In 1926, as hundreds of thousands of migrants from India and China disembarked from the steamers in port, their countrymen working on the docks unloaded ships' cargoes of cattle and birds' nests, salted fish and arrack, several million dollars' worth of opium, nearly 4 million books and maps, 48,391 cinematographic films, 232 printing and bookbinding machines, 2,448 typewriters, 46,848 sewing machines, 8,454 cars, and nearly 3 million tons of car parts—plus 531 pistols and revolvers.[7]

The years between the wars marked the juncture where the life of the Bay of Bengal merged fully with the "Asian Mediterranean": the maritime world that reached from southern China to Indonesia.[8] From this encounter came new forms of urban life and a great deal of cultural mixing and intellectual creativity. But tensions simmered—conflict loomed between ever-greater integration and louder assertions of national or cultural difference.

The commercial economy of the Bay of Bengal transformed the ecology of its entire coastal rim. This change reached inland, along the banks of the Irrawaddy River, and into the highlands of the Malay Peninsula. The sea's "metabolism" dislodged the soil and moved it long distances in the form of rice, rubber, and tea; it dislodged the young men of southeastern India and began their circular journeys across the Bay. To serve the demands of this traffic, so central to the expansion of trade and markets, the port cities of the Bay grew into large conurbations, propelled by migrant labor. The cities cast a wider net than the plantations. Traders crossed the sea as their fathers and grandfathers had done before them; merchants set up businesses and opened shops; artificers and craftsmen found new demand for their skills; laborers took their chances and ventured overseas. Migrant workers made modern cities of fishing villages and old imperial courts, just as today they raise cities from the desert sands of the Persian Gulf. And then, as now, these were cities full of strangers who spoke different tongues and ate different foods.[9]

The cities were strangely disorienting places for some who encountered them, though just as many people found their bright lights immediately seductive. Because of the sheer speed of their development, the port cities appeared, to those discomfited by them, as alien growths upon rural societies. When Rabindranath Tagore stopped in Rangoon on his way to the United States, in May 1916, he saw that "the city of Rangoon is not a city of Burma, it appears to stand in opposition to the entire country. . . . This city has not grown like a tree from the soil of the country."[10] Tagore's response is unsurprising: Rangoon was in almost every respect an "Indian" city by the early twentieth century. Indian migrant workers made up three-quarters of the city's unskilled, and around 70 percent of its skilled workforce. For their part, Penang and especially Singapore were dominated by Chinese; in both places South Asians of many regional origins moved in and out, and an increasing number of them stayed. In all three cities, the "native" people—Burmese or Malay—were a small minority.

The port cities of Southeast Asia, Singapore and Rangoon in particular, grew faster than the cities of South India. They were an overseas urban frontier for India and China, as much as for their immediate hinterlands. Such was the intensity of connection across the Bay of Bengal that the Madras-born populations of Rangoon, Singapore, Penang, and Colombo were greater, in each case, than the overall population of most South Indian towns, few of which had more than 100,000 inhabitants. The number of South Indians living in cities across the Bay was greater than the South Indian population of *any* Indian city outside Madras Presidency, including even Bombay. For millions of people along India's southeastern coast, the world they knew stretched east across the Bay more than it stretched north and west across the Indian subcontinent; their first journeys to the city were also, often, journeys overseas.

"Till recently second only to New York in importance as an immigration port," a British labor official wrote in 1933, Rangoon "now occupies pride of place as the first immigration and emigration port of the world."[11] It was from observing social life in Rangoon that John Sydenham Furnivall devised his description of the "plural society." After a long career as a scholar-administrator in Burma, Furnivall had retired in the 1930s; he sold Fabian literature from a stall in Rangoon's Scott Market, and compiled more systematically the social observations he had published in essays over many decades. "The first thing that strikes the visitor," Furnivall wrote of Southeast Asia's port cities, with Rangoon foremost in his mind, "is the medley of peoples—European, Chinese, Indian and native," but "it is in the strictest sense a medley, for they mix but do not combine. Each group holds by its own religion, its own culture and language, its own ideas and ways. As individuals they meet, but only in the marketplace, in buying and selling." Furnivall's description resonates across the decades. It has remained a touchstone in studies of urban Southeast Asia; my own students in twenty-first-century London often read it as a prophetic description of the hyperdiverse but divided city they inhabit today.[12] But Furnivall's account is an artifact of its time and place: it was a product of 1930s Rangoon, which had experienced severe economic contraction and interethnic violence. It would be a mistake to turn Furnivall's description into a timeless account of Southeast Asia's port cities.

Indian migrants arrived in Rangoon on ships that remained overcrowded and often squalid—"the tween or lowermost deck is nothing better than a black-hole," Gandhi had written upon inspecting an emigrant ship in 1929. They arrived, most of them, "with only a mat and an earthen receptacle which contained their food for the voyage." They disembarked in a port where the lightermen, launch operators, ship's chandlers, and dockworkers were all from India, too. And they arrived to be fleeced by Indian porters (or "baggage coolies"). A notorious court case in the early 1920s brought to light the existence of a "bribe book" kept by the port authority, showing the complicity of every level of the organization in the extortion of money from deck passengers; the culprits tried, unsuccessfully, to deny knowledge of the practice, and they even sued their accuser for libel.[13]

Rangoon sprawled across an extensive waterfront, "extending from the Hlaing river on the west right round by the south to the Pazundang Creek and the Pegu river on the north-east." The waterfront was ringed with jetties, where workers loaded and unloaded steamboats and sampans. Moving out from the city center, one saw the smokestacks of Burma's factories, mills, and oil refineries. By 1928 Burma had nearly a

Figure 17 Crossing Rangoon harbor toward Dalah; in the 1920s, Dalah was a thriving shipyard, and Rangoon was the world's greatest port of immigration. *Photograph by Sunil Amrith.*

thousand factories, employing more than 100,000 people; almost half of them worked in rice mills. The labor market was segmented by ethnicity, regional origin, and class. A self-replicating pattern of specialization was evident by the early twentieth century. Telugus were in a clear majority among Indian migrants to Burma, and they formed the labor corps of Rangoon—they worked the mills and factories, they worked as porters and carriers, as rickshaw and handcart pullers. More locally still, men (and a few women) from Nellore district provided "the bulk of the sweepers found in Rangoon and its suburbs." Tamils in Rangoon specialized in clerical work, and in its outskirts they worked in the rice mills and the coal mines. Oriyas formed the "bulk of the railway and public works department labour," and the boatmen of Orissa had a significant presence in Rangoon's harbor. Chittagonians, many of whom crossed the land and river border rather than arriving by sea, were prominent in the dockyard workforce—they worked as pilots and stevedores, and they crewed the launches. The Irrawaddy Flotilla Company employed "10,000 to 15,000 Chittagonians, dependent on the season, as deck and engine room hands"; in comparison, there were under a hundred Europeans on the Company's payroll, though inevitably they dominated the senior positions "as commanders and chief engineers."[14] Middle-class Bengalis, most of them Hindus, staffed the colonial administration and provided skilled technical labor for the foundries and factories; Punjabis worked as "artificers, turners, and overseers" on the railways, in the motor workshops, and in the dockyards. Entry to these fields of employment was guarded jealously.[15]

The hundreds of thousands of Indian laborers who arrived in Rangoon left home for periods ranging from a few months to a few years; not many of them stayed longer than five. When they landed in the city, they found lodging in cramped and unsanitary tenements, twenty or more to a room. English and Indian observers described the misery of Rangoon's working poor in a familiar idiom that drew on the imagery of the "dark satanic mills" of London or Chicago. One of the most detailed accounts of Rangoon's underbelly comes from E. J. L. Andrew, who had worked as the city's assistant protector of immigrants and served on many of the commissions of inquiry that the Rangoon Corporation undertook in the 1920s. "Anyone who cares to visit some of the side streets of the town inhabited by the coolies after ten o'clock at night," he wrote, "will realize the truth of conditions which he would

otherwise have found incredible." ("Incidentally," Andrew added ironically, the intrepid visitor would "see a phase of the night life of this
great city.") The "steady boom in house and land values" had put decent
housing out of reach of most working people. Andrew cited case after
case of workers living in "dilapidated" conditions; their houses were
"dismal, dark, filthy, and badly ventilated." He expressed "astonish-
ment" that employers and local government in "an important industrial
and commercial center" such as Rangoon should be so neglectful of the
need for affordable housing. When the Rangoon Corporation's health
officer, Dr. K. L. Dalal, was interrogated about the city's sanitation by a
municipal committee of inquiry, he insisted that the Corporation's slum
clearance plan was "tyranny" when people had no alternatives. "Where
are people to go?" he demanded when the committee asked him why he
had not evicted residents of substandard housing. "Am I to throw them
out on the street?" As the committee's questions grew fanciful, Dalal
responded with dark humor. One member asked, "If two-thirds of the
most insanitary classes were removed from the town, do you not think
the health of Rangoon would be a very simple matter?" Dalal replied, "If
you remove all the poor there will be no necessity for the health department." Singapore was little better: new arrivals from India lived forty or
fifty to a house in Tanjong Pagar and Serangoon Road. Tuberculosis was
a perennial hazard.[16]

Rangoon's migrant workforce found a fearless champion in Narayana
Rao. Rao, an economist from the Telugu-speaking region of Madras, arrived in Burma in 1920. Within three years of his arrival, he sat on the
Legislative Council as the representative for Rangoon East; he served
intermittently until 1928. Rao's voice was impassioned, his tone biting
and ironic. "The Indian is not welcome, but his money is quite welcome,"
Rao observed during a debate on whether to impose a tax on arriving
passengers.[17] Rao edited the *Karmika Patrika,* a weekly journal that
exposed the malpractices of *maistries* and recruiters. He was involved
in the "bribe book" case, a defendant in the libel suit brought (unsuccessfully) by the British India Steam Navigation Company. He champi-
oned the cause of Rangoon's Telugu rickshaw pullers in 1923, proposing
a bill in the Legislative Council to regulate the trade, and he organized
cartmen's and bag lifters' associations in 1928. British authorities saw
him as a dangerous figure and kept him under surveillance; in 1930,
after interethnic violence on the docks of Rangoon, they expelled him

to India. He returned to Burma a year later and continued his efforts, publishing an exhaustive and passionate account of Indian labor in Burma. "Burma could not have built her splendid Railway systems, cleared her inaccessible, extensive forests and transformed them into smiling fields, operated her factories amidst dust, fumes and high temperatures," he argued, "but for these patient, long suffering, obedient, faithful and grateful but much maligned sons of India."[18] Rao's is yet another fragmentary biography—he was an insightful commentator on his world of the Bay of Bengal, and a courageous advocate for the rights of migrant workers, but his story remains incomplete.

Tensions simmered beneath the appearance of ceaseless activity; they erupted in May 1930, as the world economic depression arrived in Rangoon. Protesting against a cut in their wages, Indian dockworkers went out on strike; in response, the shipping company brought in a group of Burmese workers to replace them. After negotiations, the Indian dockworkers returned to the job, only to find that their Burmese counterparts were there, too. A fight broke out between the two groups of workers, and quickly developed into a more serious conflict. Violence consumed Rangoon. Groups of Indians were targeted by large mobs. At least 120 Indians were killed and about 900 injured in the fighting. Narayana Rao estimated that up to 25,000 Indian "women, men and children left their homes and sought protection in public schools and buildings." Since most of the city's sanitary workers were Indian migrants, "sanitary service was paralysed, and the city was rotting in filth."[19] The violence in Rangoon was an isolated episode, but it dramatized the political and economic fault lines beneath the Bay's web of connections.

The world of the Bay of Bengal was, for centuries, a world of men. Men crossed the sea while women stayed behind. In the eighteenth and nineteenth centuries Muslim traders from South India maintained families on both sides of the Bay as they made second wives of local women. Intermarriage was less likely, and less possible, once tens of thousands of young men from India and China arrived in Southeast Asia, most of them of humble background and limited means. In 1911 there were just three women to every ten men within the Indian community in Malaya, and even fewer in Burma; overseas Chinese society was more imbalanced still. Indian nationalists feared that "frightful immorality" would result from the absence of women among the migrants: they repeated this often in the debate over indentured labor. "Their moral degradation is indescribable," an Indian newspaper wrote of Malaya's plantation workers in the early 1920s, expressing a common view. "There is hardly a place where ten males have more than a single female."[20] British officials, like elite Indian men, saw vice wherever they turned. "No Tamil women can go to the Federated Malay States and return with a rag of reputation left," one Madras official declared.[21]

The problem of housing was inseparable from the question of family life—what new forms would it take in a society of transient people? The struggles of factory workers and rickshaw pullers were joined by the struggles of women workers to make a living overseas; public violence on the streets was mirrored by violence behind closed doors. Where the Indian Ocean met the South China Sea, where millions of young men struggled to make a living far from home, pimps and hustlers and brothel keepers saw their opportunity. The demand from Southeast Asia for young women from China was so great by the turn of the twentieth century that it could hardly be met. The poverty that drove young men to seek their fortunes overseas impelled desperate parents to send their daughters away with recruiters—"seamstresses" or madams, flush with cash—who roamed the countryside. Working women passed through a familiar network of brokers and creditors. But the vulnerability of women in the sex trade was acute and probably exceeded even the worst conditions that male tin miners or rubber tappers faced. Most Chinese prostitutes ended up in the brothels of Singapore; from there, many went on to other destinations in the region. They suffered unimaginable violence and abuse, which worsened the farther they traveled from Singapore.[22] The movement of women across the Bay of Bengal to work as prostitutes was similarly widespread, and they moved to Burma in the greatest numbers. Violence was an unremitting feature of these women's lives, but no more than indentured laborers were they simply victims of circumstance.

In the migrant worlds across the Bay, a complex ecology of relationships developed between men and the much smaller number of women in their midst—from prostitution through many forms of temporary relationship to marriage. The boundary between commercial sex work, on one hand, and domestic or entertainment work, on the other, shifted with time and circumstance. As so often happens, most women who crossed the Bay left no written or oral record of their journeys—we see them through the eyes, and through the prejudices, of men in authority. But some observers were more perceptive than others, among them the retired protector of immigrants, E. J. L. Andrew. "The life of a prostitute is pitiable in the extreme," Andrew wrote. He recounted the central role of labor recruiters in this, as every other, path of migration across the Bay. "Once in the power of a keeper the girls are not allowed freedom of any kind," he noted, "and they eventually become wrecks."

Yet Andrew recognized the wide variety of relationships that developed in this migrant society; he even allowed for the possibility of love. "In many cases the alliance is based on sentiment," he wrote of the temporary relationships that were a common feature of social life in Burma, but in other cases "a peculiar system of selling women is common." A laborer returning to India (very often to his wife and children) would "sell" his local mistress to another man, "reserving his right to purchase her on his return." Andrew observed that it was usual for a woman to cook for and look after a group of men, but insisted that it was unusual for such women to maintain sexual relationships with more than one of the men in the house. Some Indian observers suspected otherwise; one journalist alleged that "gangs of dock labourers employ a single woman to cook their food for them, and use the same women for the purpose of prostitution. These things are told to me openly, shamelessly."[23] "Shame" is a recurrent theme in Indian nationalist discussions of women in the diaspora; the struggles and aspirations of the women themselves rarely entered the equation. Least likely of all to be discussed—both at the time and subsequently—was the presence of sexual relationships between men. Only on one occasion—amid thousands of pages of official correspondence, reams of newspaper reports, and hours of oral interviews—have I seen reference to the possibility of homosexual relationships, and that reference is colored by innuendo and ethnic stereotype: Chittagonian migrants in Burma, Andrew wrote, "are stated to be addicted to an evil the knowledge of the practice of which would bring them within the pale of the law."

Patterns of labor recruitment reinforced ethnic segmentation. The *kangany* system matched localities in South India with specific Malayan plantations; Indians worked the rubber plantations, while Chinese worked the tin mines. The same was true when it came to the traffic in women. The variety of the migrant populations of Southeast Asia's port cities was reflected in the sex trade. Many of the Japanese prostitutes *(karayuki-san)* in Southeast Asia, for instance, served only Japanese clients. A similar pattern was evident in Burma. The "Oriya hotels" of Rangoon provided for "the comforts of the thousands of Oriyas that pass through," including the provision of Oriya prostitutes. Some "Tamil" brothels in Rangoon were "open only to Chettiars": for the most part, to those Chettiars not wealthy enough to "keep women of the weaver class from Madura and adjacent districts of Madras presidency," as their richer brethren did.[24] But on the whole, the sex trade was no respecter of racial boundaries. A Cantonese prostitute put it quite simply in her testimony to a Singapore court: "My customers are of various nationalities, including Tamils."[25]

The men who wrote about women, steeped in patriarchy and obsessed with "immorality," looked askance at every sign of independence on the part of Indian or Chinese migrant women. But in the open, urban world of the port cities, affective relationships thrived—and with them the pain of loss and separation. Often the details of these relationships made their way into the archives only when things went horribly wrong. They are found most often in the coroner's inquests that pried into the lives of those who had died suspicious or unexplained deaths.[26] Hundreds of such cases remain in the National Archives of Singapore, each drama of suffering cataloged by serial number; the series is incomplete, and browsing through it left me with the uncomfortable sense of being a voyeur to other people's pain. But such records go where official reports do not, touching on regions of life that almost every oral history would rather suppress, and so they provide us with a richer picture of the social world that emerged at the confluence of Asia's great oceans.

For many working people in Singapore, the ordinary tensions of domestic life were compounded by debt and sharpened by a visceral lack of privacy. "The rooms are partitioned off with wooden latches covered in paper and above the wooden partition is sacking," said the landlord of 27-1 Sambau Street after two of his tenants had met violent deaths: a Tamil man killed his wife and then himself. The inhabitants of neighboring rooms—a Malayali couple, a Tamil man, and a Chinese man—claimed to have heard nothing, but they whispered, all the same, about the visitors the murdered woman would receive during the day while her husband was out at work. In a world where people moved house and even changed their names from year to year, relationships were often built on deception. Many were the cases of violence sparked by one partner's discovery that the other had a spouse and children elsewhere, across the sea in India or China, or in the Malayan hinterland. Relationship breakdown ranked alongside debt as the most common cause of suicide in the coroner's inquests, and very often the two were connected. "He has a wife and children in India so he may have sent the money to them," one woman testified after her partner's death. "I am only his mistress. His wife doesn't know that he kept me here." And reunion could be as devastating as separation. "There is no return after departure," a Chinese woman wrote to her mother-in-law back in China. She had arrived to join her husband in Singapore, only to find that "[he] had changed greatly in his conduct of life. He indulged in gambling and prostitution and was unmindful of worldly affairs." In her tragic death—she committed suicide by hanging, pregnant with her third child—we are reminded how much of life is lost when we abstract migrants into statistics and talk only of "networks" and "webs" and "flows."[27]

Love could transcend ethnicity, only to founder on dishonesty. Such was the case of a Tamil clerk in Singapore's public works department who fell in love with an actress from Medan; what he did not tell her was that he had a wife and children on a rubber plantation in Perak. When it all came apart, the man took his life in distress on the third of January 1937. A Chinese friend and colleague in the public works department told the coroner that "he was in love with a Malay woman who had left him to join a theatrical troupe"; her version of the story was that he had asked her to go see her parents in Medan while he sorted out a problem. Before his death, he left very specific instructions with his Chinese friend to "write to her, in Romanized Malay, what happened to me." His wife in Perak excused herself from attending the coroner's inquest, "on the grounds of penury."[28]

If relationships across the boundaries of ethnicity were widespread, ethnicity itself was plastic. Very often in the legal records the same individuals are identified by different witnesses as, alternatively, "Tamil Muslim" or "Boyanese" (from Bawean, in Sumatra). Others were "Malay" as well as something else: "Muslim Chinese," "Indian Muslim," or

"Java." However rigid the categories of the colonial census, in practice ethnic affiliation could be malleable and difficult to ascribe to others— and never more so than when it came to personal relationships. One of the saddest and strangest cases from the 1930s concerned the murder of a "Hailam woman," also described as "Malay" and as "China Islam," and known by many names. The web of her acquaintances—dramatized in the list of witnesses to the coroner's inquiry—was like a microcosm of Singapore's migrant society, including a Eurasian sailor (chief suspect in her murder), a Chinese water carrier and his wife (to whom the victim had given up her two-year-old daughter for adoption), a Tamil "municipal coolie" (witness to the broken door on her house), a Chinese pathologist, and Malay, Eurasian, Chinese, and Indian police officers.[29] In the end, the world of friendships, encounters, and violence that the victim and the witnesses inhabited proved too complex for the coroner to decipher: he delivered an "open" verdict.

Malaya's rubber changed the world. In 1910 Malaya produced 100,000 tons of rubber, accounting for 70 or 80 percent of the world market; by 1930 this had increased to 1 million tons. In the 1920s the American automobile market expanded so rapidly that it reached an average of one car per household; the 5.3 million cars manufactured in the United States in 1929, on the eve of the crash, called for 752,000 tons of rubber for tires, tubing, and gaskets, much of it coming from Malaya.[30] The Bay of Bengal's circuits of migration—themselves a product of both ancient and modern mobility—left an imprint on the urban cultures of most of the world. The rubber estates of Selangor and Perak fed the rise of Detroit. Rubber would eventually be found from other sources, including synthetic ones, but at the dawn of the automobile age, the connection between the Bay of Bengal's labor and North American manufacturing ushered in the beginning of humanity's fatal addiction to oil.

The cities of South and Southeast Asia themselves became enthusiastic consumers of automotive technology. The products of the Malayan forests arrived back on the streets of Singapore on cars, buses, and bicycles imported from the United States, Britain, and, increasingly, Japan. In Rangoon the first private cars appeared in 1905, with electric trams replacing noisy and polluting steam trams by 1908; buses arrived a few years later, and "by 1915, Rangoon had 8 buses, 139 motorcycles, 28 taxicabs, and 426 private cars and lorries operating on 183 miles of road." The tramways connected the docks, piers, and outer suburbs, and they were so popular that they were used even by monks collecting alms. In Singapore trolley buses proved more popular than trams, but there, too, new forms of transportation completely changed the city's geography.[31] India also embraced the automotive revolution: by 1936 British India had 123,315 registered motor vehicles, and the specter of chaotic traffic—noisy, unruly, and dangerous—haunted the streets.[32]

The speed of transit through urban life brought new risks as well as new pleasures. Traffic accidents were an alarming new pathology of modern times, and many people lost their lives on Singapore's roads. On April 19, 1921, Pavadi fell out of a truck, drunk, "returning from a joy ride in MacKenzie Road," and was killed by the truck behind. On October 2 of the same year, Sinappah, a telegraph messenger for the Eastern Extension Company, was run over in the middle of the night by a car driven by Haroon bin Abdul Rahman; Haroon had been hired by a couple with two small children to take them from the Sea View Hotel to Neil Road, and "felt a bump as though we had run over a piece of wood."[33] However smooth the roads, however fast the cars, drivers had to share space with pedestrians, bullock carts, and rickshaws, which invariably were blamed for traffic accidents. A member of the Rangoon Corporation complained that "this increase in the number of rickshaws has naturally affected the traffic problem of Rangoon, and has almost certainly resulted in an increase of accidents on the streets." The problem was that "the rickshaw is a popular form of conveyance and has been called the 'Poor Man's Motor Car.' It takes its passenger to his destination—a convenience in the rains—whereas the tramcars and motor buses are confined to fixed routes."

Even as motor transport colonized the roads, visitors to Singapore—as to each of the other port cities around the Bay—would have witnessed other, older ways of using the public streets. In 1931 Elizabeth Lewis, a writer and photographer for *National Geographic* magazine, visited Singapore to witness the annual *thimithi* procession—an act of atonement that involves devotees walking over hot coals. "We stepped into a twentieth century automobile and were whisked away to see an ancient rite," she wrote. Observed by "thronged" crowds of "Hindus, Chinese, Malays and others," the *thimithi* festival involved acts of willed pain on the public streets, celebrating the endurance of Draupadi in captivity. Lewis found the ritual performed with immense devotion. "When all seemed in readiness," she recounted, "we heard the sound of drums and a stir of excitement swept over the crowd. . . . Finally, the priests who held back the devotees began to lash them with whips, and one by one they made a dash, bare-footed, across the red-hot coals into the pool of milk." "The women," she observed, "seemed much calmer than the men."

After the experience of *thimithi*, Lewis decided to stay on to observe the performance of *thaipusam*, a ritual of penance in commemoration of Lord Murugan's victory against the demon Itumpan on Palani Hill. "Faith in the efficacy of these ceremonies is absolute," Lewis decided. She described a "martyr" being prepared for his three-mile "pilgrimage" to the Tank Road temple by "thrusting pins into his flesh. His chest, his back, his forehead and his thighs were entirely covered with small, shining, V-shaped pins." The "step of the devotees was elastic at the start, but grew slower as they proceeded," she wrote. "Sometimes the followers danced, sometimes chanted a weird chorus."

Lewis herself became part of the crowd, more so than she bargained for. "As the celebrants drew near, I pressed the button in an endeavour to put within the confines of a motion-picture film an indelible impression of the ceremony," she wrote. Jabbed inadvertently by a "spear-like needle" carried by one of the participants, she fell: "Down came my movie machine and there I was, in the centre of an excited mob." I have tried, and failed, to locate her film. Repeatedly Lewis emphasized the importance of the audience: "throngs wearing their brightest and best [clothes] . . . gazed with eager hopefulness." Having described the "self-torture" of the devotees, she concluded, oddly, that "the scene was closely related to a country fair." Similar processions took place in Penang and, perhaps most dramatically of all, in Kuala Lumpur, where they culminated in the Batu Caves—as they do to this day.[34]

Men and women traveled long distances to work in difficult, even unbearable conditions. But the city promised new opportunities for leisure and distraction as new forms of transportation loosened their segregated geographies. "Merchants have no business, workers have no work, and rubber has no value," a Singapore-based Tamil newspaper observed at the onset of the depression—but this had barely dented the sales of cinema tickets; cigarette sales had held up as well, and spending on liquor had not fallen. "Where," the writer wondered, "does all the money come from?" The economic depression of the 1930s—which hit export-dependent Malaya brutally hard—coincided with the rise of mass consumption, boosted by the development of the local advertising industry. For those who kept their jobs, falling prices brought desirable products within easier reach. In the Malay as well as the Tamil and Chinese press in Singapore, the slump saw companies marketing new goods. Sales of newspapers, journals, and theater tickets rose in times of economic adversity.[35]

Women—the "modern girls" of the port cities—were a clear target of the new advertising that filled the pages of newspapers and blared from billboards on the streets. Craven A Virginia cigarettes soothed the throat; Guinness Stout strengthened the constitution; Tiger Beer, a local entrant to the market in 1933, was good for the health, and its advertising targeted specifically Tamil and Malay women. Many of the advertisements were for healing potions, tonics, purgatives, and soaps. To be modern, in so much of Asia and Africa, was to be *clean*. Tiger Balm, a camphor ointment that remains popular in Singapore and around the world, was marketed to a Tamil audience in advertisements typeset in three languages: English, Chinese, and Tamil. Advertisements were themselves a testament to the circulation of things, and now brands, across the Bay of Bengal. The Aryan Book Agency of 212 Batu Road, Kuala Lumpur, published lists of the new Tamil novels it had received from India; authorized dealers of Columbia Records listed additions to their stock each month, drawing particular attention to the records of M. S. Subbulakshmi, the great Carnatic singer. And throughout the 1930s cinema advertising was most prominent of all. Film reels crossed the Bay, with films in Tamil, Telugu, and Hindi playing in theaters across Singapore and Malaya—the same theaters that also projected English, Chinese, and Malay films, making them among the most polyglot in the world at that time.

Migrants to the city remembered the 1930s as an age of consumption. In many oral histories, the prices of things—the passage out, a cup of coffee, a plate of rice and curry, a transistor radio, a bicycle—remain vivid in memory even after numerous other details have faded. "It was because of unbearable hunger" that A. N. Maideen traveled from the Tamil weaving village of Kadayanallur to Singapore in 1920 as a boy of seven, voyaging with his father and four others. But how much more open his story is than the circumstances of his migration would lead us to expect. Maideen left a self-published memoir, and he was interviewed for several hours (in Tamil) in the 1980s as part of an ambitious project by the National Archives of Singapore to compile the life histories of ordinary people. I listened to his oral history in the archives' overly air-conditioned reading room, on a scratchy cassette tape replete with the background noise of traffic and chirping birds. Places of public consumption and entertainment feature especially prominently in Maideen's memory. He remembers the profusion of Tamil Muslims in the food business, their stalls a site of interaction for working-class men from all communities. They served up plates of "rice and curry, mee goreng, rojak, mee siam, iced thanneer"; a culinary mix of Tamil Muslim, Tamil Hindu, Malay, Chinese, and Thai styles of cooking. Maideen was a regular at the Anson Road football stadium, where "the Calcutta Gymkhana team visited, and Hindus and Muslims played together," and at the horse races, on which he (and everyone else) would bet.

For Maideen, the cinema defined the era, as did the periodicals and the books of stories from India that he would line up to purchase as soon as they arrived. "The necessities for us were films, books, books of film songs," he remembered. From seven until midnight each day, the Empire Theater played silent films for fifteen cents; English films ran for a week each, and during the intermissions, vendors flooded the cinema halls, selling iced drinks and fried noodles. The first Indian talkie to arrive in Singapore, he said, was *Kalidas;* its soundtrack was partly in Tamil and partly in Telugu. New releases played at the Alhambra Theater and at the Capitol, where most people sat crowded together on benches, unable to afford the price of an individual seat. Enterprising gangs—conspicuously mixed in their ethnicity—bought up tickets to popular films and sold them at a profit on the black market. Maideen read voraciously, a habit inculcated in him by his teacher Abdul Rahman. "I used to follow the stories of Gandhi's salt *satyagraha,*" he recalled. He particularly enjoyed short stories—collections of twenty stories, each by a different author, were bundled together and sold for twenty-five cents. "A man ringing a bell" would announce the departures and arrivals of ships across the Bay of Bengal; new arrivals brought news from home—and a supply of magazines and newspapers from Madras.[36]

P. Singaram's *Puyalile Oru Thoni (A Boat in a Storm)* is perhaps the only great Tamil novel about the Southeast Asian experience of the first half of the twentieth century; it opens with evocative descriptions of this urban world of many diasporas. The setting for Singaram's novel was the Sumatran town of Medan; his imagination was shaped by his experience of Penang, where he lived in the 1930s and 1940s. Singaram writes that in the crowd of Mosque Street in Medan, "many melodies melded" (he uses the word *rakankal*, or *ragas*): the dulcet tones of Malay, and what this Tamil-speaker heard as the sharp staccato sounds (he uses the onomatopoeic *paraparapara* to describe them) of Chinese.[37]

On the plantations of the Malay Peninsula, a quiet but significant shift was under way in the 1920s and 1930s. Writing in 1936, the Malayan labor commissioner, C. Wilson, noted that "the recent slump brought to light an important social phenomenon that might have remained concealed . . . and that is the existence, over all the western States [of Malaya] of a large resident Indian population that has more or less settled down here." He cited reports of rubber tappers "refusing" repatriation to India when there was not enough work for them, insisting instead that they be given subsistence plots to farm until demand picked up again. The proportion of women migrating to Malaya crept up slowly beginning in the 1910s; by the mid-1920s, women made up on average a quarter of those who crossed the Bay to Malaya, though a much smaller proportion moved to the cities. The 1930s were a turning point. As the depression created mass unemployment, the Malayan government for the first time introduced restrictions on the entry of new migrant workers. Since women and children were exempt from these immigration rules, the 1930s saw a significant rise in the number of Indian and Chinese women in Malaya. Many moved to join their husbands, though a significant proportion of Chinese (and some Indian) women traveled as laborers in their own right. Families divided across the Bay of Bengal reunited when they realized that the old, circular patterns of migration were now subject to arbitrary reversals.

The 1930s saw an improvement in the gender balance among both the Indian and Chinese populations of Malaya. By the mid-1930s there were 515 women to every 1,000 men on Malaya's estates, whereas in 1911 there had been just 308. The number of local-born Tamil children, too, testifies to the shift: there were some 17,300 local births in 1934, and more than 21,000 in 1936. The census commissioner pointed out that the local-born were overwhelmingly likely to settle in Malaya. This brought Malaya more closely in line with Ceylon, where the Tamil plantation workforce had included a significant proportion of women for a much longer period, the migration of whole family groups was common, and the workers were more permanently settled. That pattern was a result both of Ceylon's proximity to India and of the different demands of tea as compared to rubber production.

The most optimistic British observers believed that caste would disappear as a result of emigration. "Emigration is a great teacher of self-respect, for caste is to a large extent put away when the Indian emigrant crosses the sea," the Madras census commissioner wrote in 1931, and he argued that "it is probably the existence of the emigration current that has contributed most to the growth of consciousness among the depressed classes in India."[38] In practice, caste distinctions did not disappear, but, just as in India, they changed. Barriers of purity and pollution were enforced on the estates, embedded in the architecture of the workers' housing and in hierarchical relations between *dalits* and those of higher caste. But social life on the plantations could be a leveler. Based on ethnographic research conducted on a Malaysian plantation in the 1960s—this retrospective study remains the best evidence we have—Ravindra Jain concluded that caste distinctions lessened over time, and that estate temples and their rituals played an incorporative role; workers, irrespective of their caste background, contributed to the upkeep of each plantation's Mariyamman temple. Marriages on the plantations became more widespread and, increasingly, took place across the lines of caste. Here the authority of the *kangany* remained strong: often his blessing would be required before a marriage could take place between workers, and invariably he officiated over the ceremonies—with or without the presence of priests.[39]

Tamil workers' claim to the land lay in the power of the temples that dotted the landscape; it lay in the landscape itself, which their labor had transformed from jungle into the ordered rows of plantation monoculture. Workers built grander, more permanent temples where once there had stood simple tree shrines. These temples affirmed an imaginative geography connecting the plantations with the workers' Tamil villages, while rooting them firmly in their locality. The South Indian temples of Malaya became more recognizably Malayan in the 1930s—in unexpected ways. A worker from the social research department of the Malayan government found, in 1936, that a temple in Negri

Sembilan had displayed on its altar "a figure representing 'Mickey Mouse'"; he interpreted this, not unreasonably, as the workers' way of evoking the world of modernity and consumption that wage labor promised to bring about. In Ceylon, for similar reasons, plantation workers were observed to have placed sewing machines on their altars.[40] In the 1930s Indian and Chinese sacred sites came together in a convergence of their attempts to make Malaya home. Chinese observers of the annual *thaipusam* procession became participants; shoreside temples continued as sites of interaction between different spiritual traditions.

Perhaps the biggest innovation in social life was the humble bicycle, which gave Tamil laborers a stake in social life beyond the plantations. Japanese-manufactured bicycles flooded the market in the 1930s, their tires, perhaps, made of the very rubber that the estate workers had tapped. A labor department official estimated in 1937 that half of all estate workers owned a bicycle, and he noted that this was "changing their habits." Mobility allowed Tamil estate workers to "mix easily with their Malay or Chinese neighbours," to "accumulate information," and to "improve their own standards." "The growing knowledge" of Malay "among Tamils has become marked in recent years," he concluded.[41]

The establishment of more-permanent Tamil settlements overseas did not lessen the connections that migrants maintained with their villages. The "habit" of migration transformed the migrants' home regions in India through a constant flow of people, investment, and ideas—in a sense, Malaya, Burma, and Ceylon became a more permanent part of the South Indian rural landscape. If overall emigration from India was small relative to population, consider that around 27 percent of the working-age male population of Tiruchi and of Tirunelveli had migrated for at least part of the period between 1921 and 1931. The first detailed social survey of rural South India, undertaken in 1918, made constant reference to the impact of emigration on the villages under study—and a further study in 1940 reached a similar conclusion. In the village of Eruvellipet, for instance, the survey concluded that "emigration to Ceylon opens out possibilities of very considerable economic advantage to the landless labourer or peasant with a very small holding and a large family." Of Kshetralampuram village in Tanjore District, researchers observed that "the whole Pariah population of this village consists of persons who have migrated at least once to foreign parts, such as Penang, Singapore and Mauritius. All of them have returned after a stay of one or two years in those parts." One British observer in the early 1930s noted that returning emigrants "bring back to their village some of the ideas on cleanliness, food and comfort acquired while abroad"; he wrote that he had "on several occasions had pointed out to me a house differing markedly from its neighbours as being that of some one who had been to Malaya or Ceylon." Such distinctions in housing can be seen in Tamil Nadu even today—just as they can be seen in those parts of Kerala that now depend on labor migration to the Middle East.[42]

By the early twentieth century, the scale and pace of Asian migration had given rise to new ways of imagining the world. Technology bridged distance. New ideas of citizenship refigured the link between land, migration, and political representation. Newspapers addressed, and in the process created, new publics: their debates, and their readership, crossed colonial and national borders. Benedict Anderson's analysis of the role of the daily newspaper in forging national consciousness—the sense of simultaneity and "mass ceremony" that it invoked within an imagined yet "inherently limited" community—remains a touchstone. Yet from a vantage point in the waters of the Bay of Bengal, Anderson's assumption that the *only* "imagined community" was the nation seems misplaced. The vernacular press in urban Southeast Asia spoke of— and spoke to—many "imagined communities," appealing to constituencies defined in local, regional, religious, and ethnic terms, which were not always mutually exclusive.[43]

The local press of the port cities was well established by 1900. The introduction of the movable-type lithograph sparked the proliferation of small-scale publishing in Southeast Asia starting in the 1870s.[44] Newspapers (most of them short-lived) and books (which ranged from manuals of Islamic instruction to genealogies of saints) flew off the presses of Singapore and Penang.[45] The press was as polyglot as the society it served. The first Tamil-language newspaper in the Straits Settlements, *Tankainesan* (Our Friend), appeared in 1876; it was edited by Muhammad Sa'id and published by the Jawi Peranakan company. The very same publishers started the first local Malay-language newspaper, the eponymous *Jawi Peranakan*.[46] The Tamil-Malay community of the Straits, descended from mixed marriages, stood quite naturally astride

the Tamil and Malay cultural worlds. In content, the early urban newspapers mirrored their world in motion. A typical issue of *Jawi Peranakan* began with a list of market prices, government circulars, and
notices from the government gazette; local news and correspondence
were followed by news from the surrounding region, "and it is worthy
of notice that so large a number of places contribute news from this
part of Malaya. Such names are found as Semarang, Serubaya, Bogor,
Pariaman, Menado, Bantan, Cherbun, Ambun, Karawang and Pulau
Banda." News of the world came from other newspapers (including the
Rangoon Times and the *London and China Express*); telegrams were "cop-
ied from the *Straits Times*" with stories from France and Russia and
Ireland and the Bolivian Republic.[47]

The Chinese press in the Straits was slower to develop, but it took off
in the 1880s. Some newspapers were printed in the romanized Malay
favored by local-born Peranakan Chinese, while others were written in
Chinese characters and still others in English, including the *Daily Advertiser* and the *Straits Chinese Magazine*. The newspaper *Lat Pau*—
established by See Ewe Lay, a Straits Chinese who worked for the Hong
Kong and Shanghai Bank—had 800 subscribers by the 1890s, and correspondents from Rangoon to Saigon.[48] The early newspapers of the
Straits were cosmopolitan in their production: most presses churned
out newspapers and books in many languages. Many of the early Tamil
Muslim publishing houses were backed by Tamil Hindu or Chinese
capital.[49] Penang's first Tamil newspaper, *Vidya Vicarini* (which debuted
in 1883), was mobile in a more literal sense: the press followed its
founding editor, poet Ghulam Kadir Navalar, back across the Bay of
Bengal to Nagore.[50]

The first of the early Tamil newspapers to survive in a full run is *Singainesan* (Friend of Singapore). It was published between 1887 and
1890 by the Denodaya Press, which also printed texts in English and
Malay. The very first edition declared (in English) that it was "designed
to commemorate the Jubilee of Her Majesty the Queen-Empress Victoria" and was dedicated to "the monarch whose sway extends to every
quarter of the globe, and whose beneficent reign will mark an epoch in
the history of the world"; it also contained a small dedication, in Tamil,
to Sultan Abdulhamid II, ruler of the Ottoman Empire and the symbolic leader of Muslims everywhere. Layers of loyalty were nothing
strange in the fluid cultural world of the port cities. In his insightful

analysis of its contents, Torsten Tschacher shows that *Singainesan* had subscribers across the Malay Peninsula, in Sumatra, Java, Siam, Indochina, and India. He shows, too, that the newspaper's authors addressed different audiences, and adopted shifting terms of self-identification. "Tamils," in the newspaper's terms, referred largely to Hindus; the term "Tamil Muslim" did not often appear. However, the paper did refer to "we Kling Muslims," and also to "Kling Hindus."[51]

In an early message to its subscribers, *Singainesan* vowed that "from now on, we will print news of Singapore, Penang, Melaka, Europe . . . Nagapatnam, Nagur, Karaikal, Madurai, Chennai [and] Jaffna," suggesting the span of its subscribers' interests. The layout of this newspaper, like that of all the others, resembled a collage. The juxtaposition of stories, from the serious to the trivial, from the proximate to the very distant, conveyed a sense of simultaneity and of worldliness: the globe was laid out on the page in columns and paragraphs. The order of news ranged from the local (the committee politics of local mosques and temples; cases in Singapore's high court; celebrations of the queen's jubilee by Singapore's Chinese associations; the racing results; robberies and murders and people running amok) to the regional (covering the Malay states, "Netherlands India," Siam, and Indochina) and from there to news of India, China, and Europe. *Singainesan* borrowed liberally from other newspapers, often English-language papers, and reproduced Reuters telegrams from around the world, encompassing everything from war reports to news of the king of Bulgaria. It gave its readers a history of Malaya's colonization—and a history of the Zulus. In its second year, the newspaper attracted more advertisers, including the Bombay Dispensary, and the Netherlands Trading Company.[52]

The early Tamil newspapers such as *Singainesan* were limited by their small audiences, and none of them lasted long. In the 1920s, as migration peaked, the Tamil-language press in Singapore, Penang, and Kuala Lumpur put down deeper roots—many of the newspapers founded in that decade are still alive today. Journalists, editors, and typesetters moved from coast to coast. Whereas at the turn of the century Tamil-speaking Muslims had dominated the press, by the 1920s Brahmin and elite non-Brahmin Tamils contended for leadership. The press became an arena for intensive debate on the future of the Tamil community in Southeast Asia. Two newspapers in particular emerged to dominate the Tamil public sphere. *Tamil Nesan* was strongly influenced by the politics of Indian nationalism and was edited by Narasimha Iyengar, a Tamil Brahmin.[53] *Munnetram* ("Forward" or "Progress"), its main rival, was edited by G. Sarangapany and projected a strong Dravidian message of social reform, setting the indigenous "Dravidian" peoples of South India against the "Aryan" Brahmin invaders from the north, and promoting Tamil cultural revival and social reform.[54] In its first year *Munnetram's* circulation was 1,500 copies; in its second year, that doubled.[55] In the 1930s Sarangapany founded *Tamil Murasu*, which remains to this day Singapore's main Tamil newspaper.

The editors of both papers had connections across the Bay. Narasimha Iyengar was born in Tiruchirapalli and in 1912 became a Congress Party volunteer in Madras. In 1915 he traveled to Rangoon to work in the accountant general's office. He dabbled in journalism, writing for the *Rangoon Mail* under pseudonyms and contributing the occasional "Current Chat" column. He was, the British authorities feared, "an intimate friend of political suspects." Iyengar then moved from Rangoon to Kuala Lumpur, where he became editor of the newspaper *Tamilakam*. He "always quotes very freely from the advanced Indian papers," complained the British agents who kept a careful eye on Iyengar's activities, and they warned that "the tone of his articles is open to exception." Iyengar's family, like so many at the time, was dispersed across the Bay: he had relatives in South India; one of his brothers, Rajam Iyengar, was manager of the Industrial Press in Kuala Lumpur; another brother, Seshadivi Iyengar, was a clerk in the financial commissioner's office in Rangoon.[56] In 1924 Narasimha Iyengar founded *Tamil Nesan*, which became the largest Tamil newspaper in Southeast Asia at the time. The man who would become his main rival, G. Sarangapany, followed a similar trajectory from commerce to journalism. He arrived in Singapore in 1924, aged twenty-one, to work as an accountant in a Tamil Muslim firm. He, too, gravitated toward journalism. In 1929 he launched *Munnetram* to challenge Brahmin dominance of public life and journalism in the Straits.[57]

The newspapers of the port cities grappled with the overarching issue of the age: the question of nationalism. By the early twentieth century, "nationalist reformers in China, Japan, and other places regarded the unified nation-state as the universal—not merely European—political form of modernity."[58] Nationalism provided the most persuasive way to discuss questions of freedom and political action across Asia, but it proved more limited as a way to capture the particular dilemmas of belonging provoked by migration. Though it spread around the world by borrowing and appropriation, the ideology of nationalism was never unalloyed. It coexisted with many other sorts of community and other circles of affiliation. Nationalist politics spread along the shipping lines and postal routes that crisscrossed the Bay of Bengal, but the experience of migration complicated the certitudes of nationalism, even as in other ways it made the pull of nation stronger.[59] By the 1920s, audiences in the port cities of Southeast Asia had front-row seats to the great dramas of Indian and Chinese nationalism, which had exploded into mass movements, but for the most part they remained spectators.

At an earlier moment in the development of nationalist politics in Asia, the links between homelands and communities overseas were closer. In the ferment of the early 1900s, Chinese reformers and revolutionaries, including Liang Qichao and Sun Yat-sen, crossed Southeast Asia to garner support among the overseas Chinese; the Ghadar movement raised arms and money for insurrection from Indian communities along the Pacific rim. But the Chinese revolution of 1911 set that country on a new course, as it was consumed by internal conflicts and the struggle to consolidate the new state. By the end of World War I, Indian politics, too, had undergone a transformation in scale. Under Gandhi's leadership, the Indian nationalist movement became an instrument of mass mobilization, and the Congress Party became a tightly organized political machine. Under these conditions, links between nationalist politics at home and Indian and Chinese communities abroad were harder to sustain. The institutions of mass politics—provincial assemblies, regional and local party branches—pulled the focus of politics toward the given boundaries of colonial and national territories. Gandhi's own transformation is revealing: though he forged his political career in South Africa, he reinvented himself upon his return to India as a figure much more rooted in the Indian soil, closer to the Indian peasantry than to the sea-facing commercial community into which he was born in Porbandhar.

Though concrete political links diminished, symbolic connections flourished. In this "age of mechanical reproduction," a profusion of images crossed the Bay of Bengal.[60] In the early 1920s a vogue for photographs of Gandhi and other Indian nationalist leaders swept

Malaya—their portraits appeared as prints or on calendars. British authorities watched nervously as nationalist images from Madras publishers made their way to Tamil Muslim vendors throughout the Straits and the Malay Peninsula. "Subversive" newspapers from the homeland followed. Muhammad Kassim, a shopkeeper in Klang, "is known to have imported a few copies of a book in Tamil entitled *Swaraj*," the Malayan intelligence service reported. Police spies noted obsessively the names of Tamil Muslim vendors of undesirable material, and they traced the stashes of print that crossed the Bay. "Booklets of songs and verse in praise of Indian leaders," they wrote, "are common in the three western states," and "those received so far originate from a press in Madurai." The symbols of Indian nationalism reached the writing desks of Penang's households. Notepaper "with a photograph of Gandhi in the top left hand corner" was sold in three shops in Penang—at an eating house on Campbell Road, at a moneychanger's on King Street, and by a "sundry shopkeeper" on Penang Street. The notepaper came from Ganesh and Company booksellers in Madras; the first shipment sold out quickly.[61] The flow of texts went in both directions—back to as well as out from India. Officials at the British customs post in Dhanushkodi watched anxiously as "objectionable" Tamil books flowed across the maritime border with Ceylon.[62]

The journeys of Indian thinkers and political leaders to Southeast Asia drew huge crowds and brought the images to life. On July 20, 1927, Rabindranath Tagore arrived in Singapore aboard the French ship *Amboise,* destined for Haiphong. His reception was enthusiastic and "attracted a large number of ordinary Indians—small traders; automobile drivers; security guards"—and every section of the local Indian community, from Tamil Hindus and Muslims to Sikhs and Sindhis. Tagore met with luminaries of the Straits Chinese community, including Dr. Lim Boon Keng. He traveled from Singapore to Melaka and Penang, where he delivered a public lecture on the perils of nationalism.[63]

More influential in this respect was the visit to Malaya of E. V. Ramasamy, known as Periyar, leader of the Self-Respect Movement in Madras. Ramasamy set sail for Penang from Nagapatnam in December 1929, accompanied by his wife, Nagammal, and a small entourage. He was fifty years old at the time of his journey. Four years earlier he had broken away from the Tamil Nadu Congress Party, which he had served as president, and founded the Self-Respect Movement to promote a radical program of caste reform and gender equality. His aim was to unseat Brahmin dominance in South Indian society.[64] On the invitation of a Malaya-based Indian association, Periyar took his message of reform to the cities and plantations of the peninsula, and "thousands of people attended every meeting at which he spoke." At the Tamils Reform conference in Ipoh in December 1929—the showpiece of his visit to Malaya—he called for Tamils in Malaya to "sink their differences of caste, and of the place whence they came," and "to love their mother tongue." He called on Tamils in Malaya to reform their religious processions "in accord with the times and the country (in which they are living)." He proceeded to Singapore, addressing a large reception at the New World entertainment complex; from there, Periyar moved through the Malay peninsula, addressing crowds in Taiping and Sungai Petani and visiting rubber plantations. Periyar's visit brought out the tensions of caste, faith, and social class that divided the Tamil communities of Malaya, and it highlighted the limitations of Indian nationalism overseas. His appeal in Malaya, as in Tamil Nadu, cut across religious lines. The orthodox Hindus of Penang pleaded with the colonial government to ban Periyar's visit to Malaya, offended by his assault on the caste hierarchy; Penang's Tamil-speaking Muslims welcomed his visit warmly.[65]

The polarized reactions to Periyar's visit mirrored the fault lines of Indian politics, but the Malayan setting gave them different contours. The tenor of anticolonialism was at a lower pitch in Malaya. Distance had a muffling effect on the clamor of Indian politics. Far from the heat of political conflict, it was easier for Singapore's Tamil journalists to focus on the excitement of mass politics itself. Ignoring the tensions between, say, the Self-Respect Movement and Gandhi, or between the Congress Party and the Muslim League, it was as if mass politics itself was what merited attention, especially when seen from sleepy Malaya. Editors and journalists feared censorship or even deportation—but many of them retained a more active loyalty to their British rulers, which they managed to combine with the nationalist sympathies they directed toward India. The idea of the Straits government as "clean" and efficient, allowing multiple communities to live together without undue interference, had a long life. More important, the concerns of the

Indian (and Chinese) diasporas in Southeast Asia were, at least in some respects, quite different from those of their countrymen at home.

Until the 1920s, the world of circulation around the Bay of Bengal was simply too fluid to sustain the sense of there being a lasting, settled Indian diaspora in Southeast Asia. This began to change as the media, and new social and political institutions, gave it a concrete reality and a presence in public life. Tamil diasporic consciousness filtered currents of Indian nationalism, blended them with the debates of local politics, and infused them with a regional imagination of a Tamil-speaking world across the Bay, rather than an "Indian" one. Diasporic consciousness was forged not only in distinction to nationalist and indigenous claims but also from the interaction between multiple diasporas.[66] In the port cities of Southeast Asia, shaped to an unusual extent by mobility, being part of a diaspora was, by the 1930s, an essential part of what it was to be modern.

Pride in the Indian nationalist movement made many in Malaya more likely than before to identify themselves as "Indians," but so, too, did their growing awareness of other Indian communities overseas, which developed gradually into the consciousness of a global diaspora, connected laterally as well as vertically. In writing of the condition of Indians in South Africa, Fiji, Ceylon, and Burma, Tamil newspaper editors evoked a sense that Indians in Malaya formed part of a broader dispersion of people who shared similar problems and struggled together for equal status and recognition.

Through the steady accumulation of detail, in tones both plaintive and informative, the Tamil newspapers of the Straits Settlements outlined a world of Indians overseas. The condition of Indians in South Africa, where white supremacy denied them rights and respect, attracted regular comment.[67] A feature on the Indian diaspora in Fiji took a different tack and cited a flurry of statistics: the 76,722 Indians there owned 110,000 acres of land, 776 shops, 196 motorized trucks, 6 music halls, and 2 newspapers.[68] Closer to home, the "loot and murder" faced by Indians in Burma evoked in the 1930s a sense of threat. Burma was, after all, part of the same Bay of Bengal world as Malaya, its fate a portent of a dark future. An impassioned editorial in *Munnetram* wrote of the suffering of Chettiar moneylenders in Burma, who had been singled out by radical Burmese nationalists; Chettiars "do not understand why the Burmese have such hatred for them," the newspaper wrote, while granting that the Chettiars had amassed "limitless" amounts of money. Like the Chinese and the Sinhalese, the editor wrote, the Burmese claimed to follow Buddhist principles but seemed far from living up to them. Until the Burmese government brought the perpetrators of the atrocities to justice, *Munnetram* declared, "Indian newspapers" throughout the world had a responsibility to draw attention to the situation.[69] A sense of fellow-feeling and shared responsibility emerged within the diaspora—together with a sense that Indians overseas shared experiences that politicians at home in India did not quite understand.

If comparisons with Indian communities elsewhere in the world lent a global frame to discussions of Indians' problems in Malaya, local debates sharpened a more specific sense of Tamil diasporic consciousness at the point where the Tamil diaspora encountered others in Malaya. The Tamil diaspora's self-appointed spokesmen confronted a strident Malay nationalism that questioned their right to live in Malaya. Early in 1932, the Malay newspaper *Majlis* attacked "foreigners" in Malaya: the government should inform Indian and Chinese migrants to Malaya, the paper declared, "that the 'protection' of the Malays isn't like the protection of the deer in the forest by the game warden, who sees to it that the deer isn't killed by hunters but allows it to be preyed upon by other enemies such as the tiger and other carnivorous animals living in the same forest."[70] The editors of *Tamil Nesan* responded immediately, and in the process defined more sharply the boundaries of the Tamil diaspora in Malaya.

The editors of *Tamil Nesan* berated *Majlis* for its "childish" editorial, which they characterized as a cry of "Malaya for the Malays." The newspaper reminded its readers that it was migrants from South India and China who had "struggled to clear the forest . . . attacked by tigers and bitten by mosquitoes," and who had worked the tin mines and the rubber estates; they were overwhelmingly responsible for Malaya's prosperity and development. Of particular concern to *Majlis* was the fact that Tamils and Chinese in Malaya maintained bonds with their lands of origin or ancestry. The editors of *Tamil Nesan* expressed dismay that *Majlis* impugned such "great personages" as Gandhi and Sun Yat-sen in condemning the destabilizing effects of foreign political ideas on Malaya. *Majlis* appeared to think that "people can be blind and deaf to the world around them," the editors argued, yet they asked whether one could really "sit idly and ignore" the world. Indians and Chinese could never develop "devotion to the country" (*desa bhakti*), the article concluded, "if they have no life in the country of their birth." Among those born in Malaya, there was "no law in God's court" to discriminate between Malays and others.[71] The conflict over the entitlements to citizenship in Malaya—diasporic claims as opposed to indigenous ones—posed stark choices for those caught between the two. Tamil Muslims, and particularly those who had intermarried with Malay families over generations, found themselves rejected by Malay nationalists, deemed not to be *betul Melayu,* or "truly Malay," while sitting outside the bounds of the Tamil diaspora as it now emerged.[72]

The defense of the rights of Tamil residents in Malaya against the demands of indigenous nationalism soon translated into a more assertive claim to citizenship. At the heart of the argument was the proposition that Malaya's entire history had been shaped by migration, and that entitlements to citizenship had to recognize this; before the great migrations from India and China, there was no civitas, only jungle. "Let us try to understand," one Tamil journalist wrote in 1935, "that not long ago Malaya was nothing but a jungle land with only some scattered fishing villages, there was no civilization, culture or tradition."[73] In search of a historical narrative to support their claims, Tamil writers in Malaya—many of them writing in English—invoked the notion of "Greater India" (the idea that Malaya and most of Southeast Asia was deeply shaped by Indian cultural influence, even Indian "colonization") in order to argue that "Indians are not foreigners in this part of the world, and . . . their traditions are not alien to this land."[74] Conversely, Tamil writers began to challenge the Malay claim to indigeneity, arguing that "the correct meaning of the term 'Malay'" is "an immigrant from Java or Sumatra belonging to the race called 'Malay.'"[75]

Tamil leaders in Malaya urged that the number of fresh arrivals from India should be curtailed in the aftermath of the economic depression that devastated the rubber industry after 1930.[76] Their argument for limits to fresh immigration from India crafted a sharper distinction between "local-born" (that is to say, Straits- or Malaya-born) and "foreign" (or India-born) Tamils in Malaya. In the words of the Singapore-based Tamil Brahmin journalist R. B. Krishnan, there was a difference in "attitude and mental ability" between local-born Tamils and "their India-born brothers." "Their native country is Malaya," he wrote of the local-born, "and their interests, life and associations are entirely Malayan and local." The "Malayan Indian," he insisted, "has a better and more tolerant outlook than his compatriot born in India. For example, he is ignorant of, or if not ignorant he contemptuously disregards, the silly notions of caste and creed held across the Bay."[77]

When Jawaharlal Nehru visited Singapore in 1937, thousands lined the streets to greet him. He insisted that the future of Indians in Malaya was "intimately and irrevocably bound up with the future of India, and on India's freedom depends their status, the protection of their interests, and the place they occupy in the world."[78] But he also warned Indians in Malaya—as he would do again when he became India's first prime minister—that their future lay in Malaya, not in India. In a letter to the editor of the *Straits Times*, the newspaper of Singapore's European elite, a Singapore-based Tamil writer urged Tamils in Malaya to rethink their connections with the other side of the Bay:

> So long as he considers himself to be a sojourner here, and allows only his carcass to move about here allowing his soul to cross the Indian waters and wait there anxiously for that blessed day when he can return, so long will he be looked upon with some suspicion and consequently never expect the status of a native or a domiciled citizen in this country.

Members of the Tamil diaspora in Malaya, he argued, "must boldly choose one of the two alternatives—and consequently stand for the chances a sojourner might get, or be a full-fledged citizen."[79] Within the settled Straits Chinese community of Singapore and Penang, a similar plea went out. Lim Cheng Ean, a member of Penang's Legislative Council, told his audience at a local school that "you must do your best to smash the idea that this is not our country. . . . If you do not wish to do so, you are free to pack your belongings and go back to China leaving we Straits-born Chinese here alone so that our position may not be jeopardised."[80] This was in practice an exceedingly difficult and painful choice for many to make.

Few among the millions who crossed the Bay of Bengal joined political movements; more of them resorted to protest in the workplace, as chapter 6 will show. A still-larger number asserted themselves by writing petitions to the authorities, detailing their struggles and the injustices they faced, or even taking their grievances to the courts. Nationalist sentiment fired the hearts of many thousands who lived, either temporarily or more permanently, outside their homeland. But the question of *nationality*—a term in wide use across the British Empire, though never fully defined—was a more practical matter bound to the question of political representation.

Starting at the turn of the twentieth century, Indian professionals, civil servants, and merchants in Malaya had formed small associations to represent their views to the authorities.[81] The first of these was the Taiping Indian Association, formed in 1906, soon followed by the Selangor Indian Association in 1909.[82] Singapore and Penang housed countless social and sports clubs, including the Peranakan Club, the Mohammedan Cricket Club, the Muslim Recreation Club, and the Singapore Mohammedan Football Association; village and regional groups, such as the Tenkasi Muslim Association and the Kadayanallur Muslims Association; and commercial, cultural, and caste organizations, including the Muslim Merchants' Society of Penang and numerous Nattukottai Chettiar associations (the last of these were found in a wide area, from Rangoon to Singapore and throughout Malaya). These societies bridged religious and secular purposes, with cross-cutting concerns and overlapping memberships.[83]

For those far from home, the choice of nationality—Indian, Chinese, Burmese, or Malayan—assumed tangible importance. The question of citizenship preceded the expansion of democracy. Citizenship mattered in practical terms because it determined to whom people could turn for justice. The Indian and Chinese imperial governments asserted themselves more forcefully in support of their subjects overseas; in doing so, they made claims on their subjects' loyalty and placed restrictions on their movements. After World War I, Indian authorities stepped up their interventions across the Bay of Bengal. The Indian Emigration Act of 1922 created offices of the government of India in Malaya and Ceylon. These agents—now Indian rather than British officials—acted increasingly as consular officers in foreign lands, even though they remained within the British Asian empire. Over the next decade the Indian agents in Malaya received thousands of letters, petitions, appeals, and visits from Indian laborers seeking their intervention in work and family disputes. In 1925 the first Indian agent in Malaya, Arulanandam Pillai, received an urgent telegram about the case of a young woman who claimed to have been held hostage and raped by the plantation manager of Tambang Estate in Johor, only days after she had arrived from India with her family to work there. The girl's father and brother, instead of going to the police, wrote directly to the Indian agent. Within days, what became known as the "Tambang Rape Case" had turned into a scandal, with the imperial government in New Delhi pressing the Malayan authorities for a prompt investigation; popular fears about the dangers that Indian women faced abroad seemed to be vindicated.[84] The accused plantation manager was eventually found not guilty, yet the case makes clear that many plantation workers were, by the 1920s, well aware of the structures of government that spanned India and Malaya; many chose to appeal directly to the government of India in times of distress.

Much of what was at stake emerges from a letter written to the Reverend C. F. Andrews—a veteran campaigner for the rights of Indians overseas, and a close friend and confidant of both Gandhi and Rabindranath Tagore—by three Tamil railway workers from Sentul (on the outskirts of Kuala Lumpur) in 1924, the year of his visit to Malaya. The railway workers said, "We live in a foreign country, hundreds of miles away from our motherland, among different races, with different culture and slowly but surely we lose our moral training." They echoed, directly, the language of Indian reformers who lamented the "demoralization" of Indian labor overseas. Taking a skewer to the motivations of Indians such as themselves who voyaged overseas to work, Andrews's correspondents lamented that "we live for money, money and money alone." The writers asked their "countrymen" in India "not that they should help us materially, but morally." They requested that Andrews encourage "the frequent visits to this country of some of our eminent countrymen of Congress fame." Reinforcing the concern of Indian reformers and nationalists, the Tamil railway workers wrote that their greatest shame lay in the fact that "not only to Europeans but to the Chinese, Malays, Eurasians and to a certain section of Ceylon Tamils, Indians (especially the Indian Tamils) are nothing but a nation of coolies."[85] The writers' concern illustrates, among other things, how powerfully a racial category of the colonial census, "Tamil," now grouped together urban elites and rural plantation workers, Muslims and Hindus, high caste and low caste, in a single representative category.[86]

But the Indian authorities soon recognized how limited their power really was. Often it was too late to intervene once emigrants had departed, and particularly once they were ensnared on the plantations. Colonial governments were too close to the planters to be reliable protectors of migrant workers' interests. It would be better to intervene, many felt, by preventing emigration altogether. This had been the response of the British Indian government after the initial outcry over the movement of indentured labor to Mauritius and the West Indies in the 1830s—though the decision was quickly reversed. Over a period of centuries the Chinese state had tried to impose a ban on emigration, though this had limited effect in practice. Rising nationalist sentiment underpinned hostility to emigration both in India and in China: why allow Indians and Chinese to travel overseas only to be exploited and humiliated?

From the Indian perspective, there emerged a new way of thinking about the economic rationale for overseas migration, until then seen as a necessary "safety valve" for India's growing population. World War I was the moment when an industrial future for India began to be debated, and when the aspiration for "development" within an enclosed national economy took hold of the political imagination.[87] "The gross wealth of India has increased, is increasing and will continue to increase, and it is the better distribution of this wealth that must be our chief concern," one imperial official wrote. In this context, the "few thousands of rupees which returning emigrants may bring back with them are of no account"; their contribution to India's development was "infinitesimal." The collector of Thanjavur, H. S. Thomas, had seen this as early as the 1870s.[88]

The idea of a Tamil—or, more broadly, Indian—diaspora in the world is, quite clearly, of recent origin. Not until the 1970s and 1980s did scholars use the term, once reserved for the Jewish Diaspora (with a capital "D"), to describe the groups of Indian and Chinese migrants who had traveled and settled throughout the world in the age of empire. In both academic writing and public discourse, the term "diaspora" has come to denote almost any migrant group of shared origin; today, "almost every ethnic group, country, or separatist movement has its diaspora."[89] We have histories of diaspora where once there were histories of immigration, and they emphasize the enduring links—imaginative, familial, economic, or political—maintained by mobile people with their lands of origin. This has been analytically useful, if anachronistic; but perhaps, too, "diaspora" has grown anemic through overuse.

But what language, what vocabulary, did people use at the time? Tamil writers of the 1920s and 1930s deployed a wide range of expressions to describe what we might now call a Tamil diaspora in Southeast Asia. The terms "Indians overseas," "South Indian workers," "South Indian coolies," "Tamils," the "Tamil world" *(Tamilakam)*, "Indians in Malaya," "Tamils in Malaya," "Ceylon's Tamils," "Tamil coolies in Ceylon," "Indians in Burma," and "Indians in the Empire" all appeared frequently. Despite its widespread use in recent scholarship, the term "Indian Ocean" appears infrequently, suggesting the importance of more specific, regional itineraries. Each of these terms drew different boundaries around community, and each evoked a different geography—greater or lesser proximity to India, shifting emphases on national as opposed to regional origin, different levels of rootedness overseas. The awareness of being part of an imperial diaspora was balanced against a more specific sense of a Tamil-speaking world connecting South India and Southeast Asia—an imagined map that encompassed the Bay of Bengal.

One of the first to write explicitly of a Tamil diaspora in the world was an English clergyman, Norman Sargant. He began his 1941 book, *Dispersion of the Tamil Church,* by quoting Ezekiel 35:6, which evokes the original sense of the term *"diaspora"*: "My sheep were scattered upon all the face of the earth." Sargant described the "Tamil people of the dispersion"—the small churches they had established in Ceylon, Burma, Malaya, and further afield. "It has been said that the dispersion of the Jews was a preparation for Christianity in the ancient world," he wrote hopefully. "May it also be said that the dispersion of the Tamil church was of great help to the apostles of the nineteenth century?" Tamil Christians were but a small minority among those who crossed the Bay, but Sargant's sense that the Tamil diaspora was best charted by the spiritual marks it left upon distant lands might have been shared by many Hindus and Muslims, too.[90]

The experience of modernity in the Bay of Bengal in the 1920s and 1930s left few novels or works of art that have stood the test of time. There was nothing in Malaya to compare with Diego Rivera's stunning murals on the courtyard walls of Detroit's Institute of Arts, commissioned by Edsel Ford in 1932, depicting the mechanics, managers, typists, accountants, and machines that powered Detroit's industrial modernity—even though Detroit was umbilically linked to the plantations of Malaya. But expressions of migrants' struggles to make themselves "at home in a constantly changing world" are there if we look for them: in popular culture, in patterns of social life, in advertising billboards, and in the pages of newspapers. Those who crossed the Bay tried, in their own ways, to live in the "maelstrom" of the modern world, moving "within its currents in search of reality, of beauty, of freedom, of justice."[91] But never, not even at the height of migration in the 1920s, did a *political* narrative emerge to unite Bay of Bengal. No politician said of the Bay's coasts, as they did of the nations they imagined, "This is the world we share, and our fates are linked." The Bay appeared, by contrast, as the realm of markets, its rhythms governed by "buying and selling " alone.

The life of the Bay of Bengal did generate what the philosopher Charles Taylor calls "social imaginaries." Taylor describes social imaginaries as the particular ways people "imagine their social existence, how they fit together with others, how things go between them and their fellows, the expectations which are normally met, and the deeper normative notions and images which underlie these expectations." Ramasamy Narayanasamy, A. N. Maideen, and thousands of their fellow migrants all would have shared elements of a social imaginary shaped by migration across the Bay, and they would have shared aspects of this imaginary—"how they fit together with others, how things go between them and their fellows"—with their Chinese and Malay neighbors. Taylor insists that such social imaginaries are "often not expressed in theoretical terms" but "carried in images, stories, [and] legends"; they refer to a "common understanding which makes possible common practices."[92] The "common practices" on the streets of the port towns—practices of eating together, of sharing public space, of participating in others' festivities—have had an enduring life, and they constitute, in themselves, an archive of interactions. Perhaps the key "expectation" that was "normally met" was the expectation of mobility—this was a world in which people expected that they would move back and forth across the sea. In the 1930s, that expectation would fall apart.

6

Crossings Interrupted

Under pressure of economic competition, squeezed by falling prices, and spurred by rising nationalism, the cords that held up the world of the Bay of Bengal broke. Writing in early 1939, the Indian government's agent in Burma reported that "for more than six months past, Indians in Mandalay . . . have had to endure what can only be described as organised persecution; their business has been boycotted, their shops picketed." They faced isolation, marooned in upper Burma as the political tide turned. Many of the shopkeepers affected were Tamil-speaking Muslims, or "Chulias," from the Coromandel Coast. They had crossed the Bay of Bengal for centuries. The shopkeepers' families had moved to Burma in the nineteenth century, alongside mill workers, coal miners, and rickshaw pullers. Now the security and prosperity that had brought them all to Burma collapsed.

Nationalist monks (*pongyis*) camped on their doorsteps, preventing Burmese customers from entering their shops. One monk purchasing goods from Rahim and Company in Yondawgyi was assaulted by three of his fellows, who abused him verbally, calling him a "son of a bitch"; they raised a crowd to compel him to return his purchases to the Indian shop. K. A. Naina Mohamed, another Tamil shopkeeper, reported that a local woman was buying things from his shop when "a pongyi came and took the goods from the hands of the buyer and threw [them] away." M. N. Mohammed Esoof, who traded at H. Block in Mandalay's Municipal Market, alleged that one of his customers had been threatened with a knife by a monk. "I pitied the lady for having trouble on account of her buying goods at our shop," he wrote, so "I had to return the money."[1]

Flashes of violence visited Rangoon's docks in 1930. They spread to the Burmese countryside during the millenarian rebellion of 1931–1932, led by the monk Saya San, during which rioters targeted Indian households and businesses. An uneasy calm held after that, but the path of Burmese nationalism was set. Separation from India occurred in 1937—the first and least-remarked of South Asia's "partitions." Governments around the Bay now treated migrants as people out of place. If the change was sharpest in Burma, it seeped into the political language of Malaya, of Indonesia, of Vietnam. Who belonged where now, across waters so many had traversed? With remarkable speed, the Bay of Bengal closed down. Its borders tightened. States viewed each other with suspicion. Migration became a zero-sum game. This was the world under strain that World War II shattered.

Bruno Lasker, a German-born veteran of social reform movements in London and New York, traveled extensively around Asia in the 1930s, working for the Hawaii-based Institute of Pacific Relations. He wrote a masterly survey of patterns of Asian migration: looking back after World War II, he noted that in the 1930s "international migration in eastern Asia was to a large extent arrested and even reversed in its course." John Furnivall, the British administrator who coined the term "plural society," was even quicker to judgment. Writing in 1939, Furnivall declared that "we can already see that 1930 marks the . . . close of a period of sixty years, beginning with the opening of the Suez Canal, and, although less definitely, the close of a period of four hundred years from the first landing of Vasco da Gama in Calicut."[2] Furnivall was prescient. But for most people who lived through them, the changes of the 1930s did not feel so decisive. The depression—with its bouts of unemployment and deflation, its new controls on migration—seemed more like a harsh setback than a lasting shift. Only in hindsight, after World War II, did these cracks in the web connecting lives around the Bay of Bengal appear to be a permanent reversal. Things changed suddenly in the 1930s: arbitrary rules blocked movement and fluctuating markets undid fortunes. But the rules were not always enforced, and markets soon recovered. In personal and collective memory, the era still appears one of openness and opportunity, if only because of the contrast with what followed.

In the assessment of one economic historian, "few economies can have undergone a macroeconomic shock more severe than that experienced in the 1930s depression by Malaya." Few economies were as dependent on the export of nonfood commodities, in this case rubber and tin. The market for both collapsed after 1929. The decline in rubber's price was almost entirely because of reduced demand from the American automobile industry; the general slowdown in the industrialized world weakened demand for tin. The value of rubber exports from Singapore fell by 84 percent between 1929 and 1932, and real wages across the Malay Peninsula fell by half.[3] The market value of rice dropped even faster than that of most other commodities, and it took much longer to recover.[4] Burma and the other rice-growing regions of Southeast Asia competed for markets; the cheapness of rice prevented the depression from sliding into a much more severe crisis of subsistence in Asia's most densely populated regions.

In Burma, the pressure on rice growers provoked a crisis in social relations in the countryside. When the bottom dropped from the world market for rice, the web of debt on which Chettiar moneylenders' fortunes were built went awry. Unable to recover loans, and with pressure being heaped on them by the European banks from which they had borrowed capital, Chettiar firms foreclosed on mortgages and acquired a significant proportion of Burma's agricultural land. In 1930 Chettiars held 6 percent of all occupied land in Burma; by 1938 that figure was 25 percent. Liquidity was essential to the Chettiars' business model; now they found themselves saddled with property they could not sell. Indebted Burmese cultivators suffered a loss of land and livelihood. In testimony to a colonial commission, one witness from the Karen community described Chettiar banks as "fiery dragons that parch every land that has the misfortune of coming under their wicked creeping." In this climate of fear, some Burmese turned against not only their Chettiar creditors but also all "immigrant" Indians on their land.[5]

The depression, as Lasker observed, saw Asian migration "arrested and even reversed in its course." While movement around the Bay of Bengal and the South China Sea had always been circular, the overall pattern was one of net immigration: a steady excess, year after year, of arrivals over departures. When crisis struck, this pattern was inverted. The number of Indians departing Burma and Malaya exceeded the number of arrivals between 1930 and 1933; the same was true of the Chinese throughout Southeast Asia, despite the civil strife prevailing in China at the time, compounded by Japanese military intervention. Well over

600,000 people left Malaya between 1930 and 1933; around 240,000 Tamil workers were repatriated from Malaya to India in those years, nearly 200,000 of them at government expense. But that was the limit of government assistance. Few if any provisions were made for their welfare when they arrived home. The Indian government's agent in Malaya noted that repatriation to India in times of distress "is proving less and less effective as a remedy against unemployment." Repatriation meant that "no relief is . . . afforded" to Tamil workers: "their suffering is merely transferred from Malaya to South India." Plantation workers who remained in Malaya had their wages cut unilaterally. Throughout Southeast Asia, migrant workers who were not repatriated moved onto marginal lands as squatters, scrabbling for subsistence—and tasting economic independence.[6]

Legislators compounded what labor markets began. During the depression, formal migration restrictions were imposed for the first time in Southeast Asia. Malaya and Singapore acted in 1930 to exclude new Chinese migrants. Indian migration to Malaya was restricted by more indirect means, since as subjects of the British Empire, Indians were in theory free to move around within it. In 1930, with unemployment on the rubber estates escalating, the state suspended the issuance of *kangany* licenses. These rules were unprecedented, but they were not rigidly enforced. The exemption of women from the immigration controls—by a colonial state still anxious about the gender imbalance in its immigrant society—led to a new wave of female migration to Malaya; this was an important step toward the more permanent settlement of Indian and Chinese families across the Bay. In the case of Indian migrants, the old nineteenth-century distinction between "free" and "assisted" migrants came back into view. So long as migrants could pay their own passage, no laws could stop them from crossing the Bay, and thousands continued to move to the cities of the Straits.[7]

The ethnic division of labor that pitted Indian landlords against Burmese tenants and immigrant plantation workers against local cultivators was partly a matter of design—the classic imperial strategy of "divide and rule"—and partly unplanned, in the sense that, once established by intent or by accident, these patterns tended to replicate themselves. Contracting economies heightened competition for scarce jobs. Local resentment turned against migrants across Southeast Asia—it is an all-too-familiar story. Immigration restrictions and repatriations aimed to forestall tensions but created new problems. Burma experienced the worst conflict, since Indian workers dominated the urban economy of Rangoon and Indian moneylenders possessed much land. A massive anticolonial rebellion broke out in Burma in 1930, led by the charismatic monk and preacher Saya San. One of the largest anticolonial revolts in Asia during the 1930s, the Saya San rebellion began as a protest against the colonial capitation tax but swelled into a millenarian movement. Attacks on Indian moneylenders and shops followed, particularly in Lower Burma—Hanthawaddy, Insein, Pegu, Pyapon, Myaungmya. A British administrator stationed in the region wrote to Rangoon that "it is very difficult to prevent villagers from going out at night, one or two at a time, and setting fire to isolated huts where Indians are living alone in the fields."[8]

British authorities used brute force to suppress the rebellion. Saya San was executed after his trial. A grudging peace returned to the Burmese countryside, but the damage to social relations ran deep. Frightened by their experiences, many Indians in Burma boarded ships for home, but most of those who left planned to return to Burma when things calmed down. By 1934 a return to business as usual seemed imminent.[9] That year arrivals in Malaya once again exceeded 100,000; in Ceylon immigration "has nearly gone up to the record figure of 1927." More than 200,000 Chinese arrived in Southeast Asia that year. The *kangany* system of recruitment never recovered from the depression, however. Most migrants to Malaya after 1933 either were "repeat migrants" or had friends and relatives living there. The control of official agencies over migration weakened. The Madras Emigration Commissioner noted in 1935 that "a large number of persons are going to and returning from Malaya as ordinary passengers," paying their own fare and so falling outside the colonial state's definition of labor migrants. Migrants to Malaya carried letters from estate managers confirming that they had previously worked there or containing a specific offer of employment and confirmation that the migrant had family or friends on the estate in question. A thriving market developed in such letters. "Old laborers," one British official complained, "take under their wing loiterers at the gate [of the emigration depot] and represent them as their relations or friends"—a familiar problem. To both Malaya and Ceylon, serial migration was now the norm. Migration became a constant and repeated part of the life experience of many families in South

India—almost a habit.[10] It looked as though Indian and Chinese migration to Southeast Asia would resume, continue, intensify; few could see, in 1936 or 1937, that it would soon come to a grinding halt. If the trends of the postdepression recovery had continued, the proportion of Malaya's population that was of Indian origin might have risen from an eighth to a quarter, and the Chinese population looked set to become an overall majority on the peninsula. This very real prospect underlay many Malay fears of being "swamped in their own land"—but it was not to be.

Markets recovered after the depression. But a shift in political structures and ideologies refigured the relationship between India and Southeast Asia, and between the different communities and ethnic groups that lived around and across the Bay. As we have seen, the aspirations of the Indian and Chinese diasporas had found expression in the language of nationalism beginning in the early twentieth century; now they found themselves the target of a rising tide of local nationalism in Burma and Malaya and throughout the region. Young local men blamed "immigrants" when they found their paths to employment in the colonial administration blocked and their prospects as entrepreneurs limited. "Through eye and ear," wrote one sympathetic British observer, "the Burman is continuously and acutely made aware of the alien control of the business activities of the country, of the steady infiltration of immigrant workers."[11] Rising awareness of inequality provoked competing claims of entitlement. The shock of the depression sharpened debates that had brewed in the 1920s about who belonged where, but now they were no longer abstract or confined to newspaper columns—much more was at stake.

Neither Burmese nor Malay nationalism emerged suddenly. Both grew from the crisis provoked by British conquest and by the destruction (in Burma) or subordination (in Malaya) of an old monarchical world. Debates over the *bangsa Melayu*, or Malay race, thrived in the polyglot world of the Straits Settlements in the nineteenth century, spurred by cultural encounters between Malays and Europeans and between Malays and other Asians. On the account of U Tin Tut of the Indian Civil Service, Burmese nationalism was rooted in a deep attachment to land and people. "A Burmese child is brought up on history and traditions which have as their background the ancient glories of the past," he said, "and it is with a shock that he realises in his adolescence that he is a member of a subject race." Burmese nationalism did not become a mass movement until the 1920s; Malay nationalism only reached those levels in the 1940s. But both grew steadily, their newspapers and journals and letter-writing clubs clamoring for recognition amid others' assertions of belonging. The Malay press expanded fast in the 1930s: newspapers were "available at every Malay bookshop and some of them at the various Malay clubs, and read even by the motor car drivers." In Burma, long one of Asia's most literate societies, vernacular texts spread a new, self-conscious nationalism, dispersed by the pervasive influence of lay monks. U Ottama, a monk of Arakanese origin, toured Burma in the early 1920s, delivering impassioned and increasingly anticolonial speeches on behalf of the Young Men's Buddhist Association.[12]

By the end of the 1920s, the goal of Burmese nationalists was clear: "separation" from India. This, more than freedom from British colonialism, motivated their efforts. They intensified their demands after the ravages of the depression and in the wake of the Saya San revolt. Burma's Legislative Council first tabled the separation bill in early 1929; in 1931–1932, as part of a wider series of constitutional negotiations over India's political future, the Burma Round Table set a date for "separation," which would take effect on April 1, 1937. Burma's Indian residents were unsure what to think. Many felt that political change would make little difference to their daily lives; others feared for their futures. Playwright and journalist V. Swaminatha Sarma wrote for the Rangoon-based Tamil newspaper *Jothi* in the 1930s, and published a book in 1936 on the coming separation. He began with an account of Burma's links with India going back to the earliest times, traced the rise of Burmese nationalism through the Young Men's Buddhist Association, outlined the coming constitutional change, and ended with the biggest question of all: "The two peoples—do they have a common future?"[13]

By the later 1930s, the youthful and assertive movement of "Thakins"— Rangoon University students, for the most part—brought new energy to Burmese nationalism. Among the student leaders was the young Aung San, who would lead Burma to independence, only to fall to an assassin's bullet. A prolonged strike in 1936 brought the university to a standstill. In 1938 student activists led attacks on local Indians after an Indian Muslim writer "insulted" the Buddha in an initially obscure pamphlet that eventually circulated like wildfire through Burma's book bazaars. Such ethnic and religious anxieties combined with sexual ones in a toxic way when the spotlight was turned upon Muslim men of Indian origin who had married Burmese women: their families constituted the mixed Zerbadi community of Arakan. India's own intercommunal tensions spread to Burma: right-wing Hindu leaders in India lent their support to their Burmese Buddhist "brothers" in their fight against Islam. Yet for the most part, Burmese nationalists grouped "Indians" together, whatever their religious affiliations.

A familiar language of nationalist resentment echoed around the Bay. A scurrilous pamphlet published in Burma in 1938 thundered against the *kala*—the local term for an Indian, derived from the word for "outsider."

> Kala at Pan Shop; Kala at bayagyaw shop; Kala at big hosiery stores; Kala at spiking the soles of shoes; Kala at the undervest factory; Kala at vendor of sand soap; Kala at vendor of toilette; Kala at lending money; Kala, Kala, every where Kala; Kala as durwans; Kala as judge of High Court; Kala as vendor of powder; Kala as doctors; Kala as jemadars; and Kala as jailors.

Burmese nationalists looked forward to a future free from Indian domination. In early 1941, a Burmese newspaper invoked Hitler approvingly in discussing the "Indian problem." The newspaper "now remembers a speech delivered by Hitler before he came into power. Hitler said, 'I have studied the histories of all countries; and I find that the retardation of a country's progress is not due to its economic affairs, but due to the influx of foreigners.'" The article concluded that in Hitler's words lay a lesson for Burma. It was the language of anti-immigration activists everywhere, though few in Asia could foresee the bloody limits to which Hitler would take his vision. And if it was sharpest in Burma, nativism was on the rise in Malaya, too, as it was in Indonesia and Vietnam.[14]

Resentment of Indian immigration across the Bay was mirrored by Indian nationalists' increasing hostility to emigration. Writers and politicians denounced the continued movement of Indian laborers to lands where they were not wanted, and where their humiliation would bring shame upon the nation. The Congress Party's *Searchlight* newspaper lamented the resumption of emigration to Malaya after the depression.

India, they argued, risked becoming "the great suppliers-general of black coolies for European plantations," where they would be treated "as mere beasts" and denied "all rights and privileges—economic as well as political—that belong . . . to other emigrants or settlers—be their skin black or white." The writer stated categorically that Indian emigrants "do not go of their own accord but are invited, persuaded, coaxed and cajoled." If Indian workers overseas could not live in dignity, journalists suggested, then they should not go at all; if need be, the state should intervene to prevent them from emigrating, for their own protection, and for the protection of India's reputation abroad. At the same time, Indian nationalist commentators took a harsh view of the "colonial-born," discouraging them from returning to India, distancing the citizens of the future nation from the "coolies" overseas.[15]

The Bay of Bengal was crossed over and over again, but it was land that underpinned the politics of belonging. Though coastal towns around the Bay were as connected with one another as each was with its hinterland, this produced neither a coherent space for political mobilization nor a collective sense that the peoples of the Bay of Bengal rim had as much in common with each other as they did with their fellow Indians or Malays or Burmese. Though mostly under British rule, the Bay's arc was divided into multiple jurisdictions. Its component parts were ruled differently: as colonies and protectorates, by direct and indirect rule, under different rules for immigrants and natives, for Asians and Europeans. The increasing territorial integration—politically, intellectually—of India or Burma or Malaya only heightened the lack of political integration around the ocean's rim, even as economic and cultural connections flourished. Partha Chatterjee writes of the "normative acceptance over a wide spectrum of political opinion of the nation-state as the universally normal, legitimate form of the modern state" during the early decades of the twentieth century, and particularly in the 1920s and 1930s.[16] Even within the British Empire, colonial administrators and nationalist politicians alike began to act according to these norms; in 1930 the Indian economist Lanka Sundaram argued that the government of India should use "India's membership of the League of Nations" as a means of "retaliation and arbitration respectively in the case of unjust treatment of her nationals overseas."[17]

Nationalism in the 1920s and 1930s provoked powerful emotions of attachment to land and landscape but not to the sea, which remained an "empty" space—crossed but not inhabited, unmarked by monuments, untroubled by memory. The Bay of Bengal was a region in the mind, a "social imaginary" mapped by shrines and journeys and longings. It made intuitive sense to many who lived in and around it; for them it was a coherent and connected part of the world. But this sense remained unspoken—and it came as a shock when this world was pulled apart.

"Burma divorces India," John Christian wrote in *Current History* in 1937, marking Burma's autonomy from Indian control after a century. It was an apt metaphor, and it applies beyond Burma. The gradual disintegration of the Bay of Bengal world was like a protracted divorce, with more than one custody battle in the years to come. It was a scholarly separation, too. For the second half of the twentieth century, the 1937 boundary between British India and British Burma marked the point where "South Asia" ended and "Southeast Asia" began. Academic departments, disciplinary institutions, and regional conferences have cleaved to that division until very recently.[18] In the 1930s the states around the Bay behaved autonomously despite their British imperial bond. The Indian government (and, more specifically, the provincial government of Madras) pursued something akin to a "foreign policy," negotiating with Burma, Malaya, and Ceylon over the future of Indian labor migration and the rights of migrants. Legally and constitutionally the unity of the Bay of Bengal world faded from view, if not yet from everyday life.

The most immediate question surrounding the Burmese "divorce" concerned the future of Indian immigration to Burma and the status of Indians already in the country. Community, residence, and loyalty emerged as the trinity that bedeviled mapmakers and constitutional lawyers across the region. For Abdul Karim Gani—a Tamil-speaking Muslim journalist who spent the 1930s in Rangoon and sat in Burma's legislative assembly—there was a clear distinction between Indians rooted in Burma, on one hand, and the sojourners whose loyalties were across the Bay, on the other. Gani was pointed in distinguishing between "Indians who have no stake in India" and those with "vested interests"; as he spoke those words, his eyes were firmly on the Chettiar representatives across the debating chamber. Gani decried the Burmese nationalists' tendency to lump together these different groups of

Indians "for ever and ever" and demanded that full rights of Burmese citizenship should be open to "anybody who is born, or who has permanently settled, in this country provided he does good to the country and provided he is true to the country."[19]

Long negotiations between the colonial governments of India and Burma aimed to draft an "immigration agreement" between the two countries.[20] The government of India "depredated the proposal to have passports as a condition of entry to Burma," yet it had little power over the Burmese authorities. At the heart of the controversy was the definition of "domicile," a concept that continued to shape debates about migration after 1945. "The determination of intention" to settle, or to return, was difficult to prove when the movement between India and Burma was circulatory. The lawyers sought, in vain, to recognize a distinction between Indians who were "settled immigrants" in Burma and those who were "useful temporary residents of varying degrees of permanence," who would enjoy "civil and political rights as British subjects" but not as Burmese citizens. On the eve of the war, different kinds of citizenship—imperial, colonial, and national—came into contention.[21]

Faced with eviction, the Chettiars cried foul. The immigration agreement, they wrote, "causes Chettiars and all Indians considerable disquiet and concern." The assumptions under which they had invested millions in Burma had been overturned; the imperial rug had been pulled from beneath them. Dark signs were everywhere. Many Chettiars had been expelled from Indochina in the mid-1930s as the French colonial administration brought in new legislation to restrain creditors; they suffered loss and violence in Burma. The immigration agreement took no account of the long-standing pattern of circular migration across the Bay. Anyone who happened to be in India when the act came into force, despite "having spent long years in Burma and acquired knowledge of language and local conditions," would be "excluded . . . and dealt [with] as new immigrants." Free circulation was at an end. Talks between India and Burma dragged on until 1941. Fearing the worst, some Chettiars moved their money out of Burma; others did the opposite, traveling to Burma in even greater numbers in case their entry should be restricted in the future.[22]

As discussions in Burma festered, other routes across the Bay closed down. Migration from India to Ceylon and Malaya came under strict control—and the initiative came from the Indian side. After the elections of 1937, held under a restricted franchise, Congress Party governments took control of eight of India's eleven provinces. Indians rose to positions of greater responsibility within the civil service, though ultimate power remained in English hands. Policy increasingly was made not by British administrators but by Indians, many of whom had nationalist sympathies. The keen humiliation that the Indian elite had long felt over the status of Indians overseas began to shape emigration policy directly. The Congress Party, by this time, resembled a state-in-waiting as much as a mass protest movement, and its eyes were on plans for India's economic development. The entity for development was the colonial (soon to be national) territory, not the wider region around the Bay. Abandoning the laissez-faire policy that gave free play to market forces, the colonial state in the 1930s embraced the cause of agrarian and industrial development.[23] Emigration now featured rarely in discussions of India's economic future; it seemed no solution at all to the overwhelming problem of poverty.

In this context, Indian officials questioned the future of labor migration to Malaya and Ceylon. The Indian agent in Malaya declared that until there were signs that "there will be no differentiation between the Malay and non-Malay subjects," the government of India "should not, under any circumstances, encourage settlement of Indians on the land."[24] In Delhi, Sir Girija Shankar Bajpai had a different sort of concern. He worried that "making the planter independent of India, by having a settled local workforce," would lead to the loss "of our only sanction to secure economic and political equality for the resident Indian population."[25] The same year, the agent in Malaya called for a formal treaty on emigration between India and British Malaya, which would "confer sufficient initiative for intervening on behalf of immigrant workers in a foreign territory." The Bay of Bengal's divorce was under way. Tamil workers in Malaya were now "immigrant workers" like any others, and Malaya was a "foreign territory." Only through an instrument of foreign policy between states—a treaty—did the Indian government now feel that it could intervene overseas. In 1938, as negotiations between the Indian and Malayan governments over wages and conditions ground to a halt, the government of India's committee on emigration declared a ban on Indian emigration to Malaya "for the purposes of labor"—the language contained an echo of the nineteenth-century legislation on indenture. A similar restriction of unskilled emigration to Ceylon came into effect the following year.[26] In neither case did migration simply cease. Now, as in the past, the rules did not restrain "free" migrants who paid their own passage, so the flow of traders and merchants and urban workers continued, as did the movement back and forth of family members. Still, with little fanfare, the emigration acts reversed the patterns of a century.

The Bay of Bengal's closure produced unexpected political openings. As migration was restricted, as the Indian government's influence in Malaya waned, Tamil workers experienced political radicalization. Where in the 1920s they had petitioned the Indian agent and the labor commissioner in plaintive tones, by the late 1930s they resorted directly to protest. The shift in political consciousness began, as it so often did, in the towns. There were strikes on the railways as early as 1924; in the 1930s these grew in scope and scale.[27] In late 1936 around 7,000 Tamil workers in Singapore's municipal services went on strike—the largest such labor action to date. Assertiveness was on the rise among Chinese workers in Malaya. The Malayan Communist Party, predominantly Chinese in membership and growing in strength, supported a series of strikes on smallholding rubber plantations in March 1937 through its General Labor Union. When the police moved to round up the "agitators," they were surprised to find that one of them was a Tamil teacher, Thangaya, who worked in an estate school. "The case of Thangaya is of more than ordinary interest," a police officer reported, "as it is the first instance in the Federated Malay States of a Southern Indian taking any active part in Communist agitation." Thangaya was alleged to have encouraged Tamil workers on a number of estates to strike in sympathy with the Chinese workers.[28]

The pressure escalated in 1940, when the outbreak of war in Europe brought a rubber boom in Malaya. The unions seized their opportunity to press for a wage increase. Again Chinese workers took the lead. A strike wave began early that year, culminating in the occupation of the Firestone tire factory in Singapore. On May 1, 1940, the unions called a general strike. The date was rich with symbolism, and the strike itself evoked the great American railroad strikes of the nineteenth century and the shared struggles of workers around the world. The police fired on the crowd, killing two and injuring two more.[29] Among the

materials they seized were several copies of a Tamil pamphlet support-
ing the strikers. "May Day will bring all the laborers under one banner," the pamphlet declared, "and caste and creed will exist no more." It
was signed by the "India Socialist Republic Army." British authorities
were alarmed.[30]

The spread of radicalism within the Tamil working class of Malaya
took the Indian urban leadership unawares and left them scrambling to
catch up. The urban elite of Singapore and Penang sought, beginning in
the 1920s, to engage more closely with plantation labor, but a gulf remained between them. Factionalism prevailed: the great concern of the
journalists and public figures in the cities remained representation on
official bodies, and they were tangled in internal conflicts. Community
remained a primary affiliation—Tamils, Malayalis, Ceylon Tamils, and
North Indians vied to be the representatives of the "Indian" community
to the colonial state that grouped them together as such. The Central
Indian Association of Malaya, formed in 1936, contained all of these
tensions. But it also included a group of younger, bolder voices.[31]

Among them was R. H. Nathan. Nathan was a Tamil-speaking Brahmin, not even thirty years old when he rose to prominence within Malaya's Indian community. He arrived in Malaya in the mid-1930s and
lived with his brother, a police court interpreter, in Klang. Nathan
found work as a clerk for Paterson, Simons and Company; when he lost
his job, he worked as a correspondent for a Japanese-owned newspaper,
the *Singapore Herald,* which brought him to the notice of British intelligence. From there, Nathan moved to *Tamil Nesan,* one of the leading
Tamil newspapers in Malaya, and became its assistant editor. Malaya's
Tamil press became more assertive in its anticolonialism by the late
1930s; under Nathan's influence, *Nesan* took a greater interest in the
plantation workers' struggles. Nathan sought to build an infrastructure
of Indian institutions across the peninsula. In 1940 he helped to form
the Klang district Indian union; he organized unions of municipal
workers, unions of railway men, unions of shop assistants. He told his
audiences to "pray for complete independence" from British colonialism; he also "urged Indian coolies [to] join the Chinese laborers and
form associations."[32]

By 1941 the plantations were restive. Blinded by their belief in the
"docility" of Tamil workers—an old stereotype that went back to Ceylon's earliest experiments in coffee planting—British officials sought

the "agitators" who alone, they believed, could bring about strikes on the rubber estates. They identified Nathan, along with Y. K. Menon, and prepared to arrest the two men. Strikes erupted before they could act. The colonial government was divided within itself over how to respond. The labor commissioner was concerned that workers' legitimate wage demands should not be ignored, and he supported the development of trade unions; hard-liners took the opposite view, urging discipline and repression. In March 1941 as many as 5,000 workers on estates across the Klang Valley went out on strike, demanding wage equality with their Chinese counterparts (which Tamil workers in Malaya had never enjoyed). The planters granted a small increase, which fell short of the workers' demands. The strikes continued to spread in April; colonial authorities were now seriously concerned. When the police moved to arrest Nathan in early May, Tamil workers mounted the biggest strike Malaya's plantations had ever seen.[33]

The day after Nathan's arrest, E. Bagot, inspector general of police, wrote in his diary that "several hundred coolies appeared . . . armed with sticks, spears, iron bars, broken bottles and bricks." He ordered a baton charge. One of the injured workers died in hospital. By May 12, "nearly all rubber estates in the coastal area were on strike." The army was called in—and an Indian regiment at that. Troops fired on protesters, killing three and wounding four. The social changes of the 1930s, which labor officials had once lauded, now turned against planters and the state. Accounts of the strike emphasized the workers' use of bicycles and motor transport. Bagot noted that strikers were "travelling around the district in buses and on cycles." The army was called in to prevent "the unrestricted use of the roads by coolies." Strikers escaped detection by making their way "from one estate to another by riding bicycles along estate roads and paths"; after one raid, "eight protestors and twenty-two bicycles were captured." The strikers' targets were symbolic: many toddy shops on the estates were attacked. "The choice of toddy shops is of interest," the police noted, "as showing there were political motives behind the destruction." Repression prevailed. Nearly two hundred people were arrested, and the "leaders"—including Nathan—were deported to India. But life on the plantations would not be the same again.[34]

Until the 1920s the Bay's political currents were directed toward social reform and quiet survival more than anticolonial revolution. That would change, and change dramatically, in the years between 1941 and 1945. But even before the war, the connected world around the Bay was jolted into political action. Tamil plantation workers in Malaya were pushed into radicalism by intolerable pressures on their livelihoods. The sense of security that had, for so long, come from the possibility of circulation was undermined. The Bay of Bengal resounded with many competing ideologies—nationalism, socialism, communism. And then it was pulled apart, and pushed together in new ways, by total war.

Early on the morning of December 8, 1941, Japanese forces landed at Kota Bahru on Malaya's east coast. It was still the morning of December 7 across the Pacific, so these landings took place hours before the assault on Pearl Harbor dragged the United States into World War II. Within weeks European power in Southeast Asia had collapsed. From Kota Bahru, Japanese forces moved down the Malayan Peninsula's tarred roads on trucks and on bicycles. Japanese bombs rained on Singapore. On December 10, Japanese bombers sank the British ships *Repulse* and *Prince of Wales* in Singapore's harbor; the "impregnable fortress" of the empire in the east crumbled. Dutch power in Java and Sumatra soon dissolved. From Thailand, which was allied to Japan in the war, Japanese troops moved into southern Burma. Japanese bombers attacked Rangoon, and panic ensued. On February 15, 1942, Lieutenant General Arthur Percival surrendered to the Japanese in Singapore. It was the biggest and most humiliating defeat in British military history. More than 130,000 Allied troops became prisoners of war, the majority of them Indians.

Japan's daring assault on Southeast Asia was, above all, an attempt to secure the oil, tin, and rubber that had turned the region's forests into a magnet for migrants and investors half a century earlier. Dependent on imports of raw materials, encircled by an American embargo, the Japanese military moved to seize the resources for themselves. Japan's Axis alliance with Germany and Italy paved the way for their advance after war broke out in Europe: Japanese forces established strategic bases in Vichy-controlled Indochina in 1940. The Japanese advance through Southeast Asia was electrifying. The rapidity of their military victory undermined European imperial claims to political supremacy and racial superiority. The unseemly haste with which European empires retreated, abandoning their Asian subjects to their fate, damaged their prestige irreparably. Many young Asians were attracted to the Japanese rhetoric of pan-Asian solidarity. Undoubtedly Japanese leaders used such political language in pursuit of their own ends, but so, too, did the Asian nationalists who worked with the Japanese in Burma, Indonesia, and Malaya.[35]

War overturned the balance of power in the Bay of Bengal. It had been a "British lake" for a century; now, again, the region became a strategic battleground, as it had been in the eighteenth century. "After the fall of Singapore and Java," a British air force commander observed, "the Japanese had command of the sea in these waters. There was no effective naval force of ours based in the Bay of Bengal."[36] The Japanese sought to exploit their advantage and conquer the Bay. In March 1942 they overran the strategically essential Andaman Islands, and then they advanced toward Ceylon. From March 31 to April 10, 1942, the Japanese carried out their "Indian Ocean Raid" under the command of the veteran admiral Chuichi Nagumo; a supplementary force commanded by Vice Admiral Jusaburo Ozawa sailed from the Mergui archipelago and attacked commercial shipping in the Bay, sinking twenty-three merchant ships in one day. Ozawa's fleet raided the Indian ports of Cocanada and Vishakapatnam—ports from which millions of emigrants had embarked for Burma. The attacks on eastern India did little damage; more serious was the Japanese attempt on Colombo. Ceylon sat between the Bay of Bengal and the Arabian Sea, and in Trincomalee it had one of the Bay's best ports, fought over by British, Dutch, and Portuguese in centuries past. Nagumo's aircraft carriers attacked Colombo in early April 1942, inflicting heavy damage on British forces. A few days later they attacked the British naval base in Trincomalee. Admiral Somerville withdrew his fleet hastily to Mombasa, concerned about a repeat of the attack on Singapore.[37]

But the feared Japanese invasion of Ceylon failed to materialize. Within two months the Japanese navy met with a heavy defeat by American forces at the Battle of Midway, diverting their naval resources away from the Indian Ocean and to the Pacific. The British, for their part, had few forces to spare. "The problem of retaining control of the coastal waters of Burma was quite beyond our powers," Ceylon's commander, Admiral Geoffrey Layton, wrote.[38] Even after the fortunes of war turned in the Allies' favor, the demand for shipping in the Mediterranean and Atlantic theaters of war left British naval forces in the

Indian Ocean weak, and they were confined to limiting Japan's maritime supply lines to Burma by launching submarine raids from Ceylon and laying mines in Burma's coastal waters. Allied forces planned a seaborne invasion of Burma and Malaya from across the Bay, but, in the end, it was over land that they advanced. The war immobilized the Bay of Bengal—this was truly unprecedented.

The Japanese conquest of Southeast Asia was a political revolution as well as a military one. Before the war, the arc of coasts around the Bay of Bengal was all, with the exception of Thailand, under British rule, though its various pieces were governed differently: a complex of colonies and protectorates and territories under different forms of administration. Subjects of many other empires—French, Dutch, Japanese— moved across their frontiers. With the Japanese conquest of Southeast Asia, the political settlement was shattered and the map redrawn. For the first time in centuries, territories that had been divided between Western empires—British Burma and Malaya, the Dutch East Indies, the American Philippines—came under a single administration. But beneath this new unity, a line was drawn across the Bay, separating India from "Southeast Asia." Because the Japanese never advanced beyond the eastern frontiers of India, the division between India and the other side of the Bay followed the lines of Japanese conquest and Allied reconquest. The establishment of South-East Asia Command, under Lord Louis Mountbatten, in 1943 gave a new reality to the idea of "Southeast Asia," distinct from India; this division, born of the contingencies of war and of administrative decisions taken in its midst, lasts to this day. South-East Asia Command, headquartered in Ceylon, came close in 1945 and 1946 to exercising control over most of the Bay, with the great exception of India.[39]

The sense of liberation that many Asians felt as they witnessed the Japanese advance soon soured. The Japanese military's brutality too often undermined their promise of pan-Asian solidarity. Soon after their occupation of Singapore, Japanese forces turned against the local Chinese community in the notorious Sook Ching massacre, which singled out for torture and public execution alleged nationalist sympathizers, intellectuals, and those recently arrived from China. Tensions arose between the war aims of the Japanese and the goals of their Asian nationalist collaborators. Japanese occupying forces had to deal, like

Europeans before them, with the challenge of Southeast Asia's cultural pluralism. And often it was migrants, or the descendants of migrants, who suffered most during the war. But the abrupt collapse of European power in Southeast Asia created new political possibilities.

The links between India and Southeast Asia were not forgotten during the war. They were central to the mission of the Indian National Army (INA), which fought against the British in pursuit of India's freedom from imperial rule. The INA emerged from the efforts of British Indian soldiers who were held as prisoners of war and who accepted Japanese support to raise an anticolonial army. The INA was initially weakened by conflicts between its leaders—drawn from an older generation of anticolonial radicals and exiles—and Japanese commanders. It gained strength with the arrival in Singapore of Subhas Chandra Bose, former president of the Indian National Congress, who had escaped detention in India and set out for Germany, via the Northwest Frontier and Afghanistan, to seek support for an armed uprising against British rule in India. Frustrated by lukewarm German backing, Bose traveled by submarine to Japan, where he received a more enthusiastic reception. He saw in Southeast Asia the grounds for his Indian revolution. Under Bose's leadership, the INA attracted the enthusiastic participation of Indians of widely different class, caste, and religious backgrounds. Women played a central role in the army, which had a dedicated women's wing, the Rani of Jhansi regiment, named after the legendary heroine of the rebellion of 1857.[40] When Bose declared the Provisional Government of Free India, the Japanese granted this exiled state a small and symbolic piece of territory—the Andaman and Nicobar Islands, right at the heart of the Bay of Bengal. It was India's freedom that the INA sought, and under pressure of war, the INA's leaders had little time to imagine how this free India would relate to the lands across the Bay. Nor were they clear where the foot soldiers of the INA, many of whom called Malaya and Burma home, would belong in the new world they fought to create.

As traffic across the Bay of Bengal ceased, cutting a path through the jungle took the place of seaborne passage in the search for safety. The exploitation of natural resources became central to the remilitarization of the Bay in an age of global warfare, and this intensified—as much as it interrupted—the process that had first dragged the region into the heart of global capitalism in the nineteenth century. Soldiers, refugees, and forced laborers experienced the war as a desperate assault on the environment of the Asian frontier. Memories of the war—hacking through the jungle to clear land for rail tracks, walking through the mountain passes of Burma toward Assam, fording and crossing rivers while advancing or retreating in battle—are bathed in an intense tropicality. In many war stories the damp heat of the jungle represents the trauma of displacement, the unpredictability of life, or the hand of fate.

Many INA soldiers—including four-fifths of the women in the Rani of Jhansi regiment—had been laborers on the plantations of Malaya. Their experience of warfare in the jungles of Burma echoed the harshness of their experience clearing and cultivating the Malayan forest, now made more lethal by Allied bombs. They fought with a passion for India's freedom, inspired by the charismatic Subhas Bose. Plantation life had prepared them well for the sacrifices they would have to make in their armed quest.[41] Advancing through Burma, the INA met its military defeat at the battles of Imphal and Kohima; Subhas Bose ordered the beleaguered army to retreat, but their bravery was never in doubt. Those who reached India's frontiers during those two battles had arrived overland at the borders of a homeland that many of them had never seen and which their parents or grandparents had left by sea decades earlier. Janaki Thevar, second in command of the Rani of Jhansi regiment, wrote years later of the "marathon walk from Rangoon to Bangkok" as the INA retreated: "Covering more than twenty-three days through virgin jungles and the most difficult terrain often in blinding darkness, crossing turbulent rivers and streams, marching in absolutely drenched and tattered uniforms and blistered feet under the constant vulturous eyes of enemy planes."[42] She remembered, more than half a century later, the moon in the night sky over Burma, and she recalled thinking then of Dorothy Lamour's song of 1940, "Moon over Burma," a strange echo from a more innocent time: "Moon over Burma / Smiling above / They say that you are / The wonderful goddess of love."[43]

They moved through a landscape with which the Indian diaspora in Southeast Asia had an intimate connection—the green carpet of paddy fields that lined Burma's river valleys, Malaya's jagged spine. Abid Hasan, Subhas Bose's trusted lieutenant, recalled a conversation with Janaki Thevar about landscape and memory. "I remember a walk I had once, not far from Rangoon, with Capt Thevar of the Rani Jhansi Regiment," he wrote. "We went to a hillock and sat there looking at the ground around us. 'Doesn't the countryside remind you of home?' I enquired, adding 'it looks so typically Indian.'" Her response surprised him: "'I do not know,' she replied simply, 'I have never been to India.'"[44] Janaki was only eighteen years old when she joined the INA; she had been born to an urban middle-class family in Malaya, and it was the only land she knew.

When the tide turned, Allied forces reoccupied Burma overland, led by General William Slim's Fourteenth Army, nearly 100,000 strong. After two disastrous attempts to invade Arakan, Allied forces succeeded in 1944–1945. They inflicted heavy defeats on Japanese regiments augmented by the Indian National Army at Imphal and Kohima. By March 1945 the Allies had captured Mandalay and moved across the Irrawaddy River to Rangoon; the March 1945 revolution of General Aung San's Burmese Independence Army, initially allied to the Japanese, eased the Allied advance. The reconquest of Malaya, too, proceeded through the forests, spearheaded by the guerrilla activity of the Communist force, the Malayan People's Anti-Japanese Army.

The INA shared the landscape with their wartime opponents; the terrain is as prominent, and as symbolic, in the memories of Indian soldiers who fought on the Allied side. As Allied forces recaptured Burma, in the winter of 1944–1945, they advanced overland toward the Irrawaddy River. Their march reenacted, in such different circumstances, the conquest of Burma's frontiers by capitalists, adventurers, and laborers in the nineteenth century. Desecrated by years of total war, by the scorched-earth tactics of the retreating British in 1942, and by the weight of Japanese exploitation, the land appeared to have reverted to its original state as an untamed frontier. In the official history of the Indian armed services in the war—a history compiled as a moving collaboration between Indian and Pakistani officers, a decade after Partition—the Irrawaddy, "this wide and treacherous river," is described as "one of the most difficult water obstacles that faced either side in the Second World War." North of Mandalay, "the river flows through thick forest and jungle for forty miles," and when the land flattens out, "navigation is obstructed by sand-banks which change position after each monsoon." British planners discussed the logistical difficulties presented by the great river, observing that "the slightest obstruction such

Figure 18 An aerial view of the Irrawaddy delta, a battleground during World War II. *Photograph by Sunil Amrith.*

as a grounded tree trunk will cause a shifting of the sand." They thought, somewhat wistfully, of old expertise: the Irrawaddy Flotilla Company had once "kept a service of Burmese pilots employed in watching the river," but "they will now, more than probably, be dispersed and not available."[45]

Military forces improvised their way over land when the Bay could not be crossed with troops and supplies; an even greater number of refugees forged a path through the jungle when the ships that carried them back and forth across the sea stopped sailing. In the atmosphere of panic that set in as Japanese bombings intensified over Burma in early 1942, hundreds of thousands of Burma's Indian residents prepared to leave. The government of Burma collapsed. Burma's British rulers were the first to leave, and the Indian population feared for their safety, the memories of the violence of the 1930s now swollen by rumors of Japanese atrocities to come.

Among the refugees was V. Swaminatha Sarma, a Tamil journalist and playwright who had moved to Rangoon from Madras in 1932 to work on a Chettiar-owned Tamil newspaper, *Jothi*. Sarma was already well known as a Tamil writer for his 1922 play *Banapurathy Veeran*, inspired by the story of Robert Bruce and banned by the British authorities, as well for as his popular biographies (his subjects included Hitler and Mussolini) and his translations of Plato from English into Tamil. Toward the end of his life he penned a memoir of his "long walk" from Burma. After the "Christmas present" of Japanese bombs over Rangoon in December 1941, the city's panicked residents began their exodus. Passage by air was reserved for Europeans and Anglo-Indians, so desperate Indian families tried to pass for Anglo-Indians, relying on accidents of complexion and assumed names: "Ramasamy became Ramsay . . . Lakshmi became Lucy." Once the aircraft were full, places on ships were rationed, reserved for Europeans and a few wealthy Indians. The racial hierarchy of colonial society and its deep divisions of class were laid bare in times of emergency.

Faced with no alternative, Sarma embarked with his wife on a journey from Mandalay to Monywa, from there by boat along the Chindwin River to Kalewa, and by truck and on foot through the jungle to Tamu, close to the Indian border. They depended on the kindness of strangers— Oriya laborers who pointed them in the right direction; a Tamil

Christian called Joe, from Tirunelveli, who drove their open-backed truck toward Tamu. They faced discrimination to the very end, for even once the refugees reached Tamu, British authorities distinguished between the "black route" (for Indian refugees) and the shorter "white route" (reserved for Europeans) across the border into India.[46] Sarma was one among thousands. Dr. Krishnan Gurumurthy, whose family also fled Burma on foot, recounted his experience of the long march to Amitav Ghosh. Gurumurthy's grandfather had moved to Burma in 1902; his father was born there, and worked on the railways. Dr. Gurumurthy himself was born in Toungoo in 1933. When they set off for India in February 1942, Gurumurthy was just nine years old. His memory of the final part of the march, the "fifty miles by foot through dense forests," is particularly powerful. "My feet were heavy out of tiredness and I could hardly lift them," he remembers; "often I hit stones on the path and bled from the nail beds."[47] Theirs was a "forgotten long march" of World War II; at the time, it was one of the largest population movements ever known.[48]

More than 140,000 Indian refugees embarked on the long march. Trekking through treacherous conditions, assailed by disease and rogue militias, around 40,000 of them died. Exhaustion alone killed scores of refugees. K. N. C. Ayyar, a man of fifty-eight, died on the road of "starvation, exposure, and exhaustion," four miles west of Tamu. Another refugee, named Abdolla, died in July 1942 of "heart failure, exhaustion, and an amputated leg."[49] These are but two names that came to the attention of the relief and rehabilitation authorities in Assam; thousands of victims remained nameless. When the rains came, malaria spread rapidly, condemning many of the refugees to death. Traveling through Burma in 1951, the British writer Norman Lewis heard many accounts of the refugees' dreadful journey, the trauma still fresh: from the night the rains broke until the refugees crossed over into India, he wrote, "they were never out of the sight and smell of death."[50] The registers of "evacuees" in the National Archives of India give a poignant sense of how diverse the body of refugees was. The occupations listed included fishermen and cloth merchants, sweepers and milkmen, "coolies" and cultivators, boatmen and machinists, a "spare motor driver," a *paan* (betel leaf) seller, and a postman. Most of them were headed back to towns in the Telugu-speaking districts of Madras and to the Bengali-speaking regions bordering on Burma, particularly

Chittagong, but the refugees' destinations included places across the Tamil south, and even Lahore and Amritsar.[51]

The "evacuees" who made it to India were housed in makeshift refugee camps in Assam, aided by the Tea Planters' Association. Conditions in the camps were dire. There were shortages of rice and water. One camp official reported that "sanitation was at a standstill at the outset, but a force of sanitary sweepers was obtained from the refugees," many of whom had worked as sweepers and night soil removers in Burma before the war. People died each day "of exposure, undernourishment, and sheer exhaustion."[52] A British officer stationed in Bengal described the influx of refugees across the border from Burma. "They were finding their way down through Assam," he wrote, "and they were moving into the country. They were arriving diseased: bringing in a particularly virulent type of malaria, and bringing in hair-raising stories of atrocities and suffering." He explained that a general air of panic followed the refugees through Bengal: "The natural effect of that on the people in Bengal . . . was to feel that times were extremely uncertain and that terrible things might happen."[53] Eastern India was in turmoil. The Quit India movement began in August 1942 and escalated into a massive and violent anticolonial rebellion, the most widespread since 1857. Large parts of eastern India became ungovernable. District administrations collapsed. The movement was fed by rumors of the collapse of British power in Burma and an imminent Japanese invasion, and fueled by the stories that the returning refugees brought with them.[54] It took massive force, including aerial bombs, for the British to subdue the movement. But the agony of Bengal was only beginning.

The experience of forced laborers was just as brutal. They built supply lines to compensate for the loss of shipping, and many of them died in the effort. Most lethal of all was the largest Japanese construction project in Southeast Asia: the Thailand-Burma railway, which was built on the blood of forced labor. The railway was constructed by around 62,000 Allied prisoners of war along with nearly 200,000 Asian workers from Thailand, Burma, Malaya, Indochina, and Indonesia—the majority of them Tamil plantation workers from Malaya. The story of the Allied prisoners of war is well known, thanks to survivors' memoirs (and the film *The Bridge on the River Kwai*). By contrast, the fate of the Asian workers is almost forgotten. Tens of thousands converged upon the site of the railway's construction. They came by train, packed into freight carriages; they came by foot, through dense jungle. Like the European planters before them, Japanese recruiters worked through the *kanganies* and foremen on Malaya's plantations. As the Japanese authorities grew desperate, they turned to more coercive methods of recruitment. They announced free screenings of motion pictures, then rounded up all of the men who attended; they picked people off the streets, out of restaurants, and from amusement arcades. Luck, or fate, determined who would be caught up in these recruitment drives: Palanisamy Kumaran recalls beating a hasty retreat to escape from the recruiters' clutches and losing his bicycle in the process. One survivor of the railway told his story to investigators after the war, in the context of Japanese war crimes trials:[55]

> I was working on Kuala Selangor Estate. One day I was walking along the road towards Bukit Rotan near my house. A Japanese military lorry stopped, and the soldiers said something to me in Japanese. I could not understand them. The soldiers forced me to get into the lorry. There were already thirty other people there. I was wearing only a pair of shorts and sandals. I begged them to let me go home to put on a proper shirt and pick up a blanket. The Japanese soldiers did not allow me to go home; instead they sent me directly to K[uala] L[umpur] and loaded me onto a freight train for Siam. There we started by cutting dense jungle. The Japanese did not give me a proper shirt or blanket for seven months. I had to work in the jungle and sleep on the bamboo floor in a hut, half naked and without any blanket.[56]

The half-starved laborers worked long hours and lived in cramped hovels without sanitation.[57] Immediately after the war, Allied forces estimated that 182,496 Asian laborers had worked on the Thailand-Burma railway. Of these, only 21,445 were repatriated at the end of the war; 74,025 were confirmed dead, and the rest were unaccounted for. This is almost certainly an underestimate of the number who died, since the Allied figures did not take into account the large number of people who deserted along the way—among those who escaped, mortality was probably even greater.

The diaries of Second Lieutenant Richard Middleton-Smith paint a harrowing picture of the railway's survivors as they spilled into relief camps in Thailand and Burma at the end of the war. Middleton-Smith served as a private in the Straits Settlements volunteer force and spoke

Tamil fluently—in later years he would serve as Singapore's Tamil examiner for the Cambridge University Examinations Syndicate. His handwritten diary, scrawled on the squared paper of Chinese exercise books and on account ledgers, noted that Tamil laborers "had to spend agonising days clearing the jungle, building a camp of sorts . . . It was into conditions such as these that the Japs pitchforked over 150,000 Asiatic labourers from Malaya—mostly Indians." "Asked whether they wanted repatriation to India or Malaya, all said Malaya," he observed; "their first wish was to get back to Malaya and see their relatives." He noted the moving spectacle at Anak Bukit camp of the "first celebration of Deepavali for many years." Middleton-Smith estimated the death toll among Tamil laborers at 100,000, a higher number than subsequent historians' figures; he was perhaps keen to emphasize Japanese brutality after his own experience as a prisoner of war.[58]

In times of trauma throughout the twentieth century, human suffering and environmental harm have been entwined. In this respect, World War II was far from unique. During the forced migrations and relocations of Mao Zedong's Cultural Revolution, there was an "intimate link between the suffering of people and the abuse of land, because of forcible . . . relocations."[59] For numerous survivors of World War II, physical suffering was inextricable from the desperate assault on the forests in which so many participated. For many who lived through it the war felt like a compressed experience of the entire history of migrant labor on Southeast Asia's frontiers, a concentration into six years of the experiences of their forefathers who had cleared the Malayan jungle. When traffic across the Bay of Bengal ceased, the blood of thousands seeped into the soil—the same soil that earlier generations of migrants had turned into plantations and paddy fields. In memory, the urgency and the displacement of war blurred into this longer history.

Wet rice cultivation had always been a cultural and ecological link between the territories bordering the Bay of Bengal. The traffic in Burmese and Thai rice was the glue that held the Bay's economies and societies together. During the war the rice trade collapsed—and disaster ensued. In the first three decades of the twentieth century, Burmese rice exports to India grew rapidly. City dwellers in Madras, and especially in Calcutta, relied on this imported rice. Between 1891 and 1910

India imported 571,000 tons of rice each year; this grew further in the 1920s, to nearly 800,000 tons annually.[60] During the depression, exports of Burmese and Thai rice increased. If falling prices caused cultivators hardship, falling food prices are one reason depression did not turn into catastrophe in eastern India and Southeast Asia. Many observers at the time saw cheap rice as a mixed blessing. Burmese rice was highly processed and of relatively poor quality; experts in the 1930s held its consumption responsible for many of the nutritional deficiency diseases that afflicted large parts of the South Indian population.[61] And dependence on imports allowed the ecological degradation of India's rice-growing lands to continue unchecked.

When the Japanese invaded Burma in 1942, British India lost, in an instant, 15 percent of its total rice supply. This was not inevitably disastrous. In some areas that took large imports of Burmese rice, such as Madras, the shortfall was overcome by local production. In Bengal, however, a concatenation of factors both long-term and immediate conspired to cause a catastrophic famine. Food shortages in Bengal were a dire consequence of the collapse of the Bay's trade. That this shortage turned into a famine that killed 3 million people was a result of political mismanagement on an unprecedented scale, compounded by the furies of nature, ecological decline—and a gradual and then abrupt loss of entitlements by the most vulnerable parts of the population.[62]

During the winter monsoon of 1942, a massive cyclone struck eastern Bengal, flooding fields and destroying crops. That year the Bay of Bengal showed its familiar fury. "In violence and devastation it surpassed any other natural calamity that befell this country," one contemporary account observed. "It forced from the Bay a high tidal wave" that reached 140 miles per hour. The cyclone "swept the standing crops, blew off the roofs, uprooted most of the trees, demolished the huts"; the floods that followed "washed away nearly [three-quarters] of the livestock, and some 40,000 human beings."[63] Panicked by the prospect of a Japanese invasion from Arakan, local officials imposed a ruthless scorched-earth policy, denying local cultivators the transportation on which they relied to take their rice to market. The Bengal government, divided within itself, failed to act, or acted incompetently. The British cabinet chose deliberately to ignore Indian officials' alarm. Churchill's well-known hatred of India was clear to all, as he insisted that starving Bengalis would simply "continue to breed." British authorities continued to *export* Indian rice to feed troops in other theaters of war and refused to consider the use of Allied shipping to send relief to India. Appalled by the suffering of his countrymen, Subhas Chandra Bose made an offer of rice from Singapore; British authorities turned it down. As shortages intensified, the most vulnerable people—landless laborers, fishermen, women, and children—starved. Calcutta's wealth leached from rural Bengal the rice that normally would have been for local consumption.[64]

The vulnerability of the Bengali poor had increased over many decades. By 1942 it was acute. Over decades they had suffered land alienation on a massive scale. In the crisis of 1942, their patrons deserted them, choosing to pay them in cash rather than in kind when inflation put rice beyond the workers' reach. Landlords turned out their sharecroppers and day laborers; families abandoned their weaker members. All of this took place amid slow ecological strangulation. The productivity of Bengal's lands had declined and the ecological balance had skewed over the twentieth century as railway embankments stemmed the flow of rivers and invasive water hyacinth choked streams.[65] Hit by the successive blows of a loss of imports, the state's confiscation of local boats to forestall their use in a Japanese invasion, a devastating cyclone, and a lack of relief, the economy and society of Bengal buckled.[66]

The result was mass starvation. The normally conservative *Statesman* newspaper published photographs of starving children and abandoned corpses, scenes that were reminiscent of the 1870s and the 1890s. A sense of moral collapse gripped those who lived through the famine. The Bengali novelist Bhowani Sen wrote that "women sell themselves literally in hordes, and young boys act as pimps for the military. After having tolerated theft, bribery and deception we have come to a stage where we fail to stand up even to this barbarism."[67] The British government was directly responsible for starvation. "It was a man-made famine which could have been foreseen and avoided," Jawaharlal Nehru wrote from Ahmadnagar jail. "In any democratic or semi-democratic country, such a calamity would have swept away all the governments concerned with it." But even more disturbing was the callousness of wealthy Indians. Nehru expressed disgust at the "dancing and feasting and a flaunting of luxury" in Calcutta while millions starved.[68] S. G. Sardesai, a Communist, decried the "unbridled profiteering" of hoarders and speculators, and argued that "total mobilization means vigorous and just procurement of the genuine surplus from rural areas, vigorous price controls, and total rationing in cities."[69] To finally secure London's commitment to relief, in the autumn of 1943, Indian officials had to emphasize the potential consequences for the war effort of Bengal's continued starvation.

One enduring consequence of the Bengal famine was the decisive rejection of any postwar return to the old ways of unregulated markets and interregional trade in rice. Indian planners, politicians, technocrats, and populists all emphasized the need for self-sufficiency in the future. The British government, too, pushed India back upon its own resources under the "grow more food" campaign. The sight of starvation now furnished an imagination of disaster that scarred Nehru's generation of Indian leaders. Having asserted that national sovereignty would alleviate the problem of starvation, Nehru and his contemporaries were haunted by the prospect of failure. "We live continually on the verge of disaster in India, and indeed disaster sometimes overwhelms us," Nehru wrote.[70]

Three moments marked the Bay's rise and fall as a region at the heart of empires and of global capitalism. The first was the British conquest of eastern India and the establishment of Penang and Singapore on the other side of the Bay in the midst of the revolutionary upheavals of the early nineteenth century. The second was the steamship revolution in the last quarter of the nineteenth century, which produced a new level of interconnection across the Bay as people, goods, and ideas moved back and forth at higher velocity and on a greater scale than before. The third came with World War II, which brought to a sudden and decisive end the connected world of the Bay of Bengal, breaking bonds that the depression had already put under strain.

The war gave new life to questions that had lingered through these transformations: Who belonged where in this mobile world? How did the place in which one was born, the place in which one lived, and how one traveled map onto the new kinds of political community that everywhere demanded loyalty? What forms of citizenship—imperial or national, individual or collective—did statesmen, lawyers, and migrants each imagine to be possible? One experiment in citizenship during the war took place under the aegis of Subhas Chandra Bose's Provisional Government of Free India. With its nominal territory at the heart of the

Bay, in the Andaman and Nicobar Islands, the Provisional Government claimed the allegiance of the 2 million or so Indians who lived in Southeast Asia. As Bhulabai Desai demonstrated in his defense of the INA soldiers tried for treason at Red Fort, more than 200,000 Indians in Malaya had signed oaths of allegiance to the Provisional Government. For many of them, drawn from Malaya's plantations, it was the first time they had been recognized as citizens of any kind. Though the state's power was limited—by Japanese control and by its own lack of resources—it was a bold experiment in imagining a citizenship of the future.[71] Many more experiments would follow.

7

The Pursuit of Citizenship

In the tumultuous years between 1947 and 1950, the French photojournalist Henri Cartier-Bresson crossed the Bay of Bengal twice. Cartier-Bresson's Asian sojourn produced the iconic images of his career: the line of people outside a Shanghai bank on the eve of the Communist victory, the journey of Gandhi's ashes through India, portraits of Asia's new leaders. The New York Museum of Modern Art's 2010 retrospective *The Modern Century* included a large map showing Cartier-Bresson's itinerary. Traveling mostly by sea and by road, he followed routes across the Bay that millions of pilgrims, laborers, and soldiers had taken before him. He crossed from Colombo to Dhanushkodi by ferry, as Tamil tea plantation workers had done for decades; he went by steamer from Calcutta to Rangoon, following the old route of Telugu bricklayers and Bengali lawyers; his journey from Singapore to Colombo took him via Port Klang and Penang and Medan, tracing the stops of Tamil Muslim shopkeepers and Chettiar moneylenders. With the dawn of the jet age, the formation of new nation-states, and the reorientation of patterns of trade, however, these routes were becoming history.

In Cartier-Bresson's work, "the overarching story was the vast transformation of Asia—the revolution in China and the independence of India, Pakistan, Burma, Malaysia and Indonesia." Yet "most of what Cartier-Bresson did photograph . . . were examples of traditional patterns of life."[1] Stopping in Singapore in 1950, he photographed—as Elizabeth Lewis had photographed for *National Geographic* in 1931— the *thaipusam* procession, performed with fervor after the interruption of war. In the nearby jungles of Malaya the Emergency raged, but the

212

diaspora rituals of the city streets appeared timeless. Cartier-Bresson photographed the wet-rice landscapes of the Bay of Bengal rim, frozen in time as though they were not, at that very moment, subjected to massive state intervention through five-year plans and "grow more food" campaigns. He pictured "traditional" life in an Indonesia caught up in regional and religious rebellions. Overcoming his aversion to flying, Cartier-Bresson took the four-hour journey from Sumatra to Java, and from above he saw the unchanging Java Sea, "caramelized with the colors of old bronzes." But change was never far away. The photographer's images of a steam dredge reclaiming land from the waters off Sumatra— mining the tin that lay on the seabed—signaled the coming industrial age. And his departure from Medan to Colombo was delayed by the intrusion of politics when dockworkers went out on strike.

Unchanging, in flux—Cartier-Bresson's photographs depicted an Asia on the precipice of change. Old cultural patterns were revived in the aftermath of war, shutters were raised and houses rebuilt, businesses salvaged and families reunited. The bombed cities of Southeast Asia still invoked "the memory of other lands and people."[2] But a new world was in the making. One by one, the lands that bordered the Bay of Bengal gained independence from colonial rule between 1947 and 1957. They renegotiated their relations with one another; they jostled for position in a world divided by the new tensions of the Cold War. The Bay of Bengal that had cohered over centuries—a world of competing empires and overlapping diasporas—gave way to a sea of nations. "Every monument of civilization," Walter Benjamin wrote, "is also a monument to barbarism."[3] Monuments to civilization lined the boulevards and *maidans* of the old colonial capitals. They praised new powers, powers that excluded as well as included peoples in the world they made. Already in the 1930s, migrants appeared as people out of place— shipped home as employment dried up, excluded by border controls, abused by the gutter press. Now migrants and the descendants of migrants became "minorities"; they troubled the architects of new nations, who erected high walls around the prize of citizenship.

Amid revolution and political transition, the Bay of Bengal's history was submerged in the vaults of national archives. Throughout South and Southeast Asia, national archives were part of the institutional apparatus of independence. As European empires crumbled, their documentary traces were parceled out between their constituent units, with some files returned to London and others moved from Delhi to Karachi, or from Calcutta to Rangoon. As recent revelations have shown, the process was never complete; in Malaya (as in Kenya) the British went to great lengths to prevent certain documents from passing into the hands of successor states.[4] Documents that had acquired their meaning through circulation from department to department, annotated along the way—from Madras to Rangoon to Singapore, and then back to Delhi or London—now created new series. The very organization of the archive took as natural, and permanent, the political boundaries that emerged in the 1940s. Upon this logic, the totality of Burmese, Malayan, or Indian history was now contained within those countries' national archives, and what lay beyond, scattered in archives elsewhere, no longer mattered. In the indexes and handlists of the new national archives, entries for "Bay of Bengal," "emigration," and even "Indian Ocean"—all mainstays of the colonial archive—disappear after the 1950s.

The war tore through the fabric of the Bay of Bengal, and when the conflict ended, it was unclear how its threads would be woven together again. Immediately after the end of the war, the Bay remained in hiatus: not until 1947 were controls lifted on civilian shipping. Uncertainty permeated every decision, every act, every plan. Would the Bay be restored to its old patterns of movement? Would "evacuees" return—and to which of their homes? Few families were unaffected by the war. Over and above the millions dead, the displaced, the broken, and the desperate lay scattered across the "great crescent." They sought to rebuild their lives, but the war's changes were irrevocable. New ideologies—more aggressive, more martial than before—claimed the postwar order, and few of them had room for people between homes, between countries, between journeys. Malayan authorities insisted that they did not "want Malaya to become a province of either China or India," instead favoring "the importation of Javanese laborers who are Mohammedans like the Malays, speak the same language, and are easily absorbed by the Malay population."[5] The Burmese government was wary of allowing "evacuees" to return, and more wary still of admitting new migrants. The future population of the Bay of Bengal's rim—the balance between old and new migration, between migration and return, between sojourning and settlement—remained unstable. The war had unsettled the ways in which sovereignty mapped onto territory and citizenship onto residence. In contention within these competing plans for the future were very different architectures of the region; plans changed as Asia's postcolonial revolutions battled colonial attempts to reassert control.

The return of Indians to Burma commenced soon after the end of the war. Already by the end of 1945, Indian labor in Burma was "employed in a large number of occupations, e.g. at docks, on rice fields, in saw mills, in oil refineries, in the Public Works Department, in Railways [and] as rickshaw coolies."[6] In the chaos of the immediate postwar period, policies bore little relation to practice. Desperate to reopen the factories, impressed by the urgency of getting rice production going again, the returning Burmese government brought with it "many hundreds [of Indians] who were not evacuees, nor even skilled or semi-skilled": precisely the kinds of Indian "immigrants" barred from Burma under the Immigration Agreement of 1941.[7] Indian and Burmese authorities struggled to differentiate between returning residents and fresh migrants. The Indian envoy in Rangoon outlined different categories of migrants in postwar Burma, including "numbers recruited by the military after the war" for help with postwar reconstruction, "evacuees recruited from India after the Japanese collapse," and "others brought over here from India who are not evacuees." There was also the problem of the internally displaced—those Indians who had remained in Burma during the war and who had been "compelled to leave their places of residence and to migrate to various places chiefly on grounds of personal safety."[8]

Such a fluid population in unsettled conditions proved difficult to control. Jamnadas Mehta, the Indian envoy in Rangoon, estimated that by April 1946 there were 600,000 to 700,000 Indians in Burma, "scattered all over the country." Most of them endured "atrocious" housing conditions, and "medical relief hardly exists." Mehta lamented that "in a country with an area of 260,000 square miles, these thousands of unfortunate workers are scattered here and there absolutely at the mercy of their employers."[9] Chinese networks were just as quick to revive. In the middle of 1946 British officials in Rangoon noted that thousands of Chinese "evacuees" had returned to Burma, armed with "a knowledge of business conditions in Yunnan," where many of them had spent the war years. While Burma faced shortages of essential goods, they "formed syndicates carrying on trade between Burma and Yunnan by road, exporting tinned goods, toilet requisites, and luxury articles"— and profits on each of these runs fell from 300 percent to a mere 100 percent as the market grew more crowded. A quarter of the housing stock in Rangoon's Chinese neighborhood had been bombed during the war; in 1946, its slow reconstruction began. Rents were expensive at fifty rupees per month on average, with a thousand rupees required as down payment. The black market in cigarettes, canned food, and other small luxuries thrived in austere times.[10]

Old Burmese fears of immigration resurfaced. The Burmese nationalist press returned to an old theme: the country was being "swamped" by Indians and Chinese. A British labor official in Burma, B. O. Binns, looked forward to a future in which Burma would be freed from dependence on Indian labor. "The job is . . . one for serious organization, not for the *laisser faire* methods of European and Indian businesses here," he wrote, confident in the power of state planning to orchestrate economic transformation. "It will mean adjustment of the ideas of employers," he wrote, "and these are mostly antediluvian." Moreover, "it will mean the substitution of bull-dozers and mechanical navvies for coolies carrying baskets of earth on their heads. . . . But surely if we want to reconstruct our roads and railways quickly it is to modern methods we must look and not to methods out-dated in every progressive country in the world—and indeed abandoned in this country during the campaign."[11] Binns's vision was an indictment of the Bay of Bengal's economy of free trade. Revisiting the immigration rules that had come into place in 1941 only to be suspended because of the war, Burmese authorities adapted legislation from around the world, bringing their laws into line with those of the United States and the white settler colonies in their explicit provisions to exclude "undesirables." Under the emergency immigration law of 1947, these included "idiots, imbeciles, feeble-minded persons, epileptics, insane persons," those "guilty of moral turpitude," and "persons who believe in or advocate the overthrow by force or violence of the Government or law of Burma or who disbelieve in or are opposed to organised Government." The old fear of anarchists lived on.[12]

Burma's rules did not pass uncontested. The Indian government raised concerns over the discriminatory provisions of the new laws.

British authorities, still in control of Burma, worried about international pressures: "Any failure on our own part to accept in principle the return of displaced persons, would be extremely difficult to defend." They worried even more about the Indian reaction if Burma appeared more ready to readmit Chinese than Indian evacuees. "It would be idle to pretend that the question of displaced persons can long be kept separate from that of Burma's place in the international world as a whole," wrote Sir Raibeart MacDougall to Burma's Executive Council. British officials were in an anomalous position, having to plan for the future of Burma's international relations as certainties about Britain's own international role crumbled. They clung to a vision of imperial cooperation (within the Commonwealth) as Burmese officials set their own course. "It must be our effort," MacDougall declared—too late—"to ensure that the rise of nationalism does not cause too narrow a concentration on purely nationalist objectives." His comment reads as an epitaph for an imperial cosmopolitanism that never lived up to its promise.

The greatest constraint on migration law was the fragility of South Asia's new borders. As shipping across the Bay remained in suspension, it was over land that the new frontiers were tested. At the boundary between Burma and Yunnan, "there was no passport check of any kind, nor was there any restriction on entry" in the middle of 1946. And control "behind the frontier" was illusory given the absence of a "comprehensive system of registration" for the documentation of individual identity. Guards at isolated border posts gave the new frontiers substance, yet their plaintive dispatches show how little power they had. Burma's first-ever immigration officer, posted to a small office in Chittagong, reported every week to Rangoon: in the week ending January 10, 1948, he had endorsed 207 evacuee identity cards, issued 65 reentry certificates to Indians, and collected 299 rupees in immigration fees. But even his reports did not necessarily make it past the border. "This is the third time when such statement from this office is not received [in Rangoon]," he complained; "to avoid loss in transit, this copy has to be sent under registered cover."[13] Burma's semblance of control over its borders was lost in the mail.

In Malaya, the "problem" of Indians' postwar role revolved around two related questions. The first concerned the political status of long-settled Indians; the second, the future supply of Indian labor to Malaya. In postwar Malaya, too, there was a permeable boundary between "return migration," and new migration occasioned by the demands of postwar reconstruction. Compared with Burma, far fewer Indians had left Malaya during war, yet the problems of return and rehabilitation were universal. Of the 180,000 or more Asian laborers forced to work on the Thailand-Burma railway during the war, a significant proportion were Tamil estate workers. Only 21,445 workers on the railway were repatriated at war's end, and Allied tallies of overall mortality are almost certainly an underestimate. Over and above the number of dead, tens of thousands "deserted" on the way to the railway's construction sites, and many were lost in the jungle, their whereabouts never determined.[14] The Indian agent in Malaya, S. K. Chettur, toured the plantations and saw family life devastated by the loss of large numbers of able-bodied men. A Congress Party medical mission to Malaya found the plantations in a parlous state, with malnutrition widespread and sanitation having collapsed. Particularly distressing for many estate families was not knowing what had become of their husbands, fathers, or sons. The rubber estates of Malaya were filled with widows and orphans.[15] More fortunate families, separated during the war, took the first opportunity after 1945 to reunite. The family of Palanisamy, a *kangany* on a rubber estate, found themselves on a visit to India when the war broke out. Only in 1946 were they able to return to their home in Malaya and rebuild their livelihoods. When they returned, they found the women on the plantations wearing white: mourning their dead.[16]

Malaya was indispensable to the postwar revival of the British Empire, as it produced a significant proportion of the world's timber and rubber. The colony's dollar-earning capacities were essential to Britain's own economic reconstruction, a situation that created significant opportunities for a resumption of Indian labor migration.[17] The old feud between Malayan and Indian authorities still rankled. The Indian government, on the verge of independence, upheld and extended the ban on unskilled emigration from India. Every Indian passport issued after 1946 differentiated between skilled and unskilled workers seeking to depart India's shores—only skilled workers received a stamp exempting them from the need to obtain formal emigration clearance from the state. The Malayan government maintained a studied ambivalence: aware of the attractions of a steady supply of Indian migrant labor, yet reluctant to countenance fresh migration that might upset the conservative Malay nationalists who had emerged as the most important potential allies—and the most dangerous potential critics—of British authority in Malaya.[18]

Nevertheless, the postwar boom brought Tamil migrant laborers to Singapore and Malaya as cable layers, road builders, food vendors, petty traders, and essential labor at British military establishments. Abdul Aziz, a Tamil Muslim who made his living in Singapore as a provision-shop keeper, remembers how easy the journey still was in 1946–1947. "India was still in the British Raj, and Indians were still British subjects—we could go elsewhere within the British Empire" without hindrance, he said. Even as British rule in India teetered on the brink of collapse, Indians made full use of the imperial connections that remained open to them. Passports, Abdul Aziz recalled, were issued from Delhi, and checks on identity were rudimentary. "You could fool them," he recalled, "and come as Ramasamy, or Kuppusamy, or whoever [you liked]."[19] Tamil newspapers in the late 1940s were full of advertisements for jobs in Singapore. Regular notices in those papers announced schedules for the steamer services, which were deregulated in 1947. M. K. Bhasi, who traveled to Singapore in 1946, had a similar memory of easy mobility: "At that time there was no restriction, no immigration controls; you could just buy a ticket and come [to Singapore]."[20] Fewer than 10 percent of Indians resident in Singapore in 1946–1947 had first arrived there after the war. The majority had been in Singapore for many years, even decades; others had returned there after the war as second-, third-, or even fourth-time migrants, reviving in new circumstances the patterns of circulation that they had followed in the 1930s.[21]

Indian authorities recognized the weakness of border and identity checks. The Indian Passport Office conceded that passports had been issued "liberally for Indian nationals bound for Malaya," and they were issued "solely on the basis of the Statutory Declaration" of identity and a "certificate of *bona fides*" issued by the passport applicant's village headman. K. S. Seshan, who acted as the controller of emigration in Madras, stated bluntly that "my experience has shown that 9 out of every 10 Statutory Declarations are either faked or otherwise ungenuine." He concluded that "as an international document," the passport "certainly deserves much more respect than what it now receives."[22] Seshan pointed to the durability of the old migrant recruiting networks operating beyond the control of the authorities. The cast of characters was a familiar one: "the omnipresent tribe of landsharks known by a variety of denominations, such as passage brokers, travel agents, guides, etc.," indulging in "recruitment on the sly." Seshan concluded that "there will be a certain amount of legalised leakage of manpower from India into Malaya which is going to be very difficult to prevent."[23]

By this time the tide had turned: Malaya's immigration controls grew stringent. The declaration of the Emergency in 1948 signified a shift from postwar reconstruction to counterinsurgency in Malaya. Persistent, low-level confrontation between the colonial state and the Malayan Communist Party spiraled into open warfare, with neither side really in control of its escalation.[24] Security concerns reinforced migration control, in a process eerily familiar from the vantage point of the twenty-first century. "Political and economic conditions had made it necessary," the Immigration Department decided, "for Malaya to guard against any large influx of aliens." As such, "strict control was particularly important in relation to adjacent countries"—among which the report's author included India—"from which there was continual pressure by large numbers of potential immigrants."[25] One classic study of Malaya's Indian communities concluded that "in the period after 1947, the Indian population settled down to a natural and internally-ordained growth, unaffected by the vagaries of inflow and outflow that had caused constant changes in the years before the war."[26] For the Malayan sons and daughters of those who had crossed the Bay, the next journey was the quest for citizenship.

In March 1947 Asia's future leaders met in Delhi's old fort, the Purana Qila. Independence had yet to arrive for any of them, but the prize of freedom was within sight. The stage for the meeting was set to awe visitors with reminders of Asia's historic bonds: on display were monuments of the civilization that the new nations shared, restored to them after the violence of colonization. With a nod to this "golden age," the Asian Relations Conference was primarily about the future. Behind the dais stood an illuminated map of Asia, marking the air routes connecting its capitals. "We stand at the end of an era and on the threshold of a new period of history," Jawaharlal Nehru intoned in his opening address. European domination had led to "the isolation of the countries of Asia from one another," he said, but now "the land routes have revived and air travel suddenly brings us very near to each other." Beneath the fraternal sentiments, dissension lurked.

As the leaders convened in Delhi, the complexion of Asia's political future remained murky. The negotiations that would culminate in the Partition of India were under way—the Asian Relations Conference began just before Lord Louis Mountbatten's arrival as the last viceroy of India—but few predicted the final form the division would take, or the brutality with which it would occur. Nationalist forces in Indonesia and Ho Chi Minh's army in Vietnam were fighting wars against colonial reoccupation; the support they sought from their fellow nationalists in Delhi was offered lukewarm. As European empires fought rearguard actions or prepared to retreat, Asian leaders shaped their successor states. Many of the delegates at the Purana Qila were busy crafting constitutions: sifting models from around the world, processing legal advice, digesting an onslaught of ideological temptations (socialism, Communism, and shades of liberal democracy), considering the balance between religious and secular polities and between unitary and federal states. A crucial problem they all faced was that of citizenship.

Because of their interbraided populations—created by centuries of interregional migration—the citizenship laws of any Asian state would have implications for its neighbors. The delegates at the Asian Relations Conference recognized this. "The existence of large groups or minorities in many Asian countries racially different from the majority of the people," the conference organizers conceded, "raised racial and migration problems which must be tackled on an all-Asian basis." They were willing to open Pandora's box in a way that their successors just a few years later were not, preferring instead to ignore the issue. The conference constituted a committee to consider "Racial Problems and Inter-Asian Migration."

The committee's discussions tackled two related questions—the citizenship rights of past migrants and their descendants, and the control of future migration across Asia's frontiers. On the subject of future migration, there was virtual unanimity that it would be restricted, with no return to the free movement of the 1920s. "Any country has the right to determine its future population," a delegate from Ceylon insisted; on the other hand, "no law can discriminate against groups who had already been resident in the country." In theory, Asia's new states had a blank slate on which to draft their laws on migration and citizenship;

in practice, each inherited a patchwork of mixed populations. Communities that had grown accustomed over generations to circular migration now faced a binding choice. "It was generally agreed" by the Asian Relations Conference that "at any *one* time a person can have only *one* nationality." A Malayan representative put it starkly: "The Indian and the Chinese are called upon to make a final and vital choice, whether or not he wants to be a citizen of Malaya today." Confronted with the "final" choice of "only one" nationality, many people found themselves caught in between. "India did not have space" to "take back" the Tamil population of Ceylon who might not qualify for Ceylonese citizenship, one representative declared; furthermore, they had "lost all touch with India." He hoped they would be treated with "justice" and "generosity"—but by whom? The Indians pointed out that the question of citizenship was complicated by "the existence of what may be termed a common British nationality" that encompassed most of the Bay of Bengal's rim; a representative from Ceylon countered, with finality, that "British nationality must be considered to have ceased to exist" at the moment of independence.[27]

In practice, these anomalies took longer to iron out. India, like many of its neighbors, achieved political independence *before* its citizenship laws had been decided. Until the citizenship clause of the Indian Constitution was introduced in November 1949—and it would not take final form until 1955—the British Nationality and Status of Aliens Act remained in force; that is to say, for two years after India's independence a "common British nationality" did continue to unite India, Ceylon, Pakistan, Burma, and Malaya, even after the British departure from South Asia. However incongruous this might seem in retrospect, it was an era in which hardheaded pragmatism underpinned the loftiest declarations of new beginnings. Consider that in December 1948 the Indian embassy in Rangoon issued a passport to an accountant called Subramania Natarajan—his passport, and his wife's, have survived in the collection of Singapore's National Library, as a small trace of the tortuous politics of citizenship around the Bay of Bengal in the 1940s. Though issued after the independence of India and Burma, the passport identified Natarajan as a "British subject"; yet under "nationality," the document identified him as "Indian (by birth)." To make things more complicated, it was valid only for travel to "India, Burma, Pakistan, Ceylon, Siam, Indonesia, Singapore, Malayan Union, United Kingdom."

Embedded within this group of countries were three conceptions of space and sovereignty: a primarily British, imperial Asia (with the addition of Indonesia and Siam); an oceanic region around the Bay of Bengal (plus the United Kingdom); and a collection of sovereign nation-states. The passport gave his "home address" in the Old Town of Cuddalore, in Tamil Nadu, but also attached to the passport was a "certificate of identity" entitling Natarajan to stay "permanently" in Malaya. It contained transit visas for each of the countries around the Bay, and a list of foreign exchange transactions. If this appears to resemble the "flexible citizenship" that anthropologists have identified with contemporary globalization, it is because in the 1940s the basic categories of citizenship—and the documents that affirmed it—remained under construction.[28]

Gradually the space for ambiguity narrowed. Already at the Asian Relations Conference, the conflicts of the 1930s over migration had resurfaced, though now in an international rather than imperial setting. "Burmese national policy of the future must always be shaped by the ever present fear of being swarmed by either Indians or Chinese," Burma's delegate declared—his emotion is clear even from the indirect speech of the conference minutes, reported in the passive voice. Fears about migration touched a deeper concern about the world after empire. "Burma was naturally frightened," the same delegate said, "by the possibility that British imperialism may be substituted either by an Indian or by a Chinese imperialism."[29] By 1948 the Indian state faced an unprecedented and unexpected refugee flow across the borders from Pakistan. Nehru's government feared entanglement in the conflicts of neighboring states and was as keen as its Burmese counterpart to differentiate between citizens and aliens.

The year after the Asian Relations Conference, the new states of Asia faced a direct challenge from a very different vision: that of a region linked by simultaneous revolutions. The Communist-organized Calcutta Youth Conference of February 19–24, 1948, presaged the outbreak of Communist uprisings a few months later in Burma, Indonesia, Malaya, and the Philippines. Recent evidence has strengthened the consensus that there was no direct Soviet involvement in coordinating the Asian uprisings, beyond furnishing a sense of global urgency imbibed by local Communist parties. But there was little sense of interregional connection, beyond solidarity in the broadest terms, among the Communist parties of the "great crescent"; they, too, adapted to a world of nation-states, and organized their revolutions along national lines, albeit within the wider context of the Cold War.[30] Fear of political subversion, fear of illicit mobility, fear of external influence—all contributed to the closing of the borders in 1948–1949.

From the outset, the makers of India's constitution decided on a civic and territorial definition of citizenship, based on the principle of *jus soli*—"every person born in the Union or naturalised according to its laws . . . shall be a citizen of the Union."[31] The meaning of Indian citizenship was transformed by the influx of refugees across the borders of 1947's Partition, their assertions and their claims upon the state reflecting competing notions of entitlement and belonging. The inherent suspicion of Muslim loyalty that permeated Indian political culture after Partition left India's Muslims in the position of "minority citizens." Laws commandeering "evacuee property" made it difficult for Indian Muslims to return to their homes, as so many tried to do after the carnage subsided—in many cases, the state construed temporary movements in search of safety as declarations of intent to emigrate to Pakistan.[32] The presence of "foreign" Muslims on Indian soil caused further anxiety to Indian administrators. As they incorporated forcibly the princely state of Hyderabad into the Indian Union in September 1948, military and civil authorities aimed to identify and repatriate Muslims of Afghan, Pathan, and Arab origin—though in practice this proved difficult to do.[33] The reverberations of India's Partition were felt around the Bay of Bengal rim.

The border between East Pakistan and Burma was another frontier on which whole communities found themselves trapped on the "wrong" side. Representatives of the Arakanese Buddhist community of Chittagong—descendants of settlers who moved there when Chittagong was still under the rule of the Kingdom of Arakan, in the seventeenth century—wrote anxiously to the Burmese government in Rangoon, asking to be repatriated. In Burma, as in Bengal or Punjab, minority communities feared reprisals from their neighbors should news filter through of atrocities on the other side. "We are apprehensive that a small spark in the form of a communal riot across the border in Aykyab district would inflame the Mohammedan people and place our life and property in great danger," the Arakanese representative wrote.[34] As if in mirror image, many among the Muslim Rohingya community on the Burmese side of the border chose the relative safety of East Pakistan, while those who remained faced persecution in Burma, as they still do today.[35]

The presence of large Indian communities across the Bay of Bengal and elsewhere appeared more as a liability than as an asset as India closed in on itself and sought to exclude those who did not belong. Speaking in India's Constituent Assembly in March 1948, Nehru indicated the attitude that his government would take toward the question of Indians overseas:

> But the real difficulty is the question of citizenship. Now, these Indians abroad—what are they? Are they Indian citizens? Are they going to be citizens of India or not? If they are not, then our interest in them becomes cultural and humanitarian, not political. . . . This House wants to treat them as Indians and, in the same breath, wants complete franchise for them in the countries where they are living. Of course, the two things do not go together.[36]

This echoed the advice he had given to Malaya's Indian community during his visit of 1937 and again, more forcefully, in 1946: Indians overseas should commit themselves to acquiring citizenship in their lands of residence, focusing on local freedom struggles rather than looking to India for support. But many Indian communities across the Bay struggled to find acceptance within the societies in which they lived. Like so many others in very different circumstances—Jews, Armenians, Chinese, Eurasians—they became "orphans of empire" as their world, in this case the world of the Bay of Bengal, fell apart.[37] Laments for a lost world must always sit alongside recognition of the promise of freedom, the prize of citizenship, the pull of belonging. For those who fell between the lines, the minimal security of an imperial world—a security that came from looking outward for family survival and reproduction—was replaced by the minimal security of a world of nations, to which access was rationed by new kinds of citizenship.

The "immigrant minorities" of Southeast Asia faced different choices and compulsions. In Ceylon, preparations for independence failed to address the question of who could become a citizen of the new state. The Soulbury Commission of 1944, sent to draft a new constitution, sidestepped the question of citizenship; during negotiations in London,

D. S. Senanayake, leader of Ceylon's independence movement, insisted that the country's citizenship laws be defined by a future elected government. The Ceylon Indian Congress demanded full franchise for Indians in Ceylon, citizenship rights for all who could prove residence on the island, and proportional representation for Indians in the legislature. The political tide pulled the other way. Negotiations between Nehru and Senanayake broke down in December 1947 over the terms on which Indians in Ceylon would qualify for citizenship—the Indian state feared another influx of returnees and wanted to see as many as possible of Ceylon's Tamils obtain citizenship there. Failing to reach an agreement, Ceylon defined its citizenship laws in the most restrictive terms possible.[38]

With their provisions masked by prosaic titles, a barrage of legislative acts disenfranchised hundreds of thousands of people. In succession, the Ceylon Citizenship Act (1948), the Indian and Pakistani Residents Act (1948), and the Ceylon Parliamentary Elections Amendment Act (1949) denied citizenship to the estate Tamils—approximately 12 percent of the population. They denied the vote to all noncitizens. The Citizenship Act differentiated between two kinds of citizenship, that by descent and that by registration. Implicitly, only citizens by descent were true citizens; a question mark of suspicion would hang over "registered" citizens. Both categories of citizenship selectively demanded documentary proof—that is to say, demanded them from those of Indian origin and not from most Sinhalese "natives." This automatically disqualified Tamil estate workers from consideration. Some among the Tamil estate population had circulated, paperless, across the porous frontier of the Palk Strait. Others had been settled, paperless, in Ceylon for generations. Many had been born on the estates, paperless, before the state thought to record births. Notwithstanding these formidable obstacles, more than 800,000 Indians in Ceylon applied for citizenship. Though the applicants were more likely to be urbanized and educated, nevertheless only 16 percent of applications received before the 1951 deadline were approved.[39] For decades afterward there remained a strong collective memory on Ceylon's estates of application forms "lost" in the mail, of intimidation, and of bureaucratic obstacles placed in the way of those with legitimate claims.[40]

Tamils in Ceylon faced statelessness and political marginalization. Denied citizenship by Ceylon, few met the criteria for Indian citizenship, and even fewer applied for it. The political rift grew between Tamils on the plantations—who had moved, or whose forefathers had moved, to Ceylon—and the much longer-settled Jaffna Tamils; adding to this division was the distinctive community of Tamil-speaking Muslims, known as "Moors." The elite Tamil leadership abandoned its demands for the franchise on behalf of the estate Tamils, focusing instead on concessions at the national level, including cabinet positions and Tamil language rights. But still the Sri Lankan state enforced policies in support of the ethnic majority. In 1956 Sinhala was decreed the only official language of the island nation, leading to public protests and retaliatory violence against Tamil communities by young mobs of Sinhalese nationalists. The 1958 riots, which targeted Tamils, were a portent of the violence that would blight Sri Lanka's political future.

Denied citizenship and status, Ceylon's Tamil population saw that their future depended on negotiations between the Indian and Sri Lankan governments. After dragging on for over a decade, the parties reached an accord in 1964, agreeing upon the repatriation of "Tamils of Indian origin" from Sri Lanka's estates. Over the next two decades, more than 330,000 people were repatriated to India. Many of them had been born in Sri Lanka and had few connections with the Indian "homeland" to which they were returned, mostly against their will. Tamil workers from Sri Lanka returned to their "ancestral villages" to find themselves strangers, with no recognition and few prospects of employment. Born and raised on the soil of Sri Lanka's highlands, many of them found the arid climate of South India oppressive—in their narratives, as in the accounts of their nineteenth-century forebears, unfamiliarity of climate was an index of displacement.[41] Gradually, grudgingly, the Sri Lankan state granted citizenship to all the estate Tamils who remained on the island—but for them, as for so many minorities around the Bay of Bengal, it was an unequal and incomplete citizenship.

When the political demands of Sri Lanka's Tamils escalated in the 1970s and turned to armed struggle in the 1980s, they followed the same territorial logic that consumed the region's states: territorial autonomy was the goal of the Liberation Tigers of Tamil Eelam (the "Tamil Tigers"). When the Indian state intervened in the Sri Lankan conflict, as it did, disastrously, in the 1980s, it was through the cynical exercise of interstate diplomacy. The old world of circulation had no place in a sea of nations. Yet movement across the watery frontier between Sri Lanka and South India never ceased completely. The continued movement of fishing communities, refugees, and labor migrants in both directions gave rise to the label *kallattoni* ("illicit boat immigrant"), used as a blanket term for Indian Tamils in Sri Lanka, including those who had lived there for generations; all movement between India and Sri Lanka was suspect.[42]

In Burma, too, the search for citizenship was elusive. The constitution of 1947 introduced two kinds of citizenship, distinguishing, again, between citizens by descent (those who "belonged to any of the indigenous races of Burma") and citizens by registration. The latter were given a deadline of April 1950 by which to submit applications for citizenship. In Burma, as in Ceylon, the documentary bar was high, and amid the uncertainties of the time, many Indian residents failed to realize the importance that pieces of paper would hold. After his return to India, W. S. Desai, a retired history professor at Rangoon University, wrote in tones of regret of the "elaborate procedure applicable to those who desired to elect the citizenship of Burma. The applicant is required to approach the court, of the district concerned, with an affidavit concerning the particulars of his residence in Burma." Those who lacked documentation of their journeys and their intentions had to create a convincing narrative. But any local resident was free to object to an application within six weeks of its submission, opening the way for personal rivalries and feuds between neighbors to block applications for citizenship.[43]

Soon after independence, the Burmese state drew firm lines between citizens and outsiders. The Land Nationalization Act of 1948 removed most property rights from noncitizens and, together with new laws on tenancies and land transfers, marked the start of "sweeping measures to liquidate Indian landed interests" in Burma.[44] Distraught Indian landowners wrote to India's Ministry of External Affairs, detailing their dispossession by Burma's new laws. Hem Chandra Bannerjee, formerly an advocate at Rangoon's High Court, wrote that "Indian nationals in Burma hold nearly one-fourth of the arable lands . . . and it will be a great tragedy if they lose them." In the general atmosphere of the time—when India, too, redistributed land from its largest *zamindars*—outward sympathy for Indian landowners in Burma, and for the

Chettiars in particular, was limited. For all their losses, they appeared to be precisely the "vested interests" that freedom and socialism would sweep away everywhere in the new Asia. Mindful of this, other petitioners took a different approach, emphasizing that "poor and middle class people" of the Chettiar community, too, suffered "as a result of their inability to discharge their debts raised in India for their Burma business during the pre-war days."[45]

The next step in consolidating a territorial nation-state in Burma was to secure the borders—stopping the circular migration that had shaped Burma's population beginning in the late nineteenth century. Indians who failed to apply for Burmese citizenship were permitted to remain as temporary residents, though they had to register with the police and acquire identity cards. If a temporary resident left the country for more than sixty days, "the identity certificate lapses and with it his privilege of residence in Burma." In an instant, circular migration became impossible. The movement of money was stemmed as decisively as the movement of people. In 1948 remittances from Burma were limited first to 1,500 rupees and then to just 250. Each exchange transaction required the permission of the controller of foreign exchange, who refused to recognize the obligations of Indians in Burma to support families back in India. In limiting remittances, "the Burmese government struck at the root of the Indian family system."[46]

Restrictions on entry and exit, and on the import and outflow of goods and currency, stimulated border crossings of all kinds. Just one example of many can be found in the oral histories collected by the Burmese writer, journalist, and folklorist Ludu U Hla in the late 1940s while serving time in Insein jail. One of his interviewees, a fellow prisoner, was a Tamil youth called Kanniya, who gave an account of how Indian merchants and laborers maintained their links across the Bay after 1945:

The Indian merchants who did business on Moghul Street usually sent diamonds and jewellery to India on ocean-going steamers plying between Rangoon and Indian ports. The ships' officers acted as couriers, the gems being packed in boxes of Cuticura face powder. I remember seeing on one occasion the European captain of a ship being handed such a box. Other favorite places of concealment were false compartments in suitcases, hollow heels of European style shoes and handles of umbrellas and bicycles.

Kanniya himself went back and forth between his father's family in Madras and his mother and stepfather in Burma, continuing a long tradition of circular migration. Restrictions on entry and residence could be overcome if one knew how they worked and where their loopholes were. Making movement illicit made it more dangerous; borders were never sealed, but there is no question that they became harder to cross.[47]

In the climate of fear that gripped Burma—beset, from the moment of independence, by multiple ("Red Flag" and "White Flag") Communist insurrections and by ethnic rebellions by the Karen and other minorities—many chose to cross the border back to India once and for all. "Owing to widespread insurrections and disturbed economic conditions," one Chettiar businessman wrote to the government of India, "landlords found that the collection of rent was impossible." He detailed cases of Chettiars assaulted, abducted, or even killed as they were caught up in the violence that swept Burma. The Indian government worried about having to accommodate yet more refugees. When India's president, Rajendra Prasad, toured Burma in 1948, he warned an audience of Indian cultivators not to return—he emphasized how difficult other returnees had found it to make a living in India. As the situation worsened, Nehru relented. In early 1949 he arranged for the evacuation of 4,000 Indians living near Insein, and nearly 30,000 Indians of Bihari origin who had moved to Burma in the nineteenth century to found a sugar-cultivating agricultural colony on Ziawadi Estate.[48] As ever, unplanned movement outran official plans for resettlement. Writing from a small intelligence post near the Burma-India border, an Indian Army officer reported in early 1949 that "many Indians are reported to be making ready to come back to India." He feared—yet again—that "apart from creating serious security problems, these refugees will also create problems of relief and rehabilitation."[49]

As movement stopped, interstate relations between Burma and India congealed. Worried about Communist subversion at home, Nehru lent support to U Nu's government in its fight against insurgency. In 1951 Burma and India signed a treaty of friendship. The view of the Bay of Bengal broken up into sealed units was enshrined in treaties and enforced by border guards. But traces of another, older world remained. Bhimrao Ambedkar—the fiercely independent leader of India's *dalits* and brilliant legal architect of India's constitution—looked across the

Bay in his search for a spiritual alternative for India's former "untouchables," convinced that Hinduism offered them only humiliation. Ambedkar considered both Islam and Christianity, but eventually he settled on Buddhism as the most appropriate path for himself and for his followers. In 1954 he visited Ceylon and made two trips to Burma; he looked to the past—to the ancient Buddhist "highway" connecting the Bay of Bengal—to provide a better future for India's *dalits*. In 1954 Ambedkar attended the World Fellowship of Buddhists in Rangoon, where he met E. V. Ramasamy, himself on a tour to Burma and Malaya to preach his message of rationalism and reform. Two years later, shortly before his death, Ambedkar led a mass conversion ceremony in the central Indian city of Nagpur, when half a million *dalits* embraced Buddhism.[50] The reasons of state governed relations across the Bay of Bengal in the postcolonial age, but an older universalism was still alive and continued to animate the flow of ideas across the water.

In the lives of migrants, there was a permanent sundering of ties between India and Burma. Many returned to their homes in India—in Andhra, Orissa, or Tamil Nadu—and for them, Burma lived on in memory as a "golden land." The poorest, those whose family ties had been sundered by migration, were resettled by Indian state governments: many of the archival files on their resettlement are missing, and the detailed story awaits its historian.[51] The exodus of landowners and laborers in the late 1940s was followed, after Burma's military coup of 1962, by further pressure on Indians to leave; a second "return" of Indians followed, nearly 200,000 of them.[52] Traces of their history remain on the landscape. Many Tamil towns still have a "Burma colony," though few of them are still inhabited by the "Burma-returned." For years after the return, however, these colonies were marked by the material influence of Burma (in the small pieces of teak furniture and the distinctive kitchen utensils that even poorer people brought back) and by its cultural influence (above all in styles of cooking). In Chennai, the "Burma bazaar" was established by returnees to sell goods imported from Burma; in time it became a thriving market (and often a black market) for imported electronic goods from across Southeast Asia, bringing to mind a very old world of commerce across the Bay. Some of those who returned remained in India's northeast: today there are still Tamil- and Telugu-speaking villages near the Indian-Burmese border, settled by people who left Burma, and now inhabited by their children. Their numbers grew through the continued influx of refugees from Burma in the 1980s, including a number of Burmese student radicals.

In the popular imagination, Burma was a land "lost" to India. For cinema-goers across the Tamil-speaking world, the loss of Burma passed into legend through *Parasakti* (1952), one of the iconic Tamil films of the twentieth century. The story opens on the eve of World War II, at a Tamil cultural performance in Rangoon. The film's protagonists— three brothers—are well-settled and prosperous members of Rangoon's Tamil community. One of them introduces the cultural show with an impassioned speech about the sacrifices of the sons of the Tamil country toiling overseas, yearning for the soil of their homeland. The three brothers are separated when Japanese bombs fall on Rangoon. The eldest brother makes it home. The middle brother is caught on the "long march" back to India and ends up in a squalid refugee camp. The youngest brother—played by Sivaji Ganesan in his film debut—wanders, lost, in the Tamil Nadu countryside after being robbed of his belongings; he begs for shelter, then turns to crime. Eventually he locates his younger sister, now widowed, and saves her from the depredations of a corrupt priest, for which he is put on trial. The moral of the story is clear—for Tamil Nadu to be a home worthy of its brave sons, social reform, justice, and the eradication of caste oppression were essential. The devastating loss of Burma showed that Tamil Nadu had to welcome its diaspora home and turn its back on the sea. This very real loss no doubt fed into a less tangible sense of cultural loss as Tamil Nadu was incorporated into the Indian nation-state—a sense of loss that motivated a fascination with "fabulous" geographies, including a quest for the lost land of Lemuria.[53]

Despite this breaking of links, an Indian community remained in Burma. Around half a million strong, linguistically and religiously diverse, most of its members were settled in Rangoon. The old port city of Moulmein, too, retained some of its maritime links of trade and movement. In the 1950s the old political institutions of Indian life in Burma— the Burma Indian National Congress, the labor unions—were depoliticized, and remained only as "cultural organizations." Even then, political connections across the Bay continued to exist. In 1952 local Tamils established a Burmese branch of the Dravida Munnetra Kazhagam (DMK), the political party that was a vehicle for Tamil nationalism in

India.[54] The Indian community in Rangoon remained—and still remains today—integral to the life of the city. Crowded around the narrow streets near the Sule Pagoda in the city center, Rangoon's Little India is a living archive of migration. Food vendors sell Indian regional specialties, though many of their waiters are now Burmese. Hindu temples, a Surati mosque, a Telugu Methodist church, and a "Chulia" dargah have remained sites of worship. In their dress, most Indians in Burma are indistinguishable from other residents, the men all opting for the ubiquitous *longyi*. This is not a diaspora in the classic sense of the term, since most of its connections with India have long disappeared. Many Indian residents in Rangoon told me that their people had come from India "long, long ago"—when they said this, even their body language gestured to the distant past—and only the very old had visited India in their youth. Connections with ancestral villages and extended families had lapsed. In a sense, the Indians settled in Burma resemble most closely the Indian communities in the former sugar

Figure 19 Signboard of the Chulia Dargah mosque in Rangoon. The streets of central Rangoon are still home to a large and long-settled Indian community. *Photograph by Sunil Amrith.*

colonies most distant from India, Trinidad and Guyana and Fiji, and there is little indication of just how closely connected the Bay of Bengal once was.

The position of Indians in postwar Malaya was tied to British plans for sweeping reforms in citizenship. The quest to create a unified political community under crown rule—a Malayan Union—proved short-lived. The Malayan Union proposal provoked a Malay political response, led by Dato Onn bin Jaafar, and the depth of reaction took British authorities by surprise. The United Malays National Organization (UMNO), formed in March 1946, rallied to the defense of Malay rights and the sovereignty of the Malay rulers. Confronted with the loss of conservative Malay support, British administrators backtracked. They abandoned the Malayan Union plan and replaced it with a Federation of Malaya that was far less accommodating to the demands of the Indian and Chinese minorities. Singapore, with its large Chinese majority, would remain outside the Federation.[55]

The conservative Anglo-Malay agreement met spirited opposition. Other visions of the political future clamored for attention, with equally persuasive narratives of citizenship and belonging. An alternative political formation—including the left-leaning Malayan Democratic Union of English-educated intellectuals, Communist-supported trade unions, and the newly formed Malayan Indian Congress (MIC)—came together to form the All-Malayan Council of Joint Action (AMCJA), chaired by the veteran Chinese business leader Tan Cheng Lock. To the alarm of the colonial authorities, AMCJA forged an alliance with the progressive wing of the Malay nationalist movement that was opposed to UMNO, spearheaded by the Malay Nationalist Party and brought under the umbrella of the Pusat Tenaga Rakyat, or "Center of People's Power." AMCJA's proposals on citizenship in Malaya—drafted in a series of meetings in the middle of 1947—provided an alternative vision, one much truer to Malaya's migrant history, and more creative than anything that emerged in Burma or Ceylon. Crucially, the AMCJA citizenship proposals "dissolved the distinctions between nationality and citizenship—between indigenous and non-indigenous."[56] In deference to Malay nationalist opinion, they abandoned the idea of "Malayan" citizenship—which implied a distinction between immigrant "Malayans" and indigenous Malays—and proposed a unitary "Melayu" nationality, open to anybody who called Malaya home, regardless of descent or origin. The term was rich with meaning. For centuries "Melayu" had been a flexible banner of identification, incorporating newcomers in this mobile, maritime world; the citizenship proposals harked back to this more open world of the nineteenth century. The council's proposals sought to start afresh, to build a modern Melayu citizenship from the diverse population that history had brought to Malaya's shores. This was not, however, a vision of diasporic citizenship. The Council was as intolerant as its opponents of multiple loyalties, insisting that "a divided allegiance is, in our opinion, a contradiction in terms." Rather, they argued that loyalty was not a question of ethnicity or origin, but one of conscious political *choice*. "The country in which a man would prefer to bury his bones," they wrote, "and which he is prepared to die to defend, is his real home."[57] The People's conception of citizenship accommodated the complex legacies of past migrations but rooted itself firmly in a world of nations.

After the war, the Indian political leadership in Malaya was weak and divided. Although the MIC participated in the AMCJA, many of its leaders continued to look to India as their source of political inspiration and the object of their allegiance. A perceptive contemporary account observed that Indian politicians in Malaya "appeared to be concentrating their efforts at unravelling the somewhat confused tangle of opinions which existed among the Indian community in general." The "tangle" included "the disbanded sympathisers of the INA, the powerful supporters of the Indian Congress, and the compact and energetic Labour wing of the Indian community"; added to these was "the small but financially strong nucleus of the Indian business class represented by the Indian Chamber of Commerce."[58] The old leaders of the prewar years—the urban elite of the Central Indian Association of Malaya—tried to reassert control. Many of them had been active in the Indian Independence League and the Indian National Army during the war, and they sought to capitalize on the sense of Indian unity that Subhas Bose had inspired. But the old tensions returned: between the urban elites and the working class, between North Indians and Tamil-speakers, between Indian-focused strategies and Malayan-focused ones.

Indian estate workers were gripped by the social and political ferment that swept Malaya after the end of the war. The "Malayan Spring" saw an unprecedented opening of the public sphere, freer of restrictions than at any time before. The Malayan Communist Party had played a key role in the Allied reoccupation of Malaya, and now they were out in the open after decades underground. The limits of openness were redefined in a constant tug-of-war between British administrators and the new political forces. Trade unions proliferated, and combined in federations. Countless newspapers and journals erupted into the public sphere, then folded just as quickly. In this time of openness and uncertainty, "many previously disempowered groups in society—women, the young, workers and peasants—took the political initiative."[59] After the trauma of the war, when so many Tamil estate workers had died and even more had been separated from their families, a new generation of labor leaders organized the estate workforce.

Though Malaya's rubber, tin, and timber were crucial to Britain's economic survival after the war, wage rates for rubber tappers remained at prewar levels. Beginning in late 1946, a series of strikes erupted on the rubber estates, starting in Kedah—the largest protests on the plantations since the Klang Valley strikes of 1941. A. N. Samy, a truck driver on Harvard Estate about whom we know very little, emerged as the movement's leader, and by early 1947 around 15,000 workers on neighboring estates were under his authority. Building on the legacy of the INA's wartime mobilization, Samy organized the men into *thondar pedai* gangs: they drilled in military formation, enforced strikes, and picketed toddy shops. Toddy shops, a source of revenue for the planters and the state, were a lightning rod for protest. In contrast to 1941, solidarities formed between Tamil and Chinese workers: unrest escalated when a Chinese laborer was killed by police on Dublin Estate after going out on strike in sympathy with Tamil rubber workers. In 1947 there were 280 strikes on rubber estates alone. Estate workers' unions were drawn into the Communist-dominated Pan-Malayan Federation of Trade Unions; two of its leaders, S. Ganapathy and P. Veerasenan, were Tamil labor activists.[60]

By the middle of 1948, rising tension between the Malayan Communist Party (MCP) and the British authorities spilled over into open confrontation. With neither side in control of the "revolt on the periphery," the colonial authorities declared a state of emergency, and the MCP launched an insurrection.[61] In the cycle of repression and reprisal that ensued, the radical wing of the Indian labor movement in Malaya was crushed. The small number of Indian activists who joined the MCP's revolution were early victims of the Emergency: S. Ganapathy was convicted of possessing explosive weapons and hanged, while P. Veerasenan was shot dead. Altogether, by 1949 more than 800 Indians had been arrested under Emergency rules. The fragile bonds of solidarity that united Tamil rubber tappers and Chinese workers unraveled in a climate of fear and suspicion. The vacuum was filled by leaders of a very different kind. After the proscription of the radical unions, John Brazier, a former British Rail union man who served as trade union advisor to the government in Malaya, lent his support to "moderate" unions of estate workers. Several of them came together in 1954 as the National Union of Plantation Workers (NUPW) under the leadership of P. P. Narayanan, a pragmatic negotiator and committed anti-Communist. It focused on securing piecemeal improvements in wages and working conditions—and not without success. Over the following decade, the NUPW participated in the purchase of estates being sold off by departing Europeans, and ran them as cooperatives.[62]

At the same time, the unions formed a closer relationship with the Malayan Indian Congress, which sought to break free of its elite, urban, and primarily North Indian origins. Led by V. T. Sambanthan, who himself was an estate owner, the MIC was taken over by Tamil-speakers in the early 1950s; they succeeded in registering large numbers of estate workers as party members. Sambanthan was Malayan-born but had studied at Annamalai University in Madras in the 1930s. There he, like so many others, was drawn to socialist ideas and devoured left-wing literature, "which they would hide in the rafters every time there was a raid."[63] He supported, but was not directly involved with, the Indian National Army. After the war, Sambanthan emerged as a voice of compromise who could also reach out, as few of the old guard of the MIC could, to the primarily Tamil constituency to which the party had to appeal in a democratic age. The MIC focused entirely on Malaya, stripping itself of its last vestiges of Indian nationalism. The final stage in the party's reinvention began in 1955, when the MIC opted to form part of the conservative Alliance—together with UMNO and the Malayan Chinese Association—in the legislative elections. The Alliance won a sweeping victory, and remains in power in Malaysia to this day. This marked the beginning of modern Malaysia's "ethnic bargain." In exchange for acceptance of Malay political and economic primacy, most

Indians and Chinese in Malaya gained citizenship rights, but the conservative, communal parties secured a monopoly on representing the views of "their" ethnic minorities within government. Political organization along lines other than ethnicity became very difficult.[64]

The cultural traffic across the Bay of Bengal between South India and Malaya flourished after the war, far more than did such traffic between India and Ceylon or Burma. If the movement of people across the Bay never resumed on the scale of the 1930s, the traffic in ideas, publications, and—more than ever—films continued after the war. In the 1920s and 1930s, as we have seen, the Tamil press of Singapore and Malaya provided a heady mix of Tamil regionalism and Indian nationalism. After the war, it was almost exclusively Tamil cultural revival that prevailed. Many prewar cultural organizations revived their activities, among them the Tamils Reform Association. New periodicals—*Dravida Murasu, Ina Mani*—took up the cause of caste reform, spearheaded by Tamil teachers' associations and labor leaders. Local branches of the Dravida Kazhagam (the Dravidian Association, which grew out of the Self-Respect Movement in Madras) were established across Malaya. Self-Respect marriages, performed with minimal ceremony and without upper-caste priests, grew in popularity in Malaya and crossed the lines of religious community: in April 1948 a young Tamil Muslim woman used a Self-Respect marriage as an occasion to make "an impassioned plea for women's rights and equal status."[65] In August 1949 a coalition of cultural associations organized the Malay Tamil Pannai, a three-day festival. Starting in 1952, an annual Tamil cultural celebration in Malaya coincided with the Pongal harvest festival. Despite the efforts of social reformers, however, old rituals intensified in scale and devotion after the war—above all the annual *thaipusam* procession, which Cartier-Bresson had witnessed on Singapore's streets in 1950.[66]

The message of social reform arrived in Singapore and Malaya in film reels, in pamphlets, and in the performances of traveling theater companies. Many of them performed in Singapore's entertainment palaces—Happy World and New World, named for their inspiration in 1920s Shanghai—alongside Malay *joget* musicians, Chinese opera troupes, and international wrestlers. Singapore remained a cultural whirlwind after the war; performances in many languages and styles shared the stage and competed for audiences' attention. A young Tamil shop assistant who worked in Happy World in the 1950s remembers the scene:

> Happy World was full of Indians, Chinese, Malays—all were there. Outside there were bars and things, all in the open air; the Malay guys would all dance joget. There were all kinds of dances going on, man . . . in the end, the government shut it all down! Many people would come down from Johor just to come to Happy World. The big shot, that biscuit factory guy, would come often, with lots of bodyguards and all.
> . . . Boxing matches would be held. King Kong! Tara Singh! Wrestling too. But boxing matches would attract the biggest crowds.[67]

In this mix was the reformist theater of South India. In November 1955 the Paari Group from Madras performed *Inbam Engai* (Where Is Happiness?) to large crowds in New World's Sunlight Hall; the following year, K. R. Ramasamy's Drama Group performed *Velaikkari* (Maid), a tale of abuse and exploitation, at Happy World stadium.[68] From the city stage, reformist theater spread to the plantations of the hinterland: workers with a taste for drama added plays with a social message to their usual repertoire of stories from the Tamil classical tradition.[69]

The cinema was, by the 1950s, the most popular medium of all. Tamil films flooded the Singapore and Malayan markets.[70] The burgeoning Malay film industry of the late 1940s and 1950s relied, still, on Indian narratives and Indian talent, and on the funding of the (Chinese) Shaw brothers. Often the story lines of such films depicted a rural Malay idyll—the *kampung*—free from external influences, but the production of Malay films was entirely cosmopolitan. Among the most prolific film directors in Malay cinema in the 1950s was L. Krishnan. He was born in India and arrived in Penang with his family in 1928, at the very height of migration between India and Malaya. During the war he joined the INA and acted as an interpreter for Japanese forces. Repatriated to India by the British, he made a career within the Tamil film industry. As an assistant director, he worked on the Sinhala film *Amma* at a time when most Sri Lankan films were still shot in Madras. In 1950 he moved back to Malaya and directed *Bakti* (Devotion), the first film to feature P. Ramlee, who would become the iconic Malay actor of his generation. In the world of cinema, the multilingual world of the Bay of Bengal continued to revolve, even as in the political sphere it cracked.[71]

In December 1954 E. V. Ramasamy returned to Malaya, which he had first visited in 1929. Periyar came from Burma, where he had met Ambedkar at the World Buddhist Congress. Periyar's first visit to Malaya had a dramatic effect on Tamil politics in the country, but in 1929 his audience was much more closely connected to India than they would be in 1954, by which time most Tamils across the Bay considered Malaya to be their home. Periyar's message of social reform was as powerful as ever, given the enduring poverty, factionalism, and division within the Tamil community of Malaya. His visit emboldened and sustained the Tamil cultural revival that was by then in full flight. Many of his speeches, and the writings of his supporters, focused on the social marginalization of the Malayan Tamil community, diagnosing their ills and prescribing the medicine of social reform and education.[72] But the political context was completely changed. Immediately after the war "Tamil populism, particularly expressed in the Dravidian movement, tended to be linked with or absorbed in the left-wing working class alliance"; by the 1950s it had been depoliticized and "stood forth as the only form of Tamil politics that was acceptable to the government."[73]

Only in Singapore did the political edge of cultural politics remain sharp. There, a progressive anticolonial alliance remained powerful through the 1950s, as Singapore was freer than Malaya from Emergency-era proscriptions. Many stalwarts of the working-class movement in Singapore were of Indian origin—James Puthucheary, a member of the Indian National Army during the war, became one of its most incisive intellectuals, and Dr. M. K. Rajkumar emerged from the University of Malaya Socialist Club as a leading voice on the left. The language and the promise of Afro-Asian solidarity thrived amid the clamor of political ideas. Dockworkers played a leading role in labor protest. Many of them were recent migrants from Kerala, part of the movement of skilled Malayali workers to Singapore and Malaysia that began after the war—their skills were in such demand that they got around the new migration controls. They brought with them a political culture of activism, inspired by the rising power of the Kerala Communist Party. Malayalis worked on the British naval base in Singapore and clustered in Sembawang, a neighborhood in equal parts Tamil, Chinese, and European, filled with countless bars and food stalls selling *vadai* and *murukku* and *sarabat*. Activists among them galvanized their fellow dockworkers, painters, and fitters with literature and regular study sessions, at times reaching well beyond the Malayali community.[74] This was a generation that had its political vision shaped by the astonishing cosmopolitan sweep of Jawaharlal Nehru's *Glimpses of World History* and by the ecumenical thought of Gandhi and Tagore as much as by Marx or Lenin. By the late 1950s, however, the political world of Singapore, too, had narrowed. The politics of state-managed "multiracialism" and a clampdown on dissent paved the way for a city-state focused on economic growth above all else.[75]

What remained was a cultural diaspora. Political and familial links, both so strong in the 1930s and 1940s, faded in intensity, and the Tamil diaspora in Southeast Asia stabilized as a permanent community, linked to India mostly through language and cultural practice and memory. In April 1966 Kuala Lumpur hosted the first international conference on Tamil studies. More than 130 delegates and 40 observers attended the conference—they came from India and Ceylon, and from across Europe and the United States. The location was symbolic, affirming that Malaysia was an integral part of the Tamil-speaking world, but in fact that world lived mostly in the past. The Malaysian prime minister, Tungku Abdul Rahman, opened the conference with reference to the long historical connections across the Bay of Bengal. With the exception of Sinnappah Arasaratnam, few speakers said anything about the recent history of migration between India and Southeast Asia, and fewer still mentioned the contemporary political and economic conditions of Malaysia's or Sri Lanka's Tamil minorities. Rather, the conference focused on the glories of Tamil classical culture, careful to avoid the raw wounds of war and the difficult politics of citizenship in the postcolonial world.[76]

Beginning in the nineteenth century, Tamil migrants to Malaya developed a sense of belonging through their intimate relation with the land. The plantation landscape of Malaya was shaped by the world of the Bay of Bengal. As that world fragmented, the plantation economy changed. The social and economic security of Tamils in Malaya became as tenuous as their political rights. The 1950s saw fundamental changes in land use in Malaya: highly mechanized oil palm plantations replaced large tracts of rubber land as the market for natural rubber declined and synthetics advanced. As European planters departed, their estates were subdivided and sold off to mostly Chinese buyers. Between 1950 and 1967 more than 320,000 acres of estate land were divided in this way; by contrast, the Tamil cooperative movement remained small in scale. For Tamil workers this spelled mass unemployment. The number of Tamil workers employed on rubber estates fell from 148,500 in 1950 to under 80,000 two decades later. Tamil estate workers, many of them born and raised on the plantations, were resettled in urban tenements; the education they had received in estate schools left them ill-equipped for the industrial economy, however, and their fragile bonds of community were broken in the process of resettlement. The result was an enduring, structural poverty for a large section of Malaysia's Tamil minority, though for many others, including some *dalits*, departure from the plantations brought social and economic mobility.[77] It was a process so traumatic that many former plantation workers I spoke to looked back on the European estates with nostalgia.

The insecurity of Tamil estate workers in postcolonial Malaysia was laid bare in May 1969 when "racial riots" broke out in and around Kuala Lumpur. Following a general election in which the Chinese-dominated opposition parties made significant gains, public demonstrations spilled into violence on May 13, 1969. Nearly 200 people died, and many more were injured or made homeless. Most of the victims of the violence were Chinese; the riots emerged from the frustration of the Malay working class, which had failed to taste the fruits of independence, and which was encouraged to protest by ambitious young politicians within the ruling UMNO party. A political revolution culminated in the New Economic Policy and sweeping measures of affirmative action in favor of ethnic Malays, including a program of land redistribution. The National Operations Council, which ruled by emergency decree, passed legislation requiring noncitizens to acquire special permits to work, which would be issued only if no citizen could do the job. Indians on the estates were the chief victims of this move—many had not applied for citizenship in the 1950s, though most of them would have been eligible. Like their counterparts in Sri Lanka, they had failed to acquire citizenship "for reasons of remoteness, illiteracy, . . . [or] bureaucratic obstruction." Now thousands found themselves under pressure. Around 60,000 Indian workers left Malaysia permanently; many of those who remained, without citizenship, found their economic positions even more insecure, reliant on informal or short-term employment. The story continues: in 2012, there are still elderly people in rural areas of Malaysia without citizenship, which excludes them from entitlements in a country that, more than most states, relies on biometric documentation of identity as a key to access state services.[78]

Envisaging a world after empire, there were political possibilities other than a world of nation-states.[79] If these alternative visions faded from prominence by the 1950s, this owed as much to the political constraints of state building and the international context of the Cold War as to any failure in their persuasive powers. By the mid-1950s the idea of the Bay of Bengal as a sea bordered by nation-states appeared natural; what was less clear was whether it could any longer be seen as a coherent region at all. When people in the nineteenth century spoke of "the Bay"—British administrators and Tamil migrants alike—their meaning was clear. By the middle of the twentieth century, this could no longer be taken for granted.

The Bay's disappearance from view was gradual. Even after India's independence, Jawaharlal Nehru continued to speak of the possibility of an "Asian federation." He was not alone in believing that the borders of 1947–1948 might prove temporary: General Aung San of Burma, too, spoke of an "Asiatic federation" in the "not very, very distant future."[80] Sarat Chandra Bose—veteran nationalist leader from Bengal, and the elder brother of Subhas—wrote in 1948 of his vision for a "United Nations of South Asia," encompassing India, Pakistan, Ceylon, and Burma. This would be a supranational body that, while respecting the sovereignty of its constituent states, would move toward economic integration and "enunciate a doctrine somewhat similar to the Monroe Doctrine for the Indian Ocean."[81] These visions of political integration proved short-lived. The violence and refugee flows of Partition, the inability to agree the contours of international borders, the "minority" problem, multiple insurgencies—their combination made Asia's new states acutely anxious about their borders. Malaya was still under colonial rule and in the grip of British counterinsurgency. By the time of the Asia-Africa Conference, held at Bandung in 1955, sovereignty had trumped every other value: Bandung was "a conclave of sovereign nation-states, and not a parliament of peoples."[82]

The concern with nation building, in turn, reshaped perceptions, so the Bay of Bengal no longer made intuitive sense as a region. A sharp division arose between "South Asia" and "Southeast Asia"—a division that drew a proverbial line directly through the Bay, where East Pakistan (now Bangladesh) met Burma. The very notion of "Southeast Asia" emerged from World War II as a new way to describe a part of the globe that had been known to colonial geography as "further India," "the Indies," "the Indian archipelago," or simply "the other side of the Bay"; in Chinese thought, it was always *nanyang*, "the southern ocean." The Japanese occupation of Southeast Asia brought under a common rule territories previously distributed among Western empires—Burma, Malaya, Indonesia, and the Philippines. In response, the Allied counteroffensive grouped them together under its South-East Asia Command. The boundaries of Southeast Asia remained flexible—South-East Asia Command was, after all, headquartered in Ceylon. But the regional political structures that developed in the 1950s and 1960s tended to reinforce the division between South and Southeast Asia. The first regional institution—the Southeast Asian Treaty Organization (SEATO), an Asian counterpart to NATO—included Pakistan; its membership of pro-American, anti-Communist Asian states followed the political geography of the Cold War. The formation of the Association of Southeast Asian Nations (ASEAN) in 1967 took the process of regionalization further. ASEAN institutionalized the distinctive identity of Southeast Asia as separate from South Asia and East Asia, and not until the 1990s would ASEAN renew its ties with the giants to its east and west. Perhaps more than any other regional organization of the postwar period, ASEAN took respect for state sovereignty and noninterference in other member states' "internal affairs" as its guiding principles.

The boundaries of Southeast Asia solidified, too, under the postwar political and academic organization of knowledge known as "area studies." Because American policy makers saw Southeast Asia as a key arena for the battle against Communism (as indeed it proved to be), funding flowed to university departments of Southeast Asian studies at Cornell, Berkeley, and elsewhere. For good intellectual reasons—and by no means simply responding to material incentives—scholars in the 1960s sought to write "autonomous" histories of Southeast Asia, freeing it from the shadow of "Greater India" or "Greater China"; they argued that the region had enough in common culturally and politically to distinguish it from the two regions that surrounded it, South Asia and East Asia.[83] The great task of the era, for scholars and policy makers alike, was to understand the origins and the nature of Southeast Asian nationalisms. Southeast Asian states, like all others, needed usable pasts to legitimize their present structures. Departments of Southeast Asian studies tended to treat Southeast Asia simply as a collection of individual nation-states, their contemporary borders projected back in time. A wealth of insights emerged from this flourishing field of scholarship—much of what we know about the history of modern Southeast Asia emerged from the work of the postwar generation of area scholars. But there were intellectual losses, too. One historian puts it thus: "Having helped to create these Frankenstein's monsters [the areas of area studies], we are obliged to praise them for their beauty, rather than grudgingly acknowledge their limited functional utility." It meant that Burmese and Malaysian history, both firmly on the side of "Southeast Asia," were completely separated from the study of India; they were studied in different departments, by scholars who attended different conferences. The deep, intensive connections that so significantly shaped their history were lost from view.[84]

As passports and visas stemmed the flow of people across the Bay, economic connections shriveled. The very fabric of material exchange that had knit the Bay together split. The nation-state became the default unit of economic planning. Trade found new channels. We can trace this diminution through the story of rice, that most essential and symbolic of the Bay of Bengal's commodities. After the war, the connected rice economy of the littoral gave way to autarky. The wartime return of starvation—not only in India but elsewhere in Southeast Asia— imprinted on Asia's new leaders the importance of self-sufficiency in food: "grow more rice" was a basic tenet of economic management in postcolonial Asia, in communist and capitalist states alike.

Intensive negotiations surrounded the resumption of Burmese rice shipments to India in the immediate postwar years. Famine was a very real fear among India's policy makers in 1946 and 1947.[85] The government took control of the food supply. Within a year of the war's end, a team of American economists visiting India declared that "no country in the world, with perhaps the exception of Russia, has gone so far in controlling basic food distribution."[86] Burmese exports to India resumed, despite the effects of Burma's multiple insurgencies, but the government of India was committed to boosting domestic food production.

The trade in rice that did flow across the Bay was now entirely in government hands, organized on a state-to-state basis—a far cry from the rice trade structured by Chettiar finance, Chinese brokers, European agency houses, and British shipping companies in the 1930s. Burma remained the world's largest exporter of rice through the 1950s, but average annual exports were only a third of what they had been in the 1930s: much less rice was being traded internationally, as more and more countries sought to meet their own needs. Possibilities for expanding acreage were relatively limited in postwar Asia. The frontier had closed. Governments of very different ideological hues looked to technological advances and mechanization to boost productivity. The availability of high-yielding strains of rice ushered in the "Green Revolution," which began in Mexico in the 1940s and spread to Asia by the 1960s. New technology permitted significant improvements in rice production around Asia, and in India in particular—though these gains were often shared unequally, and sharpened inequalities in the countryside.

By the late 1960s there was no meaningful economic integration around the Bay. The changing patterns of the rice trade now reflected the new geography of the Cold War and the dominance of national capitalism. The greatest shift was the rise of the United States as one of the world's largest exporters of rice. Much of this reached Asian markets through "concessional trade," often channeled through Public Law 480 (the "Food for Peace" scheme), organized on a bilateral basis to strengthen the links of alliance and dependency on which Cold War strategy was based, while at the same time finding captive markets for the subsidy-funded surplus in American agricultural production. The People's Republic of China, too, reentered the market as a large exporter, using bilateral agreements to earn hard currency, or barter arrangements to meet its import needs: the Chinese rubber-rice exchange agreement with Ceylon, in the 1950s, cut out the market altogether.[87] Even the fish in the sea were now "forms of national wealth." One major international endeavor that took the eastern Indian Ocean as its region of focus—the UN Food and Agriculture Organization's Bay of Bengal Program—was an attempt to govern the Bay's fisheries in such a way as to regulate competing national interests.[88] Offshore oil prospecting stimulated attempts to further divide the sea, enshrined in the Continental Shelf Convention that came into force in 1964: "a new need was felt to divide the seabed, and also the waters above it, into bordered national territories, numbered blocks . . . or 'maritime zones.'" The sea, too, became a form of territory in the postcolonial age.[89]

Asian nations imagined a future less tied to the life of the sea. Human migration would be restricted, and economies self-sufficient. Technology—above all, large dams—would liberate the countries around the Bay from the capriciousness of the monsoons. At the center of many postcolonial "development" projects was the quest to transcend the natural frontiers of energy that had moved the Bay of Bengal over centuries: wind energy, solar energy, the energy of human labor that circulated freely. Malaysia underwent a fresh wave of deforestation—now linked no longer to the economy of the Bay but to plans for national development and to schemes intended to satisfy the new global hunger for timber and palm oil.[90] As the assault on nature intensified in the late twentieth century, human actions began to affect the sea itself.

When Henri Cartier-Bresson crossed the Bay in 1950, he traveled primarily by sea; the jet age was on the horizon, but for at least another decade the ocean crossing remained most common. By the end of the twentieth century the American photographer and art critic Allan Sekula argued that the sea had become "the forgotten space." While an overwhelming proportion of global trade continued—and still today continues—to be transported by sea, awareness of the sea faded from public consciousness. Maritime labor disappeared from port cities as new harbors were built further offshore. As a result of containerization, which spread globally by the end of the 1960s, "factories become mobile, ship-like, as ships become increasingly indistinguishable from trucks and trains, and seaways lose their difference with highways." This brought about a fundamental historical shift, reversing "the 'classical' relationship between the fixity of the land and the fluidity of the sea." Sekula charted the sea's "disappearance" with a simple index: in the 1960s, the *New York Times* devoted a page to shipping news, "alongside the weather, which was charted far into the Atlantic." Twenty years later, the shipping news had disappeared from the national newspaper of record, and "the weather maps, placed elsewhere, were more likely to hug the Eastern seaboard."[91]

In many ways the Bay of Bengal, like the Atlantic of which Sekula writes, was "forgotten" in the 1960s. It vanished from the newspaper columns of the countries around its coastal rim. It is nowhere in the indexes to the national archives that organize the histories of postcolonial nation-states (unlike the colonial archives, in which "Bay of Bengal" is a common entry). The British admiralty produced its last edition of the *Bay of Bengal Pilot* in the 1960s. But if the *New York Times's* weather maps cut off the Atlantic, the weather watchers of India and Southeast Asia did not have that luxury—to this day, the weather maps of South Asia encompass the Bay of Bengal, source of both life-giving rains and destructive cyclonic storms.

The "death" of the Bay of Bengal was plain, though, in the decline of many of its port cities. In the early modern era, the Coromandel Coast was known for its sheer profusion of ports, whose fortunes rose and fell as rivals emerged and competitors diverted traffic. In the third quarter of the twentieth century, the names of ports that once evoked maritime adventure now brought to mind decaying provincial towns, places left behind. There would have been little in Kakinada or Nagapatnam, in Masulipatnam or Parangipettai (once known as Porto Novo) or Tranquebar, to suggest that these were once great ports of emigration, through which tens or hundreds of thousands passed—though some of those old memories have been revived more recently. Until their renewal through "heritage tourism" in the 1990s, Melaka and Penang, too, had fallen into steep economic decline. Singapore, on the other hand, rose to become one of the world's largest ports. But its trade was no longer oriented across the Bay, and, as its huge container port banishes sailors from view, few would think of it anymore as a "port city." The Indian port of Vishakapatnam, once the heart of emigration to Burma, grew explosively in the postcolonial period, but its connections with Burma dwindled to almost nothing.

Because of its sheer power, the Bay is ever-present as threat as well as opportunity for the peoples who live along its coasts. The monsoon rains that shaped the Bay's history continue to be fickle, however much states and scholars might have looked the other way. Cyclone Bhola, which swept in from the Bay of Bengal and hit East Pakistan in November 1970, was one of the most brutal tropical cyclones ever recorded, and the death toll reached half a million. The Pakistani government's shortcomings in providing relief boosted the Awami League, whose electoral victory in December 1970 set the stage for the conflict that would end in the creation of an independent Bangladesh the following year. South Asia's most recent nation-state was forged through a liberation struggle that entangled Indian and Pakistani forces in their third war—this one fought almost entirely along the Bay of Bengal's northern basin. Since independence, the people of Bangladesh have never had the luxury of "forgetting" the sea, which visited disaster upon them every few years. By the 1980s it had become clear to scientists—and all too clear to many local residents—that the sea's most fundamental characteristics were beginning to change. The life of the Bay of Bengal once more began to attract the attentions of those with power: no longer Europeans now, but Asians.

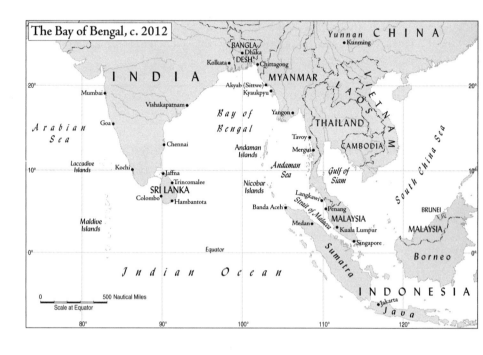

The Bay of Bengal, c. 2012

CHINA
Yunnan
• Kunming

BANGLA-
• Dhaka
Kolkata • DESH • Chittagong

I N D I A

MYANMAR

Akyab (Sittwe) •
Kyaukpyu •

Mumbai •

Vishakapatnam •

Bay of
Bengal

Yangon •

V I E T N A M

L A O S

THAILAND

Arabian
Sea

Goa •

Chennai •

Tavoy •

CAMBODIA

Andaman
Islands

Mergui •

South China Sea

Laccadive
Islands

Kochi •

Jaffna •
• Trincomalee

Andaman
Sea

Gulf of
Siam

Nicobar
Islands

SRI LANKA
Colombo • • Hambantota

Langkawi •

BRUNEI

Banda Aceh •

Strait of Malacca

• Penang

MALAYSIA

MALAYSIA

Maldive
Islands

Medan •

• Kuala Lumpur

Borneo

• Singapore

Equator

I n d i a n   O c e a n

Sumatra

I N D O N E S I A

• Jakarta

Java

0   500 Nautical Miles

Scale at Equator

80°   90°   100°   110°   120°

20°

10°

0°

8

When the Waters Rise

In the twenty-first century the Indian Ocean has reemerged as a region of strategic and political significance. Today even American leaders draw parallels between the Indian Ocean's importance in the age of sail and its role in the world today. Visiting Chennai in July 2011, U.S. Secretary of State Hillary Clinton provided a resonant narrative of the decline and rise of Chennai as a port city of the Bay of Bengal, facing east once again, after a half century's interruption. "There is no better place to discuss India's leadership in the region to its east than here in Chennai," she said. "In this port city, looking out at the Bay of Bengal and beyond to the nations of East and Southeast Asia, we are easily reminded of India's historic role in the wider region." She told her audience that "for thousands of years, Indian traders have sailed those waters of Southeast Asia and beyond." "Indian culture has left its mark" across the Bay, she noted, and she evoked the temples of Angkor Wat, which "bear the influence of Tamil architecture," while "the Hindu god Ganesh still stands guard against homes in Java." She moved directly from the ancient past to the proximate future, to the world she sought to shape. "Today, the stretch of sea from the Indian Ocean to the Pacific contains the world's most vibrant trade and energy routes, linking economies and driving growth." The Bay's position as "a stretch of sea from the Indian Ocean to the Pacific" puts it, once again, at the heart of global history.[1] The Bay of Bengal is now a pivotal arena for the competition between India, China, and the United States for influence in Asia. As environmental change brings a new volatility to the region, renewed migration around the Bay of Bengal will be central to the shape of Asia's possible futures.

At the height of British imperial power, India was a "nodal point" of empire. From India, capital, labor, and military force fanned out across the Indian Ocean. Outposts around the ocean's rim—from Aden in the west to Singapore in the east—secured British dominance, providing refueling stations for ships and bases for military forces. In emphasizing the "primacy of geopolitics," British imperial historians treat the expansion of British power around the Indian Ocean as a natural consequence of the need to defend India. The East India Company's settlement of Penang in the 1780s was motivated by the need for a "Port to the Eastward, the situation of which would connect the Bengal trade with that of China and at the same time serve as a Windward Port of refreshment and repair." In time Singapore grew to be even more important, situated at the entrance to the Straits of Melaka. The strategic challenges facing the British Empire in the Indian Ocean were familiar, having been encountered by the Dutch and the Portuguese, the Mughals and the Acehnese, and the rulers of so many small states along the littoral. Control over the ocean's "choke points"—the Straits of Hormuz and the Straits of Melaka—was crucial, and most difficult to maintain.[2]

Many observers argue that these very same challenges face the rising powers of the region today. Contemporary commentators on the Indian Ocean's military affairs draw, without discrimination, on the writings and actions of the fifteenth-century Chinese admiral Zheng He and the Portuguese conqueror Vasco da Gama, on the British viceroy Lord Curzon and the late nineteenth-century American naval theorist Alfred Thayer Mahan, to derive "lessons" for the present day.[3] If some of these suggested continuities over centuries are simplistic, to say the least, historical echoes are strong: places that have been important in the past are important again, some of them after years of neglect. Consider the example of Sri Lanka. After decades of absorption in the politics of ethnic conflict and civil war, Sri Lanka's old strategic role as the "hinge" of the Indian Ocean is again central to international politics. And within Sri Lanka, two resonant places—one precolonial, the other colonial—are at the heart of new developments.

The port of Hambantota on Sri Lanka's southern coast was for centuries visited by Malay and Arab sailing ships. Its name is derived from the word *sampan*, referring to an indigenous boat common in Indonesian waters: Hambantota was the harbor where sampans would call. In the early fifteenth century the Chinese admiral Zheng He arrived at Hambantota with his fleet of warships. Zheng He's forces launched an attack on the inland kingdom of Kotte, capturing its royal family and exiling them to Nanjing; Sri Lanka served as a base for Zheng He's expeditions to the eastern coast of Africa. The Chinese invasion of Ceylon, mostly forgotten, would be the first in a series of attempts over four centuries to capture this island at the frontier between the Arabian Sea and the Bay of Bengal. The sole trace of Zheng He's expedition is an inscription in Hambantota—written in Chinese, Tamil, and Persian characters—invoking blessings for free trade and navigation. By the twentieth century, Hambantota was a sleepy coastal town. It was in Hambantota district that Leonard Woolf served as assistant government agent from 1908 to 1911. In Woolf's fictional depiction of a rural, isolated community—based on his experience in Hambantota—there is little trace of its seafaring history. "These vanished villages and the desolation of the jungle had a curious fascination," he wrote in the preface to the American edition of *Village in the Jungle*, yet "it had once many hundreds of years ago been populous, a country with powerful kings and a civilization of its own"—and with thriving trade across the sea.[4]

Since the late 1990s Hambantota has been the site of one of the largest port construction projects in the world; an American observer describes it as a "massive dredging project—literally the creation of a new coastline." Financed by Chinese investment, Hambantota has emerged as "an oil-age equivalent of a coaling station" and a foothold of Chinese power in the Bay of Bengal.[5] The first commercial ship to dock at its facilities, the *Ellison Sun*, carried cars manufactured in Chennai by a South Korean company, destined for transshipment to Algeria—symbol of a new "south-south" globalization, to which the Indian Ocean is central. But tensions underlie this vision of mutual benefit: Indian fears of a future Chinese military base at Hambantota persist. Funds for the construction of the port were accompanied by billions of dollars in military assistance, likely used to purchase weapons that the Sri Lankan state used to crush the decades-long insurgency by the island's Tamil ethnic minority.[6]

Chinese investment has renewed the precolonial port of Hambantota; Indian interest resides in the colonial port of Trincomalee, on the eastern coast of Sri Lanka, which the British navy deemed the best harbor in the Bay of Bengal. The Japanese attack on the port in 1942 proved one of the most urgent moments of the war for the British navy. Cut off for decades by the Sri Lankan civil war, Trincomalee is experiencing a twenty-first-century revival. Its development reflects a new spirit of economic and military cooperation between the Indian and Sri Lankan governments. On the Indian side, the calculus of strategic interest now greatly outweighs the pressure from Tamil politicians in South India to champion the cause of Sri Lanka's Tamil minority, particularly after the disastrous Indian intervention in Sri Lanka in the 1980s. The fuel storage facilities at Trincomalee port are run by the Indian-owned Lanka Indian Oil Corporation on a long-term lease. Indian funding has also gone toward the development of the Palaly airfield on the Jaffna Peninsula. "India has moved from its past emphasis on the power of the argument to a new stress on the argument of power," writes one Indian commentator on foreign affairs; scholars in the field of strategic studies quote this approvingly.[7] Far from undermining the power of nation-states, strategic competition between India and China in the Bay of Bengal increases regional states' capacity to contain solidarities they see as subversive—transborder solidarities rooted in the region's history and forged by its diasporas.

In the nineteenth century, Europe's industrial revolution transformed the Bay of Bengal. The demands of British factories precipitated a rush for the commodities of Southeast Asia's frontiers—for rubber and tin and minerals and oil. Massive migration followed. The movement of people reshaped the landscape, knitting the Bay's littoral together in a circular flow of rice and labor, capital and commodities. In the twenty-first century it is China's industrial revolution that animates the Indian Ocean. China's industrialization since the 1980s—the most rapid the world has ever seen—has been fueled by an insatiable appetite for energy. China first became a net importer of oil in 1993. In the decade after 1995, China's energy consumption more than doubled, and it is forecast to double again in the next decade; the country now imports around half of its energy, and over 80 percent of those imports come through the Straits of Melaka. This dependence on the Indian Ocean's shipping routes led Chinese president Hu Jintao to lament China's "Melaka dilemma."[8] By road and by rail, by pipeline and by canal, China's Indian Ocean policy seeks to circumvent the Straits of Melaka, where American (or perhaps Indian) naval intervention could too easily choke off its energy supplies. In the process, the Chinese state has revived plans, much beloved of British investors in the second half of the nineteenth century, to connect the Bay of Bengal directly with China's southwestern region of Yunnan.

A 2004 report on Asia's "energy futures" by an American defense contractor first coined the term "string of pearls" to describe China's strategy in the Indian Ocean; American and Indian commentators were quick to adopt the phrase.[9] On this view, Chinese investment in port facilities along the Indian Ocean rim from Oman to Burma appears as a concerted strategy; refueling and port facilities, the story runs, are the thin end of the wedge, and military bases will follow. Particular concern is directed toward the Chinese financing of the Arabian Sea port of Gwadar, in Pakistan, close to the Iranian border. Hambantota and the Chinese-backed container port facility in Chittagong, Bangladesh, are the other pearls on the littoral string, together with smaller sites dotted around the Indian Ocean's islands. The reality appears more complex.[10] There is little firm evidence of Chinese military intention; Gwadar, for instance, was given to the Port of Singapore Authority on a forty-year lease, though a lack of profitability led the Singaporeans to renounce it in 2013. A thoughtful American naval analyst concedes that commentary on Chinese intentions in the Indian Ocean is built on "rampant speculation" and "superficial evidence"—and he points out that Chinese officials take seriously their self-image as a noncolonizing (and, indeed, anti-imperial) power.[11] Stories matter. Chinese leaders on their diplomatic tours commemorate Zheng He as a peaceful Chinese emissary to the Indian Ocean world, in contrast to the Western colonizers who followed him; this narrative of the past provides legitimacy for China's contemporary rise and creates a lineage for Chinese power in the Indian Ocean. But critics of Chinese expansion would point out that the legend of the eunuch admiral is shrouded in myth and even misinformation—recent scholarship suggests that Zheng He's journeys were far from peaceful, and more akin to an early (if mostly unsuccessful) attempt at maritime colonization.[12]

Amid the uncertainty, Burma plays a central role in Chinese strategies to circumvent its "Melaka dilemma"—and in India's attempt to
"look east." A recent, optimistic account hails Burma as the pivot of
Asia's future, the point "where China meets India." It has not always
proved a comfortable position: at the Asian Relations Conference of
1947, the Burmese delegate expressed his fear that "Burma was between two great powers. It was terrible to be ruled by a Western power,"
he said, "but it was even more so to be ruled by an Asian power."[13] Now
those fears have mostly given way to a sense of opportunity. Isolated by
the sanctions applied by Western governments after Burma's military
junta annulled the results of the 1990 elections and imprisoned leaders
of the democratic movement, Burma has benefited from Chinese investment on a massive scale. Burma's Bay of Bengal coastline, which
languished as the sea was enclosed, is now fevered with activity. Along
the northern arc of Burma's littoral, the new port at Kyaukpyu, on Ram-
ree Island, has been built and financed by the Chinese government and
private investors; the old Arakanese port of Sittwe has been revived,
despite heavy silting; and another new, Chinese-funded facility is located at Hainggyi island, along the Irrawaddy delta, together with a
large shipyard at Thilawa (Kyauktan), south of Rangoon.[14] In 2009 the
Chinese and Burmese governments concluded deals worth U.S. $2.5
billion to build oil and natural gas pipelines through Burma, linking
the Bay of Bengal directly to Yunnan.[15] The oil pipeline will allow Chinese imports from the Persian Gulf to avoid the Straits of Melaka. The
natural gas pipeline will take supplies from Burma's Shwe gas fields
directly to the Chinese provinces of Guizhou and Guangxi, comple-
menting ambitious overland schemes to construct pipelines from Russia and Kazakhstan to northern China.[16] From a military standpoint,
historical memories are powerful: "Beijing undoubtedly remembers
Burma's role in World War II when it provided China access to the Indian Ocean, thereby sustaining Chinese resistance to Imperial Japan."[17]
Crucially, while China is a littoral power in the western Pacific, in the
Indian Ocean it is landlocked.

In the Bay of Bengal, as in the South China Sea (where tensions run
higher still), states are anxious to claim part of the sea as an extension
of their national territory. Uninhabited islands invite competing claims.
Conflicts over energy heighten this sense of possessiveness. The Bay of
Bengal is not merely a conduit for Middle Eastern oil but also an "energy

frontier" in its own right, rich in oil, natural gas, and minerals.[18] In recent decades states around the Bay of Bengal have contested their coastal frontiers. In 2008 Bangladesh took its maritime dispute with Burma to the International Tribunal on the Law of the Sea. "Despite extensive negotiations over 35 years," the Bangladeshi submission to the court declared, "Bangladesh and Myanmar have not succeeded in agreeing upon a maritime boundary." At stake were their conceptions of "territorial sea," "exclusive economic zones," and the reach of the continental shelf. Each of those frontiers is challenged by new attempts to harness the resources of the sea through "drilling and other exploratory activities." The tribunal found in Bangladesh's favor in 2012, sparking a rush in prospecting activities.[19]

The Indian response to the new international politics of the Bay of Bengal has been fundamental—a reorientation of military strategy and diplomacy toward the Indian Ocean, and toward Southeast Asia in particular. Ironically, this has led some Indian military analysts back to a view of themselves as inheritors of the British Raj's maritime strategy, as they aim to recapture the dominance that British India exercised over the "eastern seas" in the early twentieth century.[20] On the eve of India's independence, K. M. Pannikar—a historian and diplomat who foretold the end of the "Vasco da Gama era" in Asian history and served as India's ambassador to China—wrote of the "strategic challenges" an independent India would face. In his view, the Bay was crucial. "With the islands of the Bay of Bengal properly equipped and protected with a navy strong enough in home waters," he wrote, "security can return to that part of the Indian Ocean which is of supreme importance to India."[21] Preoccupied with the conflicts in its own neighborhood and guided by a foreign policy of nonalignment, the Indian military turned away from the Indian Ocean for decades after independence. Its navy was a "brown-water force," focused on protecting India's coastal waters. That the Indian navy now seeks to be a "blue-water force"—with the capacity to act around the Indian Ocean rim—shows how the sea has been transformed in the imagination of those with power in India.[22]

Here again, the echoes of history are profound. The proposed Indian "Seabird" naval base at Goa, encompassing the old Portuguese fortress of Anjadip Island, will be the largest in Asia. At Kochi, close to where the Portuguese first landed, the Indian military maintains "unmanned aerial vehicles" while providing maintenance facilities to the American navy, now ally rather than antagonist. On the eastern coast, India's naval fleet is based in Vishakapatnam, from where hundreds of thousands embarked for Burma in search of fortune in the early twentieth century. Now Indian military power, too, crosses the Bay of Bengal. In 2001 the establishment of the Andaman and Nicobar command consolidated India's military presence in the islands that sit at the heart of the Bay—islands that were the symbolic territory of Subhas Chandra Bose's Provisional Government of Free India during World War II.[23] From the Baaz naval station on Great Nicobar's Campbell Bay, inaugurated in 2012, Indian forces "keep a hawk-eye on the strategically important Malacca strait."[24] Alongside closer relations with Sri Lanka, the Indian state competes with China for Burma's coastal resources: taking a share in the natural gas fields off the coast, investing in the construction of airfields, contributing to a deepwater harbor in Dawei. At the same time, India's trade with Southeast Asia has grown rapidly, though it lags far behind China's trade with that region. As a result of Free Trade Agreements in goods and services, signed in 2009 and 2012 respectively—in the face of substantial domestic opposition in India—the value of India's trade with Southeast Asia has more than doubled in a decade, reaching US$80 billion in 2012.[25]

The new international politics of the Indian Ocean, one scholar observes, are "deepening the identity and coherence of the Indian Ocean region"; they will "blur the boundaries and weaken the salience of some of Asia's traditional sub-regions."[26] Seen from the newly militarized Andaman Islands—closer to Malaysia than to southern India, closer to Yunnan than Yunnan is to Beijing—the boundary between South Asia, East Asia, and Southeast Asia has never been more tenuous.

The plans of states face a radical new element of instability. Because of global climate change, the monsoons grow ever more unpredictable. Rajendra Pachauri, chairman of the Intergovernmental Panel on Climate Change, writes that "climate change challenges the traditional assumption that past hydrological experience provides a good guide to future conditions." Recent decades have witnessed changes in average temperatures and rainfall, changes to the chemical composition of the seas and the diversity of life-forms that inhabit them, and an increased frequency of extreme climatic events. This, then, is the other story of the

Bay of Bengal's recent history, distinct from the calculations of military strategists: it is no longer the same sea.[27]

The changes in the world's oceans are remarkably recent. "With an ever-accelerating tide of human impact," a leading marine biologist writes, "the oceans have changed more in the last thirty years than in all of human history before."[28] And so, in our biography of the Bay of Bengal, the changes in the sea come last. The ease of crossing the water transformed the landscape. The force of capital turned virgin forests into plantations. The demands of commerce implanted cities along the banks of rivers and at their mouths where they met the seas. Throughout all these changes, "the oceans themselves seemed changeless" and "contrasted with the world above water, where landscapes underwent dramatic alterations." This contrast holds no more.[29] Starting around the 1950s, and with accelerating effects since the 1970s, a concatenation of changes has altered the seas' substance: human population has grown rapidly; large coastal cities have burgeoned, and continue to expand; the "fishing frontier" extends farther into the deep sea, propelled by commercial trawling; the parts of the world once under European colonial rule have undergone substantial if uneven industrialization; agricultural production has intensified, buoyed by massive pesticide use; and the region's appetite for fossil fuels has become insatiable.

The forces that now choke the life from the Bay of Bengal began as unintended, initially unseen consequences of the political choices that states and peoples made as a new world arose from the ruins of war and the remnants of empires. This is only partly a story of blindness to consequence, or of the hubris of "high modernism."[30] The policies that finally "extended human dominion to the sea"—projects to increase food security, schemes of industrialization to provide employment—represented an advance in human freedom around the Bay of Bengal. They emerged in reaction to an imperial world where lives were cheap: where labor was uprooted for the profit of European planters, where migrant workers were denied their humanity, where colonial policies left millions to starve. The Bay's imperial world of specialization and migration had permitted its own margins of freedom: the freedom to move in search of fortune, or at least to avert family catastrophe. When these margins narrowed, in the 1930s and 1940s, it was at least partly in order to secure a different—and, many felt, *greater*—freedom: the political rights of citizens of free nations, and the rights to livelihood that these new nations would provide. Starting in the mid-twentieth century, the Bay's political and economic fragmentation had important consequences, which are clear only in retrospect. As the avenues of emigration and interregional trade were closed off by new national borders, the growing populations of the region could be sustained only by a massive intensification of domestic agricultural production. As they turned away from oceanic commerce, coastal cities grew rapidly: port cities turned inland and became industrial centers. The final enclosure of the Bay—the treatment of the sea as an extension of national territory—facilitated its overexploitation as a resource.

Around four-fifths of the pollutants that spill into the Bay of Bengal every year come from the land. They flow out with the great rivers that empty into the Bay—the Ganges, the Brahmaputra, the Meghna, the Godavari, the Kaveri, the Krishna, and the Salween. They trickle in as refuse from the large coastal cities that ring the sea's littoral, places that were the departure points of millions of journeys in the age of sail and steam and which are now swollen with people and riven with the new inequalities of globalization. The Bay is a "sink of organic and inorganic wastes." Because of the size and number of the rivers that feed into it, and the density of population around its rim, "the total amounts of nutrients reaching the Bay of Bengal . . . must be close to the highest in the world." Every day the Bay ingests a noxious cocktail of "organic matter, nutrients, metabolized drugs, medical wastes, cytotoxic, antibiotic and hormone-mimicking materials, bacteria, viruses and worms, chemicals such as detergents and a significant quantity of sediments."[31] Floods and storm surges dislodge pollutants and carry them over long distances. A plague of plastic floats out to sea. The rivers themselves are in "dire" health. And around 80 percent of the world's population lives in areas where human water security and the biodiversity of river systems is under cumulative threat.[32] The excess of nutrients that flows through the rivers—most damaging is the nitrogen from agricultural fertilizer runoff, and from vehicle and factory exhausts—creates "dead zones" starved of oxygen (though the Bay of Bengal is less badly afflicted in this respect than the notorious Gulf of Mexico or the waters around Japan).[33] Writing from the southeastern edge of the Bay in the early nineteenth century, John Crawfurd declared that "no part of the world abounds in more fine fish."[34] Two centuries later, the fish are disappearing. Nearly 85 percent of the world's fish stocks are "fully exploited, over-exploited, or depleted."[35]

The coastline is shifting. Deforestation and aquaculture encroach on the mangrove swamps that provide coastal zones with their best natural flood defenses. And aquaculture expands as deep-sea fishing provides diminishing returns. "Mangroves," Rachel Carson wrote, "are among the far migrants of the plant kingdom, forever sending their young stages off to establish pioneer colonies." Since her lyrical account, penned in 1955, her beloved mangroves have almost everywhere been pushed back, their "colonies" disbanded. Mangroves excelled in "creating land where once there was sea." As they give way to industrial (and often state-subsidized) shrimp farms, the land recedes with the loss of the "complex matrix of roots and stems" that "traps and binds sediment and stabilizes the coast."[36]

The coasts are destabilized, so much so that many of the world's river deltas are sinking. On one account, the deltas—which host some of the

Figure 20 Pichavaram mangrove forest on the Tamil Nadu Coast. Pichavaram is one of the largest mangrove forests in the world. Mangrove forests have disappeared from the Bay of Bengal's coasts at a rapid rate. *Photograph by Sunil Amrith.*

largest concentrations of population on earth—are sinking at up to four times the rate at which sea levels are rising. In the past decade, more than 10 million people each year have experienced severe flooding due to storm surges alone; most of them live along Asia's littorals. As a result of human intervention, much less sediment reaches the river deltas than would occur naturally—sediment that is essential for the deltas to sustain and replenish themselves. The "predominant" role is played by projects of hydraulic engineering, epitomized by large dams, which proliferated in the second half of the twentieth century. The trapping of sediment by dams far outstrips the effects of land clearance and construction in displacing it; rather, bypassing "an important natural filtration system," storm surges and floods carry displaced sediment directly to the sea, while large quantities remain trapped in reservoirs. The attempt to engineer away the smaller tributaries that feed the great rivers breaks the "critical links between channels and their floodplains" and "starves delta systems of necessary sediments." Reservoirs

Figure 21 Sign at Pichavaram encouraging mangrove conservation. *Photograph by Sunil Amrith.*

have increased by 600 or 700 percent the volume of water held by rivers.[37]

Governments around Asia retain their enthusiasm for dam building, despite their many social and environmental costs: since so many of Asia's great rivers flow out into the Bay of Bengal, it will be particularly badly affected.[38] So much water is diverted for irrigation that the Kaveri River, among others, is reduced to a trickle by the time it reaches the Bay through some of its tributaries. A further cause of the subsidence of deltas is the sediment compaction caused by the overextraction of groundwater for urban and agricultural use—a perennial problem in India and China—and, increasingly, the effects of removing oil and natural gas from the delta's underlying sediments. The sinking deltas of the Bay of Bengal, particularly around its northern basin, are among the most densely populated on earth—and there, offshore drilling is only just beginning. Half a billion people face a greatly increased risk of flooding in the coming decades.[39] Geologists write that the current state of the world's river deltas "represents the legacy of natural history, human decisions, and ongoing sea-level rise"; to account fully for this process is the task of a new sort of environmental history, one that we are only beginning to write.[40]

The Bay of Bengal receives the refuse of a vast swath of eastern India, and the trash discharged by most of Asia's great rivers; it also receives the discarded hulks of the world's unwanted ships. The Bangladeshi port of Chittagong, at the northern edge of the Bay—once ruled by the kingdom of Arakan, and a port of emigration to Burma in the nineteenth century—houses one of the world's largest shipbreaking yards. The industry began through an accident of climate: in the 1960s one of the Bay of Bengal's notorious cyclones blew a 20,000-ton tanker off course and onto the beach in Chittagong. Local people used their ingenuity to recycle the ship's components, stripping out what was most valuable—and opening the eyes of investors to a new opportunity. The average tanker can provide 50,000 meters of copper cable, 35,000 kilograms of aluminum, and 20,000 kilograms of zinc. Eighty percent of the world's shipbreaking industry is located in Bangladesh, India, and Pakistan; in Chittagong alone, around 30,000 people are employed in the trade. Shipbreaking is one of the most dangerous occupations in the world: young men, even boys as young as ten, wade through toxic, oily sludge to take the ships apart. Every day the workers inhale a brew of dangerous chemicals, including lead and asbestos. But for those with few other options, shipbreaking pays, and many resent the intrusion of environmental and labor activists who want to regulate the industry. Canadian photographer Edward Burtynsky's photographs of the Bangladeshi shipbreaking yards bear witness to the detritus of globalization—he finds both beauty and horror on this stretch of beach where ships go to die.[41] Though shipbreaking has expanded into a global industry, it is an old trade. Mr. Nevil, a character in Michael Ondaatje's novel *The Cat's Table,* reflects wistfully on his life as a ship dismantler in the first half of the twentieth century: "In a breaker's yard you discover that anything can have a new life, be reborn as part of a car or railway carriage, or a shovel blade. You take that older life and you link it to a stranger."[42]

In the coming century, the world's oceans are likely to rise at an unprecedented rate due to planetary warming. If the causes of coastal erosion and marine pollution can be traced to the regions that surround particular rivers and seas, the causes of the rising oceans are both global and cumulative. They are the outcome of the accumulation of greenhouse gases in the atmosphere, a consequence of humanity's addiction to fossil fuels from the time of the Industrial Revolution—but especially since the 1950s. As the earth heats up, sea levels rise as warmer water expands and as ice melts into the sea. The Intergovernmental Panel on Climate Change (IPCC) estimates that globally the sea level will rise between 18 and 59 centimeters by 2100, an estimate that some scientists believe to be conservative; if we reach a "tipping point," sparking the rapid melting of land-based ice, the figures will be dramatically greater, a question of meters rather than centimeters. To put this in perspective, "we are reaching the end of an era of around 5,000 years of unbroken stability in the volume of water in our oceans."[43]

One consequence of climate change—the moral and political conundrum of our time—is the "geographical separation of emission source from environmental consequence."[44] Though the Bay of Bengal region accounts for a small proportion of global greenhouse gas emissions, it is likely to be among the world's worst-affected regions as the waters rise. Facing the Bay of Bengal are 2,350 kilometers of Indian coast. Coastal regions have depended on the life of the sea for nutrition, and on the winds and currents for the opportunities they offered on the far horizons of Southeast Asia's shores. The vulnerability of many of these low-lying settlements is great: between 1990 and 2006, an area of 93 square kilometers along the Andhra Pradesh Coast, between the Krishna and Godavari deltas, has been lost to coastal erosion, and nearly 450 kilometers of that coast is under "very high risk" from rising waters.[45] Bangladesh is perhaps the country in the world most threatened by rising sea levels, for it is low-lying and densely populated; only the small islands of the Indian Ocean and the Pacific are more vulnerable.[46] The melting of the Himalayan glaciers could prove catastrophic for coastal areas of the Bay. The Himalayan ice provides the meltwater for seven of Asia's largest rivers—the Indus, Ganges, Brahmaputra, Salween, Mekong, Yangzi, and Huang He—three of which spill into the Bay of Bengal. The effects of planetary warming on the region attracted controversy due to a careless claim in the IPCC's Fourth Assessment Report suggesting that the Himalayan glaciers could melt by 2035—this was subsequently retracted, but seized upon cynically by those who would deny the reality of climate change. Recent studies, however, suggest that the Himalayan region is warming faster than the global average.[47]

Climate scientists project that it is not only the mean sea level that will rise but also its "extreme" level—the maximum level the sea reaches during storm surges, which are predicted to become more frequent, more devastating, and more erratic in the coming years. These storms are among the greatest threats to the Bay and its coastal peoples, because the Bay has always been "a hotbed of generation of tropical cyclones." As we have seen, the Bay's turbulence is its distinguishing feature: familiar to mariners and fishermen, to poets and prophets, and to millions of migrants who crossed the rough seas. "Cyclones in the Bay of Bengal are more dreaded than any other form of storm known to mariners in other parts of the world," a Singapore newspaper wrote in 1924. "For sheer, confused danger there is nothing equal to the tumultuous seas raised by a cyclone in the Bay."[48] The tumult looks set to increase. Though there has been no clear trend in the overall number of cyclones in the Bay in recent decades, the frequency of *intense* cyclones has risen.[49] The people of Burma's coast experienced the full horror of a violent storm in May 2008, when Cyclone Nargis swept in from the Bay of Bengal and across the Irrawaddy delta. Comparing satellite images of the delta taken before and after the storm, journalist Emma

Larkin remarks that "it seemed as if a bucket of water had been sloshed across an ink drawing; the carefully marked lines [of the delta's waterways] had been erased and the paper beneath was buckled and distorted." Nearly 85,000 people died, with tens of thousands more missing; up to 2 million were displaced immediately after the storm. The catastrophe was worsened by the failure of the military government to provide adequate relief.[50] It is discomfiting to see this as a portent of the Bay's future.

The effects of a warming earth on the Asian monsoons are unpredictable. Recent experience points to a more erratic monsoon, and to a devastating combination of drought and flooding—average rainfall is likely to decline, while the incidence of abnormally powerful storms will increase. Climatologists sound a note of uncertainty about the future: "Global warming . . . would tend to favor a stronger summer monsoon in the long term, yet in detail there is much potential complexity. Melting of the Greenland ice sheet may disrupt the overturn of waters in the North Atlantic and result in the cooling of that region. . . . [S]uch an event would result in weaker summer monsoons" in Asia.[51] The combination of unreliable monsoons and extreme climatic events has produced "spine-chilling" estimates that India and Pakistan will experience a decline in food production of more than 20 percent.[52]

If the future of the monsoons is unpredictable, the displacement of people by rising waters appears a virtual certainty. The majority of those displaced will be in Asia, a significant proportion of them along the Bay of Bengal's rim. The specter of "climate refugees" looms large in political discussions of climate change–the fear of uncontrolled migration brings climate change firmly within the realm of "national security" in many parts of the world. In one sense, climate-induced migration is nothing new, as each year millions of people in Asia flee their homes to escape flooding. Most of the time, however, these are temporary and short-distance moves. The crisis will come if coastal regions have to be abandoned permanently. "Climate refugees" have a geography but not a history. The space of their displacement is "monsoon Asia"—an old colonial term that is back in fashion. They live in a state of permanent emergency, buffeted by the furies of nature. They provoke a fear of chaos among those with power. "The monsoon is nature writ large," one American commentator writes, "a spectacle of turbulence that suggests the effect of the environment on humankind living in increasingly crowded and fragile conditions in places like Bangladesh." The stark image of poor people forced from their homes by floods or by sinking habitations haunts the imagery of climate change in the wealthy world.[53] When one looks at maps projecting population displacements along Asia's coastal rim, there is little sense that these are regions connected in other ways: by a deep history of movement.

In the nineteenth century, too, many observers saw the movement of people across the Bay as driven by climate—not by climate change as such, but climate's cyclical volatility, heightened in the 1870s and the 1890s by El Niño events of exceptional severity. Self-interestedly, British officials saw the flood of migrants to Burma, Malaya, and Ceylon as people "pushed" from India's shores by an inhospitable nature. The compulsion of the monsoons, wrote Bowness Fischer, the verbose consular agent of Karaikal, meant that there could be "no analogy" between Asian and European migrants. The latter were a "free and intelligent people" who made a rational decision to move, whereas Asian migrants were the victims of climatic circumstance. Treating South Indian emigrants as refugees from the monsoon allowed British officials and rubber planters to justify indenture abroad as preferable to starvation at home, and the failure of the rains made the work of *kanganies* and labor recruiters that much easier. Few administrators asked why some villagers responded to the droughts of the 1870s by uprooting themselves, while others moved temporarily over short distances and still others clung to their homesteads, however desperate their circumstances. In practice, the relationship between climate and migration was as complex in the nineteenth century as it is today. Only where migration was thinkable and feasible—because of prior local experiences, because of the presence of contacts and relatives overseas, because of the availability of credit, however usurious—did episodic crises provoke large-scale movement. Colonial policy in the late nineteenth century vacillated between encouraging movement, tolerating it, and preventing it. Some of that indecision remains in international debates on migration.

Today the borders drawn by the mid-twentieth century's partitions complicate long-distance journeys. In an age of globalization, borders are more heavily guarded than ever, even as capital is freed from restraint. Indian officials talk regularly of constructing a wall along the border with Bangladesh as a deterrent to migration. The naval patrols that now police the Straits of Melaka are at least as concerned with detecting "illegal immigrants" as they are with pirates or enemy ships. The patrols and the walls are just the latest in a long line of attempts, going back to the early nineteenth century, to close the "porous borders" of the region.[54] They are unlikely to succeed. Where policy makers see closed borders, many local people see a more open frontier. If the old plantation frontier has long since closed, migrants gravitate to the new frontiers that have emerged from the inequalities of Asia's economic growth. This is hardly a surprise. Coastal regions have been shaped by movement. The places most threatened by environmental catastrophe—the great river deltas—are also places with long histories of migration.

After the political revolutions of the mid-twentieth century, overseas movement declined while internal migration grew. But the old interregional networks did not disappear—they stood in the shadows, awaiting their opportunity. Since the 1970s they have reemerged, and they have reinvented themselves. Bangladesh, for instance, remains connected with the eastern arc around the Bay of Bengal. Connections with Burma were interrupted by Burma's closure to the world, though the Burma-Bangladesh border has long been crossed by traders and traffickers and cross-border communities. Links with Malaysia have strengthened since the 1980s. As the construction and plantation industries of Malaysia boomed in the 1980s, and as economic development provided more lucrative employment for local workers, Bangladeshi migrants gravitated to Malaysia and to neighboring Singapore. Malaysia occupies a powerful place in the Bangladeshi social imagination, alongside the Middle East, as a land of hard-won opportunity. The connections between Tamil-speaking South India and Southeast Asia have also experienced a revival. Tamil labor migration to Singapore and Malaysia is substantial, if not on the scale of the 1920s. Today it takes place alongside diversified and growing movements of people between India and Singapore—software engineers and students and investment bankers.

Now, as in the early twentieth century, working-class Tamil migrants are excluded from the clubs, societies, and newspapers that constitute the "Indian diaspora" in contemporary Southeast Asia. Now, as then,

Tamil workers can expect little consular support from the representatives of their government. In a recent discussion of labor migration in contemporary Southeast Asia, the political philosopher Pheng Cheah argues that migrants' "rights can be effectively promoted in the present and near future only by affirming the importance of political citizenship or membership in a nation-state." Furthermore, he argues that the governments of "labor-sending" countries "need to have a strong bargaining position, and the political will to demand just treatment for their workers."[55] In the 1930s such an argument would have struck many Indian nationalists and reformers, British Indian administrators, and Tamil journalists as both reasonable and familiar. But in the twenty-first century the Indian and Bangladeshi governments face the same dilemmas that were faintly visible to their colonial predecessor in the 1930s: under what powers, and with what chance of success, could they intervene in a "foreign country" to protect or advance the interests of their nationals overseas? And would not the mistreatment of their working-class nationals reflect poorly on the global ambitions of their diasporic elites?

The ambivalent status of migrant workers—unable to garner protection from their home states, and without the power to effect change in their places of work—can have direct and devastating consequences. For the most part, South Asian migrant workers in Singapore and Malaysia do the hardest, most dangerous work. They work for low wages—but wages greater than what they would earn at home. Many have undefined legal status, often because employers confiscate workers' passports on arrival and then threaten them with exposure as "illegals." Industrial accidents—from broken limbs to paralysis caused by falls from great heights—are widespread, and often go unreported. An experienced eye surgeon in Singapore described to me cases she has seen regularly since the 1980s of workers who have lost part or all of their vision after sustaining injuries on construction sites. Many of the injured workers are uninsured, despite laws obliging their employers to take out insurance. Cases have come to light since the 1990s of injured workers being denied even minimal compensation—they are simply put on the next flight home. Transient migrant workers lie entirely outside the bounds of the national population that an intrusive and sophisticated state such as Singapore seeks to improve and develop and care for. They are, quintessentially, people without power.

Yet today, just as in the exploitative imperial world of the 1920s, some workers succeed in using legal provisions to fight for their rights. They appeal to multiple authorities—to their home governments, to the labor departments of their host countries, now to international nongovernmental organizations—for redress. They develop an intimate knowledge of how bureaucratic power works; they use the state's promises, its language, and its ubiquitous pieces of paper to further their aims. Anthonysamy Charles—the charismatic, loquacious protagonist of Vicknesh Varan's short documentary film *Special Pass*—began, as a sixteen-year-old, cleaning and washing dishes in a restaurant in a small town in Tamil Nadu. In his twenties he migrated to Singapore to find work as a chef in a local restaurant. When he lost his job, dismissed without being paid his wages, he began a campaign to claim compensation for himself and a few colleagues. Supported by a local charity, Charles appealed to every level of government, from the (unsympathetic) Indian High Commission to Singapore's Ministry of Manpower and various industrial tribunals. Over the two years that their case dragged on, Charles and his colleagues remained in Singapore on sufferance—their "special pass" limited their right to work, and even prevented them from leaving the country. Charles and his colleagues eventually returned to India, their fight for compensation only partially successful—but theirs is one story among many of quotidian struggle in the new world of migration that spans the Bay of Bengal.[56] In the rise of nongovernmental organizations concerned with migration in Singapore and throughout the region, we can see the beginnings of a new inter-Asian politics of migration that tries, not always successfully, to bridge the gap between transnational networks of migration and the resolutely national framework of migration policy.[57]

Today migrant workers who cross the Bay participate enthusiastically in the digital world of images and stories that circulate on mobile-phone cameras and through online social networks. To a much greater extent than the working-class sojourners of a century ago, today's migrants are telling their own stories.[58] But in other ways the social life of male migrants bears striking similarities to that seen in Singapore or Rangoon in the 1920s. A decade ago Indian cultural critic Rustom Bharucha described his experience of walking through Singapore's Serangoon Road on a Sunday—where migrant workers from across South

Asia gathered, and still gather, on their sole day off—as "one of the most saddening experiences of my life." He continues:

> As you jostle through the crowds, picking up snatches of conversation in Tamil, Bangla, Sylheti—common talk about family and prospects of going home, bargains in shopping centers, quarrels and bitter regrets—you see men talking their lives out in a state of chaos and cacophony. For once, the sterile image of Singapore is completely shattered. One is left confronting the most profound isolation of the foreign workers that has yet to be addressed adequately in the multi-cultural discourse of Singapore.[59]

I have known this neighborhood all my life. Alongside the sadness and isolation, which are all too real, there is a profound sense of ambition for a better life among migrant workers of diverse origins. They delight in the ordinary pleasures of sociability, and a sense of solidarity that at once affirms and transcends their places of origin. Rarely do migrant workers in Southeast Asia present themselves as victims—quite the contrary. Most commonly, stories of migration are stories of self-realization. "Malaya" Samy, a twenty-four-year-old driver who started out as a plasterer when he first traveled to Singapore at age eighteen, put it simply: "Singapore is a good place for earning—here you can advance in life."[60] There is more than an echo here of the stories, even the precise language, of much older migrants' life histories stored in the National Archives of Singapore's Oral History Department—the same parallels emerged from my own conversations with contemporary migrant laborers and with older people whose experience of crossing the Bay was many decades ago.

What leads South Asian migrant workers overseas is a pervasive rural crisis of reproduction that cannot be reduced to the effects of climate change but is not unconnected to it. Most migrant laborers come from families with small, fragmented landholdings: in most cases, landless laborers in India are too poor to finance long-distance migration in the first place. In many parts of Tamil Nadu and Bangladesh, climate change has exacerbated a deep agrarian crisis, the result of decades of neglect and of rising social inequalities. Many, if not most, migrants do manage to redeem their families' debts; they invest in house construction and even expand their families' landholdings after several years' labor overseas. But the difficulties faced by those who fail to prosper—and their ranks are large—are sharpened by the debts they incur in migrating. The majority of migrants departing Tamil Nadu or Bangladesh for Southeast Asia begin their journeys several thousand dollars in debt to agents and recruiters; anticipating their foreign earnings, many migrants' families mortgage or even sell land to finance their odysseys. These debts add immeasurably to the pressure migrants feel to make good on their promises—and they are the chief source of migrants' anxiety when their jobs across the Bay do not turn out to be all they expect, or were led to believe, they would be. The networks that facilitate migration—the agents and agencies, the "tribe of landsharks," or the *kanganies* of the twenty-first century—have long histories. They are back in business.[61]

But for Tamil workers as much as for Bangladeshis, Singapore remains a place where they imagine that they could, through hard work and with luck on their side, transform their families' fortunes.[62] As new wealth circulates through the Indian diaspora in Southeast Asia, there is a new demand for very old forms of migration—the movement of Tamil priests and temple architects takes place alongside that of construction laborers. Sometimes these disparate trades involve the very same people. A young priest at a small temple in Kuala Lumpur told me that he had been in Malaysia for four years, working on a "temple visa" (a religious visitor's visa); he had initially been there as a student, and then had worked in construction, interspersed with periods back home in Tamil Nadu. His dream was to get to Singapore, where one of his brothers worked as a forklift operator and another brother worked "repairing stadiums." "Singapore is a good place," he said; "they give pensions, medical, regardless of race. Not in Malaysia—it's tough here." In the young man's story were many features of an earlier phase of labor migration between Tamil Nadu and Malaya: an oscillating pattern of migration (a few years abroad, alternating with periods in India) and the sort of occupational flexibility that was more characteristic of Indian migration to Burma.

Partway through our conversation, it became clear that these were not just parallels but also continuities: circulation between South India and Malaysia was embedded in the young man's family, interrupted only in the third quarter of the twentieth century. His mother was born in Malaysia in the 1940s; her own parents were plantation workers who had moved there in the early twentieth century. Like so many families divided by the choices of citizenship they made, part of her family had returned to India in the 1960s, while her brother stayed on in Malaysia. With the increasing pressure on rural livelihoods in India, and with the growing opportunities for construction work in booming Malaysia and Singapore, the family reestablished their tradition of circulation across the Bay in the 1990s.[63] Theirs is a common story. Mr. Balu arrived in Singapore to work in construction in the early twenty-first century; his grandfather had been there, washing cars, in the 1940s and 1950s; Mr. Balu's mother, Vijayalaksmi, whose father and son both worked in Singapore forty years apart, said that "every time I see Singapore on TV, I feel like it's my own country"—even though she had not been there. Migration across the Bay was part of the family's collective experience.[64]

Many of the region's migrants in the age of globalization come from places, or even from families, that had been mobile in the past. The town of Nagore, for centuries tied to Southeast Asia by its merchants and seafarers, now sends many of its young men to the Middle East and to Southeast Asia as contract workers. In other port towns, including Parangipettai, deep histories of mobility across the sea are being revived—contemporary paths of migration are located in these traditions that, for part of the twentieth century, were forgotten. It would be a mistake to separate a discussion of "climate migration" from a broader consideration of movement around the Bay of Bengal, both in the past and in the present. Even the Asian Development Bank acknowledges that "migration flows associated with climate change" will use "existing migration corridors . . . already used by family or community members."[65] That is to say, people will follow old routes—routes traversed by their sisters or uncles, or perhaps even by their grandparents before them. Migration is not just a response to a changing climate but also—where it is an option—a means of insurance and security, "no longer an act of abandonment, but part of what allows people to stay." The migration of some family members, and the remittances they send back, allows others to maintain their homes against the rising waters.[66] And yet the treatment of migrants as a security threat—often involving the criminalization of migration itself, save for the migration of the already wealthy—will have its effect. The overwhelming majority of "climate-change migration" will be internal, short-distance, and destined for urban areas. Much of the burden will fall on the megacities of the great river deltas: already vulnerable, already overstressed.[67]

In a vital contribution to the debate, Dipesh Chakrabarty argues that the crisis of planetary climate change poses a challenge to the discipline of history, which "exists on the assumption that our past, present, and future are connected by a certain continuity of human experience." As humankind becomes a "geological agent"—as, through our actions, we transform the very structures of the earth—the old distinction between "human" and "natural" history breaks down. The scale of our impact on the earth is such that many scientists argue we need to conceive of our role in the largest possible terms: as a species. Chakrabarty rightly points out that historians "feel concerned about their finely honed sense of contingency and freedom in human affairs having to cede ground to a more deterministic view of the world." But if we seek to explain how humanity "stumbled into" its geological role, a "finely honed sense of contingency" can be helpful; interregional history can help to illuminate a planetary history of unintended consequences.[68]

Throughout these pages I have argued that the millions of men and women who crossed the Bay of Bengal—rubber tappers and river pilots, rickshaw pullers and railwaymen—"made their own history," in Marx's words, "but not just as they pleased." Their choices were constrained by nature (the monsoon winds, the hard landscapes their hands transformed), by the power of capital, by colonial laws of contract and imperial ideologies of free trade, and by brute force. Within those constraints, the small decisions taken by these "minor characters" on the stage of modern Asian history contributed to changing the world in ways they could not see. If the history of the automobile industry has had a disproportionate influence in pushing our collective addiction to oil—"the mechanical bastard-child of oil demanded so much feeding that by mid-century, black blood flowed through every vein and artery of our restless civilization"—the Bay of Bengal, as we have seen, fed the beast with rubber.[69] The paddy fields along the river deltas of Southeast Asia swelled to meet the demand from migrant workers on the plantations of the frontier; only recently have we recognized that rice fields are among the greatest emitters of methane (twenty-five times more powerful than carbon as a greenhouse gas) into the atmosphere. These great migrations, with planetary consequences, were a result of countless small decisions and small acts of coercion as much as they were driven by policies crafted on an imperial level.

Let us be clear: the policies and ideologies of European imperialism bear a heavy burden of responsibility in humanity's path toward environmental crisis. British imperial policy dragged the Bay of Bengal region into a central role in global capitalism for a half century after 1870. The forces of empire and capital energized the life of the sea and sowed the seeds of its slow death. The elevation of private profit over public good, of environmental destruction over preservation, was integral to Victorian imperialism, notwithstanding its occasional communitarian urges and the stirrings of early environmentalism. Despite a few dissenting voices, postcolonial states learned these lessons well, and tried to apply them better. Alternative ideas of common wealth were crushed by colonial and postcolonial states, wedded as they were to a "developmental project" that transcended political divisions. We must not forget the very close association between human suffering and ecological harm. In the history I have told, moments of the most intensive environmental destruction—the land clearances on the Southeast Asian forest frontier in the 1870s, the wartime attempts to hack a jungle path around the Bay of Bengal—rested on the exploitation of labor at its most unfree. In collective memory, trauma and the transformation of landscape are in intimate embrace. With few exceptions, struggles for political freedom in the twentieth century failed to make that connection.

Seeing the Bay of Bengal whole again—as poets and migrants and labor activists and some colonial administrators did a hundred years ago—can shed new light on its most urgent problems. The rising waters of the Bay are due to global causes, but it is at the level of the region that their effects will be felt. The region has the cultural resources to generate a new ethic of hospitality and aid to strangers: a store of collective memories, intercultural understandings, and stories that allow the imagination of solidarities over long distances, though many of these have been forgotten or lie buried beneath the surface of official ideologies. The triumph of narrow nationalism over more expansive political visions in the mid-twentieth century need not be permanent. The utter necessity of managing shared water resources is as likely to produce a new spirit of cooperation across borders and regional divisions as it is to provoke "water wars." Ecologists treat the region as a whole, writing of the "Bay of Bengal Large Marine Ecosystem." The maps of social scientists and humanists remain fractured by the boundaries of area studies. This book is a small tug toward greater wholeness. The Bay of Bengal's coastal rim provokes an "ecology of fear"—but its history could also harness ecologies of hope.[70]

Crossing the Bay of Bengal

The design of the Loyang Tua Pek Kong temple in northeastern Singapore is unlike any other I know. Approached along a road lined with bright yellow flags, the temple's roof, pictured in figure 22, is an architectural hybrid—it blends within the same structure the roofs of a Chinese temple and a Hindu one.

Inside the temple complex, shrines to Daoist, Buddhist, and Hindu deities and the grave site *(keramat)* of a Muslim holy man sit next to one another. Worshippers do a round of the shrines. Each person approaches with the gestures ingrained by habit—Hindus with hands together in prayer, Chinese clasping incense sticks and bowing to the shrines. Some boundaries are preserved while others are crossed. The Hindu shrine and the *keramat* are adjacent, but a small sign by the *keramat* asks those who have consumed pork that day not to approach it. The temple attracts tens of thousands of people each month; it is open all hours. These religious mixtures retain the capacity to surprise, but here such mixing feels entirely natural, and never more so than in the early hours. On a whim, I arrived at three o'clock one morning, to see a steady trickle of people stopping by the brightly lit temple in the fading heat of a tropical night.

The Loyang temple is a site where two oceans and many diasporas meet. It provides a dwelling for many divinities: gods that crossed the Bay of Bengal and the South China Sea to find a home at the edges of empires. The temple is relatively new, but it embodies much older movements of people and spirits. Sometime in the 1980s "a group of fishing buddies stumbled across Buddhist, Hindu, and Daoist statues strewn across the isolated beach at the end of the Loyang Industrial

277

Area." The men built a hut "made of bricks and zinc sheets" to house the figures, and soon a Muslim *keramat* was built next to them by local people who had "received a sign" that this should be done. The temple gained a following initially among workers on the local industrial estate. In a city-state that prizes rational efficiency, the power of enchantment remains. The shrine by the sea was driven inland as Singapore's coasts shifted through land reclamation. The original complex burned down in a fire in 1996. By this time, the popularity of the temple was so great that donations poured in to build a new one; in 2003 it moved again, to its present site.[1] Long after the ocean was "forgotten"— receding physically as well as culturally, as Singapore's container port was pushed offshore—traces of the sea orient people's consciousness of the hidden powers that shape their fortunes.

In his Nobel Lecture of 1992, the poet Derek Walcott evoked the living traces in his native St. Lucia of a history of indentured migration from

Figure 22 The Loyang Tua Pek Kong temple in Singapore. The structure blends the architectural styles of a Hindu temple and a Chinese temple. *Photograph by Sunil Amrith.*

India. Walcott invited his audience to "consider the scale of Asia reduced to these fragments: the small white exclamations of minarets or the stone balls of temples in the cane fields." Faced with these "fragments," marooned as islands amid a sea of sugarcane, "one can understand the self-mockery and embarrassment of those who see these rites as parodic, even degenerate." Walcott disagreed with that diagnosis. What he saw in the cane fields was not just a historical artifact but a living tradition—a tradition that had gained new life from its global dispersion in the age of empire. Here is Walcott:

> I misread the event through a visual echo of History—the cane fields, indenture, the evocation of vanished armies, temples, and trumpeting elephants—when all around me there was quite the opposite: elation, delight in the boys' screams, in the sweets-stalls, in more and more costumed characters appearing; a delight of conviction, not loss.[2]

The "delight of conviction" is visible around the Bay of Bengal's rim; it is the living legacy of many crossings past. At so many sites both around the ocean's rim and deep inland, at places such as the Loyang temple in Singapore, the "fragments of Asia" come alive. Each provides a glimpse of the whole arc of the Indian Ocean's coasts, scattered with holy places and linked by millions of journeys. The "delight of conviction" enlivens the annual *thaipusam* procession that still takes place every year in Singapore, Kuala Lumpur, and Penang: spectacular acts of ritual suffering have dimmed not a bit in the century since the first peak of Indian emigration across the Bay. The Singapore government today—like the colonial authorities 150 years ago—regulates the procession's use of music, its beating of drums, the routes it takes through the city, but the ritual continues, year after year.[3] Among the most enthusiastic participants each year are a few Chinese devotees who interpret the ritual in their own ways—a ritual that has been a familiar feature of the city streets their families have shared with Indian migrants for well over a century.

Across the Bay of Bengal, in the South Indian coastal town of Nagore, old paths of pilgrimage live on. Today, as in centuries past, the *dargah* to the saint Shahul Hamid attracts local Hindu as well as Muslim devotees. It also connects Nagore with Southeast Asia. During the saint's annual festival, thousands of pilgrims converge on Nagore from Burma and Indonesia, and especially from Singapore and Malaysia. Pilgrims from Malaysia include Tamil and Malay Muslims,

Tamil Hindus, and even Chinese Buddhists. "Kindly also let me know your inner desires, so that I should whole heartedly pray on your behalf on the solemn occasion for fulfillment and beseech Allah to grant you with success in every walk of life," the shrine's trustee wrote in his invitation to the festival in 2009: thousands do, and they do so with the "delight of conviction."[4] Signs around the shrine complex commemorate donations from the faithful in Southeast Asia over more than a century: for marble for the courtyard floor, for canopies to shelter the shrine's outdoor school. Old geographies acquire new resonance. In the nineteenth century, the steamship and the printing press energized old religious networks as much as they unleashed modernist, secular political movements; the cheap flights and electronic communications of the twenty-first century allow older kinds of movement to flourish.[5]

Loss plays a part in the story, but in many cases, this loss is recent—the loss not of an original homeland but of the landscapes that people have *made* through generations of migration and settlement. For many Tamil Malaysian families, the old rubber plantations are invested with layers of memory and meaning: memories of suffering or of triumph over adversity, memories of the physicality of work, memories of chance and its role in shaping their lives. From the outset, these were localities produced by a history of imperialism, capitalist expansion, and mass migration. They became sacred landscapes. Small tree shrines, replicas of temples far away, acquired moral power in the Malaysian soil. In the second half of the twentieth century, as migration between India and Malaysia declined, the estate temples' power derived, more and more, from their sense of place rather than from their ability to evoke an original site in India. The most insightful scholar of contemporary Tamil society in Malaysia writes that "working-class Tamils are constructing a Malaysian Hindu identity that, while modeled on the *bhakti* pilgrimage tradition, is not directly related to the consumption of transnational culture flows, nor does it involve a diasporic longing for return to the motherland." Rather, they commemorate the "local *presence* of the Lord in various temples and shrines."[6]

That "presence" is now threatened with loss. Estate shrines and temples have been demolished in growing numbers since the 1990s, as plantations are sold off and redeveloped as industrial estates or as suburban housing. However traumatic the memories associated with the plantation landscapes, their disappearance is even worse. The demolition of Hindu temples across the peninsula for the construction of highways or housing developments provoked the largest Tamil protest movement in Malaysian history, led by the Hindu Rights Action Force (HINDRAF) in 2007. Some went so far as to speak—with exaggeration, since interethnic violence has been very rare in Malaysia—of the "mini–ethnic cleansing" of Tamils, linking the condition of Tamils in Malaysia to the fate of their Sri Lankan counterparts. More than 10,000 people protested on the streets of Kuala Lumpur in November of that year; ranks of police met their protest with water cannons and tear gas. The movement's leaders were detained under Malaysia's notorious, colonial-era Internal Security Act.[7]

Though the conflict was framed in terms of the rights of an ethnic and religious minority, the loss was more widely shared: small mosques, too, fell victim to the same process of developer-led land clearance. A voracious hunger for development consumes Malaysia's sites of memory as rapidly as its forest cover and its biodiversity. The loss of Malaysia's Tamil landscapes is felt by other Malaysians, too. A recent collection of work by Malaysian Chinese artists depicts in oil and watercolors the Hindu temples of the country. Lee Weng Fatt's painting of a Hindu temple in Falim, Ipoh, shows the structure as an inherent part of the landscape; that is just how generations of Tamil migrants would have seen it. Tham Siew Inn's picture of a temple in Seremban uses the "bleed of watercolor to suggest things seen through the blur of memory."[8]

The international politics of "heritage" have decreed a very different fate for the urban landscapes produced by migration across the Bay and across the South China Sea. The demands of global tourism, academic and popular interest in instances of "multiculturalism," sustained lobbying—all of these came together to give Georgetown (Penang) and Melaka recognition as World Heritage Sites by UNESCO in 2008. The citation from UNESCO argues that they "bear testimony to a living multi-cultural heritage and tradition of Asia, where many religions and cultures met and coexisted."[9] For all the limitations of such recognition—why these two sites and not others that bear similar "testimony"?—it suggests that the history of migration might yet play a greater role in the histories that schoolchildren study or that popular culture purveys, histories that today remain still bound by the nation-state.

In advance of their campaign of November 2007, the leaders of HINDRAF wrote a letter to the British prime minister at the time, Gordon Brown, appealing for compensation from the British government for the suffering of Tamils in Malaysia. It was their opening gambit in a campaign to highlight the conditions of deprivation and "second-class citizenship" that Malaysian Tamils continue to face. They began with a narrative of their collective past. "We were removed by duplicity and force from our villages," they wrote to Mr. Brown, "and taken to Malaya and put to work to clear the forests, plant and harvest rubber, and make billions of pounds for British owners. After a century of slaving for the British, the colonial government withdrew . . . and they left us unprotected and at the mercy of a majority Malay-Muslim government that has violated our rights as minority Indians." This is one, but only one, way in which people remember the Bay of Bengal's history.

Palanisamy Kumaran was one of the makers of that world, and he remembers it differently. He arrived as a rubber tapper in 1937 with nothing but the clothes on his back. Hard work paid off and good fortune favored him; his is the sort of rags-to-riches story of migration that usually has more basis in legend than in reality. We began with Palanisamy's story, and we can now see how it turned out. Today, every one of his five children and several grandchildren is a successful doctor in Malaysia. He owns acres of land around the plantation store he built in the 1940s and through which he made his fortune. He drove me around those lands, proudly, in his Land Rover; at the age of ninety-five, he inspected them every day. Using his own funds, he ordered the reconstruction of the estate temple, bringing in craftsmen and architects from India to lend it an air of grace. A new estate school bears his name. He is proud of what he has achieved. His land is his own. Malaysia is his home. It is where his children and grandchildren were born, and where his family has flourished. No migrant experience is "representative"—each is necessarily singular. What holds them together is a geography, the Bay of Bengal; a set of institutions, imperial and postcolonial; and shared cultural symbols.

When Ahmad Rijaluddin crossed the Bay of Bengal in the early nineteenth century, he moved within a familiar cultural world. The world of his travels was welded together by Islam and by commerce. It was the trading world of the Indian Ocean that brought "people of different races—English, Portuguese, French, Dutch, Chinese, Bengalis, Burmese, Tamils and Malays"—into contact and into conflict. In the two centuries that separate his journey from our own time, millions followed the same paths, in both directions, across the Bay. Many of them were of humbler origin; they went to work and had neither the luxury nor the time—nor, in many cases, the learning—to leave a travelogue, as Rijaluddin did. They did leave traces of their journeys in the shrines they built and in the things that they made.

Crossing the Bay of Bengal, they crossed frontiers both natural and political. Their journeys invented new ways of seeing the world—not the world as it appeared in maps, but a world shaped by the movement of names and stories. In the imagination, distance became relative—measured in the length of a crossing, in the time it took a letter to arrive, in the density of people from home who clustered together in a neighborhood or on a plantation across the sea. Crossing the Bay of Bengal involved encounters between peoples and between languages, often for the first time. These encounters were not abstract: they had a place, an architecture, a flavor. Emotion, as much as reason, shaped what one embraced and what one pushed away.

The half century after 1880 was pivotal: a period of relentless energy that altered permanently the societies and the ecology of the entire coastal rim. A more discordant movement followed the crescendo of the 1920s—the Bay was fragmented by depression and broken by war. After the war, threads across the Bay were woven back together, but never with the same density of weave. Although migration across the Bay declined after 1945, the velocity of those earlier circulations had a cascading effect: they produced a permanent transformation, left a lasting echo. By the second half of the twentieth century, that transformation became visible on the sea as it was already visible on the land. Over centuries, the dance of land and sea shaped the coastal arc—here the "colonies" of mangrove expanding, there the force of the waves eroding the coastline. Human intervention, light at first, accumulated over centuries; over the past fifty years it has accumulated on an irrevocable scale.

However connected the coasts of the Bay have been, there has never emerged a set of regional political institutions to encompass it. Not even the imperial scaffold could hold the Bay together—in the age of

Victorian imperialism, it was governed as a patchwork of separate territories, often deliberately kept apart. The more recent institutions that have emerged, such as the Bay of Bengal Initiative for Multi-Sectoral Economic Cooperation (BIMSTEC), are technocratic, narrowly focused, and very limited in their reach. The Bay of Bengal inspired many imaginations and many visions of solidarity across distance, but it never developed into an *idea* with the force of territorial nationalism. However much people's lives were shaped by circulation around the Bay, few would have identified with the sea and its coasts as their home. What the region does possess, richly, is a practical ethic of coexistence. "We can live together without agreeing on what the values are that make it good to live together," Kwame Anthony Appiah writes. The history of everyday life in the coastal cities that surround the Bay—their coffee shops and eating stalls, their cultures of public performance and religious interaction—bear out this proposition.[10]

The moral and political questions that face the Bay of Bengal today would have been familiar at the turn of the twentieth century. To whom will the Bay belong? To the rising powers with their fevered quest for energy and resources and influence? To the forces of capital that seek to extract value from the land (and now from the very bed of the sea)? Or to the diversity of peoples that inhabit its coasts? We can no longer ignore the costs—to human beings, to the species that give life to the sea, to the sea itself—of our collective hunger for energy. The Bay of Bengal rises each year, with consequences that have been uneven but already catastrophic. The urgency of the environmental and political challenge opens a small window for reimagining the Bay of Bengal: an opportunity to link communities' struggles for cultural recognition with an acknowledgment that the region's history spills over national borders, an opportunity to link struggles against environmental destruction with struggles for the welfare of those who make their living from the Bay. Migration around the Bay is on the rise again. The problems of global climate change can no longer be addressed by national governments alone. A new sense of connectedness is wanting. In the Bay of Bengal's history are resources, narratives, and memories upon which to build one.

To see the world anew, we need new maps. Journalist and strategic commentator Robert D. Kaplan makes this point to an American audience used to seeing Mercator projections with the United States dead center, with the Indian Ocean "split up at the far edges of the map." The "Greater Indian Ocean," he argues, "may comprise a map as iconic to the new century as Europe was to the last one." Seeing the Indian Ocean whole, on one map, makes the world look different.[11] The map Kaplan describes is a map of power—a map of the (possible) redistribution of power in an Asian century. But there are other maps that reshape our vision in other ways. Artist T. Shanaathanan begins his moving work *The Incomplete Thombu* with an unsettling, upside-down map of Sri Lanka, with the Jaffna Peninsula at eye level. It is a map that inverts the official view. Michael Ondaatje observes that the "southern part of the island, where the power and the narrative voice usually reside, are now somewhere to the distant north." It is this "re-invented and re-aligned map" that "prepares the reader and viewer for this new perspective"—a moving and painstaking documentation of the "multiple displacements" of the Tamil residents of Jaffna by civil conflict. This is just the latest in a long series of displacements around the Bay of Bengal's coastal rim.[12]

Oceanic history is itself a kind of cartography. By foregrounding the Bay of Bengal—linked by journeys, memories, and the sinews of power—we can see beyond the borders of today's nation-states, beyond the borders imposed by imperial mapmakers and immigration officials, to a more fluid, more uncertain world: a world that resembles our own. As the furies of nature grow clamorous, the fortunes of migrants are ever fickle.

Glossary

Boria Nineteenth-century Penang variant of the Muharram celebration

cartaz Shipping and trading permits enforced by Portuguese authorities in the Indian Ocean

Chola South Indian dynasty at the height of its power between the ninth and twelfth centuries AD

Chulia Derived from "Chola"; term used in nineteenth-century Southeast Asia to refer to Tamil Muslim merchants

dalit Modern term for formerly "untouchable" groups in India, often now a preferred term of self-description

dargah Tomb shrines of Sufi saints (called *keramat* in the Malay world)

Dravidian Family of South Indian languages; also used to refer to a Dravidian as distinct from an Aryan "race," and to describe a political movement for the advancement of non-Brahmin communities in South India

El Niño The El Niño–Southern Oscillation (ENSO) describes the alternation between cooler and warmer sea surface temperatures in the equatorial Pacific, with global climatic effects. The warmer phase is El Niño; the cooler phase is known as La Niña

hajj Muslim pilgrimage to Mecca

jawi General term for the Malay peoples of Southeast Asia, from the Arabic *jawah* (Java); also refers to Malay written in Arabic script

kala Burmese term used to describe Indians, originally a term denoting "foreigner," but it assumed pejorative connotations

kangany Tamil term for labor recruiter; often an existing plantation worker/foreman who returned home to recruit workers on commission. Used in Malaya and Ceylon

kapitan an office of communal representation; Portuguese term, also used by the Dutch in Indonesia

Kling Derived from Kalinga (an ancient kingdom on the Orissa coast), a term used to describe South Indians in nineteenth-century Southeast Asia. Developed pejorative connotations over time

kongsi Chinese association or cooperative brotherhood

lascar term for sailors from India or Southeast Asia, from the Urdu *lashkari,* "soldier"

lebbai Educated laymen among the Tamil Muslim community; treated by some scholars as a distinct community or "caste"

maistry Term used in colonial Burma for labor boss or recruiter (equivalent to *kangany*)

maraikkayar Tamil Muslim elite, claiming Arab descent; term drawn from a Tamil word for boat, *marakkalam;* in Malaya, Maraikkayar was rendered "Merican" and became a common name

Muharram Shi'a festival commemorating the death of Husayn, grandson of the Prophet Muhammad

Nanyang The Chinese term for Southeast Asia ("Southern Ocean")

pannaiyal Bonded agricultural workers in South India

Peranakan "local-born"; term used to describe descendants of Chinese settlers in Southeast Asia who married local women and adopted elements of indigenous culture; also used for hybrid Indian Muslim communities, as in *Jawi Peranakan*

pongyi Burmese Buddhist monk

qiyas Term used by Arabic navigators to describe stellar measurement

sampan Indigenous boats used in the Malay world

shahbandar Harbormaster; important political position in precolonial Southeast Asian port cities, often occupied by foreigners

thaipusam Tamil Hindu festival of ritual penance and procession, very popular in Singapore and Malaysia

thimithi Tamil Hindu fire-walking ceremony, popular in Singapore and Malaysia

thoni Traditional fishing boat used in South India and the Maldives; also rendered *doni*

thosai South Indian lentil and rice flour crepe, popular in Southeast Asia

waqf Endowment by Muslims for religious, educational or charitable purposes

Abbreviations

AMCJA	All-Malayan Council of Joint Action
ASEAN	Association of Southeast Asian Nations
BIMSTEC	Bay of Bengal Initiative for Multi-Sectoral Technical and Economic Cooperation
BISNC	British India Steam Navigation Company
EIC	East India Company
ENSO	El- Niño Southern Oscillation
INA	Indian National Army
IOR	India Office Records
MCP	Malayan Communist Party
MIC	Malaysian Indian Congress
NADM	National Archives Department, Myanmar, Yangon
NAI	National Archives of India, New Delhi
NAS	National Archives of Singapore
NAUK	National Archives of the United Kingdom
NMM	National Maritime Museum, Greenwich, UK
PRO	Public Record Office
RMRL	Roja Mutthiah Research Library, Chennai
SSFR	Straits Settlements Factory Records
SSR	Straits Settlements Records
TNSA	Tamil Nadu State Archives, Chennai
UMNO	United Malays National Organization
UNESCO	United Nations Educational, Scientific and Cultural Organization
VOC	Verenigde Oostindische Compagnie: Dutch East India Company

Notes

1 The Life of the Bay of Bengal

1. *Ahmad Rijaluddin's Hikayat Perintah Negeri Benggala*, ed. and trans. C. Skinner (The Hague: Martinus Nijhoff, 1982), 21, 29, 51, 75.
2. Sanjay Subrahmanyam, "Connected Histories: Notes towards a Reconfiguration of Early Modern Eurasia," *Modern Asian Studies* 31, 3 (1997): 745.
3. Interviews with the author in Penang and Sungai Petani, August and September 2007. All translations from Tamil texts and interviews in this book are my own, except where otherwise indicated.
4. E. G. H. Dobby, *Monsoon Asia* (London: University of London Press, 1961), 27.
5. William Methwold, *Relations of the Kingdome of Golchonda, and Other Neighbouring Nations within the Gulfe of Bengala, Arreccan, Pegu, Tannassery, etc. and the English Trade in Those Parts* [1626], in W. H. Moreland, ed., *Relations of Golconda in the Early Seventeenth Century* (London: Hakluyt Society, 1931), 1.
6. Willem van Schendel, *A History of Bangladesh* (Cambridge: Cambridge University Press, 2009), 3.
7. K. V. L. N. S. Sarma et al., "Morphological Features in the Bay of Bengal," *Journal of the Indian Geophysics Union* 4, 2 (2000): 185–190.
8. United States Geological Survey, Tectonic Summary: http://neic.usgs.gov /neic/eq_depot/2004/eq_041226/neic_slav_ts.html (accessed 21 March 2011).
9. Sugata Bose, *A Hundred Horizons: The Indian Ocean in the Age of Global Empire* (Cambridge, MA: Harvard University Press, 2006), 3.
10. Peter D. Clift and R. Alan Plumb, *The Asian Monsoon: Causes, History and Effects* (Cambridge: Cambridge University Press, 2008), vii; Jay S. Fein and Pamela L. Stephens, eds., *Monsoons* (New York: John Wiley and Sons, 1987).
11. Clift and Plumb, *The Asian Monsoon*.
12. E. Halley, "An Historical Account of the Trade Winds and the Monsoons, Observable in the Seas between and near the Tropicks, with an attempt to

assign the physical cause of the sail winds," *Philosophical Transactions of the Royal Society of London* 16 (1686): 153–168.

13. Clift and Plumb, *The Asian Monsoon.*

14. *Bay of Bengal Pilot,* 8th ed. (London: HM Admiralty, 1953), 28.

15. Pablo Neruda, "May Monsoon," in *Residence on Earth,* trans. Donald D. Walsh (London: Souvenir Press, 1976), 44–45.

16. *Oxford Dictionary of English,* 2nd ed. (Oxford: Oxford University Press, 2005).

17. J. F. Imray, *The Bay of Bengal Pilot: A Nautical Directory for the Principal Rivers, Harbours, and Anchorages, Contained within the Bay of Bengal* (London: James Imray and Son, 1879), 297–298.

18. *Bay of Bengal Pilot* (1953), 57.

19. K. Sivasubramaniam, *Marine Fishery Resources of the Bay of Bengal,* BOBP/WP/36 (Rome: FAO, 1985).

20. Francis Day, *Report on the Sea Fish and Fisheries of India and Burma* (Calcutta: Government of India, 1873).

21. K. N. Chaudhuri, *Trade and Civilization in the Indian Ocean: An Economic History from the Rise of Islam to 1750* (Cambridge: Cambridge University Press, 1985), 27.

22. James C. Scott, *The Art of Not Being Governed: An Anarchist History of Upland Southeast Asia* (New Haven, CT: Yale University Press, 2010).

23. Clift and Plumb, *The Asian Monsoon.*

24. John Edye, "Description of the various Classes of Vessels constructed and employed by the Natives of the Coasts of Coromandel, Malabar, and the Island of Ceylon, for their Coasting Navigation," *Journal of the Royal Asiatic Society of Great Britain and Ireland* 1 (1834): 1–14.

25. Chaudhuri, *Trade and Civilization in the Indian Ocean,* 138–159; J. H. Parry, *The Discovery of the Sea* (London: Weidenfeld and Nicolson, 1974), 3–26; Daniel R. Headrick, *Power over Peoples: Technology, Environments, and Western Imperialism, 1400 to the Present* (Princeton, NJ: Princeton University Press, 2010), 11–19.

26. Herman Melville, *Moby-Dick or, The Whale* [1851] (London: Penguin Classics, 2003), 415.

27. Leonard Y. Andaya, *Leaves of the Same Tree: Trade and Ethnicity in the Straits of Melaka* (Honolulu: University of Hawai'i Press, 2008), 22.

28. Jan Wisseman Christie, "The Medieval Tamil-Language Inscriptions in Southeast Asia and China," *Journal of Southeast Asian Studies* 29, 2 (1998): 239–268.

29. K. A. Nilakanta Sastri, *The Colas,* 2nd ed., 2 vols. (Madras: Madras University Press, 1955).

30. Christie, "Medieval Tamil-Language Inscriptions"; Hermann Kulke, "The Naval Expeditions of the Cholas in the Context of Asian History," in

Hermann Kulke, K. Kesavapany, and Vijay Sakhuja, eds., *Nagapattinam to Suvarnadwipa: Reflections on the Chola Naval Expeditions to Southeast Asia* (Singapore: ISEAS Press, 2010), 1–19; Tansen Sen, *Buddhism, Diplomacy and Trade: The Realignment of Sino-Indian Relations, 600–1400* (Honolulu: University of Hawai'i Press, 2003).

31. Kulke et al., *Nagapattinam to Suvarnadwipa.*
32. Victor Lieberman, "Charter State Collapse in Southeast Asia, ca. 1250–1400, as a Problem in Regional and World History," *American Historical Review* 116, 4 (2011): 937–963; Victor Lieberman, *Strange Parallels: Southeast Asia in Global Context, c. 800–1830*, vol. 2, *Mainland Mirrors: Europe, Japan, China, South Asia, the Islands* (Cambridge: Cambridge University Press, 2009); Victor Lieberman and Brendan Buckley, "The Impact of Climate on Southeast Asia, circa 950–1820: New Findings," *Modern Asian Studies* 46, 5 (2012): 1049–96.
33. Cited in Andaya, *Leaves of the Same Tree,* 27.
34. H. G. Quaritch Wales, "Archaeological Researches on Ancient Indian Colonization in Malaya," *Journal of the Malayan Branch of the Royal Asiatic Society* 18, pt. 1 (1940): 56.
35. A. Cortesão and A. Teixeira, *Monumenta Cartographica Portugaliae Cartographica* (Lisbon, 1960–1962), 1:79–81.
36. Ahmad ibn Majid al-Najdi, *Kitab al-Fawa'id fi usul al-bahr wa'l-qawa'id* [c. 1490], *Arab Navigation in the Indian Ocean before the Coming of the Portuguese,* trans. G. R. Tibbetts (London: Royal Asiatic Society, 1971), 124.
37. Alexander Dalrymple, *Memoir of a Chart of the Bay of Bengal,* 2nd ed. (London: George Bigg, 1787), 1.
38. Captain John Ritchie, *An Hydrographical Journey of a Cursory Survey of the Coasts and Islands in the Bay of Bengal* (London: George Bigg, 1784), 1.
39. Chaudhuri, *Trade and Civilisation,* 135.
40. Dalrymple, *Memoir of a Chart of the Bay of Bengal.*
41. *An Hydrographical Journey,* 19, 70.
42. W. Somerset Maugham, "The Vessel of Wrath," in *Collected Short Stories 2* (London: Penguin, 1963), 9.
43. *The Bay of Bengal Pilot* (1879), 307–309.
44. *Journal of the Asiatic Society of Bengal* 16, 2 (1847): 848; Gisela Kutzbach, "Concepts of Monsoon Physics in Historical Perspective: The Indian Monsoon (Seventeenth to Early Twentieth Century)," in Fein and Stephens, eds., *Monsoons,* 159–209.
45. C. W. Brebner, *New Handbook for the Indian Ocean, Arabian Sea and Bay of Bengal* (Bombay: Times of India Press, 1898), 95.
46. Joseph Conrad, *Mirror of the Sea: Memories and Impressions* (London: Methuen, 1906), 43.

47. R. E. G. Davies, *A History of the World's Airlines* (London: Oxford University Press, 1964), 170–174.

48. Richard Upjohn Light, "Cruising by Airplane: Narrative of a Journey around the World," *Geographical Review* 25, 4 (October 1935): 565–600.

49. Diana L. Eck, *India: A Sacred Geography* (New York: Harmony Books, 2012).

50. It was also widely known as Suvarnadwipa, "isle of gold." Quotations from Paul Wheatley, *The Golden Khersonese: Studies in the Historical Geography of the Malay Peninsula before A.D. 1500* (Kuala Lumpur: University of Malaya Press, 1961), 182; Richard H. Davis, *Global India circa 100 CE: South Asia in Early World History* (Ann Arbor, MI: Association of Asian Studies, 2009), 13.

51. "Mahajanaka-Jataka," no. 539, trans. E. B. Cowell and W. H. D. Rouse, in E. B. Cowell, ed., *The Jataka, or Stories of the Buddha's Former Births* (Cambridge: Cambridge University Press, 1895–1913), 6:19.

52. Wheatley, *Golden Khersonese*, 179.

53. *The Travels of Fa-hsien, 399–414 A.D., or Record of the Buddhistic Kingdoms*, trans. H. A. Giles (Cambridge: Cambridge University Press, 1923).

54. "Nuranneha and the Grave," in Dineshchandra Sen, ed. and comp., *Eastern Bengal Ballads*, vol. 4, pt. 1 (Calcutta: University of Calcutta, 1932). See also Lakshmi Subramanian, *Medieval Seafarers of India* (New Delhi: Roli Books, 1999).

55. Joseph Conrad, "Youth: A Narrative," in *Youth: A Narrative and Two Other Stories* (London: J. M. Dent and Sons, 1923), 37.

56. Bose, *A Hundred Horizons*, 109.

57. NAS, Oral History Department, M. K. Bhasi, interviewed by Ng Chang Wang, August 1985, A000590/09.

58. Derek Walcott, "Sicilian Suite," in *White Egrets* (New York: Farrar, Straus and Giroux, 2010), 15–22.

59. Chaudhuri, *Trade and Civilization;* Michael Pearson, *The Indian Ocean* (London: Routledge, 2003); Kenneth McPherson, *The Indian Ocean: A History of People and the Sea* (New Delhi: Oxford University Press, 1993).

60. Robert D. Kaplan, *Monsoon: The Indian Ocean and the Future of American Power* (New York: Random House, 2010), 10; Amitav Ghosh, *In an Antique Land* (London: Granta, 1992), 236; Bose, *A Hundred Horizons;* Isabel Hofmeyr, "Universalizing the Indian Ocean," *Proceedings of the Modern Language Association* 125, 3 (2010): 721–729; Mark Ravinder Frost, "'Wider Opportunities': Religious Revival, Nationalist Awakening and the Global Dimension in Colombo, 1870–1920," *Modern Asian Studies* 36, 4 (2002): 936–967.

61. Chaudhuri, *Trade and Civilisation*, 21–23; R. J. Barendse, *The Arabian Seas: The Indian Ocean World of the Seventeenth Century* (Armonk, NY: M. E. Sharpe, 2002).

62. Fernand Braudel, *The Mediterranean and the Mediterranean World in the Age of Philip II*, trans. Sian Reynolds (New York: Harper and Row, 1972), 1:18.
63. Orhan Pamuk, *The Naïve and the Sentimental Novelist*, trans. Nazim Dikbas (Cambridge, MA: Harvard University Press, 2010), 10–11.
64. Chaudhuri, *Trade and Civilization*, 23; Fernand Braudel, "Histoire et sciences sociales: la longue durée," *Annales: Economies, Sociétés, Civilisations* 13 (1958): 725–753.
65. Paul Ricoeur, *Time and Narrative*, trans. Kathleen McLaughlin and David Pellauer (Chicago: University of Chicago Press, 1984), 1:208.
66. "Bay of Bengal," *Encyclopedia of Oceanography* (New York: Reinhold, 1966), 110–118.
67. Ricoeur, *Time and Narrative*, 1:104.
68. David Blackbourn, *The Conquest of Nature: Water, Landscape and the Making of Modern Germany* (New York: Norton, 2006); Richard White, *The Organic Machine: The Remaking of the Columbia River* (New York: Hill and Wang, 1995); compare with, Timothy Mitchell, "Can the Mosquito Speak?" in *Rule of Experts: Egypt, Technopolitics, Modernity* (Berkeley: University of California Press, 2002).
69. Kären Wigen, "Oceans of History: Introduction," *American Historical Review* 111, 3 (2006): 717–721.

2 That Vast Sea's Emporium

1. J. F. Imray, *The Bay of Bengal Pilot: A Nautical Directory for the Principal Rivers, Harbours, and Anchorages, Contained within the Bay of Bengal* (London: James Imray and Son, 1879), 27.
2. Susan Bayly, *Saints, Goddesses and Kings: Muslims and Christians in South Indian Society, 1700–1900* (Cambridge: Cambridge University Press, 1989), 217–219; S. A. A. Saheb, "A Festival of Flags: Hindu-Muslim Devotion and the Sacralising of Localism at the Shrine of the Nagore-e-Sharif in Tamil Nadu," in Pnina Werbner and Helene Basu, eds., *Embodying Charisma: Modernity, Locality and the Performance of Emotion in Sufi Cults* (London: Routledge, 1998), 55–76.
3. *Bay of Bengal Pilot*, 27–28.
4. "Petition from Nagore Merchants," Proceedings of Committee of Investigation into the State of the Revenue, 1797–1798, NAUK, PRO, CO 55/2.
5. Bayly, *Saints, Goddesses and Kings*; Richard M. Eaton, *Sufis of Bijapur* (Princeton, NJ: Princeton University Press, 1978); Richard M. Eaton, *The Rise of Islam and the Bengal Frontier, 1204–1760* (New Delhi: Oxford University Press, 1993); A. H. Johns, "Sufism as a Category in Indonesian Literature," *Journal of Southeast Asian History* 2 (1961): 10–23.

6. Anthony Reid, *Southeast Asia in the Age of Commerce, 1450–1680* (New Haven: Yale University Press, 1993), 2:133.

7. Ibid., vol. 2; Torsten Tschacher, "Circulating Islam: Understanding Convergence and Divergence in the Islamic Traditions of Ma'bar and Nusantara," in R. Michael Feener and Terenjit Sevea, eds., *Islamic Connections: Muslim Societies in South and Southeast Asia* (Singapore: ISEAS, 2009), 48–67.

8. Ronit Ricci, *Islam Translated: Literature, Conversion, and the Arabic Cosmopolis of South and Southeast Asia* (Chicago: University of Chicago Press, 2011).

9. Sanjay Subrahmanyam, " 'Persianization' and 'Mercantilism': Two Themes in Bay of Bengal History, 1400–1700," in Om Prakash and Denys Lombard, eds., *Commerce and Culture in the Bay of Bengal, 1500–1800* (New Delhi: Indian Council of Historical Research, 1999), 47–85; Engseng Ho, *The Graves of Tarim: Genealogy and Mobility across the Indian Ocean* (Berkeley: University of California Press, 2006), 189.

10. Edgar Thurston, *Castes and Tribes of Southern India*, 7 vols. (Madras: Government Press, 1909); Bayly, *Saints, Goddesses and Kings*, 80–88; Tschacher, "Circulating Islam."

11. Ricci, *Islam Translated*, 128; David Shulman, "Muslim Popular Literature in Tamil: The Tamimancari Malai," in Yohanan Friedmann, ed., *Islam in Asia*, vol. 1, *South Asia* (Jerusalem: Magnes Press, Hebrew University, 1984), 175; Vashudha Narayanan, "Religious Vocabulary and Regional Identity: A Study of the Tamil *Cirappuranam*," in David Gilmartin and Bruce B. Lawrence, eds., *Beyond Turk and Hindu: Rethinking Religious Identities in Islamicate South Asia* (Gainesville: University Press of Florida, 2000), 74–97; Ki. Nayanar Muhammadu, "Cirappuraanathil Kaappiya Panpugal," *Proceedings of the Second International Conference Seminar of Tamil Studies* (Madras, 1968), 3:95–103.

12. Umaru Pulavar, "Vilatattuk Kantam, Nattu Patalam," in *Cirappuranam*, ed. M. Seyyihu Muhammadu Hasan (Chennai: Ulatak Tamilaraycci Niruvanam, 1984), 26; translation from Narayan, "Religious Vocabulary and Regional Identity," 86.

13. Sejarah Melayu, *Malay Annals*, trans. C. C. Brown (Kuala Lumpur: Oxford University Press, 1970), 70–71, 184–185.

14. Stewart Gordon, *When Asia Was the World* (New Haven, CT: Yale University Press, 2008), 162.

15. Tomé Pires, *The Suma Oriental of Tomé Pires*, trans. Armando Cortesão (London: Hakluyt Society, 1944), 2:268.

16. Denys Lombard, "Pour une histoire des villes du Sud-Est asiatique," *Annales: Économies, Sociétés, Civilisations* 25, 4 (1970): 842–856.

17. Eric Tagliacozzo, "An Urban Ocean: Notes on the Historical Evolution of Coastal Cities in Greater Southeast Asia," *Journal of Urban History* 33, 6 (2007): 911–932.
18. On Portuguese imperialism in Asia, see K. N. Chaudhuri, *Trade and Civilization in the Indian Ocean: An Economic History from the Rise of Islam to 1750* (Cambridge: Cambridge University Press, 1985); Sanjay Subrahmanyam, *The Portuguese Empire in Asia 1500–1700: A Political and Economic History* (London: Longman, 1993); Sinappah Arasaratnam, *Merchants, Companies and Commerce on the Coromandel Coast 1650–1740* (New Delhi: Oxford University Press, 1986); Om Prakash and Denys Lombard, eds., *Commerce and Culture in the Bay of Bengal, 1500–1800* (New Delhi: Manohar, 1999); Sanjay Subrahmanyam, *The Political Economy of Commerce: South India, 1500–1650* (Cambridge: Cambridge University Press, 1990); C. R. Boxer, *The Portuguese Seaborne Empire, 1415–1825* (London: Hutchinson, 1969).
19. Cited in Subrahmanyam, *Political Economy of Commerce*, 92.
20. Luiz Vaz de Camões, *The Lusíads*, trans. Landeg White (Oxford: Oxford University Press, 1997), 120.
21. William Methwold, *Relations of the Kingdome of Golchonda, and Other Neighbouring Nations within the Gulfe of Bengala, Arreccan, Pegu, Tannassery, etc. and the English Trade in Those Parts* [1626], in W. H. Moreland, ed., *Relations of Golconda in the Early Seventeenth Century* (London: Hakluyt Society, 1931), 40–41.
22. Cayetano J. Socarras, "The Portuguese in Lower Burma: Filipe de Brito de Nicote," *Luso-Brazilian Review* 3, 2 (1966): 3–24.
23. K. N. Panikkar, *Asia and Western Dominance: A Survey of the Vasco da Gama Epoch of Asian History, 1498–1945* (London: George Allen and Unwin, 1959); Amitav Ghosh, *In an Antique Land* (London: Granta, 1992).
24. Jonathan I. Israel, *The Dutch Republic: Its Rise, Greatness, and Fall, 1477–1807* (Oxford: Clarendon Press, 1995).
25. Giovanni Arrighi, *The Long Twentieth Century: Money, Power, and the Origins of Our Times* (London: Verso, 1994), 138; Jan de Vries and A. M. van der Woude, *The First Modern Economy: Success, Failure and Perseverance of the Dutch Economy, 1500–1815* (Cambridge: Cambridge University Press, 1997).
26. Arrighi, *The Long Twentieth Century*.
27. Lauren Benton, *A Search for Sovereignty: Law and Geography in European Empires, 1400–1900* (New York: Cambridge University Press, 2010).
28. Hugo Grotius, *The Freedom of the Seas, or the Right Which Belongs to the Dutch to take part in the East Indian Trade* [1608], trans. Ralph Van Deman Magoffin (New York: Oxford University Press, 1916); Peter Borschberg,

"Hugo Grotius' Theory of Trans-Oceanic Trade Regulation: Revisiting *Mare Liberum* (1609)," Institute for International Law and Justice Working Paper 2005/14, New York University, 2005; Benton, *Search for Sovereignty.*

29. Chaudhuri, *Trade and Civilisation in the Indian Ocean,* 84.

30. John F. Richards, *The Unending Frontier: An Environmental History of the Early Modern World* (Berkeley: University of California Press, 2003), 25–38; John F. Richards, *The Mughal Empire* (Cambridge: Cambridge University Press, 1993); Muzaffar Alam and Sanjay Subrahmanyam, eds., *The Mughal State, 1526–1750* (New Delhi: Oxford University Press, 1998); Richard M. Eaton, *The Rise of Islam and the Bengal Frontier, 1204–1760* (Berkeley: University of California Press, 1993).

31. Antony Schorer, "Brief Relation of the Trade of the Coromandel Coast, especially at the Factory at Masulipatnam, where I resided in the service of the Hon'ble Company in the seventh Year" [1615–1616], in W. H. Moreland, ed., *Relations of Golconda in the Early Seventeenth Century* (London: Hakluyt Society, 1931), 55–59; Methwold, *Relations of the Kingdome of Golchonda,* 39; Arasaratnam, *Merchants, Companies and Commerce;* Subrahmanyam, *Political Economy of Commerce.*

32. Arasaratnam, *Merchants, Companies and Commerce,* 94.

33. Reid, *Southeast Asia in the Age of Commerce,* 2:208–212.

34. Ibid., 2:148–149; Subrahmanyam, *Political Economy of Commerce,* 335.

35. For a skeptical view of the global reach of the Little Ice Age, see IPCC, *Climate Change 2001: Working Group I: The Scientific Basis* (Cambridge: Cambridge University Press, 2001), ch. 2.

36. Lieberman and Buckley, "The Impact of Climate"; Victor Lieberman, *Strange Parallels: Southeast Asia in Global Context, c. 800–1830* (Cambridge: Cambridge University Press, 2003; 2009), 1:101–112, 2:79–84.

37. Lieberman and Buckley, "Impact of Climate"; Lieberman, *Strange Parallels,* 2:79–84; Reid, *Southeast Asia in the Age of Commerce,* 2:291–293.

38. Lieberman and Buckley, "Impact of Climate," 1053.

39. Sinnappah Arasaratnam, ed. and trans., *François Valentijn's Description of Ceylon* (London: Hakluyt Society, 1978), 176.

40. Gordon, *When Asia Was the World,* 113.

41. Girolamo Priuli, *I Diarii,* quoted in Chaudhuri, *Trade and Civilisation,* 64–65.

42. Fernand Braudel, *The Mediterranean and the Mediterranean World in the Age of Philip II,* trans Sian Reynolds (New York: Harper and Row, 1972), 1:389–399; Reid, *Southeast Asia in the Age of Commerce,* 2:9–10.

43. Anthony Reid, "Southeast Asian Consumption of Indian and British Cotton Cloth, 1600–1850," in Giorgio Riello and Tirthankar Roy, eds., *How*

India Clothed the World: The World of South Asian Textiles, 1500–1850 (Leiden: Brill, 2009), 31–52; for an overview, see also Riello and Roy's introduction to the volume.

44. Pires, *Suma Oriental,* 3:92–93; Reid, "Southeast Asian Consumption," 36.

45. Arasaratnam, *Merchants, Companies and Commerce,* 98–99.

46. Dispatch from Jan Pieterz Coen, Jacatra, 5 June 1617, VOC 1055, ff. 113–117, in Om Prakash, ed., *The Dutch Factories in India 1617–1623: A Collection of Dutch East India Company Documents Pertaining to India* (New Delhi: Munshiram Manoharlal, 1984), 1:29; Braudel, *Mediterranean,* 406; Reid, *Southeast Asia in the Age of Commerce,* 2:28–29, 301–302.

47. Dennis O. Flynn and Arturo Giráldez, "Cycles of Silver: Global Economic Unity through the Mid-Eighteenth Century," *Journal of World History* 13 (2002): 391–427.

48. Pires, *Suma Oriental,* 2:206.

49. Roy W. Hamilton, ed., *The Art of Rice: Spirit and Sustenance in Asia* (Los Angeles: UCLA Fowler Museum, 2003), 23.

50. Arasaratnam, *Merchants, Companies and Commerce,* 102–103; Governor-General De Carpentier (Batavia) to Ysbrantsz (Masulipatnam), 26 July 1625, VOC 1085, ff. 123–130; De Carpentier to Ysbrantsz, 28 August 1627, VOC 1092, ff. 161–162, all in Prakash, ed., *Dutch Factories,* 1:164, 330; Augustin de Beaulieu, quoted in Lombard, "Pour une histoire des villes" (my translation).

51. Coen (Batavia) to Van Uffelen (Masulipatnam) and Soury (Masulipatnam), 8 May 1622, VOC 1076, ff. 76–78; Coen (Batavia) to Van den Broecke (Surat), 8 May 1622, VOC 849, ff. 85v–87v, all in Prakash, ed., *Dutch Factories,* 1:201–203.

52. Van Uffelen (Masulipatnam) to Coen (Batavia), 7 July 1622, VOC 1076, ff. 240–242v, in Prakash, ed., *Dutch Factories,* 1:209–210; Coen (Batavia) to Van Uffelen (Masulipatnam), 22 July 1622, VOC 850, ff. 4–7, in Prakash, ed., *Dutch Factories,* 1:212–213.

53. Sanjay Subrahmanyam, "Dutch Tribulations in Seventeenth-Century Mrauk-U," in *Explorations in Connected History: From the Tagus to the Ganges* (New Delhi: Oxford University Press, 2004), 200–248; Om Prakash, "Introduction," in Prakash, ed., *Dutch Factories,* 2:33–34.

54. Ysbrantsz (Pulicat) to VOC Directors (Amsterdam), 28 April 1625, VOC 1084, ff. 166–168; De Carpentier (Batavia) to Ysbrantsz (Masulipatnam), 26 July 1625, VOC 1085, ff. 123–130, both in Prakash, ed., *Dutch Factories,* 2:148–149, 162.

55. This paragraph is based on Markus Vink, "'The World's Oldest Trade': Dutch Slavery and Slave Trade in the Indian Ocean in the Seventeenth Century," *Journal of World History* 14, 2 (2003): 131–177.

56. Indrani Chatterjee and Richard M. Eaton, eds., *Slavery and South Asian History* (Bloomington: Indiana University Press, 2006), 11; Anthony Reid, ed., *Slavery, Bondage and Dependency in Southeast Asia* (St. Lucia: Queensland University Press, 1983), 27.

57. Chaudhuri, *Trade and Civilization*; Subrahmanyam, *Portuguese Empire in Asia*; Arasaratnam, *Merchants, Companies and Commerce*; Prakash and Lombard, eds., *Commerce and Culture in the Bay of Bengal*. Subrahmanyam, *The Political Economy of Commerce*.

58. Thomas Bowrey, *A Geographical Account of the Countries round the Bay of Begal, 1669 to 1679*, ed. Richard Carnac Temple (Cambridge: Hakluyt Society, 1905).

59. Ibid., 257–258.

60. Anne Bulley, ed., *Free Mariner: John Adolphus Pope in the East Indies, 1786–1821* (London: Bacsa, 1992).

61. Arrighi, *The Long Twentieth Century*.

62. Daniel K. Richter, *Before the Revolution: America's Ancient Pasts* (Cambridge, MA: Harvard University Press, 2011), 4.

3 Turbulent Journeys, Sacred Geographies

1. Francis Light's Journal on the *Eliza* and on Shore, 29 June to 30 September 1786, SSFR, vol. 2, British Library, Asian and African Studies Collection, IOR; H. P. Clodd, *Malaya's First British Pioneer: The Life of Francis Light* (London: Luzac, 1948), 5, 55.

2. Memorandum by J. Price, SSFR, vol. 2, 23 February 1786, IOR/G/34/2; Memorandum by J. Price, 23 February 1786, SSFR, vol. 2; Letter from James Scott to George Ramsay, September 1780, SSFR, vol. 1, IOR/G/34/1.

3. C. A. Bayly, *Imperial Meridian: The British Empire and the World* (London: Pearson, 1989).

4. Fernand Braudel, *The Mediterranean and the Mediterranean World in the Age of Philip II*, trans Sian Reynolds (New York: Harper and Row, 1972), 1: 116.

5. Fred Anderson, *Crucible of War: The Seven Years' War and the Fate of Empire in British North America* (New York: Knopf, 2000).

6. Peter Marshall, *Bengal: The British Bridgehead: Eastern India, 1740–1828* (Cambridge: Cambridge University Press, 1988); C. A. Bayly, *Indian Society and the Making of the British Empire* (Cambridge: Cambridge University Press, 1988).

7. Edward R. Cook et al., "Asian Monsoon Failure and Megadrought During the Last Millennium," *Science* 328 (2010): 487.

8. Adam Smith, *An Inquiry into the Nature and Causes of the Wealth of Nations* (London: W. Strahan and T. Cadell, 1776), book 4, ch. 5.

9. David Arnold, "Hunger in the Garden of Plenty: The Bengal Famine of 1770," in Alessa Johns, ed., *Dreadful Visitations Confronting Natural Catastrophe in the Age of Enlightenment* (New York: Routledge, 1999), 81–112; Ranajit Guha, *A Rule of Property for Bengal: An Essay on the Idea of Permanent Settlement* (Paris: Mouton, 1963).

10. Giovanni Arrighi, *The Long Twentieth Century: Money, Power, and the Origins of Our Times* (London: Verso, 1994); Dennis O. Flynn and Arturo Giráldez, "Cycles of Silver: Global Economic Unity through the Mid-Eighteenth Century," *Journal of World History* 13 (2002): 391–427.

11. Edward Thornton, *India: Its State and Prospects* (London: Parsbury, Allen, 1835), 89.

12. H. Dodwell, *Sepoy Recruitment in the Old Madras Army,* Studies in Indian Records, no. 70 (Calcutta: Superintendant of Government Printing, 1922).

13. Lord Minto, quoted in Bayly, *Imperial Meridian,* 72; C. A. Bayly, *The Birth of the Modern World: Global Connections and Comparisons, 1780–1914* (Oxford: Blackwell, 2004), 88–89.

14. Alicia Schrikker, *Dutch and British Colonial Intervention in Sri Lanka, 1780–1815: Expansion and Reform* (Leiden: Brill, 2007); Bayly, *Imperial Meridian,* 70–73; Michael Ondaatje, *Running in the Family* (New York: Vintage Books, 1982), 64; Robert Percival, *An Account of the Island of Ceylon: Its History, Geography, Natural History, with the Manners and Customs of its Various Inhabitants* (London: C. and R. Baldwin, 1805), 2, 57, 345–348.

15. John Bastin, *Sir Stamford Raffles's Account of the Founding of Singapore* (Eastbourne, UK, 2004); C. M. Turnbull, *A History of Modern Singapore, 1819–2005* (Singapore: NUS Press, 2009), 30–31.

16. Eric Tagliacozzo, *Secret Trades, Porous Borders: Smuggling and States along a Southeast Asian Frontier, 1865–1915* (New Haven: Yale University Press, 2005).

17. "A List of the Inhabitants of Prince of Wales Island," 25 August 1788, SSFR, IOR/G/34/3; Penang Proceedings, 5 April 1793, SSFR, IOR/G/34/5.

18. Another suggested origin for this term of identification is that it originated as "Jawi Bukan"—that is to say, *not* "Jawi," or non-Malay; an alternative rendering is "Jawi Pekan," or "town Malays." See Helen Fujimoto, *The South Indian Muslim Community and the Evolution of the Jawi Peranakan in Penang up to 1948* (Tokyo: Tokyo Gaikokugo Daigaku, 1988).

19. On the use of "creole" in a Southeast Asian context, see Sumit K. Mandal, "Becoming Arab: Creole Histories and Modern Identity in the Malay World," unpublished manuscript.

20. *The Hikayat Abdullah: The Autobiography of Abdullah bin Kadir (1797–1854),* trans. A. H. Hill (Singapore: Oxford University Press, 1969);

Anthony Milner, *The Invention of Politics in Colonial Malaya: Contesting Nationalism and the Expansion of the Public Sphere* (Cambridge: Cambridge University Press, 1995); Amin Sweeney, ed., *Karya Lengkap Abdullah bin Abdul Kadir Munsyi* (Jakarta: Kepustakaan Populer Gramedia, 2005).

21. The account of Mohamed Noordin's life is based on Fujimoto, *South Indian Muslim Community.*

22. James William Norton Kyshe, ed., *Cases Heard and Determined in Her Majesty's Supreme Court of the Straits Settlements 1808–1884* (Singapore: Singapore and Straits Printing Office, 1885), 1:255–272.

23. *Badar Bee v. Habib Merican Noordin* (1909), A.C. 615.

24. Francis Light (George Town) to Sir John Shore (Fort William), 1 August 1794, SSFR, IOR/G/34/6; Robert Percival, "Account of the Island of Ceylon," *Ceylon Historical Journal* 22 (1803): 114–115.

25. Alexander Kyd, Memorandum on Penang, 1 September 1787, SSFR, IOR/G/34/1; Francis Light to John MacPherson, 13 December 1786, SSFR, IOR/G/34/2.

26. "Proceedings Relative to Prince of Wales Island," Fort William, 5 January 1791, SSFR, IOR/G/34/4; Rajesh Rai, "Sepoys, Convicts and the 'Bazaar Contingent': The Emergence and Exclusion of 'Hindustani' Pioneers at the Singapore Frontier," *Journal of Southeast Asian Studies* 35, 1 (2004): 1–19.

27. Letter from John Brown, Provost, Prince of Wales Island, to Francis Light, 5 February 1794, enclosure in Light's letter to Calcutta, 1 August 1794, SSFR, IOR/G/34/6; Letter from James Scott, 30 January 1794, SSFR, IOR/G/34/6; Case of Syedpilly Marikan: Enclosure No. 20, January 1794, SSFR, IOR/G/34/6.

28. Dispatch from Sir T. Maitland to Viscount Castlereagh, 20 August 1808, appendix to T. Smith, *A Military History of Ceylon,* ms., 1833, NAUK, PRO, CO/59/26, WO/1/364–366; B. A. Hussainmiya, *Orang Rejimen* (Kuala Lumpur: UKM Press, 1990).

29. Letter from Francis Light, 13 December 1786, SSFR, IOR/G/34/2; Extract from Letter of F. R. MacDonald, Superintendant, Prince of Wales Island, 12 November 1796, in "Bengal Proceeding and Correspondence on Land Tenure at Penang, November 1786–August 1800," SSFR, IOR/G/34/1; Letter from W. M. Hunter to C. R. Commelin, Secretary to the Government, Public Department, 8 July 1802, SSFR, IOR/G/34/9.

30. *Ravensworth* Log, 1786–1787, IOR/L/MAR/B/565A; Dispatch from Sir T. Maitland to Viscount Castlereagh, 20 August 1808, Appendix to T. Smith, *A Military History of Ceylon,* ms., 1833, NAUK, CO/59/26.

31. Petition from "Free Bengalis" to John Prince, 28 September 1826, IOR /F/4/1184/30747.

32. Clare Anderson, "Sepoys, Servants and Settlers: Convict Transportation in the Indian Ocean, 1787–1945," in Ian Brown and Frank Dikötter, eds., *Cultures of Confinement: A History of the Prison in Africa, Asia and Latin America* (London: Hurst, 2007), 185–220; Anand A. Yang, "Indian Convict Workers in Southeast Asia in the Late Eighteenth and Early Nineteenth Centuries," *Journal of World History* 14, 2 (2003): 179–208.

33. "Memorial of the Polygar Prisoners," 6 May 1815, SSFR, G/34/49; Fort Cornwallis: Answer to the General Letter of 18 February 1814, SSFR, G/34/181; Anderson, "Sepoys, Servants and Settlers"; Yang, "Indian Convict Workers"; Kerry Ward, *Networks of Empire: Forced Migration in the Dutch East India Company* (Cambridge: Cambridge University Press, 2008).

34. Letter from H. Barlow, Register, Nizamat Adalat, to E. Hay, Secretary to the Government of Bengal, 20 November 1793, Bengal Judicial Proceedings, 20 December 1793, IOR/P/128/7; K. Duncan, Resident, Benares, to G. M. Barlow, Secretary to the Government of Bengal, 10 July 1794, Bengal Judicial Proceedings, 25 July 1794, IOR/P/128/12; see also Anderson, "Sepoys, Servants and Settlers," 190–191.

35. Minute by the President, Fort Cornwallis, 15 April 1824, SSFR, G/34/94; J. F. McNair, *Prisoners Their Own Warders: A Record of the Convict Prison at Singapore . . . : Together with a Cursory History of the Convict Establishments at Bencoolen, Penang and Malacca from the Year 1797*, assisted by W. D. Bayliss (London: Archibald Constable, 1899).

36. F. R. MacDonald, 20 July 1796, enclosure in SSFR, G/34/94 (1824); Letter from E. A. Blundell, Moulmein, to Major D. Williams, 17 September 1836, in Bengal Criminal and Judicial Consultations, 21 November–26 December 1837, IOR/P/141/18.

37. Letter from A. P. Phayre to Major D. Williams, 10 December 1845, in Bengal Criminal and Judicial Consultations, 1–15 April 1846, IOR/P/142/46.

38. Minute by the President, Fort Cornwallis, 15 April 1824, SSFR, G/34/94; Yang, "Indian Convict Workers"; SSFR, G/34/94, 15 April 1824.

39. Quotations from Yang, "Indian Convict Workers," 204–206.

40. Radha Kumud Mookerji, *Indian Shipping: A History of the Sea-Borne Trade and Maritime Activity of the Indians from the Earliest Times* (Bombay: Longmans, 1912), 246–247; David Arnold, *Science, Technology and Medicine in Colonial India*, The New Cambridge History of India, pt. III, no. 5 (Cambridge: Cambridge University Press, 2000), 102–103.

41. Amitav Ghosh, "Of Fanas and Forecastles: The Indian Ocean and Some Lost Languages of the Age of Sail," *Economic and Political Weekly,* 21 June 2008, 56–62; Anne Bulley, ed., *Free Mariner: John Adolphus Pope in the East Indies, 1786–1821* (London: Bacsa, 1992), 54; Amitav Ghosh, *Sea of Poppies* (London: John Murray, 2008).

42. Fort St. George, Public Department, Consultations, 14 January–31 December 1784, Memoranda of 27 June and 18 November, 1784, IOR/P/240/59. For further discussion, see Ravi Ahuja, "Labour Relations in an Early Colonial Context: Madras, c. 1750–1800," *Modern Asian Studies* 36, 4 (2002): 793–832.

43. Eric Meyer, "Labour Circulation between Sri Lanka and South India in Historical Perspective," in Claude Markovits, Jacques Pouchepadass, and Sanjay Subrahmanyam, eds., *Society and Circulation: Mobile People and Itinerant Cultures in South Asia, 1750–1950* (New Delhi: Permanent Black, 2003), 55–88; Sujit Sivasundaram, "Ethnicity, Indigeneity and Migration in the Advent of British Rule to Sri Lanka," *American Historical Review* 115, 2 (2010): 428–452.

44. Letter from Emerson Tennent to Earl Grey, 21 April 1847, NAUK, CO/54/235; Meyer, "Labor Circulation between Sri Lanka and South India"; Patrick Peebles, *Plantation Tamils of Ceylon* (Leicester: Leicester University Press, 2001); R. DeButts, *Rambles in Ceylon* (London: W. H. Allen, 1841), 185; James Duncan, *In the Shadows of the Tropics: Climate, Race and Biopower in Nineteenth Century Ceylon* (Aldershot: Ashgate, 2007), 58–59.

45. Patrick Peebles, *Sri Lanka: A Handbook of Historical Statistics* (Boston: G. K. Hall, 1982), 67–68.

46. Meyer, "Labor Circulation between Sri Lanka and South India"; Frank Heidemann, *Kanganies in Sri Lanka and Malaysia: Tamil Recruiter-cum-Foreman as a Sociological Category in the Nineteenth and Twentieth Century* (Munich: Anacon, 1992); Roland Wenzelhumer, *From Coffee to Tea Cultivation in Ceylon, 1880–1900: An Economic and Social History* (Leiden: Brill, 2008).

47. Jan Breman and E. Valentine Daniel, "Conclusion: The Making of a Coolie," *Journal of Peasant Studies* 19, 3–4 (1992): 268–295.

48. John Geoghegan, *Note on Emigration from India* (Calcutta: Government of India, 1873), 1; Letter from Francis Light (Penang) to Sir John Shore, Fort William, 1 August 1784, SSFR, 2: IOR/G/34/2; Prince of Wales Island, Census Department, 1823, IOR, F/4/74020284. John Crawfurd, *History of the Indian Archipelago: Containing an Account of the Manners, Arts, Languages, Religions, Institutions and Commerce of Its Inhabitants* (Edinburgh: Archibald Constable, 1820), 1:133–134; McNair, *Prisoners Their Own Warders;* T. J. Newbold, *Political and Statistical Account of the British Settlements in the Straits of Malacca,* vol. 1 (London: John Murray, 1839).

49. Letter from from Official Resident Councillor, Prince of Wales Island, to Fort St. George, MPP, vol. 832, 12 December 1848, nos. 7–8, TNSA; Letter from Governor, Prince of Wales Island, to Officiating Chief Secretary, Fort St. George, 15 May 1849, no. 7, MPP, vol. 836, TNSA.

50. Letter from Official Resident Councillor, Prince of Wales Island, to Fort St. George, 12 December 1848, nos. 7–8, MPP, vol. 832, TNSA.

51. J. W. Birch, Colonial Secretary, Straits Settlements, to the Chief Secretary, Fort St. George, 1 July 1870, NAI, Department of Revenue, Agriculture and Commerce: Emigration Branch, Proceedings 1–9, September 1871.

52. I owe this observation to Amitav Ghosh.

53. Denys Lombard and Claudine Salmon, "Islam and Chineseness," *Indonesia* 57 (1993): 115–131.

54. Philip A. Kuhn, *Chinese among Others: Emigration in Modern Times* (Singapore: NUS Press, 2008), 8; Leonard Blussé, "Batavia, 1619–1740: The Rise and Fall of a Chinese Colonial Town," *Journal of Southeast Asian Studies* 12, 1 (1981): 159–178; G. William Skinner, "Creolized Chinese Societies in Southeast Asia," in Anthony Reid, ed., *Sojourners and Settlers: Histories of Southeast Asia and the Chinese* (Sydney: Allen and Unwin, 1996), 50–93; Carl A. Trocki, *Opium and Empire: Chinese Society in Colonial Singapore, 1800–1910* (Ithaca, NY: Cornell University Press, 1990).

55. J. D. Vaughn, *Manners and Customs of the Chinese of the Straits Settlements* (Singapore: Mission Press, 1879), 16.

56. John Thomson, *The Straits of Malacca, Indo-China and China, or Ten Years' Travels, Adventures and Residence Abroad* (London: Sampson, Low, Marston, Low and Searle, 1875), 10–13.

57. Amitav Ghosh, *River of Smoke* (London: John Murray, 2011), 108–109.

58. Bulley, ed., *Free Mariner,* 90.

59. Sir Richard C. Temple, "Buddermokan," *Journal of the Burma Research Society* 15, 1 (1925): 1–33; Moshe Yegar, *The Muslims of Burma* (Wiesbaden: O. Harrassowitz, 1972), 8.

60. Janab Gulam Kadhiru Navalar, *Karunai-Kadal Nagur Andavaravargalin Punitha Vaazhkai Varalaaru* (Chennai, 1963); S. A. Shaik Hassan Sahib Qadhiri, *The Divine Light of Nagore (The Whole History and Teachings of Nagore Great Saint)* (Nagore: Nagore Dargah, 1980).

61. Torsten Tschacher, "Witnessing Fun: Tamil-Speaking Muslims and the Imagination of Ritual in Tamil Southeast Asia," in Michael Bergunder, Heiko Frese, and Ulrike Schröder, eds., *Ritual, Caste and Religion in Colonial South India* (Halle: Verlag der Franckeschen Stiftungen, 2010): 189–218. Susan Bayly, "Imagining 'Greater India': French and Indian Visions of Colonialism in the Indic Mode," *Modern Asian Studies* 38, 3 (2004): 704.

62. C. Snouck Hurgronje, *The Achehnese,* trans. A. W. S. O'Sullivan (Leyden: E. J. Brill, 1906), 1:218.

63. Koca Maraikkayar, *Pinangu Ursava Thiruvalankaara Cinthu* (Penang: Kim Seyk Hiyan, 1895), 4–6; see also Tschacher, "Witnessing Fun"; "Coroner's Inquests," *Singapore Free Press*, 26 February 1857; Anon., "Mohamedan Mosque, Penang," watercolor [photographic print, formerly in Raffles Museum], plate 162, in Lim Chong Keat, *Penang Views, 1770–1860* (Penang: Penang Museum / Summer Times Publishing, 1986).

64. "Petition from Hindoo Inhabitants of Singapore," NAS, SSR, Singapore Consultations (A), A34, May 1827.

65. "Petition from Hindoo Inhabitants of Singapore"; "Petition from Mohammedan Inhabitants of Singapore Respecting the Hindu Temple Adjoining the Mosque": NAS, SSR, A34, May 1827.

66. James Low, *The British Settlement of Penang* (Singapore, 1836); Letter to Trustees, Hindoo Temple at Singapore (Original Petition Enclosed), NAS, SSR, Miscellaneous Letters Out, 1800–1867, V30 (1860).

67. Prabhu P. Mohapatra, "The Hosay Massacre of 1884: Class and Community among Indian Immigrant Labourers in Trinidad," in Arvind N. Das and Marcel van der Linden, eds., *Work and Social Change in Asia: Essays in Honour of Jan Breman* (New Delhi: Manohar, 2003); Prashant Kidambi, *The Making of an Indian Metropolis: Colonial Governance and Public Culture in Bombay, 1890–1920* (Ashgate, UK: Aldershot, 2007).

68. M. L. Wynne, *Triad and Tabut: A Survey of the Origin and Diffusion of Chinese and Mohamedan Secret Societies in the Malay Peninsula A.D. 1800–1935* (Singapore: GPO, 1941); Fujimoto, *The South Indian Muslim Community.*

69. Letter from Harry St. George Ord, Governor of Penang, 19 August 1867, NAUK, CO/273/11; *Report of the Commissioners Appointed under Act XXI of 1867 to Enquire into: The Penang Riots* (Penang: Argus Press, 1868), evidence statements 36–39 and Appendix 16, NAUK, CO/273/26; A. E. H, Anson, *About Others and Myself* (London: J. Murray, 1920), 278–283.

70. Crawfurd, *History of the Indian Archipelago,* 1: 133–134; Thomson, *The Straits of Malacca, Indo-China and China,* 12–14.

71. *Report on the Administration of the Straits Settlements, during the year 1855–56* (Singapore: Government Printer, 1857), 20.

72. Bayly, *Imperial Meridian,* 66; Benedict Anderson, *Imagined Communities: Reflections on the Origin and Spread of Nationalism,* 2nd ed. (London: Verso, 1991), 120–121; cf. Joel S. Kahn, *Other Malays: Nationalism and Cosmopolitanism in the Modern Malay World* (Singapore: NUS Press, 2006).

73. Kenneth Pomeranz, "Introduction: World History and Environmental History," in Edmund Burke III and Kenneth Pomeranz, eds., *The Environment and World History* (Berkeley: University of California Press, 2009), 3–32; Robert Marks, "Commercialization without Capitalism: Processes of Environmental Change in South China, 1550–1850," *Environmental*

History 1, 1 (January 1998): 56–82. See also Anthony Reid, *Southeast Asia in the Age of Commerce, 1450–1680* (New Haven: Yale University Press, 1993), vol. 2; David Washbrook, "The Textile Industry and the Economy of South India, 1500–1800," in Giorgio Riello and Tirthankar Roy, eds., *How India Clothed the World: The World of South Asian Textiles, 1500–1850* (Leiden: Brill, 2009), 173–192; C.J. Baker, "Economic Reorganization and the Slump in South and Southeast Asia," *Comparative Studies in Society and History*, 23, 3 (1981), 325–49.

4 Human Traffic

1. MPP, no. 40 of 13 September 1870, IOR/P/449/10; *Friend of India*, 14 April 1870, 433; Memorandum by E. F. Webster, Collector of Tanjore, to Chief Secretary, Government, 25 March 1881, NAI, Revenue and Agricultural Department: Emigration Branch, Proceedings 19–21, January 1882; *Police Weekly Circular*, 4 February 1865, in extract from diary of Assistant Superintendent of Police, MPP, no. 40 of 13 September 1870.

2. Alexander Kyd, Memorandum on Penang, 1 September 1787, SSFR, IOR/G/34/1; Syed Hussein Alatas, *The Myth of the Lazy Native: A Study of the Image of Malays, Filipinos and Javanese from the Sixteenth to the Twentieth Century and Its Functions in the Ideology of Colonial Capitalism* (London: Frank Cass, 1977).

3. Patrick Peebles, *Plantation Tamils of Ceylon* (Leicester: Leicester University Press, 2001); MPP, vol. 832, 12 December 1848, nos. 7–8, Appendix: "Ships Arriving in Prince of Wales Island," TNSA; Kernial Singh Sandhu, *Indians in Malaya: Some Aspects of their Immigration and Settlement (1786–1957)* (Cambridge: Cambridge University Press, 1969), 304; Straits Settlements, *Reports on Indian Immigration* (Singapore and Penang: Government Printer), 1880–1911; Michael Adas, *The Burma Delta: Economic Development and Social Change on an Asian Rice Frontier, 1852–1941* (Madison: University of Wisconsin Press, 1974).

4. Adam McKeown, "Global Migration, 1846–1940," *Journal of World History* 15, 2 (2004): 155–189; Kingsley Davis, *The Population of India and Pakistan* (Princeton, NJ: Princeton University Press, 1951).

5. Joseph Conrad, "The End of the Tether," in *Youth, a Narrative, and Two Other Stories* (London: W. Blackwood and Sons, 1902), 168.

6. E. A. Wrigley, *Energy and the English Industrial Revolution* (Cambridge: Cambridge University Press, 2010).

7. Arthur Cotton, "On Communication between India and China by Line of the Burhampooter," *Proceedings of the Royal Geographic Society of London* 11, 6 (1886–1887); John Ogilvy Hay, *A Map Shewing the Various Routes*

Connecting China with India and Europe through Burmah and Developing the Trade of Eastern Bengal, Burma and China (London: Edward Stanford, 1875); Henry Duckworth, *New Commercial Route to China (Capt. Sprye's Proposition)* (London, 1861); Ifekhar Iqbal, "The Space between the Nation and the Empire: 1905 and Trans-regional Trajectories on Northeastern India, Burma and Southwestern China," paper presented at Tufts University, December 2010.

8. Wrigley, *Energy,* 242.

9. Sayako Kanda, "Environmental Changes, the Emergence of a Fuel Market, and the Working Conditions of Salt Makers in Bengal, c. 1780–1845," *International Review of Social History* 55 (2010), 123–151.

10. *The Irrawaddy Flotilla and Burmese Steam Navigation Company, Limited,* promotional leaflet, 1872; typescript dated 6 May 1940, written by R. J. Wilkinson, Irrawaddy Flotilla Company manager in Burma and later a director in Glasgow; typescript note on the IFC's "parent company," enclosed with letter to T. Cormack, 26 January 1937. All files found in NMM, Papers of the Irrawaddy Flotilla Company (uncatalogued), MS79/077, Box 1.

11. T. Braddell, Colonial Secretary, Straits Settlements, to D. F. Carmichael, Acting Chief Secretary to the Government, Fort St. George, 23 December 1874, MPP, no. 87, 26 January 1875, IOR/P/276.

12. Sandhu, *Indians in Malaya,* appendices 3–4; Michael Adas, *The Burma Delta,* 96.

13. *Report of the Deck Passenger Committee, 1921* (Calcutta: Government Printer, 1921), 1:9–10.

14. K.N. Chaudhuri, *Trade and Civilization in the Indian Ocean: An Economic History from the Rise of Islam to 1750* (Cambridge: Cambridge University Press, 1985).

15. Derek Walcott, "Another Life," in *Selected Poems,* ed. Edward Baugh (London: Faber, 2007), 76.

16. Sumit K. Mandal, "Becoming Arab: Creole Histories and Modern Identity in the Malay World," unpublished manuscript, ch. 2.

17. Manu Goswami, *Producing India: From Colonial Economy to National Space* (Chicago: University of Chicago Press, 2004); Matthew Edney, *Mapping an Empire: The Geographical Construction of British India, 1765–1843* (Chicago: University of Chicago Press, 1997); K. Sivaramakrishnan, *Modern Forests: Statemaking and Environmental Change in Colonial Eastern India* (Stanford, CA: Stanford University Press, 1999).

18. Thomas R. Metcalf, *Imperial Connections: India in the Indian Ocean Arena, 1860–1920* (Berkeley: University of California Press, 2007).

19. Burton Stein, *Peasant State and Society in Medieval South India* (New Delhi: Oxford University Press, 1980); Burton Stein, "Circulation and

the Historical Geography of Tamil Country," *Journal of Asian Studies* 37, 1 (1977): 7–26.

20. Christopher Baker, *An Indian Rural Economy 1880–1955: The Tamilnad Countryside* (New Delhi: Oxford University Press, 1984), 19–97.

21. Dharma Kumar, *Land and Caste in South India: Agricultural Labour in Madras Presidency during the Nineteenth Century* (Cambridge: Cambridge University Press, 1965).

22. David Washbrook, "India 1818–1860: The Two Faces of Colonialism," in Andrew Porter, ed., *The Oxford History of the British Empire: Volume 3: The Nineteenth Century* (Oxford: Oxford University Press 1999), 395–421; Prasannan Parthasarathi, "Historical Issues of Deindustrialization in Nineteenth-Century South India," in Giorgio Riello and Tirthankar Roy, eds., *How India Clothed the World: The World of South Asian Textiles, 1500–1850* (Leiden: Brill, 2009), 415–435.

23. Mike Davis, *Late Victorian Holocausts: El Niño Famines and the Making of the Third World* (London: Verso, 2001).

24. William Digby, *The Famine Campaign in Southern India (Madras and Bombay Presidencies and Province of Mysore, 1876–1878)* (London: Longmans, Green, 1878), 1:112–113.

25. F. A. Weld to the Earl of Kimberley, 5 May 1881, NAI, Department of Revenue and Agriculture, Emigration Branch, Proceedings 10–17, November 1881.

26. Secretary to the Chief Commissioner, British Burma, to Secretary to the Government of India, Rangoon, 3 March 1877, NAI, Department of Revenue, Agriculture and Commerce, Emigration Branch, March 1877, Proceedings 3–4 ("Emigration from Madras to Burma").

27. David Arnold, "Famine in Peasant Consciousness and Peasant Action: Madras, 1876–8," in R. Guha, ed., *Subaltern Studies III: Writings on South Asian History and Society* (New Delhi: Oxford University Press, 1984), 62–115; S. Ambirajan, "Malthusian Population Theory and Indian Famine Policy in the Nineteenth Century," *Population Studies* 30, 1 (1976): 5–14.

28. Arnold, "Famine in Peasant Consciousness."

29. Eric Meyer, "Labour Circulation Between Sri Lanka and South India in Historical Perspective," in Claude Markovits, Jacques Pouchepadass, and Sanjay Subrahmanyam, eds., *Society and Circulation: Mobile People and Itinerant Cultures in South Asia, 1750–1950* (New Delhi: Permanent Black, 2003): 55–88.

30. "Agricole," letter to the *Straits Free Press*, 9 June 1836, cited in Sandhu, *Indians in Malaya*, 48.

31. Sandhu, *Indians in Malaya*.

32. Ibid., 79.

33. William Beinart and Lotte Hughes, *Environment and Empire* (Oxford: Oxford University Press, 2007), ch. 14; Richard Drayton, *Nature's Government: Science, Imperial Britain, and the "Improvement" of the World* (New Haven: Yale University Press, 2000); Colin Barlow, *The Natural Rubber Industry: Its Development, Technology and Economy in Malaysia* (Kuala Lumpur: Oxford University Press, 1978); J. H. Drabble, *Rubber in Malaya, 1876–1922: The Genesis of an Industry* (Kuala Lumpur: Oxford University Press, 1972).

34. Calculated from Straits Settlements, *Reports on Indian Immigration* (Singapore and Penang), 1880–1911.

35. Jan Breman, *Labour Migration and Rural Transformation in Colonial Asia* (Amsterdam: Free University Press, 1990); Ravindra K. Jain, *South Indians on the Plantation Frontier in Malaya* (New Haven: Yale University Press, 1970).

36. Cited in Sandhu, *Indians in Malaya*, 101–102.

37. Muthammal Palanisamy, *Nadu Vittu Nadu* (Chennai, 2007).

38. Observations of a colonial official cited in Adas, *The Burma Delta*, 75.

39. On the Chettiar community, see Adas, *The Burma Delta*; Raman Mahadevan, "Immigrant Entrepreneurs in Colonial Burma: An Exploratory Study of the Role of Nattukottai Chettiars of Tamil Nadu, 1880–1930," *Indian Economic and Social History Review* 15, 3 (1978): 329–358; David West Rudner, *Caste and Capitalism in Colonial India: The Nattukottai Chettiars* (Berkeley: University of California Press, 1994); Sean Turnell, *Fiery Dragons: Banks, Lenders, and Microfinance in Burma* (Copenhagen: NIAS Press, 2009).

40. Preceding discussion draws on Burma Provincial Banking Enquiry (Grantham) Committee, *Volume 1: Report: Banking and Credit in Burma* (Rangoon: Government Press, 1930); *Report on Settlement Operations in the Syriam Township, Hanthawaddy District, 1880–81* (Rangoon: Government Press, 1882); *Report on Settlement Operations in the Hanthawaddy and Pegu Districts* (1882–1883) (Rangoon: Government Press, 1884); *Proceedings of the Government of Burma, Department of Revenue and Agriculture* (May 1906), IOR/P/7237.

41. Karl Marx, *Capital: Critique of Political Economy*, Ben Fowkes, trans., (London: Penguin, 1990), 1:860; John Bellamy Foster, "Marx's Theory of Metabolic Rift: Classical Foundations for Environmental Sociology," *American Journal of Sociology* 105, 2 (1999): 355–405.

42. Harry St. George Ord, Governor, Straits Settlements, to the Earl of Kimberley, 15 May 1871, NAI, Department of Revenue, Agriculture and Commerce: Emigration Branch, September 1871, Proceedings 1–9, September 1871, "Emigration of Labourers from India to the Straits Settlements."

43. A. E. H. Anson, Lieutenant Governor of Penang, to Colonial Secretary, 16 November 1880, NAI, Home, Revenue and Agricultural Department: Emigration Branch, Proceedings 17–23, April 1881.

44. J. P. James, Port Officer and Emigration Agent, Negapatam, to Collector and District Magistrate, Tanjore, 25 July 1890, NAI, Revenue and Agricultural Department: Emigration Branch, Emigration Proceedings 15–23, February 1891, "Proposed Opening of Emigration from India to British North Borneo and Labuan."

45. H. V. Cobb, Acting Head Assistant Collector of Tanjore, to Collector of Tanjore, 17 November 1890, NAI, Revenue and Agriculture Department, Emigration Branch, Proceedings 6–7, March 1891, "Mortality among Indian Emigrants in the Straits Settlements."

46. George Grierson, *Report on Colonial Emigration from the Bengal Presidency* (Calcutta: Government Printer, 1883).

47. James Low, "The Probable Effects on the Climate of Pinang of the Continued Destruction of Its Hill Jungles," *Journal of the Indian Archipelago and Eastern Asia,* 1849, 534–536; on early environmentalism in Malaya, see also Jeyamalar Kathirithamby-Wells, *Nature and Nation: Forests and Development in Peninsular Malaysia* (Copenhagen: NIAS Press, 2005).

48. Muthammal Palanisamy, *Naduppurra paatalgalil en payanam* (Chennai, 2006).

49. David Dean Shulman, *Tamil Temple Myths: Sacrifice and Divine Marriage in the South Indian Saiva Tradition* (Princeton, NJ: Princeton University Press, 1980), 46–47; Fred W. Clothey, *The Many Faces of Murugan: The History and Meaning of a South Indian God* (The Hague: Mouton, 1978); Henry Whitehead, *The Village Gods of South India* (Calcutta: Association Press, 1921).

50. Diana L. Eck, *India: A Sacred Geography* (New York: Harmony, 2012).

51. Marx, *Capital,* 1:926.

52. Richard White, *The Organic Machine: The Remaking of the Columbia River* (New York: Hill and Wang, 1995), x; Henri Fauconnier, *The Soul of Malaya* [1930], trans. Eric Sutton (Singapore: Archipelago Press, 2003), 32.

53. Fauconnier, *The Soul of Malaya,* 128–129; Beinart and Hughes, *Environment and Empire,* 240–241; Richard Upjohn Light, "Cruising by Airplane: Narrative of a Journey around the World," *Geographical Review* 25, 4 (October 1935): 565–600.

54. Memorandum by A. E. Anson, no. 4223, 4 December 1873, NAI, Department of Revenue, Agriculture and Commerce: Emigration Branch, Proceedings 10–13, June 1874.

55. Ralph Shlomowitz and Lance Brennan, "Mortality and Indian Labour in Malaya, 1877–1913," *Indian Economic and Social History Review* 29 (1992); *Report of the Commission Appointed to Enquire into Certain Matters Affecting the Health of Estates in the Federated Malay States* (Singapore: Government Printer, 1924); Malcolm Watson, *The Prevention of Malaria in the*

Federated Malay States, 2nd ed. (London: John Murray, 1921); Amarjit Kaur, "Indian Labour, Labour Standards, and Workers' Health in Burma and Malaya, 1900–1940," *Modern Asian Studies* 40, 2 (2006): 466.

56. Memorandum by W. E. Maxwell, Magistrate, Province Wellesley and others, Butterworth, 15 December 1873, NAI, Department of Revenue, Agriculture and Commerce: Emigration Branch, Proceedings 10–13, June 1874.

57. From S. H. Wynne, Protector of Emigrants, Negepatam, to Under Secretary to Government, 13 December 1880 NAI, Home, Revenue and Agriculture Department: Emigration Branch, Proceedings 17–23, April 1881.

58. Note by W. O'Halloran, Surgeon-Major, Army Medical Department, Penang, 8 December 1873, NAI, Department of Revenue, Agriculture and Commerce: Emigration, Proceedings 10–13, June 1874; Major J. F. Fitzpatrick, Zillah Surgeon, Negapatam, to Acting Sub-Collector and Protector of Emigrants, Negapatam, 2 July 1880, NAI, Home, Revenue and Agriculture Department: Emigration Branch, Proceedings 17–23, April 1881.

59. "Testimony of 3 Returned Emigrants," in letter from J. Cameron, Acting Sub-Collector of Tanjore, to H. Thomas, contained in letter from H. S. Thomas, Collector of Tanjore, to D. F. Carmichael, Officiating Chief Secretary, Fort St. George, 29 June 1875, Madras Public Consultations, no. 111 of 28 July 1875, IOR/P/276; Office Memo no. 4223, 4 December 1873, from A. E. Anson, Lieutenant Governor of Penang, NAI, Department of Revenue, Agriculture and Commerce: Emigration Branch, Proceedings 10–13, June 1874.

60. J. D. M. Coghill, Acting Colonial Surgeon, Province Wellesley, 11 December 1873, NAI, Department of Revenue, Agriculture and Commerce: Emigration Branch, Proceedings 10–13, June 1874.

61. Sverker Sörlin and Paul Warde, "The Problem of Environmental History: A Re-reading of the Field," *Environmental History* 12, 1 (2007); Alfred W. Crosby Jr., "The Past and Present of Environmental History," *American Historical Review* 100 (1995).

62. An early version of the arguments in this section appeared in Sunil S. Amrith, "Indians Overseas? Governing Tamil Migration to Malaya, 1870–1941," *Past and Present* 208 (August 2010): 231–261; they have been substantially revised here.

63. A. O. Hume, Secretary to the Government of India, to the Secretary to the Government of Madras, 2 October 1875, NAI, Department of Revenue, Agriculture and Commerce: Emigration Branch, Proceedings 10–21, November 1875.

64. Letter no. 282, Karaikal, 1 April 1873, from Captain B. Fischer, British Consular Agent, Karaikal, to Protector of Emigrants, Madras, NAI,

Department of Revenue, Agriculture and Commerce: Emigration Branch, Proceedings 38–48, February 1874.

65. B. Fischer, Consular Agent, Karaikal, to Acting Chief Secretary to Government, 23 November 1885, NAI, Department of Revenue and Agriculture: Emigration Branch, Proceedings 4–6, March 1886.

66. Lieutenant Governor of Penang to Colonial Secretary, Straits Settlements, 26 March 1875, NAI, Department of Revenue, Agriculture and Commerce: Emigration Branch, Proceedings 10–21, November 1875.

67. John Berger, *And Our Faces, My Heart, Brief as Photos* (London: Bloomsbury, 2005), 64–65.

68. Bowness Fischer, Consular Agent, Pondicherry and Karaikal, to Chief Secretary to the Government of Madras, 27 July 1886 (emphasis in the original), NAI, Revenue and Agriculture Department: Emigration Branch, Proceeding 9, September 1886.

69. Bowness Fischer to Chief Secretary to the Government of Madras, 9 August 1881, Proceedings of the Revenue and Agriculture Branch: Emigration, no. 21, IOR/P/1862.

70. Cf. Charles Taylor, "What Is Human Agency?" in *Philosophical Papers*, vol. 1, *Human Agency and Language* (Cambridge: Cambridge University Press, 1985).

71. Eric Tagliacozzo, *Secret Trades, Porous Borders: Smuggling and States along a Southeast Asian Frontier, 1865–1915* (New Haven: Yale University Press, 2005), 243–244.

72. B. Fischer, Consular Agent, Karaikal, to Acting Chief Secretary to Government, 23 November 1885, NAI, Department of Revenue and Agriculture: Emigration Branch, Proceedings 4–6, March 1886.

73. *R. v. Shaik Ismail Lebby* (1878), in James William Norton Kyshe, ed., *Cases Heard and Determined in Her Majesty's Supreme Court of the Straits Settlements 1808–1884* (Singapore: Singapore and Straits Printing Office, 1885), Vol. 3: Magistrate's Appeals, 99.

74. Bowness Fischer to Officiating Chief Secretary to the Government of Madras, 29 June 1881, Proceedings of the Revenue and Agriculture Department: Emigration, no. 21, IOR/P/1862.

75. Major A. T. Rolland, Superintendant of Police, Tanjore, to Assistant Inspector-General of Police, Madras, Tanjore, 12 November 1880, NAI, Department of Revenue and Agriculture: Emigration Branch, Proceedings 19–21, January 1882.

76. J. Douglas, Colonial Secretary, Straits Settlements, to Chief Secretary, Government of Madras, 21 March 1878, NAI, Home Revenue and Agriculture Department: Emigration Branch, Proceedings 20–26, April 1880.

77. Government of Madras, Public Department, from Consular Agent, Pondicherry and Karaikal, to Chief Secretary of Government, 25 January 1886, NAI, Department of Revenue and Agriculture: Emigration Branch, Proceedings 12–13, July 1886.

78. F. H. Gottlieb, Acting Protector of Immigrants, to Lieutenant Governor of Penang, 4 and 13 March 1879; Memorandum by Mr. MacGregor, Protector of Immigrants, 25 May 1880, Proceedings of the Revenue and Agriculture Department: Emigration, no. 21, IOR/P/1862.

79. Aloysius de Mello, *A Manual of the Law of Extradition and Fugitive Offenders, Applicable to the Eastern Dependencies of the British Empire,* 2nd ed. (Singapore: Government Printing Office, 1933).

80. "Emigration to the Straits Settlements," TNSA, Public Department, Government Order 143–44, 16 February 1907.

81. Frank Heidemann, *Kanganies in Sri Lanka and Malaysia: Tamil Recruiter-cum-Foreman as a Sociological Category in the Nineteenth and Twentieth Century* (Munich: Anacon, 1992); Tagliacozzo, *Secret Trades, Porous Borders,* 257–258.

82. On legal testimony, see Shahid Amin, "Approver's Testimony, Judicial Discourse: The Case of Chauri Chaura," in Ranajit Guha, ed., *Subaltern Studies V* (New Delhi: Oxford University Press, 1987), 166–202.

83. A. O. Hume, Secretary to the Government of India, to Colonial Secretary, Singapore, 9 June 1874, NAI, Department of Revenue, Agriculture and Commerce: Emigration Branch, Proceedings 10–13, June 1874; J. D. M. Coghill, Acting Colonial Surgeon, Province Wellesley, to Magistrate of Police and CEO, Province Wellesley, 16 November 1873, NAI, Department of Revenue Agriculture and Commerce: Emigration Branch, Proceedings 10–13, June 1874; Office Memo no. 4223, 4 December 1873, from A. E. Anson, Lieutenant-Governor of Penang, NAI, Department of Revenue Agriculture and Commerce: Emigration Branch, Proceedings 10–13, June 1874.

84. Telegram from Government of Madras, 15 January 1872, NAI, Department of Revenue, Agriculture and Commerce: Emigration Branch, Proceedings 12–34, "Emigration from Madras to Penang," March 1872.

85. H. S. Thomas, Collector of Tanjore, to W. Hudleston, Chief Secretary to the Government, Fort St. George, dated Vallam, 4 March 1876, Madras Public Proceedings, no. 882 (1876), IOR/P/1038.

86. A. O. Hume, Secretary to the Government of India, to Colonial Secretary, Singapore, 9 June 1874, NAI, Department of Revenue Agriculture and Commerce: Emigration Branch, Proceedings 10–13, June 1874.

87. Philip A. Kuhn, *Chinese among Others: Emigration in Modern Times* (Singapore: NUS Press, 2008).

88. John S. Hoyland, ed., *Gopal Krishna Gokhale: His Life and Speeches* (Calcutta, 1933), 176–177.

89. Madhavi Kale, *Fragments of Empire: Capital, Slavery and Indian Indentured Labour in the British Caribbean* (Philadelphia: University of Pennsylvania Press, 1998), 167–171.
90. Hoyland, ed., *Gopal Krishna Gokhale*, 179.
91. Marilyn Lake and Henry Reynolds, *Drawing the Global Colour Line: White Men's Countries and the International Challenge of Racial Equality* (Cambridge: Cambridge University Press, 2007); Brij Lal, "Kunti's Cry: Indentured Women on Fiji Plantations," *Indian Economic and Social History Review* 22 (1985); Marina Carter and Khal Torabully, *Coolitude: An Anthology of the Indian Labour Diaspora* (London: Anthem, 2002).
92. Cf. Ambikapat Rai, *The Indian Coolie in Malaya* (Kuala Lumpur, 1914).
93. J. D. Samy, "The Indian Coolies in the Federated Malay States: The Perils of Ignorance," typescript, reproduced in NAI, Deparment of Commerce and Industry: Emigration Branch, Proceedings 2–3 (B), July 1914.
94. Hugh Tinker, *New System of Slavery: The Export of Indian Labour Overseas, 1830–1920* (London: Oxford University Press, 1974), 288–366.
95. File note by Hardinge, 28 August 1915, NAI, Department of Commerce and Industry: Emigration Branch, Proceedings 56–73 (A), December 1915.
96. David Northrup, *Indentured Labour in the Age of Imperialism, 1834–1922* (Cambridge: Cambridge University Press, 1995).
97. From R. G. Watson, Federated Malay States, to Earle of Crewe, Colonial Office, 30 December 1909, NAI, Department of Commerce and Industry: Emigration Branch, Proceedings 3–4, May 1910; From L. H. Clayton, Superintendant of Indian Immigration, to Federal Secretary, Kuala Lumpur, 16 December 1909, NAI, Department of Commerce and Industry: Emigration Branch, Proceedings 3–4, May 1910; Colonial Office to India Office (Confidential), 11 March 1910, NAI, Department of Commerce and Industry: Emigration Branch, Proceedings 3–4, May 1910.
98. Chief Secretary to the Government of Fort St. George to the Secretary to the Government of India, 19 March 1883, NAI, Department of Revenue and Agriculture: Emigration Branch, Proceeding 24, July 1883.
99. Rebecca J. Scott, *Degrees of Freedom: Louisiana and Cuba after Slavery* (Cambridge, MA: Harvard University Press, 2005).
100. Talal Asad, "Thinking about Agency and Pain," in *Formations of the Secular: Christianity, Islam, Modernity* (Stanford, CA: Stanford University Press, 2003), 72–73.
101. B. Nukaiah and V. K. Sarma, eds., *Proceedings Volume of the Second World Telugu Mahasabha* (Hyderabad, 1981), 76–77, trans. A. Satyanarayana in "'Birds of Passage': Migration of South Indian Labour Communities to South-East Asia, 19–20th Centuries," CLARA Working Paper no. 11, 6 (2001).

102. H. G. Quaritch Wales, "Archaeological Researches in Ancient Indian Colonization," *Journal of the Malayan Branch of the Royal Asiatic Society* 18, 1 (1940): 1–85; Paul Wheatley, *The Golden Khersonese* (Kuala Lumpur: Oxford University Press, 1961).

5 Oceans' Crossroads

1. Interview with Ramasamy Narayanasamy, NAS, Oral History Department, A 001194/12, interviewed by Rajendran Supramaniam on 28 May 1990. For all oral histories from the Singapore archives, transcriptions from the original audio recordings and translations from the Tamil are mine unless otherwise stated.
2. M. K. Gandhi, "The Chinese and the Indians in Singapore," *Indian Opinion,* 1 July 1905, in *Mahatma Gandhi on Indians Overseas* (Bombay: Purshotamdas Thakurdas Reseach Centre, 1970), 39.
3. "Acknowledgement of a Telegram Stating That Trade Routes in the Region of the Bay of Bengal . . . Had Been Closed Due to Enemy Shipping," September 1914, NAUK, CO323/624/80.
4. R. W. Harper, *Singapore Mutiny* (Singapore: Oxford University Press, 1984); T. R. Sareen, *Secret Documents on Singapore Mutiny, 1915* (New Delhi: Mounto, 1995).
5. Letter from Agents of the British India Steam Navigation Company, Singapore, to Controller of Labour, Federated Malay States, 4 October 1915, NMM, Papers of the British India Steam Navigation Company, BIS/7/20, "Negapatam-Straits Mail and Coolie Contract."
6. Liew Kai Khiun, "Terribly Severe though Mercifully Short: The Episode of the 1918 Influenza in British Malaya," *Modern Asian Studies* 41, 2 (2007): 221–252.
7. Straits Settlements, *Blue Book, 1926* (Singapore: Government Printer, 1926), "Imports and Exports."
8. Denys Lombard, "Une autre 'Méditerranée' dans le Sud-Est asiatique," *Hérodote, Revue de Géographie et de Géopolitique* 88 (1998): 184–193.
9. Frank Broeze, ed., *Brides of the Sea: Port Cities of Asia from the Sixteenth to Twentieth Centuries* (Sydney: UNSW Press, 1989).
10. Sugata Bose, *A Hundred Horizons: The Indian Ocean in the Age of Global Empire* (Cambridge, MA: Harvard University Press, 2006), 109–110.
11. E. J. L. Andrew, *Indian Labour in Rangoon* (London: Oxford University Press, 1933), 5.
12. J. S. Furnivall, *Colonial Policy and Practice: A Comparative Study of Burma and Netherlands India* (Cambridge: Cambridge University Press, 1948),

304. For a recent view that echoes Furnivall, see Carl A. Trocki, *Singapore: Wealth, Power and the Culture of Control* (London: Routledge, 2006).

13. *Young India*, 11 April 1929; Andrew, *Indian Labour in Rangoon*, 20.

14. Irrawaddy Flotilla Company, "Short Statement of Activities on the Rivers of Burma," 12 February 1942, typescript in NMM, Papers of the Irrawaddy Flotilla Company (uncatalogued), MS79/077, Box 1.

15. Andrew, *Indian Labour in Rangoon*; O. H. Spate, "Beginnings of Industrialization in Burma," *Economic Geography* 17, 1 (January 1941): 75–92.

16. Andrew, *Indian Labour in Rangoon*, 2:32–58.

17. *Proceedings of the Legislative Council of Burma* (1925), 57–69, 416–441.

18. Frank Trager, "The Labor Movement," in Frank Trager, ed., *Burma*, vol. 3 (New Haven: Yale University Press, 1956); A. Narayana Rao, *Indian Labour in Burma* (Rangoon, 1933), 66.

19. Rao, *Indian Labour*, 187.

20. John S. Hoyland, ed., *Gopal Krishna Gokhale: His Life and Speeches* (Calcutta, 1933), 177; *Qaum Parasht* (Lahore), 11 June 1922, cited in *Malayan Bulletin of Political Intelligence*, August 1922, IOR L/P&J/12/103.

21. Cited in A. Satyanarayana, "'Birds of Passage': Migration of South Indian Labour Communities to South-East Asia, 19–20th Centuries," CLARA Working Paper no. 11, 6 (2001).

22. James Francis Warren, *Ah Ku and Karayuki San: Prostitution in Singapore, 1870–1940* (Singapore: Oxford University Press, 1993); Eric Tagliacozzo, "Morphological Shifts in Southeast Asian Prostitution: The Long Twentieth Century," *Journal of Global History* 3 (2008): 251–273.

23. *Indian Review* (1924), 708.

24. Andrew, *Indian Labour in Rangoon*, 182–189.

25. Testimony of Chan Yau Choi, case of Liew Soi Ngan, NAS, Coroner's Court, Coroner's Inquests and Inquiries, Certificate B, Coroner's View, S/No. 15, October-December 1937. This and all coroner's records in the notes that follow are cited by permission of the Singapore Supreme Court, obtained in March 2007.

26. James Warren pioneered the use of coroners' records to write Singapore's social history. See his *Rickshaw Coolie: A People's History of Singapore* (Singapore: Oxford University Press, 1986).

27. Case of Pakiamah: NAS, Coroner's Court, Coroner's Inquests and Inquiries, Certificate B, Coroner's View, S/No. 19, October-December 1932; Case of Ratanam: NAS, Coroner's Court, Coroner's Inquests and Inquiries, Certificate B, Coroner's View, S/No. 19, October-December 1932; Case of "Adult Female Hokchew, Aged 24": NAS, Coroner's Court, Coroner's Inquests and Inquiries, S/No. 9, April-June 1936.

28. Case of K. Kuhni Kannan: NAS, Coroner's Court, Coroner's Inquests and Inquiries, S/No. 12, January–March 1937.

29. Case of "Piah alias Puteh": NAS, Coroner's Court, Coroner's Inquests and Inquiries, S/No. 20, January–March 1933.

30. T. R. McHale, *Rubber and the Malaysian Economy* (Kuala Lumpur: MPH, 1966), 16–28.

31. Michael W. Charney, *A History of Modern Burma* (Cambridge: Cambridge University Press, 2009), 20–22; Tilman Frasch, "Tracks in the City: Technology, Mobility and Society in Colonial Rangoon and Singapore," *Modern Asian Studies* 46, 1 (2012): 97–118.

32. David Arnold, "The Problem of Traffic: The Street-Life of Modernity in Late Colonial India," *Modern Asian Studies* 46, 1 (2012): 119–42.

33. Case of "Pavadi": NAS, Coroner's Courts, Coroner's Inquests and Inquiries, S/No. 3–4 (1920–21); Case of "Sinappah": NAS, Coroner's Courts, Coroner's Inquests and Inquiries, S/No. 6, October–December 1921.

34. L. Elizabeth Lewis, "The Fire-Walking Hindus of Singapore," *National Geographic* 59, 4 (April 1931): 513–522.

35. "Thavippu Vendam," *Munnetram*, 16 July 1931; Jan van der Putten, "Negotiating the Great Depression: The Rise of Popular Culture and Consumerism in Early 1930s Malaya," *Journal of Southeast Asian Studies* 41, 1 (2010): 21–45.

36. NAS, Oral History Department, A 001211/20, A. Nagore Maideen, interviewed by Rajendan Supramaniam, October 8 1990; see also A. N. Maideen, *Nenchil Pathintha Ninaivu Suvadukal* (Kumbakonam: Tozhamaip Patippakam 1989).

37. P. Singaram, *Puyalile Oru Thoni*, 2nd ed. (Chennai: Tamilini, 2005), 18–19.

38. M. W. M. Yeats, *Census of India 1931*, vol. 14, *Madras*, pt. 1, *Report* (Madras, 1932), 93–94.

39. Ravindra Jain, *South Indians on the Plantation Frontier in Malaya* (New Haven: Yale University Press, 1970).

40. Personal communication from Professor Nira Wickramasinghe.

41. *Annual Report of the Labour Department, Malaya for the Year 1936* (Kuala Lumpur: Government Press, 1937).

42. Gilbert Slater, ed., *University of Madras, Economic Studies*, vol. 1, *Some South Indian Villages* (London: Oxford University Press, 1918); P. J. Thomas and K. C. Ramakrishnan, eds., *Some South Indian Villages: A Resurvey* (Madras: University of Madras, 1940); *Census of India 1931*, 14:93.

43. Benedict Anderson, *Imagined Communities: Reflections on the Origin and Spread of Nationalism*, 2nd ed. (London: Verso, 1991).

44. E. W. Birch, "The Vernacular Press in the Straits," *Journal of the Straits Branch of the Royal Asiatic Society* 4 (December 1879): 51–55.

45. The earliest surviving printed book in Tamil is Muhummad Abdul Kadir Pulavar, *Munajathuthirattu* (Singapore, 1872).
46. Birch, "The Vernacular Press."
47. Ibid.
48. Chen Mong Hock, *The Early Chinese Papers of Singapore, 1881–1912* (Singapore: University of Malaya Press, 1967); Mark Ravinder Frost, "*Emporium in Imperio:* Nanyang Networks and the Straits Chinese in Singapore, 1819–1914," *Journal of Southeast Asian Studies* 36, 1 (2005): 29–66.
49. Helen Fujimoto, *The South Indian Muslim Community and the Evolution of the Jawi Peranakan in Penang up to 1948* (Tokyo: Tokyo Gaikokugo Daigaku, 1988).
50. S. M. A. K. Fakhri, "Print Culture amongst Tamils and Tamil Muslims in Southeast Asia, c. 1860–1960," Madras Institute of Development Studies Working Paper, no. 167, February 2002.
51. Torsten Tschacher, "Kling, Tamil, Indian: Being a Tamil-Speaking Muslim in Singapore," unpublished manuscript.
52. See, inter alia, "Ippathirikaiyin Nokkam," *Singainesan,* 27 June 1887; "Kaioppakkaarargalukku," *Singainesan,* 4 July 1887; "Achai," *Singainesan,* 26 March 1888; "Italikkum, Abshiniyavukkum Sandai," *Singainesan,* 16 April 1888; "Malaya Desam," *Singainesan,* 22 April 1889. General comments based on a survey of issues from 1887 to 1890, consulted at the Lee Kong Chian Reference Library, National Library of Singapore.
53. Rajeswary Ampalavanar, "Tamil Journalism and the Indian Community in Malaya, 1920–1941," *Journal of Tamil Studies* 2, 2 (1970): 41–58.
54. Cf. ibid.
55. "Namathu Pathirikai," *Munnetram,* 15 January 1931.
56. *Malayan Bulletin of Political Intelligence* [Secret], July 1922, IOR L/P&J/12/103.
57. M. Elias, *Tamilavel Sarangapany* (Chennai: Arivuchudar Pathipakam, 1997).
58. Carol Gluck, "The End of Elsewhere: Writing Modernity Now," *American Historical Review* 116, 3 (2011): 678.
59. An early version of the arguments in this section appeared in Sunil S. Amrith, "Tamil Diasporas across the Bay of Bengal," *American Historical Review* 114, 3 (2009): 547–572; they have been substantially revised here.
60. Walter Benjamin, "The Work of Art in an Age of Mechanical Reproduction," in *Illuminations: Essays and Reflections,* ed. Hannah Arendt, trans. Harry Zohn (New York: Schocken Books, 1968).
61. *Malayan Bulletin of Political Intelligence* [Secret], various issues, March–September 1922, IOR L/P&J/12/103.
62. "Books in Tamil Seized by Customs Authorities in Dhanushkodi," TNSA, Government of Madras, Public Department, Government Order 1201, 19 September 1932; Government Order 1260 of 27 September

1932; Government Order 1274 of 1 October 1932; see also "Objectionable Books Imported into British India from Ceylon and Seized by the Customs Authorities at Dhanushkodi," Government Order 107 of 30 January 1933.

63. Bose, *A Hundred Horizons*, 249–250; "Arrival of Dr. Tagore in Singapore," *Malaya Saturday Post*, 30 July 1927; "Dr. Rabindranath Tagore," *Singapore Free Press and Mercantile Advertiser*, 19 July 1927.

64. M. S. S. Pandian, *Brahmin and Non-Brahmin: Genealogies of the Tamil Present* (New Delhi: Permanent Black, 2002); Robert Hardgrave, *The Dravidian Movement* (Bombay: Popular Prakashan, 1965)

65. "Penang Hindus Hot: Landing of Ramasamy Naicker Opposed," *Straits Times*, 18 December 1929; "Indian Reformer Arrives," *Straits Times*, 26 December 1929; "Singapore Tamils' Public Meeting," *Singapore Free Press and Mercantile Advertiser*, 30 April 1930; A. C. Suppaiyah, "Rabbar Tottatil Periyar," in V. Thirunavakarasu, ed., *Maleyavil Periyar* (Singapore: K. Pichaiyan, 1955), 17–18. See also the account of the Indian agent in Malaya in NAI, Department of Education, Health and Lands, Lands and Overseas Branch, Proceedings 14–15 (B), February 1930.

66. James Clifford, "Diasporas," *Cultural Anthropology* 9, 3 (1994): 302–338.

67. See, for example, "Thenafirikka Indiyar," *Tamil Nesan*, 13 August 1932; "Thenafirikka Indiyargal," *Tamil Nesan*, 15 October 1932; "Thenafirikka Indiyargalin Kavalaikkitamaana Nilaimai," *Tamil Nesan*, 23 November 1932.

68. "Fiji Indiyargal Nilaimai," *Tamil Nesan*, 10 September 1932.

69. "Barma," *Munnetram*, 25 June 1931; "Barmaavil Adaatha Kollaiyum, Kolaiyum," *Tamil Nesan*, 20 April 1932.

70. Cited in William Roff, *The Origins of Malay Nationalism* (New Haven, 1967), 171.

71. "Malay Naattil Raajiya Urimaigal," *Tamil Nesan*, 20 April 1932.

72. Fujimoto, *South Indian Muslim Community*.

73. "Indian Land Settlement in Malaya," *Indo-Malayan Review* 1, 2 (1934).

74. R. B. Krishnan, *Indians in Malaya: A Pageant of Greater India* (Singapore, 1936), 1; see also Susan Bayly, "Imagining 'Greater India': French and Indian Visions of Colonialism in the Indic Mode," *Modern Asian Studies* 38, 3 (2004): 703–744.

75. "Indian Land Settlement in Malaya," *Indo-Malayan Review* 1, 2 (1934).

76. Confidential Letter from the Agent of the Government of India in British Malaya, 3 April 1933; Confidential Letter from Agent, Malaya, Kuala Lumpur, 17 November 1933, NAI, Department of Education, Health and Lands, Lands and Overseas Branch, 1932, File No. 206-2/32-L. & O.

77. Krishnan, *Indians in Malaya*, 27; John D. Kelly and Martha Kaplan, "Diaspora and Swaraj, Swaraj and Diaspora," in Dipesh Chakrabarty, Rochona

Majumdar, and Andrew Sartori, eds., *From the Colonial to the Postcolonial: India and Pakistan in Transition* (New Delhi: Permanent Black, 2007).

78. *The Indian,* 5 June 1937.

79. "Indians in Malaya," *Straits Times,* 1 June 1934.

80. *Malaya Tribune,* 12 February 1931, cited in Chua Ai Lin, "Nation, Race and Language: Discussing Transnational Identities in 1930s Colonial Singapore," *Modern Asian Studies,* 46, 2 (2012), 283–302.

81. On the emerging sphere of "political society" in Bengal, see Partha Chatterjee, *Lineages of Political Society: Studies in Postcolonial Democracy* (New Delhi: Permanent Black, 2011); on the scope and limits of civil society in colonial India, see Sudipta Kaviraj, *The Imaginary Institution of India: Politics and Ideas* (New York: Columbia University Press, 2010).

82. Sinnappah Arasaratnam, *Indians in Malaysia and Singapore* (Kuala Lumpur, 1970),

83. For a sample of newspaper coverage: "Silangur Indiya Varthakar Sangam Kolalumpur," *Tamil Nesan,* 23 March 1932; "Mariyamman Kovil Kes Mudivu," *Tamil Nesan,* 12 November 1932; "Kola Kangksar Tamil Seerthirutta Sangam," *Desa Nesan,* 1 October 1933.

84. NAI, Department of Education, Health and Lands, Lands and Overseas Branch, Proceedings 7–25 (B), January 1926; see also *Malayan Observer,* 29 June 1925.

85. From T. V. Thillainayagam, K. Mahalingam, and R. Aiyavoo to "C. F. Andrews of India," 25 July 1924, NAI, Deparment of Education, Health and Lands, Overseas Branch, Proceeding 1 (B), September 1924.

86. Charles Hirschman, "The Meaning and Measurement of Ethnicity in Malaysia: An Analysis of Census Classifications," *Journal of Asian Studies* 46, 3 (1987): 552–582.

87. *Report of the Indian Industrial Commission, 1916–18* (Calcutta: Government Printer, 1918).

88. File note by R. H. Craddock, 1 September 1915, NAI, Department of Commerce and Inudstry: Emigration Branch, Proceedings 56–73 (A), December 1915.

89. Stéphane Dufoix, *Diasporas,* trans. William Rodarmor (Berkeley: University of California Press, 2008); Robin Cohen, *Global Diasporas* (London: UCL Press, 1997); Engseng Ho, "Empire through Diasporic Eyes: The View from the Other Boat," *Comparative Studies in Society and History* 46, 2 (2004): 214.

90. Norman Carr Sargant, *The Dispersion of the Tamil Church* (Madras: SPCK, 1940).

91. Marshall Berman, *All That Is Solid Melts into Air: The Experience of Modernity* (New York: Simon and Schuster, 1982).

92. Charles Taylor, *A Secular Age* (Cambridge, MA: The Belknap Press, 2007), 171–172.

6 Crossings Interrupted

1. Letter from Agent of the Government of India to Secretary, Government of Burma, 7 February 1939, NAI, Department of Education, Health and Lands, 1939, 143/39 OS.
2. Bruno Lasker, *Asia on the Move: Population Pressure, Migration, and Resettlement in East Asia under the Influence of Want and War* (New York: Henry Holt, 1945), 23; J. S. Furnivall, *Netherlands India* (Cambridge: Cambridge University Press, 1939), 428.
3. W. G. Huff, "Entitlements, Destitution, and Emigration in the 1930s Singapore Great Depression," *Economic History Review* 54, 2 (2001): 290–323.
4. "1930-vil Malaya Naattil Indiya Kooligalin Nilaimai," *Tamil Nesan*, 2 January 1932; "Thottai Kallu Kadaigal," *Tamil Nesan*, 3 May 1932; "Malayavukku Thozhilaalargal," *Desa Nesan*, 8 July 1933.
5. Burma Provincial Banking Enquiry (Grantham) Committee, *Volume 1: Report: Banking and Credit in Burma* (Rangoon: Government Press, 1930); Michael Adas, *The Burma Delta: Economic Development and Social Change on an Asian Rice Frontier, 1852–1941* (Madison: Univeristy of Wisconsin Press, 1974).
6. Confidential Letter from the Agent of the Government of India in British Malaya to the Government of India, 3 April 1933, NAI, Department of Education, Health and Lands: Overseas, 206-2/32-L. & O.
7. "Unemployment in Malaya: Restriction of Chinese Immigration," 1930, NAUK, PRO, CO 273/566/2; Memorandum Presented by the Agent of the Government of India in Malaya to the Indian Immigration Committee of Malaya, Kuala Lumpur, 16 July 1930, NAI, Department of Education, Health and Lands, Overseas, Proceedings 76–162 (A), June 1931; Letter from K. A. Mukundan, Agent in Malaya, to M. S. A. Hydaru, Deputy Secretary to the Government of India, 28 March 1934, NAI, Department of Education, Health and Lands, 206-2/32-L. & O.
8. Report by the Government of Burma on Recent Rebellions in That Province, 8 May 1931, NAI, Department of Education, Health and Lands, Overseas Section, 92-1/38-L. & O.
9. S. Grantham, "Indian Immigration at Rangoon," 29 September 1934, NADM, 6M-14.
10. *Annual Report on the Working of the Indian Emigration Act, 1922, for the Year 1934* (Madras: Government Printer, 1935): Government of Madras, Government Order 1464L, 26 June 1935, 1–8.

11. A. Narayana Rao, *Indian Labour in Burma* (Rangoon, 1933), 214.

12. U Tin Tut, cited in C. A. Bayly, "Ideologies of the End of the Raj: Burma, India and the World, 1940–50," in Durba Ghosh and Dane Kennedy, eds., *Decentring Empire: Britain, India and the Transcolonial World* (New Delhi: Orient Longman, 2006); William R. Roff, *The Origins of Malay Nationalism* (New Haven, CT: Yale University Press, 1967); Anthony Milner, *The Invention of Politics in Colonial Malaya* (Cambridge: Cambridge University Press, 1995); Michael W. Charney, *A History of Modern Burma* (Cambridge: Cambridge University Press, 2009).

13. V. Swaminatha Sarma, *Pirikkappatta Burma* (Rangoon: Navinakata Press, 1936), RMRL.

14. Ng Thein Pe, "Indo-Burman Conflict," pamphlet reproduced and translated in NAI: Education, Health and Lands, Overseas Section, 92-1/38-L. & O. (Confidential), Press Cuttings; translated extract from *Saithan,* 1 January 1941, NAI, Indians Overseas Department, Overseas Branch, 144-1/38-L. & O.

15. *The Searchlight* (Patna), 16 May 1934; John D. Kelly and Martha Kaplan, "Diaspora and Swaraj, Swaraj and Diaspora," in Dipesh Chakrabarty, Rochona Majumdar, and Andrew Sartori, eds., *From the Colonial to the Postcolonial: India and Pakistan in Transition* (New Delhi: Permanent Black, 2007).

16. Partha Chatterjee, *The Black Hole of Empire: History of a Global Practice of Power* (Princeton: Princeton University Press, 2012), 273; see also Mrinalini Sinha, *Specters of Mother India: The Global Restructuring of an Empire* (Durham, NC: Duke University Press, 2006).

17. Lanka Sundaram, "The International Aspects of Indian Emigration," *Asiatic Review,* October 1930, 37.

18. John L. Christian, "Burma Divorces India," *Current History,* 46, 1 (April 1937): 82; on "South Asia" and "Southeast Asia," see Willem van Schendel, "Geographies of Knowing, Geographies of Ignorance: Jumping Scale in Southeast Asia," in Paul H. Kratoska, Remco Raben, and Henk Schulte Nordholt, eds., *Locating Southeast Asia: Geographies of Knowledge and Politics of Space* (Singapore: NUS Press, 2005).

19. A. K. Abdul Karim Gani, quoted in NAI, Indians Overseas Department, Overseas Branch, 144-1/38-L. & O.

20. "Immigration Enquiry Committee," NADM, D (M) 39, no. 647.

21. File note, anon., n.d. [c. 1941], NAI, Indians Overseas Department, Overseas Branch, 144-1/38-L. & O.

22. Telegram from President, Nattukottai Chettiars Association, to Member for Indians Overseas, Government of India, Simla, NAI, Indians Overseas Department, Overseas Branch, 144-1/38-L. & O.

23. Christopher Baker, *An Indian Rural Economy 1880–1955: The Tamilnad Countryside* (New Delhi: Oxford University Press, 1984), 422–425, 516–519.

24. File Note by Agent of the Government of India in Malaya [n.d.], NAI, Deparment of Education, Health and Lands: Lands and Overseas Branch, 117/37-L. & O., Part I, 1937.

25. File Note by G. S. Bajpai, 19 February 1938, NAI, Department of Education, Health and Lands, Lands and Overseas Branch, 117/37-L. & O., Part I, 1937.

26. Minutes of the Standing Emigration Committee, 13 February 1939, NAI, Department of Education, Health and Lands: Overseas Branch, 1938, 44/38-L. & O.

27. From Agent of the Government of India in British Malaya to Deputy Secretary, Government of India, 12 August 1925, NAI, Department of Education, Health and Lands, Overseas Branch, Proceedings 95–98 (B), September 1925.

28. Memo by E. Gent [n.d.], "Labour Disputes in Malaya, 1937–8," NAUK, CO 273/632/9.

29. John Tully, *The Devil's Milk: A Social History of Rubber* (New York: Monthly Review Press, 2011), 270–274.

30. "Labour Unrest in Malaya, 1940," NAUK, CO 273/662/10.

31. Sinnappah Arasaratnam, *Indians in Malaysia and Singapore* (Kuala Lumpur, 1970).

32. Special Branch Report on R. H. Nathan, NAUK, CO 717/145/12.

33. H. E. Wilson, "The Klang Strikes of 1941: Labour and Capital in Colonial Malaya," Research Notes and Discussion Paper, 25, Institute of Southeast Asian Studies, Singapore, 1991.

34. "Report on the Strikes in Selangor," E. Bagot, Inspector General of Police, Federated Malay States, 13 June 1941, NAUK, CO 717/145/12.

35. Christopher Bayly and Tim Harper, *Forgotten Armies: The Fall of British Asia, 1941–45* (London: Penguin, 2004).

36. Despatch on Air Operations in Burma and the Bay of Bengal, Jan 1st to May 22nd, 1942, Air Vice Marshal D. F. Stevenson, NAUK, AIR 23/1924.

37. Jeremy Black, "Midway and the Indian Ocean," *Naval War College Review* 62, 4 (Autumn 2009): 131–140.

38. Cited in ibid.

39. Bayly and Harper, *Forgotten Armies*, 34.

40. Sugata Bose, *His Majesty's Opponent: Subhas Chandra Bose and India's Struggle against Empire* (Cambridge, MA: Havard University Press, 2011).

41. Joyce Chapman Lebra, *Women against the Raj: The Rani of Jhansi Regiment* (Singapore: ISEAS Press, 2008), ch. 6.

42. Janaki Athinahappan, "The Rani of Jhansi Regiment," *Oracle* 2, 1 (1980): 32.
43. Interview with Janaki Athinahappan on BRM Radio, Malaysia, "Merdeka" Series, Part 2, 26 August 2010.
44. Abid Hasan Safrani, "The Men from Imphal," *Oracle* 15, 1 (1993): 35.
45. Bisheshwar Prasad, ed., *Official History of the Indian Armed Forces in the Second World War, 1939–45: The Reconquest of Burma* (New Delhi: Combined Inter-Services Historical Section, India and Pakistan, 1959), 2:255–257; "Use of Kyaukphu as Burma Naval Base," Secret Memo by Captain D. J. Munro, 5 June 1944, NAUK, ADM 1/16001.
46. V. Swaminatha Sarma, *Enathu Burma Vazhi Nadai Payanam* (Chennai: Tirumakal Nilaiyam, 1979); V. Swaminatha Sarma, *Banapurathy Veeran: Oru Natakam* (Chennai: S. Radha, 1924); *Ve. Swaminatha Sarmavil Katturai Kalainjiyam* (Chennai: Punkoti Patippakam, 1988).
47. Dr. Krishnan Gurumurthy's memoir of the walk from Burma was published in full as "Exodus from Burma, 1941: A Personal Account, Parts 1, 2 & 3," 21 June 2011, on Amitav Ghosh's blog, www.amitavghosh.com /blog/?p=432, accessed 5 June 2012.
48. Hugh Tinker, "A Forgotten Long March: The Indian Exodus from Burma, 1942," *Journal of Southeast Asian Studies* 6 (1975).
49. NAI, *Burma Evacuee Register,* Part 2, No. 403 (B).
50. Norman Lewis, *Golden Earth: Travels in Burma* (London: Jonathan Cape, 1952).
51. NAI, *Burma Evacuee Register,* Part 2, No. 403 (B).
52. Lieutenant G. C. G. Brown, Burma to Commanding Officer, Burma, 11 September 1942, Report on Kyaukpyu Evacuation, Dated 14 April 1942, NAI, Commonwealth Relations Department, Overseas Section, F. 45-21/44-OS.
53. Evidence of L. G. Pinnell before the Bengal Famine Inquiry Commission, 15 August 1944, in Partha Sarathi Gupta, ed., *Towards Freedom: Documents on the Movement for Independence in India, 1943–44,* pt. 2 (New Delhi: Oxford University Press, 1997), 1997.
54. Gyanendra Pandey, ed., *The Indian Nation in 1942* (Calcutta: K. P. Bagchi, 1988).
55. Nakahara Michiko, "Malayan Labour on the Thailand-Burma Railway," in Paul Kratoska, ed., *Asian Labor in the Wartime Japanese Empire: Unknown Histories* (Armonk, NY: M. E. Sharpe, 2005).
56. Survivor's Testimony, in Paul H. Kratoska, ed., *The Thailand-Burma Railway, 1942–1946: Documents and Selected Writings* (London: Routledge, 2006), 4:308–309.
57. Shanmugam, *Siyam Marana Rayil* (Chennai: Tamilosai Pathippagam, 2007).
58. Archives of the Imperial War Museum, London, Private Papers of Second Lieutenant R. Middleton-Smith, 02/50/1.

59. Judith Shapiro, *Mao's War against Nature: Politics and Environment in Revolutionary China* (Cambridge: Cambridge University Press, 2001), 142–143.

60. Iftekhar Iqbal, *The Bengal Delta: Ecology, State and Social Change, 1840–1943* (Basingstoke, UK: Palgrave Macmillan, 2010), 163.

61. W. R. Aykroyd and K. Rajagopal, "The State of Nutrition in Schoolchildren in South India," *Indian Journal of Medical Research* 24 (1936); Sunil S. Amrith, "Food and Welfare in India, c. 1900–1950," *Comparative Studies in Society and History* 50, 4 (2008): 1010–35.

62. Bayly and Harper, *Forgotten Armies,* 282–291.

63. *The Ramakrishna Mission: Bengal and Orissa Cyclone Relief, 1942–44* (Howrah: Ramakrishna Mission, 1944), 1–2.

64. "Note to Famine Commission" (1944), Papers of L. G. Pinnell, British Library, Asian and African Studies Collection, MSS Eur D 911/7.

65. Iqbal, *Bengal Delta,* ch. 8; Sugata Bose, "Starvation amidst Plenty: The Making of Famine in Bengal, Honan and Tonkin, 1942–45," *Modern Asian Studies* 24, 4 (1990): 699–727.

66. Amartya Sen, *Poverty and Famines: An Essay on Entitlement and Deprivation* (Oxford: Oxford University Press, 1981); Paul Greenough, *Prosperity and Misery in Modern Bengal: The Famine of 1943–4* (New York: Oxford University Press, 1982); Bayly and Harper, *Forgotten Armies,* 282–291.

67. Bhowani Sen, *Rural Bengal in Ruins,* trans. N. Chakravarty (Bombay: People's Publishing House, 1945).

68. Jawaharlal Nehru, *The Discovery of India* [1946] (New Delhi: Oxford University Press, 2003), 496–498.

69. S. G. Sardesai, *Food in the United Provinces* (Bombay: People's Publishing House, 1944), 19, 36–37.

70. Nehru, *Discovery of India,* 535.

71. Bhulabai Desai, "Provisional Government of Azad Hind and International Law," Address of Counsel for Defence, Red Fort, Delhi, 1 December 1945, reproduced in *Oracle,* 15, 4 (1993).

7 The Pursuit of Citizenship

1. Peter Galassi, "Old Worlds, Modern Times," in Peter Galassi, ed., *Henri Cartier-Bresson: The Modern Century* (New York: Museum of Modern Art, 2010), 22–23.

2. Terence McGee, *The Southeast Asian City: A Social Geography of the Primate Cities of Southeast Asia* (London: G. Bell and Sons, 1967).

3. Walter Benjamin, "Theses on the Philosophy of History," in *Illuminations,* ed. Hannah Arendt, trans. Harry Zor (New York: Schocken Books, 1968), 253–265.

4. "Britain Destroyed Records of Colonial Crimes," *Guardian,* 18 April 2012.
5. File Note, anon., n.d. [c. 1945], NAI, Commonwealth Relations Department, Overseas Section II, 43-44-OS.
6. "Burma: Indian Embassy," NAI, Ministry of External Affairs and Commonwealth Relations (CR Wing), 4/2/46-OS IV; File Note by B. N. Nanda, 29 December 1945, NAI, Ministry of External Affairs and Commonwealth Relations (CR Wing), 4/2/46-OS IV.
7. Jamnadas Mehta, Indian Representative in Rangoon, to R. N. Banerjee, Indian Civil Service, 8 April 1946, NAI, Ministry of External Affairs and Commonwealth Relations (CR Wing), 4/2/46-OS IV.
8. Ibid.
9. Ibid.
10. "Review of the Situation in Rangoon's Chinese Quarter as a Result of the Return of Chinese Evacuees from China" [Secret], July 1946, NADM, Acc. No. I-83, Reel 1; Memorandum by Lt.-Col. G. Tarr, 24 July 1946, NADM, Acc. No. I-83, Reel 1.
11. Letter from B. O. Binns to L. Waight, Financial Adviser, Office of the Financial Commissioner, Burma, 25 March 1946, IOR/M/4/9.
12. Burma Immigration, Emergency Provisions Act, 1947, IOR/M/4/1221.
13. Weekly Statement, Immigration Office, Chittagong, 10 January 1948, NADM, Acc. No. 34, R-1; Letter from Ba Maung, Immigration Officer, Chittagong, to Controller of Immigration, Rangoon, 27 January 1948, NADM, Acc. No. 34, R-1.
14. Nakahara Michiko, "Malayan Labour on the Thailand-Burma Railway," in Paul Kratoska, ed., *Asian Labor in the Wartime Japanese Empire: Unknown Histories* (Armonk, NY: M. E. Sharpe, 2005).
15. S. K. Chettur, *Malayan Adventure* (Mangalore, 1948); C. Siva Rama Sastry, *Congress Mission to Malaya* (Delhi, 1947).
16. Muthammal Palanisamy, *Nadu Vittu Nadu* (Chennai: United Writers, 2007).
17. Harper, *End of Empire.*
18. Conditions of Indian Labourers in Malaya, 1948–9, NAUK, PRO, CO 717/181/2.
19. NAS, Oral History Department, Abdul Aziz, interviewed by Rajendran Supramaniam, 6 September 1990.
20. NAS, Oral History Department, M. K. Bhasi, interviewed by Ng Chang Wang, August 1985.
21. M. V. del Tufo, *A Report on the 1947 Census of Population* (Kuala Lumpur: Government of Malaya, 1947).
22. K. S. Seshan, Controller of Emigration, to S. V. Sampath, Under Secretary, Ministry of External Affairs, 2 March 1953, NAI, Ministry of External Affairs, Emigration Branch, F 11-5/53-Emi.

23. K. S. Seshan to T. V. Ramakrishna Rao, Acting Agent of Government of India in Malaya, 21 August 1953, NAI, Ministry of External Affairs, Emigration Branch, F 11-5/53-Emi.

24. Harper, *End of Empire.*

25. Singapore, *Annual Report of the Immigration Department* (Singapore: Government Printer, 1953).

26. Sinnappah Arasaratnam, *Indians in Malaysia and Singapore* (Kuala Lumpur, 1970), 41.

27. *Asian Relations: Being Report of the Proceedings and Documentation of the First Asian Relations Conference, New Delhi, March–April 1947* (New Delhi: Asian Relations Organization, 1948), 91–99.

28. The passport has been digitized by the National Library of Singapore and is available at http://sgebooks.nl.sg/detail/6bc6bd9c-8f54-44fe-be2b-d1109e121bd4.aspx, accessed 30 March 2013; the document is also discussed in Sunil S. Amrith, *Migration and Diaspora in Modern Asia* (Cambridge: Cambridge University Press, 2011), 121. See also Aihwa Ong, *Flexible Citizenship: The Cultural Logics of Transnationality* (Durham, NC: Duke University Press, 1999).

29. *Asian Relations,* 96.

30. Ruth T. McVey, *The Calcutta Conferences and the Southeast Asian Uprisings* (Ithaca, NY: Cornell University Press, 1958); see also the special issue of the *Journal of Southeast Asian Studies* 40 (October 2009), ed. Karl Hack and Geoff Wade.

31. Joya Chatterji, "South Asian Histories of Citizenship, 1946–1970," *Historical Journal,* 55, 4 (2012): 1049–1071; Ramachandra Guha, *India after Gandhi: The History of the World's Largest Democracy* (London: Macmillan, 2007), 84–126.

32. Chatterji, "South Asian Histories of Citizenship"; Vazira Fazila-Yacoobali Zamindar, *The Long Partition and the Making of Modern South Asia: Refugees, Boundaries, Histories* (New York: Columbia University Press, 2007).

33. Taylor C. Sherman, "Migration, Citizenship and Belonging in Hyderabad (Deccan), 1945–1956," *Modern Asian Studies* 45, 1 (2011): 81–107.

34. Petition to the Governor of Burma from Bengal Arakanese Buddhist Association, n.d. [c. 1946], NADM, Acc. No. I-83, Reel 1.

35. Willem van Schendel, *The Bengal Borderland: Beyond State and Nation in South Asia* (London: Anthem, 2005).

36. Jawaharlal Nehru, Speech in the Indian Constituent Assembly (Legislative), March 8, 1948, in Jawaharlal Nehru, *India's Foreign Policy: Selected Speeches, September 1946—April 1961* (New Delhi, 1962), 128–129.

37. Robert Cribb and Li Narangoa, "Orphans of Empire: Divided Peoples, Dilemmas of Identity, and Old Imperial Borders in East and Southeast Asia," *Comparative Studies in Society and History* 46, 1 (2004): 164–187.

38. Nira Wickramasinghe, *Sri Lanka in the Modern Age: A History of Contested Identities* (London: Hurst, 2006), 161–191.

39. Ibid.

40. E. Valentine Daniel, *Charred Lullabies: Chapters in an Anthropology of Violence* (Princeton, NJ: Princeton University Press, 1996), 110–113.

41. Valli Kanapathipillai, *Citizenship and Statelessness in Sri Lanka: The Case of the Tamil Estate Workers* (London: Anthem, 2009).

42. Eric Meyer, "Labour Circulation between Sri Lanka and South India in Historical Perspective," in Claude Markovits, Jacques Pouchepadass, and Sanjay Subrahmanyam, eds., *Society and Circulation: Mobile People and Itinerant Cultures in South Asia, 1750–1950* (New Delhi: Permanent Black, 2003), 86–88.

43. W. S. Desai, *India and Burma: A Study* (Bombay: Orient Longmans, 1954), 97.

44. Usha Mahajani, *The Role of the Indian Minorities in Burma and Malaya* (Bombay: Vora, 1960), 176.

45. *Notes by the Indian Advisory Committee to Burma Nattukottai Chettiars' Association on the Land Nationalization Act, 1948* (Madras: Commercial Printing and Publishing House, 1948); Letter from Hem Chandra Banerjee, Calcutta, to K. V. Padmanabham, Deputy Secretary, Ministry of External Affairs, New Delhi, 7 June 1952, NAI, Ministry of External Affairs, Burma I Branch, 1950, 48-65/50-B.I; Letter from P. Narayanan, Rangoon, to Nehru through the Ambassador of India, Rangoon, 31 November 1950, NAI, Ministry of External Affairs, Burma I Branch, 1950, 48-65/50-B.I.; *Burma Nattukottai Chettiargal Sangam, India Alocanai Kamitti Muthal Arikai* (Chennai, 1949), RMRL.

46. Mahajani, *Indian Minorities,* 182.

47. Ludu U Hla, *The Caged Ones* [1958], trans. Sein Tu (Bangkok: Tamarind Press, 1986), 116–21.

48. Bayly and Harper, *Forgotten Wars,* 463.

49. Letter from Army Headquarters Liaison Officer, Shillong, to Military Intelligence Director, New Delhi, 26 March 1949, NAI, Ministry of External Affairs, B.I. Branch, 3-8/49-BCI (B) (Secret).

50. Gail Omvedt, *Buddhism in India: Challenging Brahmanism and Caste* (New Delhi: Sage, 2003), 258–263.

51. The following series of files were listed in the NAI's catalog but were missing, "not transferred," or otherwise unavailable for consultation: Ministry of External Affairs, Overseas IV Section: Evacuation I Section (1944–1946); Evacuation II Section (1944–1945); Evacuees Repatriation Section (1946–1949).

52. K.R.R. Sastry, "Plight of the Indians in Burma", *Swarajya* 8, 48 (1965): 12; K. Krishna Moorthy, "Indians in Burma: Problems and Prospects", *Economic Weekly* 14, 43 (1962): 1691–1694.

53. Sumathi Ramaswamy, *The Lost Land of Lemuria: Fabulous Geographies, Catastrophic Histories* (Berkeley: University of California Press, 2004).

54. Mahajani, *Indian Minorities*; Nalini Ranjan Chakravarti, *The Indian Minority in Burma: The Rise and Decline of an Immigrant Community* (London: Oxford University Press, 1971).

55. T. N. Harper, *The End of Empire and the Making of Malaya* (Cambridge: Cambridge University Press, 1999).

56. Bayly and Harper, *Forgotten Wars*, 367.

57. PUTERA-AMCJA, *The People's Constitutional Proposals for Malaya, 1947* (reprinted, Kajang: Ban Ah Kam, 2005), 19, 35.

58. Malayan Democratic Union, "Political Report for the Year Ending 1946" [typescript, n.d.]: IOR/L/PJ/8/267: Indians Overseas, Malaya, Constitutional Reforms.

59. Bayly and Harper, *Forgotten Wars*, 517.

60. Mahajani, *Indian Minority*, 193–197; Michael Stenson, *Class, Race and Colonialism in West Malaysia* (Vancouver: University of British Columbia Press, 1980); P. Ramasamy, *Plantation Labour: Unions, Capital and the State in Peninsular Malaysia* (Kuala Lumpur: Oxford University Press, 1994).

61. Harper, *End of Empire*, 94–148.

62. Charles Gamba, *The National Union of Plantation Workers: The History of the Plantation Workers of Malaya, 1946–1958* (Singapore: Eastern Universities Press, 1962).

63. Interview with Uma Sambanthan, Kuala Lumpur, July 2007.

64. Stenson, *Class, Race and Colonialism*.

65. S. Arasaratnam, "Social and Political Ferment in the Malayan Indian Community 1945–55," in *Proceedings of the First International Conference Seminar of Tamil Studies* (Kuala Lumpur: International Association of Tamil Research, 1966), 141–155; *Ina Mani*, 10 April 1948; on Self-Respect marriages in India, see Sarah Hodges, "Revolutionary Family Life and the Self-Respect Movement in Tamil South India, 1926–1949," *Contributions to Indian Sociology*, 39, 2 (2005), 251–277.

66. Andrew Willford, "The Figure of the Tamil in Modern Malaysia," in Andrew Willford and Eric Tagliacozzo, eds., *Clio/Anthropos: Exploring the Boundaries between History and Anthropology* (Ithaca: Cornell University Press, 2009), 223–273.

67. NAS, Oral History Department, Interview with Abdul Aziz, 6 September 1990, interviewed by Rajendran Supramaniam, A 001195.

68. Clippings in the files of the Singapore Indian Artistes' Association, NAS, NA 2345.

69. Arasaratnam, "Social and Political Ferment."

70. NAS, Oral History Department, Interview with Krishnaswamy Reddy Arumugam, 8 November 1990, interviewed by Rajandran Supramaniam, A 001225; NAS, Oral History Department, Interview with Ramasamy Narayanasamy, 28 May 1990, interviewed by Rajendran Supramaniam, A 001194.

71. Prem K. Pasha, *The Krishnan Odyssey: A Pictorial Biography of Dato' L. Krishnan* (Kuala Lumpur: Nasarre, 2003); William Van der Heide, *Malaysian Cinema, Asian Film: Border Crossings and National Cultures* (Amsterdam: Amsterdam University Press, 2002); Joel S. Kahn, *Other Malays: Nationalism and Cosmopolitanism in the Modern Malay World* (Singapore: NUS Press, 2006).

72. V. Thirunavakarasu, "Periyar Varukai Tanta Balan," in V. Thirunavakarasu, ed., *Maleyavil Periyar* (Singapore: K. Pichaiyan, 1955), 9–10.

73. Stenson, *Class, Race and Colonialism,* 176.

74. NAS, Oral History Department, Interview with Salleh Alikunju, No. 1236; Interview with Padmanabhan Ramachandran, No. 764; Interview with Karunakaran Nair, No. 1177. Also, author's interviews with Tan Jing Quee and Dominic Puthucheary, Singapore, July–August 2005.

75. Carl A. Trocki, *Singapore: Wealth, Power and the Culture of Control* (London: Routledge, 2006).

76. *Proceedings of the First International Conference Seminar of Tamil Studies* (Kuala Lumpur: International Association of Tamil Research, 1966).

77. Willford, "The Figure of the Tamil"; S. Nagarajan, "A Community in Transition: Tamil Displacements in Malaysia," Ph.D. dissertation, Institute of Postgraduate Studies, University of Malaya, Kuala Lumpur, 2004; Ravindra K. Jain, "Culture and Economy: Tamils on the Plantation Frontier Revisited, 1998–99," www.transcomm.ox.ac.uk/working%20papers/ravijain.pdf, accessed 1 August 2011.

78. Stenson, *Class, Race and Colonialism,* 205–206; "Malaysia to Resolve Ethnic Indians' Citizenship Issues," *Hindustan Times,* 31 December 2010.

79. Jane Burbank and Frederick Cooper, *Empires in World History: Power and the Politics of Difference* (Princeton, NJ: Princeton University Press, 2010), 443–461; Sugata Bose, *A Hundred Horizons: The Indian Ocean in the Age of Global Empire* (Cambridge, MA: Harvard University Press, 2006).

80. Amitav Acharya, *Whose Ideas Matter? Agency and Power in Asian Regionalism* (Ithaca, NY: Cornell University Press, 2010), 33–34.

81. Sarat Chandra Bose, "United Nations of South Asia," *Oracle* 1, 2 (1979).

82. Bayly and Harper, *Forgotten Wars,* 326; Acharya, *Whose Ideas Matter?*

83. John R. Smail, "On the Possibility of an Autonomous History of Modern Southeast Asia," *Journal of Southeast Asian History* 2 (1961): 72–102.

84. Paul H. Kratoska, Remco Raben, and Henk Schulte Nordholt, eds., *Locating Southeast Asia: Geographies of Knowledge and Politics of Space* (Singapore: NUS Press, 2005), 1–19; Benedict Anderson, *Spectre of Comparisons: Nationalism, Southeast Asia, the World* (London: Verso, 1998); quote from Sanjay Subrahmanyam, "Connected Histories: Notes towards a Reconfiguration of Early Modern Eurasia," *Modern Asian Studies* 31, 3 (1997): 735–762.

85. Food: Rice Study Group, February–June 1947, IOR/M/4/936; Food: International Emergency Food Council, IOR/M/4/809; Singapore Sub-Committee on Rice, October 1946–October 1947, IOR/M/4/809.

86. Henry Knight, *Food Administration in India, 1939–47* (Stanford, CA: Stanford University Press, 1954), 253.

87. Duncan Ridler and Christopher A. Yandle, "Changes in Patterns and Policies in the International Trade in Rice," *Staff Papers: International Monetary Fund* 19, 1 (1972): 46–86.

88. FAO, Bay of Bengal Programme, *Report of the First Meeting of the Advisory Committee, Colombo, Sri Lanka, 28–29 October 1978*, Appendix I of Document IOFC/DV/78f44.1 (Rome: FAO, 1978); K. Sivasubramaniam, *Marine Fishery Resources of the Bay of Bengal* (Colombo: FAO, 1985).

89. Stein Tønnesson, "Locating the South China Sea," in Kratoska, Raben, and Nordholt, eds., *Locating Southeast Asia*, 203–233; Ajantha Subramanian, *Shorelines: Space and Rights in South India* (Stanford, CA: Stanford University Press, 2009), 126–130.

90. K. S. Jomo et al., *Deforesting Malaysia: The Political Economy and Social Ecology of Agricultural Expansion and Commercial Logging* (London: Zed Books, 2004).

91. Allan Sekula, *Fish Story* (Dusseldorf: Richter Verlag, 2002), 43–53; see also the recent film by Allan Sekula and Noel Burch, *The Forgotten Space* (2010).

8 When the Waters Rise

1. Hillary Clinton, "Remarks on India and the United States: A Vision for the Twenty-First Century," speech in Chennai, 20 July 2011, www.state.gov/secretary/rm/2011/07/168840.htm, accessed 5 June 2012.

2. Thomas R. Metcalf, *Imperial Connections: India in the Indian Ocean Arena, 1860–1920* (Berkeley: University of California Press, 2007), 1; Ronald Hyam, "The Primacy of Geopolitics: The Dynamics of British Imperial Policy, 1763–1963," *Journal of Imperial and Commonwealth History* 27, 2 (1999): 27–52; Memorandum by J. Price, Straits Settlements Factory Records, v. 2, 23 February 1786, IOR/G/34/2.

3. Robert D. Kaplan, *Monsoon: The Indian Ocean and the Future of American Power* (New York: Random House, 2010); Vijay Sakhuja, *Asian Maritime*

Power in the 21st Century: Strategic Transactions, China, India, and Southeast Asia (Singapore: ISEAS Press, 2011).

4. Richard Hall, *Empires of the Monsoon: A History of the Indian Ocean and Its Invaders* (London: HarperCollins, 1996), 80–92; Geoff Wade, "The Zheng He Voyages: A Reassessment," Asia Research Institute Working Papers Series, No. 31 (Singapore: Asia Research Institute, 2004); Leonard Woolf, *Village in the Jungle* [1913] (New Delhi: B.R. Publishing, 1975).

5. Kaplan, *Monsoon*, 10, 191.

6. "Sri Lanka's Southern Hambantota Port Begins Commercial Operations," *Colombo Page*, 6 June 2012, www.colombopage.com/archive_12/Jun06 _1338967766CH.php, accessed 13 June 2012; "Chinese-Built Port in Sri Lanka Fuels Indian Fears Beijing Is Encircling Them," *Guardian*, 18 November 2010; "Chinese Billions in Sri Lanka Fund Battle against Tamil Tigers," *Times*, 2 May 2009.

7. Donald L. Berlin, "The 'Great Base Race' in the Indian Ocean Littoral: Conflict Prevention or Stimulation?" *Contemporary South Asia* 13, 3 (2004): 239–255; the quotation is from C. Raja Mohan, *Crossing the Rubicon: The Shaping of India's New Foreign Policy* (New Delhi: Viking, 2003), xxii; "India to Revive Defence Ties with Sri Lanka," *Hindu*, 24 December 2010, www.thehindu.com/todays-paper/tp-national/article973497.ece, accessed 4 June 2012.

8. Chen Shaofeng, "China's Self-Extrication from the 'Malacca Dilemma' and Implications," *International Journal of China Studies* 1, 1, (2010): 1–24.

9. Julie MacDonald, Amy Donahue, and Bethany Danyluk, *Energy Futures in Asia* (Washington, DC: Booz-Allen Hamilton for Director of Net Assessment, November 2004); Brigadier S. K. Chatterji, "Chinese String of Pearls Could Choke India," 8 September 2010, *Rediff News*, news.rediff. com/column/2010/sep/08/chinese-string-of-pearls-could-choke-india .htm, accessed 6 June 2012.

10. Billy Tea, "Unstringing China's Strategic Pearls," *Asia Times Online*, 11 March 2011, www.atimes.com/atimes/China/MC11Ad02.html, accessed 10 May 2012.

11. Daniel J. Kostecka, "Places and Bases: The Chinese Navy's Emerging Support Network in the Indian Ocean," *Naval War College Review* 64, 1 (2011): 59–78.

12. Wade, "The Zheng He Voyages."

13. Thant Myint-U, *Where China Meets India: Burma and the New Crossroads of Asia* (London: Faber and Faber, 2011); *Asian Relations: Being Report of the Proceedings and Documentation of the First Asian Relations Conference, New Delhi, March–April 1947* (New Delhi: Asian Relations Organization, 1948), 96.

14. Berlin, "'Great Base Race,'" 246–247.
15. "CNPC to Build, Run, China-Myanmar Oil Pipeline," *China Daily*, 21 December 2009, www.chinadaily.com.cn/china/2009–12/21/content_9209811 .htm, accessed 13 June 2012.
16. Chen, "China's Self-Extrication from the 'Malacca Dilemma,'" 11–12.
17. Berlin, "'Great Base Race,'" 246.
18. Sudhir T. Devare, ed., *A New Energy Frontier: The Bay of Bengal Region* (Singapore: ISEAS Press, 2008).
19. International Tribunal on the Law of the Sea, *Dispute Concerning Delimitation of the Maritime Boundary between Bangladesh and Myanmar in the Bay of Bengal:* Judgment, 14 March 2012. Judgement, notes and submissions on the case available at www.itlos.org/start2_en.html, accessed 3 April 2012; "Dividing the Spoils," *Himal Magazine,* www.himalmag.com /component/content/article/5048-dividing-the-spoils.html, accessed 18 April 2012.
20. Kaplan, *Monsoon*, 183.
21. K. M. Panikkar, *India and the Indian Ocean: An Essay on the Influence of Sea Power on Indian History* [1945] (Bombay: George Allen and Unwin, 1971).
22. "Blue Water Navy Is the Aim," *Times of India,* 1 November 2006, articles.timesofindia.indiatimes.com/2006–11–01/india/27785056_1_maritime-security-admiral-sureesh-mehta-admiral-arun-prakash, accessed 1 June 2012.
23. David Scott, "India's Drive for a 'Blue Water' Navy," *Journal of Military and Strategic Studies* 10, 2 (2007–2008); "From Brown Water to Blue," *Indian Express,* 5 December 2006; Indian Navy, *Tacking to the Blue Waters: The Year That Was* (New Delhi, 2003); "India Navy Drops Another Anchor," *Asia Times Online,* 17 October 2006, www.atimes.com/atimes/South_Asia /HJ17Df02.html, accessed 13 June 2012; "Andaman and Nicobar Command," www.globalsecurity.org/military/world/india/anc.htm, accessed 5 June 2012.
24. Sudha Ramachandran, "India Extends Malacca Strait Reach," *Asia Times Online,* 8 August 2012, www.atimes.com/atimes/South_Asia/NH08Df01 .html, accessed 10 August 2012.
25. Harsh V. Pant, "Filling the Strategic Space in South-East Asia," *The Hindu*, 22 December 2012; Simon Denyer, "India Looks to Burma to Boost Trade with South-East Asia," *The Guardian*, 26 February 2013.
26. Berlin, "'Great Base Race,'" 251.
27. Esther Conrad, "Living with an Uncertain Monsoon: IRI's Work to Benefit Farmers in India," portal.iri.columbia.edu/portal/server.pt/gateway /PTAR, accessed 19 June 2012; Asia Society, *Asia's Next Challenge: Securing the Region's Water Future, A Report by the Leadership Group on Water Security in Asia* (New York: Asia Society, 2008), 31.

28. Callum Roberts, *Ocean of Life: How Our Seas Are Changing* (London: Allen Lane, 2012), 3.

29. Ibid., 2.

30. James C. Scott, *Seeing like a State: Why Certain Schemes to Improve the Human Condition Have Failed* (New Haven, CT: Yale University Press, 1998).

31. Urusla L. Kali, "Review of Land-Based Sources of Pollution to the Coastal and Marine Environments of the BOBLME Region," Bay of Bengal Large Marine Ecosystem (BOBLME) Theme Report, GCP/RAS/179/WBG.10 (March 2004), available at http://www.boblme.org/documentRepository /Theme_%20Land%20Based%20Pollution%20-%20%20Urusla%20Kaly .pdf, accessed 31 March 2013.

32. C. J. Vörösmarty et al., "Global Threats to Human Water Security and River Biodiversity," *Nature* 467 (30 September 2010): 555–561.

33. United Nations Environment Program (UNEP), "Dead Zones Emerging as Big Threat to Twenty-First Century Fish Stocks," press release, ENV/ DEV/758, 19 March 2004.

34. Cited in John Butcher, *The Closing of the Frontier: A History of the Marine Fisheries of Southeast Asia, c. 1850–2000* (Singapore: ISEAS Press, 2004), 28–29.

35. The World Wide Fund for Nature map is reproduced in Roger Harrabin, "Shortages: Fish on the Side," BBC News, 18 June 2012, www.bbc.co.uk /news/science-environment-18353964, accessed 18 June 2012.

36. Rachel Carson, *The Edge of the Sea* [1955] (New York: First Mariner Bookers, 1998), 240; Roberts, *Ocean of Life*, 94.

37. C. J. Vörösmarty et al., "Battling to Save the World's River Deltas," *Bulletin of the Atomic Scientists* 65, 2 (2009): 31–43.

38. Kenneth Pomeranz, "The Great Himalayan Watershed," *New Left Review* 58 (2009).

39. James Syvitski et al., "Sinking Deltas Due to Human Activities," *Nature Geoscience* 2 (October 2009): 681–686; James Syvitski, "Life at the Edge: Sinking Deltas," lecture delivered at the Royal Geological Society, London, 28 March 2012.

40. Vörösmarty et al., "Battling to Save the World's River Deltas."

41. Michael Mitchell, "Sticky Assets," in *Burtynsky: Oil* (Toronto: Melcher Media, 2012); "Burtynsky: Oil," exhibition at the Photographers' Gallery, London, May-July 2012.

42. Michael Ondaatje, *The Cat's Table* (London: Jonathan Cape, 2011), 77–78.

43. O. Pilkey and R. Young, *The Rising Sea* (Washington, DC: Island Press, 2009); R. J. Nicholls and A. Cazenave, "Sea-Level Rise and Its Impact on Coastal Zones," *Science* 328 (2010): 1517–20; Roberts, *Ocean of Life*, 82.

44. Mike Davis, "Who Will Build the Ark?" *New Left Review*, 61 (2010): 29–46.

45. K. Nageswara Rao et al., "Sea Level Rise and Coastal Vulnerability: An Assessment of Andhra Pradesh Coast, India, through Remote Sensing and GIS," *Journal of Coastal Conservation* 12, 4 (2008): 195–207.

46. John Vidal, "'We Have Seen the Enemy': Bangladesh's War against Climate Change," *Guardian,* 9 May 2012, www.guardian.co.uk/environment /2012/may/09/bangladesh-war-against-climate-change, accessed 20 June 2012; Thomas Hofer and Bruno Messerli, *Floods in Bangladesh: History, Dynamics and Rethinking the Role of the Himalayas* (Tokyo: United Nations University, 2006).

47. J. Qui, "The Third Pole," *Nature* 454 (2008): 393–396; Praful Bidwai, *The Politics of Climate Change and the Global Crisis: Mortgaging Our Future* (Hyderabad: Orient BlackSwan, 2012), 49–76; Pomeranz, "Great Himalayan Watershed."

48. *Straits Times,* 10 December 1924, 8.

49. A. S. Unnikrishnan et al., "Sea Level Changes along the Indian Coast: Observations and Projections," *Current Science* 90, 3 (2006): 362–368.

50. Emma Larkin, *No Bad News for the King: The True Story of Cyclone Nargis and Its Aftermath in Burma* (New York: Penguin, 2010), 5–6.

51. Peter D. Clift and R. Alan Plumb, *The Asian Monsoon: Causes, History and Effects* (Cambridge: Cambridge University Press, 2008), viii.

52. Bidwai, *Politics of Climate Change,* 52; William Cline, *Global Warming and Agriculture: Impact Estimates by Country* (Washington, DC: Center for Global Development, 2007).

53. Kaplan, *Monsoon,* xiv; Collectif Argos, *Réfugiés Climatiques* (Paris: Editions Carré, 2010).

54. Eric Tagliacozzo, *Secret Trades, Porous Borders: Smuggling and States along a Southeast Asian Frontier, 1865–1915* (New Haven: Yale University Press, 2005).

55. Pheng Cheah, *Inhuman Conditions: On Cosmopolitanism and Human Rights* (Cambridge, MA: Harvard University Press, 2007), 180.

56. Vicknesh Varan, *Special Pass* (Rupture Productions, 2012), available at: http://vimeo.com/53857518, accessed 7 January 2013.

57. Prasenjit Duara, "Asia Redux: Conceptualizing a Region for Our Age," *Journal of Asian Studies,* 69 (2010), 963–983.

58. The Singapore theater group Migrant Voices has done creative work with migrant workers from across Asia, allowing them to tell their stories in a variety of media. Migrants' use of digital media is the subject of work in progress by anthropologist Megha Amrith.

59. Rustom Bharucha, "Consumed in Singapore: The Intercultural Spectacle of Lear," *Theater* 31, 1 (2001): 107–127.

60. "Malaya" Samy interviewed by the Made by Migrants documentary project, video available at www.madebymigrants.com, accessed 7 January 2013.

61. Aseem Shrivastava and Ashish Kothari, *Churning the Earth: The Making of Global India* (New Delhi: Penguin, 2012); Md Mizanur Rahman, "Migration and Social Development: A Family Perspective," ARI Working Paper, 91, National University of Singapore, 2007; Sunil S. Amrith, *Migration and Diaspora in Modern Asia* (Cambridge: Cambridge University Press, 2011), ch. 5.

62. Tan Hui Yee, "They Build Our Dream Homes So They May Have Theirs," *Straits Times*, 26 January 2008; Megha Amrith, "Vulnerability, Community and Resistance: A Study of Tamil Migrant Workers in Singapore," honors dissertation, University College, London, 2006.

63. Interviews in Kuala Lumpur, July-August 2007; he asked not to be named.

64. Tan, "They Build Our Dream Homes."

65. Asian Development Bank, *Addressing Climate Change and Migration in Asia and the Pacific: Final Report* (Manila: Asian Development Bank, 2012), 4.

66. Sam Knight, "The Human Tsunami," *Financial Times*, 19 June 2009.

67. Asian Development Bank, *Addressing Climate Change and Migration*.

68. Dipesh Chakrabarty, "The Climate of History, Four Theses," *Critical Inquiry* 35 (2009): 197–222.

69. Michael Mitchell, "Death of a Star," in *Burtynsky: Oil*.

70. Borrowing here from the brilliant Mike Davis, *Ecology of Fear: Los Angeles and the Imagination of Disaster* (New York: Metropolitan Books, 1998).

Epilogue: Crossing the Bay of Bengal

1. Naidu Ratnala Thulaja, "Loyang Tua Pek Kong," in *Singapore Infopedia* (Singapore: National Library Board, 2003), infopedia.nl.sg/articles/SIP_352_2004-12-27.html, accessed 30 May 2012.

2. Derek Walcott, "The Antilles: Fragments of an Epic Memory," in *What the Twilight Says: Essays* (London: Faber and Faber, 1998), 65–86.

3. "Thaipusam Rules: Court Rejects Appeal," *Straits Times*, 19 January 2011.

4. Text of the invitation I received from the shrine's trustees in 2009.

5. Cf. Nile Green, *Bombay Islam: The Religious Economy of the West Indian Ocean, 1840–1915* (Cambridge: Cambridge University Press, 2011).

6. Andrew Willford, *Cage of Freedom: Tamil Identity and the Ethnic Fetish in Malaysia* (Ann Arbor: University of Michigan Press, 2006), 288–289.

7. Subramaniam Pillay, "Hindraf Rally: A Plea of the Dispossessed?" *Aliran* 27, 10 (2007); Vinay Lal, "Multiculturalism at Risk: The Indian Minority in Malaysia," *Economic and Political Weekly*, 2 September 2006, 3764–5;

Farish A. Noor, "The Hindu Rights Action Force (HINDRAF) of Malaysia: Communitarianism Across Borders?" Working Paper No. 163, S. Rajaratnam School of International Studies, Singapore, 4 July 2008.

8. Krishna Gopal Rampal, *Sacred Structures: Artistic Renditions of Hindu Temples in Malaysia and Singapore* (Singapore: Bluetoffee, 2008).

9. *George Town: World Heritage Site Map* (Penang: Penang Heritage Trust, 2008).

10. Kwame Anthony Appiah, *Cosmopolitanism: Ethics in a World of Strangers* (New York: Norton, 2006).

11. Robert D. Kaplan, *Monsoon: The Indian Ocean and the Future of American Power* (New York: Random House, 2010), xi, 6–7.

12. T. Shanaathanan, *The Incomplete Thombu* (London: Raking Leaves, 2011); Michael Ondaatje, "A Port Accent," *A Room for London,* podcast available at www.aroomforlondon.co.uk/a-london-address/jun-2012-michael-ondaatje, accessed 4 July 2012.

Archives and Special Collections

British Library, London

Asian and African Studies Collection

India Office Records
Bengal Political and Judicial Consultations
Burma Office Records
East India Company Factory Records
Emigration Proceedings
Madras Public Proceedings
Marine Department Records
Political and Judicial Records
Straits Settlements Factory Records
Straits Settlements Records
European Manuscripts
Papers of L. G. Pinnell
Papers of Richard Carnac Temple

Maps Collection

Bay of Bengal Maps

Imperial War Museum, London

Papers of R. Middleton-Smith

National Archives of the United Kingdom, Kew, London

Admiralty Records
Cabinet Office Records
Colonial Office Records
War Office Records

National Maritime Museum, Greenwich, London

British India Steam Navigation Company Papers
Irrawaddy Flotilla Company Papers

School of Oriental and African Studies (SOAS) Archives

Furnivall Papers

National Archives of India, New Delhi

Department of Revenue and Agriculture
Department of Revenue, Agriculture and Commerce
Department of Commerce and Industry
Department of Education, Health and Lands
Indians Overseas Department
Commonwealth Relations Department
Burma Evacuee Registers
Ministry of External Affairs

Tamil Nadu State Archives, Chennai

Development Department
Fisheries Department
Department of Food and Agriculture
Public Department

Roja Mutthiah Research Library, Chennai

Rare Books and Newspaper Collection

Archives of the Netaji Research Bureau, Kolkata

Newspaper and Photographic Collection

National Archives of Singapore

Government Records

Straits Settlements Records
British Military Administration, 1945–1946

Ministry of Education
Coroner's Court Records

Private Papers

Mariyamman Temple
Singapore Indian Artistes' Association
Tamil Methodist Church
Tamils Reform Association

Oral History Department

Interviews with:
Abdul Aziz
Krishnaswamy Arumugam
M. K. Bhasi
Kasinthan Dandayodapani
Mohammed Ali Kader Ghouse
Varathar Gopal
Abdul Hameed
Shahul Hamid
Kanusamy
Nagore Maideen
Sundaresan Mariammal
Lakshmi Naidu
Karunakaran Nair
Ramasamy Narayanasamy
S. L. Perumal
Ramasamy Pillai
Thambyah Purushothaman
Alagappar Sockkalingam
Paramasiva Thambiraju

National Library of Singapore

Lee Kong Chiang Reference Library: Rare Books and Newspaper Collection

National University of Singapore Law Library

Malaysia/Singapore Collection

Arkib Negara Malaysia, Kuala Lumpur

Federated Malay States: Commissioner for Labour

Penang State Library, Butterworth

Malaysiana Collection: Pamphlets and Periodicals

Universiti Malaya Library, Kuala Lumpur

John Thivy Papers

National Archives Department of Myanmar, Yangon

Indian Immigration Enquiry: Papers
Irrawaddy Flotilla Company
Ministry of Foreign Affairs, 1948–1950

Newspapers and Periodicals

Amrita Bazar Patrika
Desa Nesan
The Hindu
Ina Mani
The Indian
The Indian Emigrant
Indian Opinion
Jawi Peranakan
The Malaya Tribune
Munnetram
Nurul Islam
Reform!
Searchlight
Seerthirutham
Singainesan
The Straits Times
Tamil Murasu
Tamil Nesan

Acknowledgments

The research for this book was made possible by a Large Research Grant from the British Academy (2007–2009), and by additional travel grants from Birkbeck College, the University of London's Central Research Fund, and from the Cambridge Centre for History and Economics. The final part of the research has received funding from the European Research Council under the European Union's Seventh Framework Programme (FP/2007–2013)/ERC Grant Agreement 284053. This marks the first stage in a larger project on the history of environmental change along the Bay of Bengal's rim, which will continue to 2017.

I am deeply grateful to the staff of the many archives and libraries where I undertook the research for this book. I would particularly like to thank the staff of the Asian and African Studies Collection of the British Library; the Imperial War Museum in London; the National Maritime Museum in Greenwich; the National Archives of the United Kingdom, in Kew; the National Archives of India in New Delhi; the Connemara Public Library, Chennai; the Roja Mutthiah Research Library, Chennai; the Tamil Nadu State Archives, Chennai; the National Archives of Singapore; the National Library of Singapore; the National University of Singapore's Central and Law Libraries; the library of the Institute of Southeast Asian Studies, Singapore; the Arkib Negara Malaysia, Kuala Lumpur; the National Archives Department of Myanmar, in Yangon; the Widener Memorial Library at Harvard University, and the Baker Library at Harvard Business School. Access to certain archives was made difficult by the continuing sensitivity that questions of migration and citizenship provoke in the region. I am especially grateful to those archivists who argued my case for access to political authorities, whether or not their efforts were successful.

Dozens of people in India, Malaysia, Singapore, Burma, and Indonesia were generous enough to share with me their own experiences of migration. Some of these were formal interviews, but many more took the form of informal conversations over many years. Most of the people I spoke with asked not to be named in this book—I did my research in Malaysia at a time when local Tamil politics was very much in the news and on the streets, and people expressed views to me that they preferred not to have attributed. I have respected their wishes, and my

343

gratitude to them all is immense. Of those who spoke to me on the record, I am especially grateful to Muthammal Palanisamy and Spencer Grant, and to their daughters in Rawang; to Palanisamy Kumaran and his family (and in particular to Sundar Ramasamy who facilitated my interviews with his remarkable grandfather); and to Uma Sambanthan.

I benefited enormously from comments on drafts of the manuscript. The two readers for Harvard University Press were generous beyond the call of duty; I am immensely grateful for the care and attention they gave to their critical readings of my work. I am equally grateful to Emma Rothschild for reading a full draft: her always-insightful comments improved it in countless ways. Although I have not had the pleasure of meeting him, Amitav Ghosh kindly agreed to read the manuscript: the influence of his magnificent fiction in shaping my imagination as a historian is incalculable, and his comments were most helpful.

I have accumulated more debts in writing this book than I can ever repay. For their kindness and for their generosity in so many ways, I owe particular thanks to my friends Sumit Mandal, Naoko Shimazu and A. R. Venkatachalapathy. They have enriched my work and encouraged me in this project from the start. Their scholarship sets the standard I aspire to. Tim Harper is my ideal historian. His friendship and solidarity have made many things possible for me. Working with him is both a privilege and a pleasure, and our conversations have shaped many of my ideas. The influence of Sugata Bose's work on this book will be evident from even a quick glance, and I have been fortunate indeed to benefit from his vision, wisdom, and kindness. I am honored by the interest that Amartya Sen has taken in my work over the years; he has inspired me in ways that reach far beyond this particular project. From the beginning of my academic career, Emma Rothschild has been an unwavering source of support and guidance; she remains my first and most trusted reader. Her own work is an inspiration to me to do the best I can. Any merit there might be in this book, I owe to what I have learned from them all.

Many others have been unstinting with their time and their advice. At the risk of omission, I would particularly like to thank Sana Aiyar, Seema Alavi, Clare Anderson, Alison Bashford, Christopher Bayly, Susan Bayly, Dipesh Chakrabarty, Sharad Chari, Joya Chatterji, Chua Ai Lin, Patricia Clavin, Debojyoti Das, Prasenjit Duara, Mark Frost, Engseng Ho, Sarah Hodges, Isabel Hofmeyr, Iftekhar Iqbal, Riho Isaka, Ayesha Jalal, Andrew Jarvis, Khoo Salma Nasution, Michael Laffan, Rachel Leow, Su Lin Lewis, Loh Wei Leng, David Ludden, Kazuya Nakamizo, Eleanor Newbigin, Chikayoshi Nomura, Susan Pennybacker, Jahnavi Phalkey, Bhavani Raman, Ronit Ricci, Taylor Sherman, Benjamin Siegel, Kavita Sivaramakrishnan, Glenda Sluga, Lakshmi Subramanian, Eric Tagliacozzo, Torsten Tschacher, Kohei Wakimura, Kirsty Walker, and Nira Wickramasinghe. I have benefited from several opportunities to present this work in progress, and I am grateful to many seminar audiences for insights and criticisms that challenged me to clarify its arguments.

I began the initial research for this project in 2004, while a Research Fellow at Trinity College, Cambridge, and I thank the Master and Fellows of Trinity for their support. Most of the research and writing has coincided with my time at Birkbeck, where I have taught since 2006. I should particularly like to thank Hilary Sapire, Chandak Sengoopta, Naoko Shimazu, and Filippo de Vivo for their warmth and solidarity. Through the exercise of their departmental responsibilities, John Arnold, Jessica Dunne, Sharon Durno, Catharine Edwards, Julian Swann, Alison Watson and Miriam Zukas have supported me in different ways over the years. My students at Birkbeck have contributed many ideas to this book with their probing questions and their varied perspectives, in particular the wonderful students who have taken my course on "Asian Diasporas." Special thanks are due to my PhD students Joshua de Cruz and Catherine Stenzl.

The Cambridge Centre for History and Economics has provided an intellectual home for me for over a decade. I am deeply grateful to the Centre—and, in particular, to Emma Rothschild and Inga Huld Markan—for its support of my work, and for its unique ability to bring interesting projects together. A semester of sabbatical leave at Harvard University in 2010 was crucial to the development of this book, allowing me time to write and access to the treasure that is the Widener Library. I am grateful to the Harvard Center for History and Economics and the Harvard History Department for their hospitality.

I owe a great deal to the advice and vision of my editor, Joyce Seltzer. At our very first meeting Joyce saw more clearly than I did what shape this book could take, and her support and enthusiasm have been vital to its creation. I could not imagine a better editor. At Harvard University Press, I would also like to thank Jeannette Estruth and Brian Distelberg for their assistance in numerous ways. Sue Warga's superb copyediting improved the text; Edward Wade oversaw the book's production with skill and efficiency, and Philip Schwartzberg of Meridian Mapping did a wonderful job with the maps: I am deeply grateful to all of them.

My extended family in India, the United States, and Britain have helped me in many ways. I would particularly like to thank my mother-in-law, Barbara Phillips, who regularly welcomes me to her home. I owe everything to the support of my parents, Jairam and Shantha Amrith, and my sister, Megha Amrith. My gratitude is beyond words, so I shall confine my thanks to their specific contributions to this book. I have discussed it extensively with Megha, and have learned a great deal from her own scholarship on migration. My father joined me on an enjoyable field trip to Malaysia in 2010 and helped with proofreading; my mother gave me invaluable advice in checking some of my translations from Tamil, and she introduced me—through old friends from medical school—to many Tamil families in Malaysia. Nothing I do would be possible without the love, generosity and calm practicality of my wife, Ruth Coffey. She has lived with this project for years. She commented on several chapters and accompanied me on many research trips, navigating us through the urban walks on which I took the photographs that illustrate these pages; I owe to her inspiration my growing interest in environmental issues. Most of all, work is only a small part of our journey together: she makes it worthwhile, and reminds me of what truly matters. This book is dedicated to her with love.

Index

Abdullah abd al-Kadir, 71–72
Aceh, 41, 49, 51–52, 55, 59–60, 63, 109
Air travel, 22–23, 220–221
Albuquerque, Afonso de, 18, 40–42
All-Malayan Council of Joint Action,
   234–235
Ambedkar, B.R., 230–231
Amsterdam, 44
Andaman Islands: convict settlement on,
   77–78; Indian military facilities on, 258;
   in World War II, 197–199, 211
Anderson, Benedict, 100, 165
Andrew, E.J.L., 150–151, 154
Andrews, C.F., 177
Anthonysamy, Charles, 270
Appiah, Kwame Anthony, 284
Arabian Sea, 11, 27–28, 36, 42, 69, 255
Arakan, 43, 49, 56–57, 77–79, 119, 188, 201,
   224–225, 256
Archives, 137, 155–156, 161, 213–214,
   248, 271
Area studies, 1, 244–245, 276
Asad, Talal, 141–142
Asian Relations Conference (1947),
   220–223, 256
Association of Southeast Asian Nations
   (ASEAN), 244
Atlantic: comparison with Indian
   Ocean, 26, 57, 141, 247–248; migration
   across, 104
Aung San, 187, 201, 243
Automobiles, 2, 29, 157–158, 180, 183, 274

Bajpai, Girija Shankar, 192
Bandung Conference (1955), 243
Bangladesh: Cyclone Bhola in, 248–249;
   impact of climate change on, 265;

maritime dispute with Myanmar, 257;
   migration to Malaysia from, 268
Bay of Bengal: as ecosystem, 276; geography
   of, 9–13; and Indian Ocean, 27–29; in
   mythology, 22–25; naming of, 18–19; and
   regional institutions, 283–284; strategic
   position of, 1, 5, 64, 197–198, 251–258;
   travel accounts of, 6–8, 24–26, 40,
   88–89. *See also* Climate change;
   Monsoons; Shipping; Trade
Bay of Bengal Pilot, 20, 32, 248
Bayly, C.A., 68
Bayly, Susan, 90
Bengal, 67, 207–210. *See also* Bangladesh;
   East India Company; Famine
Benjamin, Walter, 213
Bharucha, Rustom, 270–271
Borders, 99, 130, 134, 217, 223–224,
   229–230, 243–244, 267–268, 285
Bose, Sarat Chandra, 243
Bose, Subhas Chandra, 199–200,
   209–211
Bose, Sugata, 10
Bowrey, Thomas, 58–60, 88
Braudel, Fernand, 29–30, 52–53, 64, 105
Brazier, John, 237
British Empire: administration of, 109, 135,
   189–190; economic policies of, 70,
   112–113, 138, 216; expansion around Bay
   of Bengal, 63–68; strategic imperatives
   of, 67–68, 252
British India Steam Navigation Company,
   107–109, 151–152
Brito, Felipe de, 43
Buddhism, 14, 16, 23–25, 89, 186–188,
   224–225, 230–231
Bujang Valley, 15, 142–143